D1043875

The Taming of the Shrew

Texts and Contexts

The Bedford Companion to Shakespeare:
An Introduction with Documents
BY RUSS MCDONALD

William Shakespeare, *Hamlet*
(Case Studies in Contemporary Criticism)
EDITED BY SUSANNE L. WOFFORD,
UNIVERSITY OF WISCONSIN–MADISON

The Taming of the Shrew

Texts and Contexts

➤◄

FRANCES E. DOLAN

Miami University

Bedford/St. Martin's

BOSTON ◆ NEW YORK

For Bedford/St. Martin's
President and Publisher: Charles H. Christensen
General Manager and Associate Publisher: Joan E. Feinberg
Managing Editor: Elizabeth M. Schaaf
Developmental Editor: Karen S. Henry
Editorial Assistant: Kate O'Sullivan
Production Editor: Anne Benaquist
Copyeditor: Mary Mitiguy
Text Design: Claire Seng-Niemoeller
Cover Design: Lina Haddad Design
Cover Art: Details from valence showing hunting scenes. English, early seventeenth century. Victoria & Albert Museum, London, UK/The Bridgeman Art Library.

Library of Congress Catalog Card Number: 95–80793

For information, write: Bedford/St. Martin's
75 Arlington Street, Boston, MA 02116

ISBN: 0–312–10836–2 (paperback)
ISBN: 0–312–15858–0 (hardcover)

Published and distributed outside North America by:

MACMILLAN PRESS LTD.
Houndmills, Basingstoke, Hampshire, RG21 2XS and London
Companies and representatives throughout the world.

ISBN: 0–333–65709–8

Acknowledgments

The Taming of the Shrew from Bevington, David. THE COMPLETE WORKS OF SHAKE-SPEARE, 4th Edition, © 1992., pp. 110-146, A-103, A-104. Reprinted by permission of Pearson Education, Inc., Upper Saddle River, N.J.

INTRODUCTION
Figure 1. Skimmington beating her husband from *Divers Crabtree Lectures* by John Taylor (London, 1639). Shelfmark Douce. L.4. Reprinted by permission of the Bodleian Library.

Acknowledgments and copyrights are continued at the back of the book on page 335, which constitute an extension of the copyright page. It is a violation of the law to reproduce these selections by any means whatsoever without the written permission of the copyright holder.

*For my sister, Kate, whose
untamable spirit I have always admired.*

Preface

———————————————— ✕ ————————————————

Recent attempts to help students approach literary works historically have often confronted a daunting pedagogical obstacle: how do teachers avoid lecturing students into silence and passivity? One way to combine inter-active learning and historical approaches is to put the evidence historians use into students' own hands, inviting them to extend literary analysis to these texts as well and to work toward their own interpretations of the past. This approach opens up to question the distinction between "literature" and "primary documents." It also encourages students to read historical evidence — and the narratives of change that historians base on that evidence — critically. But this approach faces its own obstacle. How can a range of primary texts be made available to students in an accessible, affordable form? Even those teachers who have the library resources, know-how, and time to dig up and photocopy these materials find them a challenge to teach. Faintly printed or overinked and in unfamiliar typefaces, riddled with confusing (and inconsistent) orthographic and typographical conventions, offering the reader no assistance or explanation, photocopies of sixteenth- and seventeenth-century texts can easily overwhelm and discourage even the most determined student.

This edition seeks to solve these classroom dilemmas by offering students twenty-three texts in modern spelling, each with its own introduction and each with full annotation. Armed with this edition, students can interpret *The Taming of the Shrew* in a more informed and critical way. They can also use Shakespeare's play itself as evidence as they consider the social history of sixteenth- and seventeenth-century England. Thus this book offers students historical avenues of approach to Shakespeare as well as Shakespearean avenues of approach to social history. Each headnote returns students to the play with new questions and insights. In turn, the play provides the organizing principle for all of these materials, motivating students' inquiries into social history, providing an entry point into the past, and enabling students to make connections.

While this approach does not replace the Shakespearean text, it does displace it, making room on the syllabus for texts that were not there before. Presenting Shakespeare's play as one text among many, this is as much about sixteenth- and seventeenth-century debates about marriage, women, and domesticity as it is about *The Taming of the Shrew*. Hence the plurals in our title — texts and contexts. This edition does not offer one central text — Shakespeare's play — and one context through which to understand it. Instead, it suggests that any of the texts here could be placed at the center of a discussion or that discussions might focus on issues rather than a single text. Even Shakespeare's play, the best-known of the materials included here, is not a text but many texts, as the inclusion of endings from alternative versions of the play — *The Taming of A Shrew*, and Garrick's *Catharine and Petruchio* — indicates. Rather than a play in the foreground and other texts in the background explaining and enhancing it, you will find here noisy, heated, and unresolved debates among texts. In the context of these debates, *The Taming of the Shrew* seems more complicated and harder to pin down than ever. For instance, how one understands and evaluates Petruchio's strategies for taming Katharine might shift as one considers the play first in relation to sermons and guidebooks that offer advice to husbands, next shrew-taming stories, then handbooks on falconry, and finally, witchfinders' manuals.

I have understood the *con* in *context* in its meaning of "with" — texts to read with other texts — but I have also borrowed its connotation of "against" (as in *pro and con*) to suggest that these texts might be read against one another. Sometimes one text explains or illuminates the other, but often they contradict (literally speak against) one another. Some of these texts offer voices, perspectives, and attitudes distinctly different from those we find in Shakespeare's play. However vocal and various *The Taming of the Shrew* is, there are some struggles and issues that were not acted out on the stage and that we must seek out elsewhere.

The texts included here have not been selected and organized as a line of sources and influences leading up to and culminating in Shakespeare's play. This is not a story of development or evolution; these are not necessarily the books from Shakespeare's library that informed and influenced the playwright as he wrote. For instance, I have paid little attention to the subplot of the play or to its sources. If these texts, considered together, do not map out a line leading to a triumphant climax (Shakespeare), then perhaps they form the pieces in a kaleidoscope; these pieces constantly regroup to form new pictures in response to changing questions and emphases. I have cast my net wide in both chronology and genre in order to recreate debates about women, marriage, domesticity, disorder, and violence that were important in English culture from the end of the sixteenth century to about the middle of the seventeenth century. These texts were written in a broad range of genres, including ballads, a sermon in its entirety, and substantial selections from books on domestic conduct.

Although *The Taming of the Shrew* was probably written between 1590 and 1594, and thus toward the beginning of Shakespeare's career, the other selections here have publication dates ranging from c. 1550 to 1828; they thus extend across those centuries (roughly 1500–1800) that historians call the Early Modern Era in England. Most, however, were published in the first half of the seventeenth century. One rationale for this chronological sweep is that Shakespeare's play continued to be produced in various versions; it is not the product of a single moment, nor does it contribute only to those debates underway when it was first written and produced. Another rationale is that many texts published in the seventeenth century offer particularly vivid articulations of views and values already common in the late sixteenth century. Conflicts surrounding marriage, the household, and women's status and role were not resolved by the late sixteenth century. Readers will chart some differences from one genre to another, one text to another, and across time, but they will also see striking continuities. Finally, while Shakespeare responded to literary precedents and contemporary controversies, he also created influential precedents. *The Taming of the Shrew* does not "hold a mirror up to nature," statically reflecting events and attitudes; it works to shape those attitudes long after its first publication and production. The debates in which *The Taming of the Shrew* engaged and the processes of social change in which those debates played an important role raged on after Shakespeare stopped writing and continued to do so well after he was dead. As a cultural stereotype and obsession, the "shrew" was — and is — very long-lived.

EDITORIAL POLICY

In transcribing and editing these texts, I have generally used the first or only editions, except in those cases in which works were frequently revised, expanded, and reprinted. For such works, including *A Homily of the State of Matrimony*, the books on domestic conduct by Dod and Cleaver, Gouge, and Whately, and the guides to falconry by Turberville and Latham, I have selected later revised editions. My choice of copy was often determined by what was available on microfilm. The edition is always indicated.

My primary goal has been to make the texts as accessible as possible. In all quotations in the introduction and headnotes as well as in the texts themselves, I modernized, standardized, and Americanized spelling, punctuation, capitalization, italics, and paragraphing format. To regularize the grammar would often require complete rewriting; I have done my best to make sense clear through punctuation, without rearranging sentences or adding or subtracting words. I have generally expanded abbreviations and contractions, corrected obvious printing errors, but retained archaic verb endings and archaic plurals. In dramatic texts I have expanded speech prefixes to insure that students will recognize who is speaking. Although I have checked all biblical citations and expanded abbreviations to avoid confusion, I have usually reproduced biblical references as they appear in the original texts. *The Oxford English Dictionary* (*OED*) has guided me in glossing words, and *The Dictionary of National Biography* (*DNB*) has been my usual source for biographical information on authors. In the case of obsolete or archaic words, I have generally used the spelling preferred in the *OED*.

In citations of sixteenth- and seventeenth-century texts, I have used signature rather than page numbers where appropriate. Signature numbers are a now-obsolete way of indicating pagination; where they coexist with the consecutive numbering of pages with which we are now more familiar, they are often more accurate. They indicate how large pages were folded (into four to create *quarto* volumes, eight to create *octavo* volumes, etc.) and then stitched or "gathered" together to form a book. Signature numbers include a letter, which identifies all of the pages printed on a single sheet, a number, and in the case of the reverse side of a given page, a *v* for "verso." To find D4v, you would turn to the D gathering, then count only the right pages in each opening until you get to D4 (which might not be marked as such). The back of that page would be D4v.

In many of these texts, *and* or *an* bears the meaning of "if"; I have not substituted one for the other but have, instead, glossed the first instance in each text in which *and* or *an* carries this meaning.

ACKNOWLEDGMENTS

In preparing this volume, I have relied on the contributions of other scholars. These debts are acknowledged in the notes and bibliography, but I am especially grateful to Susan Amussen, Lynda Boose, Mark Thornton Burnett, Emily Detmer, Margaret Loftus Ranald, Mary Beth Rose, Scott Shershow, Valerie Wayne, and Joy Wiltenburg for offering me concrete ideas about texts I might include. David Bevington provided the edition of *The Taming of the Shrew* as well as advice. Barbara Bowen and Frank Whigham offered helpful suggestions. Michael Bristol, Jim Clark, Jean Howard, Laurie Maguire, and Valerie Wayne read various drafts of the manuscript, offering invaluable advice, corrections, and encouragement. My students at Miami University cheerfully tested out the texts; my colleagues Mary Jean Corbett, Emily Detmer, and Scott Shershow read drafts of the introduction; and my fellow Shakespeare teachers, Jim Clark and Rich Ehrlich, offered the wisdom of their experience as well as their eagerness to try new approaches. Laurie Maguire and Liza Nelligan generously shared their unpublished work on the play. Barry Chabot and Jerry Rosenberg provided much-needed computer assistance.

At Bedford Books, I am grateful to Mary Mitiguy for her judicious and careful copyediting and to Anne Benaquist for her patience, good humor, and good sense in overseeing production. My greatest debt is to Karen Henry, who first approached me with the idea for this volume and who has counseled me at every turn. Collaborating with me in thinking through how to conjoin teaching and research in fruitful and practical ways, she has made the process a rewarding one.

Frances E. Dolan
Miami University

Contents

Of Masters' Excess in Correcting Servants 241
Of Masters' Ordering That Correction They Give to Their
    Servants 242

→ *4. Shrews, Taming, and Untamed Shrews* 244

Shrews and Shrew Taming 244

"The Cruel Shrew" 247

*A Merry Jest of a Shrewd and Curst Wife Lapped in Morel's Skin,
    for Her Good Behavior* 254

"The Cucking of a Scold" 288

From *The Tragical Comedy, or Comical Tragedy, of
    Punch and Judy* 296

Analogues to Shrew Taming 304

FALCONRY 304

George Turberville, From *The Book of Falconry or Hawking* 309

Simon Latham, From *Latham's Falconry* 310

WATCHING A WITCH 312

Matthew Hopkins, From *The Discovery of Witches* 314

John Stearne, From *A Confirmation and Discovery of
    Witchcraft* 315

Thomas Ady, From *A Candle in the Dark* 316

Untamed Shrews 317

Thomas Harman, From *A Caveat for Common Cursitors, Vulgarly
    Called Vagabonds* 317

Thomas Heywood, From *A Curtain Lecture* 324

The Taming of the Shrew

Texts and Contexts

Introduction

———————————— >-< ————————————

This edition considers Shakespeare's *The Taming of the Shrew* in the context of lively controversies. In its own time the play was one text among many in heated debates about women's status, marriage, and domesticity. The history of the play's reception is also particularly contentious, for critics have long disagreed about how to interpret the play, viewing it variously as a romantic comedy in which two spouses achieve mutual satisfaction (Novy), a rambunctious farce in which we should not take the violent taming seriously (Heilman), an embarrassment (Shaw), even as a "bad" play (Garner). This introduction considers the play in relation to these two levels of controversy — the cultural contests in which the play participated in sixteenth- and seventeenth-century England, and the debates among the play's recent critics.

   Interweaving discussion of the play with discussion of the other texts included in this edition, I offer one model for how to think about the connections among diverse materials. I begin with a discussion of why Shakespeare might have chosen to dramatize the story of a "shrew" and her taming. Why were such stories so popular? How does Shakespeare's play relate to the many other versions of this story? Does it reinforce or contradict other evidence that his culture was particularly concerned about assertive women, marital conflict, and domestic disorder? The introduction then follows the structure of the play, beginning with the two opening scenes known as the Induction and concluding with Shakespeare's last scene and its relation to other possible endings. Along the way I focus on those issues and moments in the play that have attracted the most discussion and controversy, and that offer the most fruitful points of connection to other texts included in the edition. I discuss what it meant to be a "shrew"; how assumptions about authority and violence in the household shape both Petruchio's strategies as shrew tamer and Katharine's conduct; Katharine's puzzling silences and how these correspond to the conception of a married woman as a "feme covert" or a woman legally overshadowed by her husband; and how Petruchio and Katharine move toward the "ideal" marital relationship in the "sun and moon" scene. Throughout, I suggest how the diverse texts included here can help to clarify the issues at stake in various critical debates and reveal critics' assumptions. Among these texts, students can find support for different, even contradictory, interpretations of the play. Reading *The Taming of the Shrew* against other texts does not resolve conflict by providing authoritative or definitive answers; often, this process emphasizes contradictions, opening up rather than flattening out complexities.

Texts and Contexts

Probably written between 1590 and 1594,[1] *The Taming of the Shrew* stands at the beginning of Shakespeare's career. It also stands at the middle of a period in English history (roughly 1550 to 1660) in which many historians have found "an intense preoccupation with women who are a visible threat to the patriarchal system," that is, a system in which men control property and wield power, exercising authority over and taking responsibility for their subordinates in political as well as domestic settings (Underdown 119). Historians find their evidence for this preoccupation in new legislation and increased rates of prosecution targeting women for crimes such as witchcraft, disorderly speech, illegitimate pregnancy, and child murder. They also examine the proliferation of cheaply produced, widely distributed texts such as ballads (popular songs both sung in the streets and sold by the sheet) and pamphlets (short, relatively cheap unbound booklets). Many of these texts focus on women as violent criminals who kill their husbands, masters, neighbors, and children, despite the fact that, then as now, women were far more likely to be victims, rather than agents, of violent crime.

---

[1] On the date of the play, see Morris 50–65; and Thompson 1–9. (See the Secondary Sources section in the Bibliography.)

Ballads, folktales, jokes, and plays about outspoken, assertive women suggest that the English found disorderly women simultaneously threatening and fascinating; stories of their taming were, apparently, reassuring and amusing.[2] (See the texts on "Shrews and Shrew Taming" in chapter 4, "Shrews, Taming, and Untamed Shrews.")

Thinking about Shakespeare's play in relation to all these other kinds of evidence reveals that Shakespeare did not write in isolation or informed only by his own imagination; instead, he actively engaged in the controversies of his day. Since he assessed and selected among alternatives, the choices he made were neither inevitable nor entirely personal. If Shakespeare told the story of a husband who tames his shrewish wife, it was, in part, because that was the kind of story that most interested his audiences and most preoccupied his culture. We must recognize that most storytellers — from balladeers on street corners to playwrights and poets — chose to depict "the taming of the shrew" rather than, say, "the reform of the tyrannous husband." But this does not mean that we should not question why Shakespeare tells this story at all, and why he tells it as he does. It simply means that in scrutinizing this particular play, and the debates in which it engaged, we are scrutinizing a culture as well as an individual playwright. We witness a contest over changing ideals for private life, not just a handful of texts.

The primary materials in this edition are not necessarily sources or precedents for the play; many are not exactly contemporary to it; and some were published long after the play was first produced. The range of texts enables the reader to chart continuity and change across time and among different kinds of texts. In historically situating the play, these materials help us to place it as a document in multiple histories and processes of change. The play connects, therefore, to texts published long before or long after it and written in distinctly different genres — sermons, books of advice on personal conduct, ballads, puppet shows, pamphlets, and so forth. The inclusion of a script for a *Punch and Judy* show offers a good example. Transcriptions of this popular puppet show, probably first performed in England in the late seventeenth century, were not made until the nineteenth century. Like these transcriptions, many published texts offer our best evidence of ideas, values, and stories in circulation long before their publication. They also demonstrate how texts can contribute to processes of change that they may not anticipate, demonstrating how, for instance, *The Taming of the Shrew* participates in a long history of representing violent spousal conflict as a slapstick struggle for dominance. In this tradition the

---

[2] In addition to Underdown, see Amussen; Dolan, *Dangerous Familiars*; and Wiltenburg.

contenders are almost evenly matched in a protracted struggle, yet the husband usually wins. Two distinct models for marriage coexist as uneasily as do Punch and Judy: the first is a partnership between equals, and the second is a hierarchical relation in which the husband is dominant and the wife is subordinate. These models raise certain questions. How is hierarchy to be achieved and maintained if the wife will not submit but instead struggles to assert either equality or mastery? What if a husband abuses his power? Finally, what are the possibilities for spousal roles beyond these too-simple and constricting options?

As many of the texts included in this edition demonstrate, different texts addressed these questions in different ways. Contradictory views can be found within texts, as well as among them. The differences between, say, a raucous street ballad or puppet show and a sermon on marriage can be described in many ways, but one useful approach is to consider the various functions that texts perform. Some texts describe what actually happens in households and marriages; records of testimony in a court case, letters, and autobiographies might be considered *descriptive* texts. Other texts attempt to shape how people ought to behave; these texts, sometimes called *prescriptive*, might include sermons (like *A Homily of the State of Matrimony*, p. 172), and works offering advice and instruction on personal conduct (such as the works advising against beating a wife or servant); they might also include negative portraits of how people should *not* behave. Still other texts, which might be called *imaginative*, neither describe nor attempt to change readers' behavior directly; instead, they offer exaggerated versions of readers' lived experience (as in fairy tales or the excessive violence of the shrew taming in *A Merry Jest of a Shrewd and Curst Wife Lapped in Morel's Skin*, p. 257), fantasies of alternatives (as in Shakespeare's green world comedies such as *As You Like It*), or imaginary solutions to real problems, that is, happy endings resolving or repressing conflict (such as *The Taming of the Shrew*). These categories often overlap; many texts simultaneously or alternately describe, prescribe, and imagine.

But understanding the different functions of texts can help readers avoid mistaking texts for accurate descriptions of social reality. For instance, if laws and fictions about disorderly women suddenly proliferate, that may not mean that more women are breaking laws, bossing around their husbands, or talking back. It may mean, instead, that women are suddenly seen as a threat, that more people are afraid of powerful women. The question then becomes not why women are acting this way, but why women are suddenly perceived and represented this way.

Conversely, repeated injunctions that women should be chaste, silent, and obedient do not necessarily mean that all women were. If all women stayed home and kept quiet, why did so many writers need to lecture them? If all wives submitted to their husbands, neither the Church of England (in *A Homily of the State of Matrimony*), nor Katharine at the end of *The Taming of the Shrew* would have to justify such subordination and scold women into it. The possibilities for couples' relationships were more diverse and complex than those represented in texts that suggest that the husband in charge was the ideal and the woman on top was the disorderly, nightmarish inversion of that ideal. One historian, for instance, argues for "the *private* existence of a strong complementary and companionate ethos, side by side with, and often overshadowing, theoretical adherence to the doctrine of male authority and *public* female subordination" (Wrightson 92). Most people would experience "day-to-day conflicts between the dictates of the patriarchal ideal and the infinite variety of husband/wife relationships" (Ingram, "Ridings" 98). But our access to that "infinite variety," to what happened inside early modern people's minds, hearts, and households, is restricted. We know only what was recorded and what has survived. Furthermore, even texts such as letters, diaries, or court depositions in which speakers claim to articulate the "truth" of their own experience filter, mediate, and shape that experience. Although all texts are evidence, often they are evidence of people's attitudes more than of their actions. For instance, texts representing marriage and domestic relations might tell us more about what writers thought should happen, or what they feared might happen, than about what actually did.

Representations do, however, have consequences for men and women's lived experience. Couples may have turned to advice literature for help in their negotiations and for guidance as expectations and roles changed. Popular street literature might have provided fighting spouses and neighbors with standards by which to measure — and find fault with — one another, as well as a battery of insults to use when fighting.[3] To apply the standards they drew from stories circulating orally or in print, however, they had to ignore "the huge gulf between literature and experience," between ideals and what happened in most houses on the street or in the village (Gowing 10).

The Taming of the Shrew explores all these issues: the process by which husband and wife negotiate a relationship; the disparity between private and public conduct; the clash between conflicting ideals. Focusing on how spouses jockey for position *after* the wedding, *The Taming of the Shrew* differs markedly from Shakespeare's other comedies, which dwell on courtship, and end rather than begin with marriage. What happens after the

---

[3] Gowing argues that ballads and broadsides may have shaped the kinds of testimony about disorderly women that she finds in London court records between 1570 and 1640.

wedding is more often the business of tragedy (consider *Othello*, for instance) than of comedy. This may explain the long tradition of debate over *this* comedy. Is this the romantic story of two equals who struggle toward marital happiness or the dispiriting tale of a man who swells into a husband and a woman who dwindles into a wife? Does marriage emancipate or defeat Kate? Could the answers to these "either/or" questions be "both"?

The Induction

The text of the play is itself the subject of debate. Although records suggest that *The Taming of the Shrew* (in some version) was first performed in 1594, the version of the play on which most modern editions (including this one) are based was published as part of Shakespeare's *First Folio* (the first edition claiming to collect Shakespeare's complete plays) in 1623. The edition included the two opening scenes now jointly known as the Induction. Although often considered the authoritative or "best" version, it does not return to the characters it introduces in the Induction. For this reason some editors have eliminated these first two scenes from their editions. Questions then arise because another version of the play in circulation in the late sixteenth century does close the frame opened in the Induction. This play, entitled *A Pleasant Conceited History, Called The Taming of a Shrew*, was published in 1594, 1596, and 1607; at various points in this play Christopher Sly, the character introduced in the Induction, interrupts and comments on the action; *A Shrew* also closes with Sly's reflections on the play that he has watched along with the audience (see p. 146 for the final scene of *A Shrew*).

For many readers and viewers of the play, the Induction, with its story of how the Lord and his servants convince the drunken tinker, Christopher Sly, that he is a wealthy aristocrat, at first seems unrelated to the rest of the play. But some critics argue that the Induction shapes how we view what follows. First, the Induction teaches viewers that characters form their identities by playing roles and that they can switch roles and thus identities; and that characters also form their identities in relation to other characters. For instance, Sly begins to redefine himself when others' responses to, and treatment of, him change. Sly finds it increasingly difficult to determine which is the dream and which the reality of his identity.[4] In the process the Induction instructs readers/viewers that class and gender identities are not natural or fixed, but instead are roles — a matter of how one dresses, acts, and is treated — and, as such, can be changed.

---

[4] On identity and imposture in the Induction see Dusinberre; Hodgdon 540; Kahn 117; and Neely 28.

Sly's transformation introduces the inversions and impostures that recur throughout the play. Some critics argue that the idea of mistaken or transformed identity unites the play's three structural elements — the Induction, the main plot about Katharine and Petruchio, and the subplot about Bianca and her suitors (Seronsy; Thompson 31–32). This subplot is based on George Gascoigne's play *Supposes* (1566; 1572–75), a translation of Ariosto's *Gli Suppositi* (1509; on the subplot, see Hutson ch. 6). Gascoigne's play is organized around disguise, mistaken identity, and conjectures. In Gascoigne's play, as in Shakespeare's subplot, those who disguise themselves do so self-consciously and purposefully. In Shakespeare's main plot, by contrast, Katharine is persistently described as the object, rather than the agent, of transformation: "she is changed, as she had never been" (5.2.119).[5] In the Induction, Sly is transformed by the Lord's orders and for the Lord's "sport." In both cases the more powerful figure — Petruchio or the Lord — has the power to "suppose" alteration in his subordinate and through supposing to make it so, at least temporarily.

The Induction presents the Lord's game of convincing Sly that he is a gentleman, and watching the spectacle of his confusion, as an aristocratic "sport" parallel to hunting. (On the significances of hunting in the play, see the section on "Analogues to Shrew Taming: Falconry," pp. 304–312.) What pleasures will the Lord extract from making a beggar forget himself? In part the Lord enjoys the pleasure of exercising power — of reshaping this drunken beggar's sense of his own identity, of temporarily altering his reality. Through this jest the Induction also instructs readers/viewers on exactly what privilege means. Here it means access to sensual pleasure (wanton pictures, warm distilled waters, incense, rosewater, and music); servants who treat you reverently and submissively; possessions (clothes, hounds, a horse); and relations who are also depicted as property (your lady, your servants, your kindred).[6] Of this catalogue the lady or wife proves particularly important in establishing Sly as both a man and a lord.[7]

[5] The play establishes many parallels between Sly and Katharine. Sly wonders whether he dreams or wakes; later, Katharine is described as one "new risen from a dream." Sly wonders if he is mad; later Katharine begs pardon for "mad mistaking." Sly's "marriage" is unconsummated; Katharine and Petruchio seem to defer the consummation of their marriage until the very end of the play. On parallels between Sly and Katharine, see Baumlin 252; Leggatt 42–43; Quilligan 215; Slights 169–70; and Thompson 32. Also see Palmer on how Petruchio and the Lord abuse their roles as hosts, using hospitality to reform their guests (63–66).

[6] See Orlin, "The Performance of Things," on the complex operations of "things" in the play, especially their role in determining and securing status; cf. Slights 172–75.

[7] "In this play, as is frequently true in gender and class relations in general, beneath every asserted dominance is inevitably an unacknowledged, uncredited, and usually unpaid dependency of the higher on the lower" (Boose, *"Taming of the Shrew"* 224).

The Lord assures Sly: "Thou art a lord, and nothing but a lord. / Thou hast a lady . . ." (Ind.2. 56–57); Sly incredulously seeks reassurance: "Am I a lord? And have I such a lady? / Or do I dream? Or have I dreamed till now?" (63–64).[8]

This lady is played by Bartholomew, a boy page whom the Lord instructs on how to act like a wife. By dramatizing this process, the Induction reminds viewers that boys played all the women's parts on the Renaissance stage; boys would have played both Kate and Bianca in the play to follow (see Michael Shapiro and Dusinberre). Just as the Lord teaches Bartholomew to use an onion to provoke tears, Katharine accuses Bianca of sticking her finger in her eye to make herself cry (Ind.1. 121–24; 1.1.78–79). In both cases the "woman's gift" of tears is a gift for performance. Just as the Lord teaches Bartholomew how to submit to a husband "With soft low tongue and lowly courtesy," Katharine also learns how to do her husband "obeisance" (Ind.1. 110, 104). The Induction thus forces the viewer to remain conscious of the play as a play and, through the page who plays Sly's wife, of gender, class, and adulthood as scripts that can be imitated and altered. In her bravura performance as gentlewoman and wife in the final scene, does Katharine do anything different from what Bartholomew does when he plays a lord's wife?

Finally, the Induction urges viewers to reflect on the play's form before it even begins. Is the play a dream, a jest, a sport? Is it a salubrious distraction, a less risky alternative than sex, given Sly's fragile condition? Is it "household stuff" or "a kind of history"? If it is a history play, as Boose argues, it is a "kind of history" very different from Shakespeare's other histories, all of which are named after the kings on whom they focus. For it is a history not about rulers, wars, and court politics, but about "household stuff." The play raises questions about the sources of legitimate authority, about the means of achieving and maintaining power, and about negotiating conflicts, as Shakespeare's other histories do, but it explores these issues in a domestic setting. The struggles for power occur between sisters, father and daughter, husband and wife, master or mistress and servant.

Shrews and Shrew Taming

In act 1, scene 1, we learn that Baptista Minola has two daughters, Bianca and Katharine; as we meet them we also learn that, from the perspective of

---

[8] On the role of women in securing masculine class and gender identities, see Boose, *"Taming"*; and Newman 38.

Bianca's suitors, Katharine is the less desirable. It is worth questioning rather than automatically accepting this evaluation. How are Bianca and Katharine different? What marks Katharine rather than Bianca as the shrew?

Katharine is called a devil (1.1.66), a "fiend of hell" (88), and "the devil's dam" (106); her own father calls her "thou hilding of a devilish spirit" (2.1.26) after she binds and beats Bianca. The men generally agree that Katharine is unmarriageable "unless [she] were of gentler, milder mold" (1.1.60); she is "stark mad or wonderful froward" (1.1.69). Gremio concludes that "she's too rough" for him (1.1.55). Although the play makes clear from the opening scene that Katharine is the shrew of the title — the one who must be tamed — the various and vague complaints leveled against her in this opening scene raise the question: What *is* a shrew? How does a shrew act?

In the sixteenth and seventeenth centuries shrews were, first and foremost, women. The term *shrew* describes the caricature or stereotype of a bossy woman that was a familiar figure in popular culture (see "The Cruel Shrew," p. 250). One important component of shrewishness was talking — talking too much, or too loudly and publicly, or too crossly for a woman. Lacking other means to express anger or redress grievances, a shrew depended on her tongue, which "although a member bad, / Was all the 'fensive weapon that she had" (*Anatomy of a Woman's Tongue*, epigram xviii, 281). As Lisa Jardine argues, "both gossiping and scolding give her a semblance of power, which threatens disorder without actually freeing her from her multiple obligations and constraints" (107). Katharine certainly wields her tongue as a weapon. Petruchio's servant Grumio fears her tongue, should she become his mistress. Baptista warns Petruchio that if he wishes to court Katharine, he must be "armed for some unhappy words" (2.1.135).

The contrast between Katharine and Bianca is, in part, that Katharine assaults and disturbs the suitors through their ears, while Bianca pleases their eyes. As Katharine herself complains of Bianca, "Her silence flouts me, and I'll be revenged" (2.1.29). Lucentio is guided so much by his eyes that they take the place of his ears; in Bianca's silence he claims to "see / Maid's mild behavior and sobriety" (1.1.70–71); "I saw her coral lips to move, / And with her breath she did perfume the air. / Sacred and sweet was all I saw in her" (166–68). For Lucentio romantic love is not blind but deaf. He is so absorbed in gazing at Bianca that he effectively silences what little she does say.

Lucentio's admiration for Bianca's silence suggests that the most important contrast between the two sisters is that one talks and one does not. Yet the play blurs that distinction. Bianca talks more, and more assertively, as the play progresses. The play also suggests that there is more to Katharine's shrewishness than her unruly tongue. Although it is still widely assumed that shrews talked too much, the many ballads about shrewish or scolding women reveal that women were labeled as shrews for a variety of disorderly behaviors. According to these ballads, shrews force men to do "women's work";[9] they beat and humiliate their husbands;[10] they take lovers; they refuse to have sex with their husbands or blame their husbands for being sexually useless;[11] they drink and frequent alehouses; and they scold. But most of all, they strive for mastery. As a "Scold Rampant" informs her husband, "I will have my will, or I will vex every vein of thy heart, thou logger-headed booby" (*Juniper Lecture* D6v–D7).[12]

A shrew, then, is not just a talkative woman; she is a woman refusing to submit to a man's authority and aggressively asserting her independence. Since English culture at this time associated self-assertion, independence, and "mastery" with masculinity, many texts depicted such women (especially married women) as usurping men's rights and privileges, rather than as claiming their own. Assertive women were imagined to overturn the existing hierarchy that placed men above women, thus making them "women on top" (see Figure 1). Any assertion of themselves was thus construed as taking something away from their husbands, as, for instance, wresting away the one pair of breeches in the family and insisting on wearing them.[13] The possible solution of getting another pair of breeches is never imagined; instead, husband and wife must fight over that one pair. In various representations of spousal relations, "marriage emerges as a relationship governed ultimately by force. One partner has to dominate . . . violence is the fundamental arbiter" (Wiltenburg 137; cf. Garner 108). It is not simply how much Katharine talks that marks her as a shrew. Indeed, she does not talk more than many of the other characters; in the first scene she has only thirteen lines, all of them in response to provocation (Kahn).

[9] In "The Cuckold's Complaint," for instance, the husband complains: "I am forced to wash her smock, and the child's s[odd]en clouts also" (*Roxburghe Ballads* 7:431, line 31). In "My Wife Will Be My Master," the husband complains: "I wash the dishes, sweep the house, I dress the wholesome diet; / I humor her in everything, because I would be quiet" (*RB* 7:188–89, lines 45–46). For other ballads about the gendered division of labor, see those in the section on "Women's Work: Gender and the Division of Labor" (pp. 206–18).

[10] "The Patient Husband and the Scolding Wife" (*RB* 7: 182–83).

[11] "The Scolding Wife's Vindication" (*RB* 7: 194–97).

[12] Sometimes, as here, I cite a signature rather than a page number. This now obsolete method of numbering pages was usually used in sixteenth- and seventeenth-century texts.

[13] This trope shaped insults and litigations over insults. As Gowing argues, "defamers [those who attack others' reputations or slander them] who make use of anxieties about clothing and gender tend to focus simply on the metaphorical image of the breeches, the symbol of male dominance in a long tradition of ballads and broadsides. . . . The assumption of men's clothing is seen entirely in the context of the disruption of household economic order, represented by men's work garments" (Gowing 11).

Nor is it even what she says. Instead, Katharine troubles and threatens other characters through a constellation of self-assertions.

Shrewish behavior provoked various punishments, official and unofficial. Women might be brought into court under the charge of being "scolds." This was largely a female offense, although men were occasionally presented to authorities for it. Scolding upset class as well as gender hierarchies; those women charged with scolding were usually of low status and had offended against those of equal or superior status (Underdown 120).[14] The punishments exacted by the community were painful, frightening, and humiliating. An offender might be forced to wear a sharp, embarrassing "scold's bridle" or might be "cucked," that is, strapped to a stool and dunked repeatedly in water (see Figures 12 and 13 and "The Cucking of a Scold," p. 292).[15]

While some punishments were primarily designed to inflict severe pain, sometimes to mark the offender permanently, the cucking stool and scold's bridle "were devised primarily as shaming devices" (Boose, "Scolding Brides" 189). As a result, the woman being punished became a target of ridicule. As Boose argues, "both the figure of the 'scold' and the cucking stool belong to the purview of comedy in ways that the male brawler and his punishment at the pillory do not" (Boose, "Scolding Brides" 190). Native English folk traditions — including medieval dramatizations of biblical stories such as that of Noah's wife — songs, jokes, and stories that circulated orally also contributed to making the shrew what M. C. Bradbrook has called "the oldest . . . native comic rôle for women" (Bradbrook 134). In stories about the shrew and her taming, cruelty, suffering, ridicule, and laughter coexist. The texts in chapter 4, "Shrews, Taming, and Untamed Shrews," especially those that depict the punishment of scolds and shrews (such as "The Cucking of a Scold," p. 292, and *A Merry Jest,* p. 257), reveal how aggressive and violent popular entertainments — whether punishments themselves or stories about them — could be.

Women's shrewish assertions of their will might also be punished informally at home. Shrewish wives were widely presumed to provoke their husbands to violence, as popular songs reveal.

[14] While being a scold was a legal category of offense, being a shrew was not. "Scold" is a subcategory of "Shrew," easier to identify and define; "shrew" is a more capacious, ambiguous category that includes all forms of disorderly female mastery. On scolds see Boose, "Scolding Brides"; Ingram, "Scolding Women"; and Underdown.

[15] See also Boose, "Scolding Brides"; Ingram, "Scolding Women"; and Wayne, "Refashioning the Shrew." These punishments must be considered in the context of other widely used punishments during this period. For instance, men and women convicted of sedition or libel, which are also forms of disorderly speech, might be mutilated by having their ears cut off, their noses slashed, and/or their cheeks branded.

◄ FIGURE I. *A frontispiece is an illustration placed at the first opening of a volume. This frontispiece from John Taylor's* Diverse Crabtree Lectures *(London, 1639) depicts a "woman on top." The wife bends over her cowering husband, who attempts to appease her; she beats him with a ladle and scolds him for being a drunkard. Depictions of "men on top," that is, men beating or scolding their wives, are rare; this kind of inversion is depicted far more frequently."*

Dub a dub, kill her with a club,
Be thy wife's master.

. . . .

But if she persist, and will have her will,
Oh, then bang her, bang her, bang her still.   (*Juniper Lecture* G9, G9v)

Domestic violence was fairly widespread and not legally prohibited; unless a husband disturbed his neighbors' peace or beat his wife to death, there was no cause to bring him to court and little chance of any action against him. Although there were no laws against wife beating, an increasing number of didactic texts sought to convince husbands to govern both themselves and their wives and to refrain from violence. In the view of these texts, the man who allows himself to be provoked to violence has lost control rather than regained it (see "Wife Beating" in chapter 3, "The Household: Authority and Violence"). On the other hand, while neighbors objected to husbands who endangered their wives' lives or who constantly engaged in loud, disturbing fights, they also objected to husbands who submitted to abuse from their wives and allowed a "shrew" to go unreprimanded.

If authorities were reluctant to interfere in how men ran their households (unless private conflicts tumbled out into public notice), neighbors pried into every detail of events next door or down the street (Amussen, "Violence and Domestic Violence" 78). When they were dissatisfied, they might bring the couple before the church courts (which focused on regulating personal conduct).[16] Or they might take matters into their own hands, embarrassing their neighbors into conforming to community standards. Organizing a raucous parade that acted out the upside-down state of affairs in a household in which the wife "wore the breeches," neighbors sought to shame husband and wife into resuming their places in a traditional gender hierarchy — masterful husband and submissive wife. But the effects of such shaming rituals were unpredictable. On the one hand, Underdown argues that "gender inversion temporarily turns the world upside-

---

[16] Rather than concern themselves with those who broke the civil law, these courts, also known as ecclesiastical, consistory, or bishop's courts, focused on regulating personal conduct. As Laurence explains, "church courts dealt with transgressions of morality and the secular courts with matters regarding public order and property" (47).

down — but to reinforce, not subvert, the traditional order" (Under-down 117). On the other hand, Natalie Davis argues that the message of these shaming rituals was "mixed: it both exhorted the henpecked husband to take command and invited the unruly woman to keep up the fight" (Davis 140).[17] The unruly woman caricatured in a shaming ritual "was shameful, outrageous; she was also vigorous and in command" (Davis 140).

However we interpret Katharine's shrewishness, reading Shakespeare's play against other texts reveals that the play, like most other depictions of shrews, is full of resistant, disorderly self-assertions, not just outspokenness. Furthermore, the play, like most other depictions of shrews, focuses on tam-ing, whatever we may think of that process. Indeed, the play explores what Petruchio thinks, feels, and does as a tamer more fully than it explores what Katharine thinks, feels, and does as a shrew.

Authority and Violence in the Household: Husbands and Wives; Masters, Mistresses, and Servants

Many ballads and folktales recount the violent taming of shrews; in fact, those versions of shrew-taming stories in widest circulation tended to be extremely violent. In *A Merry Jest of a Shrewd and Curst Wife Lapped in Morel's Skin* (p. 257), for example, which Shakespeare probably knew, the husband secures his wife's obedience by severely beating her until she bleeds, then wrapping her in a salted horse hide; in "The Cucking of a Scold" (p. 292), the community, rather than a husband, uses pain, fear, and shame to discipline and silence a scold. But in Shakespeare's play, Petru-chio's methods of shrew taming are not quite so brutal or so overtly violent. Although Katharine slaps Petruchio, prompting him to warn "I swear I'll cuff you if you strike again" (2.1.216), Petruchio never hits Katharine. By what means, then, does he "tame" her?

In several speeches (two delivered directly to the audience as soliloquies) Petruchio outlines a series of strategies to gain mastery over Katharine. All these strategies, discussed in more detail below, correspond to the advice that ministers offered husbands in texts such as *A Homily of the State of Matrimony* (p. 172), William Whately's *A Bride-Bush* (p. 222), and Wil-liam Gouge's *Of Domestical Duties* (p. 225). According to these Protestant moralists, husbands should rule by policy rather than by blows. Even

---

[17] On how the participants in shaming rituals held husbands responsible for tolerating wives who defied their authority, see Boose, "Scolding Brides" 189–91; Ingram, "Ridings"; Un-derdown 127; Wiltenburg ch. 8; and Woodbridge ch. 8.

works less sober than these sermons insisted that policy was preferable to violence, not because it was more humane but because it was more effective.

> If she be quarrelsome, and curs'd of nature,
> Why policy will tame the fiercest creature.
>
> . . . .
>
> Some men will beat their wives, but that's the way,
> To make them obstinate and go astray;
>
> . . . .
>
> But, if thou seest her strive to wear the breeches,
> Then strive to overcome her with kind speeches.
> (*The Anatomy of a Woman's Tongue* 268)

William Heale, presenting himself as an "advocate" for women, similarly argues against domestic violence because it does not achieve the desired goal, obedience:

> Policy goeth beyond force in martial actions, wisdom beyond rigor in domestical affairs. And far safer is the obedience yielded up on fair terms, than that which is constrained on foul conditions: for the one proceeds from love, and is even filial; the other cometh of fear, and is only servile. (Heale F2)

Drawing parallels between "martial actions" and "domestical affairs," yet insisting that policy surpasses force even in the former, Heale, like many other writers about domestic conduct at this time, tries to help men draw distinctions between appropriate conduct on the battlefield and at home.

Writers like Heale or the unknown author of *A Homily of the State of Matrimony* work to convince male readers that violence is never the best way to resolve conflicts and that it is particularly inappropriate within the household. The goal of these efforts is to reinvent masculinity by proposing a domesticated, nonviolent alternative standard of manhood. *A Homily* recognizes that men who attempt to emulate this new standard will face opposition from their friends:

> Howbeit, the common sort of men doth judge that such moderation should not become a man. For they say that it is a token of womanish cowardness, and therefore they think that it is a man's part to fume in anger, to fight with fist and staff. (p. 175)

In establishing a new standard of masculinity, *A Homily* holds up Saint Peter as a more fit arbiter of conduct than such "common" men. "And yet a man may be a man, although he doth not use such extremity" (p. 175–76). By refraining from violence, husbands such as Petruchio can distinguish themselves from "the common sort of men" as gentle, in the sense of being both nonviolent and noble or wellborn. When Katharine warns Petruchio, after she has hit him — "If you strike me, you are no gentleman" (2.1.218) — she draws on the emerging association of overt domestic violence with commonness and of "policy" with gentleness or gentility.[18]

A Homily also emphasizes that this kinder, gentler mode of domestic discipline will accomplish better results: "For honest natures will sooner be retained to do their duties rather by gentle words than by stripes" (p. 175); another text similarly advises, "Better tame them by policy than blows" (Anatomy of a Woman's Tongue 271). Indeed, the husband's very survival depends on his ability to secure his wife's love rather than her grudging obedience. As John Dod and Robert Cleaver, two writers on domestic conduct, explain: "the husband that is not beloved of his wife holdeth his goods in danger, his house in suspicion, his credit in balance, and also sometimes his life in peril, because it is easy to believe that she desireth not long life unto her husband, with whom she passeth a time so tedious and irksome" (Dod and Cleaver L3; for an excerpt from this work, see p. 201).[19] Love is not an alternative to coercion or dominance. Instead, securing the love of one's dependents is depicted, in text after text, as a particularly efficacious and "politic" means of governing them.

These attempts to construct a less violent masculinity were complicated by the fact that marriage itself was viewed as a battle. A Homily of the State of Matrimony, for instance, advises husband and wife to be "armed on every side" against threats to the marriage (p. 183). The goal of such texts was to convince both husband and wife to cease fighting against one another and, instead, to join together in battling any obstacles to their marital happiness and peace. Both spouses are urged to consider themselves soldiers and warriors engaged in the heroic, perilous adventures of marriage. But these texts attempt to replace the comic antagonism between husband and wife so common in popular texts about shrews and their tamers — "often frivolous, always self-defeating" — with a model in which spouses are allies rather than opponents, striving together for happiness and salvation through marriage.[20]

In refraining from battering Katharine and in praising his own "policy," Petruchio aspires to this emerging ideal of "gentle" domestic masculinity.

[18] As policy rather than force became the mark of the gentleman, distinguishing him from the common sort, it also became a crucial component of his reputation. For instance, Heale claims that "it is a main hindrance to any public preferment" to be known as a wife beater, "for how can he be thought fit to manage the affairs of a commonwealth, who is not able to keep order in his own house?" (Heale C4). On how blame for domestic violence was displaced onto lower-class men, see p. 246, and Hunt. See also Quilligan 214–15, 219.
[19] This passage appeared first in Edmund Tilney's The Flower of Friendship (London, 1568).
[20] See Rose on the "heroics of marriage in Renaissance tragedy" (ch. 3).

But the tenacious stage tradition in which Petruchio brandishes a whip (which seems to have begun in the eighteenth century) suggests that audiences have long associated him with violence or the threat of violence, despite his claims to policy.[21] (See Figure 4 on p. 156.) Even Petruchio's claims that he will endure Katharine, rather than forcefully oppose her, can be seen as an aggressive refusal to engage with her. For instance, explicitly contrasting martial and marital struggles, Petruchio diminishes the threat posed by "a woman's tongue." Fortified by his experiences as a soldier and adventurer, he can "endure [Katharine's] loud alarums" (1.1.128).

> Think you a little din can daunt mine ears?
>
> . . . .
>
> Have I not heard great ordnance in the field,
> And heaven's artillery thunder in the skies? (1.2.190, 194–95)

In belittling the threat offered by a woman's tongue, Petruchio translates Katharine's speech into meaningless noise. His goal is to endure it rather than to hear, understand, and respond to it. This portrait of his own heroic endurance of, rather than engagement with, Katharine's speech corresponds to his taming strategy of contradicting Katharine, which he outlines in 2.1.

Refusing to listen to, or respond to, scolding was often recommended as a shrew-taming strategy. In *A Juniper Lecture*, for instance, the author advises: "There is nothing more vexing to a scold, than when she perceives the party she scolds at not to be vexed; for they cannot be angered worse than not to answer them" (*Juniper Lecture* F11). The author further counsels that, when a wife begins scolding, her husband "slight her, by doing some action or other, as singing, dancing, whistling, or clapping thy hands on thy sides; for this will make her vex extremely, because you give her not word for word"; rather than leave home, the husband should pace back and forth in front of her, performing his disregard (G7v). If all else fails, the husband should buy a drum "and when she doth begin to talk aloft, do then begin to beat aloud, which she hearing will presently be amazed, hearing a louder voice than her own, and make her forbear scolding anymore for that time"

---

[21] This tradition seems to have begun with the actor J. P. Kemble. In a promptbook from a 1788 production of David Garrick's *Catharine and Petruchio*, Kemble wrote "whip for Petruchio" as a stage direction for Petruchio's entrance in the wedding scene (Haring-Smith 24; Thompson 19). Works such as *The Anatomy of a Woman's Tongue*, which proposes binding a wife hand and foot and threatening to cut out her tongue if she does not shut up as a way of taming "by policy," also reveal that "policy" could be violent even if it did not resort to blows.

(G8v).[22] If a woman's scolding was construed as disorderly and as a kind of violence, then the husband's refusal to hear her and his raucous attempts to drown her out — singing, whistling, dancing, clapping, drumming — should also be seen as violent and disorderly. Husbands are advised to use a riotous, confusing performance for disciplining their wives and to counter disorder with disorder.

Petruchio does just this in his attempts to tame Katharine, especially at the wedding (3.2) and then in the scene at his house (4.1), treating his servants so badly that Katharine intervenes on their behalf. As many critics have argued, in these scenes "Petruchio tames a shrew by becoming one" (Wayne, "Refashioning the Shrew" 171); he shows Katharine a mirror of her own disorderly behavior (Andresen-Thom 131–35; Perret). As Petruchio's servant Curtis remarks after hearing the story of the couple's progress home from the wedding: "By this reckoning he is more shrew than she" (4.1.60). Although Tranio finds it impossible to believe that Petruchio could be "curster" than Katharine, he and Gremio draw parallels between her disruptive conduct and Petruchio's.

GREMIO: Why, he's a devil, a devil, a very fiend.
TRANIO: Why, she's a devil, a devil, the devil's dam.
GREMIO: Tut, she's a lamb, a dove, a fool to him.   (3.2.145–47)

But if many critics agree with these characters in the play that Petruchio himself acts as a shrew in order to tame Katharine, they disagree in evaluating this behavior. Some see it as a clever, playful strategy; Petruchio teaches Katharine how much she values convention, order, and social prestige (Leggatt 51–54; Hibbard). Many critics also think that by imitating Katharine's creation of chaos, Petruchio moves them both from a debased equality (as two shrews) to an elevated one (equal partners in marriage) (Bean). Other critics, however, argue that Petruchio's ability to assume the role of shrew for the purposes of taming Katharine reveals the marked inequality between the two. Petruchio can get away with this behavior, but Katharine cannot; in him it is funny and strategic, but in her it is threatening and out of control (Boose, "Scolding Brides" 193; Hodgdon 540). Furthermore, when Petruchio yells at and strikes his servants, he abuses or exaggerates power that his culture gives him as a man: householder, master, and husband (Kahn 104). When Katharine lashes out, she seizes power not properly hers; indeed she seizes it away from Petruchio (Garner 112–13). Petruchio is also a shrew in that he dominates through speech, drowning

----

[22] See Xanthippe's discussion of how her husband fiddles to drown her out, in Snawsel's *A Looking Glass for Married Folks* (p. 189).

out Katharine's words with his own, and making his account of her the dominant one. In her first lines Katharine complains that men talk about her and
that her father *lets* them. Petruchio steps in to contradict these claims made
about Katharine and to redirect the pastime of talking about her. When he
first encounters Katharine, he claims to have "heard" not those remarks she
complains about in act 1, but praise. Later in this scene when Petruchio reports his success as a suitor and his plans to marry Katharine, he deliberately
refutes the false reports of her. He also offers a fresh interpretation of her
shrewishness, correcting even her father (2.1.283–85). Yet in refusing to believe one set of stories about Katharine, Petruchio creates another. Katharine
is still talked about more than she talks. In his first soliloquy, explaining that
he'll woo by contradiction, Petruchio repeats the word "say" five times; he
uses at least eight verbs to describe speaking (*rail, tell, ask, speak, commend,
utter, bid, deny*) (2.1.166f). The whole speech is structured around what others might "say" about Katharine's behavior as opposed to what Petruchio will
"say" about it. In other words, Petruchio proposes to contradict not only
what Katharine herself says but also the "reports" of her, the ways of describing her conduct practiced by the suitors. Part of his strategy for taming
a shrew will be to insist from the start that she is not one.

   Though Petruchio never strikes Katharine (despite the fact that she
strikes him) part of his "politic" regime for taming her relies on physical
violence directed at those near her and enacted before her eyes. We see the
first instance of violence when he wrings Grumio's ears (1.2). At the wedding
Petruchio cuffs the priest and throws the winesops in the sexton's face (3.2).
We hear that on their way home he beats Grumio because Kate's horse stumbled (4.1); once at home, he kicks, strikes, and throws food at his servants
(4.1). Many critics find it significant that "the humor and violence that the
husband traditionally vents on the wife [in shrew-taming tales] are deflected
from Katharine onto subsidiary characters such as Grumio, the sexton,
Petruchio's household servants, the tailor" (Mikesell 153) and that Petruchio's disorderly behavior "is not aimed at Kate" (Wayne, "Refashioning the
Shrew" 171). But Petruchio's violence is directed at his subordinates — at
those over whom he has power — and reminds Katharine that she, too, is his
subordinate and that he could beat her if he chose. At the wedding we are
told that Katharine "trembled and shook" (3.2.157); when Petruchio abuses
his servants, Katharine intervenes to stop or reprimand him (4.1). She responds as if the violence is "aimed at" and threatening to her.[23]

---

[23] In many folktales, "a man cures his bad wife by administering cruel and irrational punishment to a recalcitrant animal" (Brunvand 345); his strategy is to frighten his wife by making
her witness displaced violence.

Once Katharine marries Petruchio and walks into his household as his wife, she enters a situation in which he controls her access to even the most basic subsistence — food and sleep. In his soliloquy describing how he has "politicly begun [his] reign" (4.1.157–80), Petruchio explains that he will tame Katharine as falconers tame wild hawks, or haggards. He will prevent her from eating or sleeping, but in doing so he will "kill her with kindness," insisting that "all is done in reverent care of her." (See the readings in "Analogues to Shrew Taming," pp. 304–16, for contexts for Petruchio's speech.) Rather than explicitly deny Katharine food or sleep, he insists that neither the food nor the bed is good enough for her. Katharine finds this the most galling aspect of Petruchio's treatment: "And that which spites me more than all these wants, / He does it under name of perfect love" (4.3.11–12). Under the appearance of solicitude he wreaks havoc at the table and in the bed, the very places where husband and wife were supposed to foster their bond. He rejects the food as inedible, throws it around the room, and breaks dishes; he also tears up the bed: "here I'll fling the pillow, there the bolster, / This way the coverlet, another way the sheets" (4.1.170–71). The table and bed were so widely understood to be the central locations of marital life that a legal separation was called a separation *a mensa et thoro*, that is, a separation from table and bed. In popular accounts of husbands or wives who murder their spouses, the murders most often occur in these locations. William Gouge explains that wives are more vulnerable to abusive husbands than servants are to abusive masters because they are "continually at board and bed with their husbands" (p. 226). Finally, texts that parody the speeches of scolding wives often depict the wives as lecturing their husbands in bed, disturbing the one place that should be most restful. As one writer warns, "if that place [the bed] which is ordained to make amends for all faults and so to renew love be polluted, either with strife or grudgings, then farewell all hope of love days or atonements" (Erasmus, *Merry Dialogue* 271). These texts are often called "curtain lectures" because they claim to record the speeches wives make behind the bed curtains (see Figures 2 and 3). In his role as politic, temporary shrew, then, Petruchio creates chaos in the two central locations of marriage, the sites of greatest intimacy and greatest risk.

Although Katharine is able to raise mayhem in her father's house through words and blows, she is at Petruchio's mercy in the conjugal bed and at the marital table. As Katharine's situation reveals, a woman's place may be in the home, but the home is not necessarily safe.[24] Yet, in both her father's house and Petruchio's house, Katharine's relationship to violence-

---

[24] "The privacy of home can be a dangerous place, especially for women and children" (Okin 129; cf. Radford 7).

A BOVLSTER LECTVRE.

Dum loquor, illa, taces?

Surdo canis.

Will: Marshall. sculpsit.

This wife a wondrous racket meanes to keepe,
While th' Husband seemes to sleepe but do'es not sleepe:
But she might full aswell her Lecture smother,
For ent'ring one Eare, it goes out at t'other.

London. Printed for R Best and are to bee sould at his shop neare Graies Inn gatte in Houlbourne.

A Curtaine Lecture.

When Wiues preach, tis not in the Husbands, pow
To haue their Lectures end within an hower
If Hee with patience stay till shee haue donn
Shee'l not conclude till twyce the Glasse hee runn

22

and to domestic authority is complicated. Katharine, like Petruchio, uses violence to assert mastery over those to whom she feels superior. She threatens to hit Hortensio in the head with a three-legged stool (1.1.63–64); she ties up Bianca and strikes her (2.1); she breaks Hortensio's/Litio's head with the lute (2.1); and she strikes Petruchio (2.1). Petruchio's servants assume that Katharine will be violent toward them. Grumio warns Curtis that he will "soon feel" their new mistress's hand, "she being now at hand" (4.1.22–23). Indeed, later at Petruchio's house, she beats Grumio for refusing to feed her (4.3).

Do Katharine's motives for resorting to violence change from 2.1 to 4.3? One critic claims that when she strikes out, she does so "because of provocation or intimidation resulting from her status as a woman" (Kahn 108). But Katharine also acts out of an empowerment resulting from her status as a *gentle*woman and a mistress. She acts simultaneously out of gender subordination and class privilege; in relation to her younger sister, her age is a factor.

In the other instances of violence in the play, superiors also lash out against inferiors. Grumio boxes Curtis's ear (4.1); Vincentio beats Biondello (Lucentio's boy servant), and threatens to slit Tranio's nose (5.1). Given that servants are the usual targets of violence in the play, when

◄ FIGURE 2. *Frontispiece from Richard Brathwaite's* Ar't Asleep Husband? *A Bolster Lecture (London, 1640). Collections of "bolster" or "curtain" lectures, like this one, claimed to offer scripts for the kinds of things angry wives said to their husbands in bed. Such works simultaneously imagined or recorded women's angry speech, and dismissed it as insignificant. The verse beneath the picture insists that the wife's speech is fruitless; the Latin tags issuing from the spouses' mouths also convey this message. The wife wonders how her husband can remain silent while she is speaking at his side; he informs her that she is preaching to deaf ears. The appropriate response to a scold's speech is to ignore it.*

In their very titles, curtain or bolster lectures indicate the centrality of the bed as a location of domestic life and marital interaction. The domestic details — the chamber pot, the slippers at the side of the bed, the substantial bed curtains and linens — indicate a fairly high level of comfort and affluence.

FIGURE 3. *Another frontispiece, this one from Thomas Heywood's* A Curtain Lecture *(London, 1637), closely resembles the preceding one. Here, too, the Latin tags indicate that the husband and wife speak at cross-purposes. She announces "I proclaim the truth," while he warns "Don't believe women" (Best edition of Markham xxiv). In both illustrations, in contrast to* The Taming of the Shrew, *it is the wife who keeps the husband awake with her nagging. The domestic setting here is even more detailed and opulent than in Figure 2.*

Katharine hits Petruchio, she treats him as a servant; she hits him to demote him, to gain the upper hand, in terms of class/status. Although we see one extraordinary instance of trust and friendship between a master and servant — Lucentio refers to Tranio as his confidant ("Thou are to me as secret and as dear / As Anna to the Queen of Carthage was" [1.1.145–46]), asks for his counsel, and trusts him to exchange identities — the play suggests that persons with power over others often abuse that power, relying on violence to assert themselves.

Under Petruchio's instruction Katharine learns not only how to be an obedient wife but also how to assert dominance in more socially acceptable ways. Throughout *The Taming of the Shrew* Katharine imposes obedience and subordination both with physical violence (from torturing her sister to "swingeing" Bianca and the widow "soundly forth unto their husbands" [5.2.108]) and with assertive speech (from her first complaint to her father to her final sermon to other wives). What Katharine learns is not to be less violent, but to redirect her violence toward more appropriate targets; that Bianca becomes an acceptable target by the end of the play suggests how the balance of power has shifted between the sisters. When Katharine uses violence to dominate servants and other women rather than to resist her father or husband, her conduct is presented as laudable.[25]

The "Feme Covert": Katharine's Silences

Although Katharine is labeled a shrew because she resists attempts to dominate her and asserts herself with fist and tongue, she is characterized more by silence than by speech at several important points in the play. These moments of silence baffle critics, actors, and directors (Rutter ch. 1). How do we know what Katharine thinks, feels, and wants? How does Katharine act in these scenes in which she says nothing? For instance, in the scene in which Petruchio reports on his success in wooing Katharine and their plans to marry (2.1), what does she do? She says she'll see him hanged rather than marry him (line 292); but as he goes on to insist on her love for him and on the bargain they have struck, she says nothing. Petruchio explains her silence by claiming: " 'Tis bargained twixt us twain, being alone, / That she shall still be curst in company" (2.1.297–98). Some critics take Petruchio at his word here, reading his statement as an

---

[25] According to Boose, "Kate's submission to the hierarchy of gender is predicated on the retention of her social position in the hierarchy of class." Petruchio gets her to that point by means of a careful strategy: "every time Kate resists submission in the arena of gender, she is punished by degradation in the arena of class" (Boose, *"Taming"* 219).

early indication that, for instance, "Petruchio and Katharine have found a mode of conjugal behaviour for public display and a mode of behaviour for private rapport" (Maguire 135). According to this interpretation, then, Katharine conforms in public but remains "free to be her own person in private" (Maguire 135). Petruchio "has gained her outward compliance in the form of a public display, while her spirit remains mischievously free" (Kahn 115). A sharply demarcated boundary between public and private thus frees both partners to negotiate their relationship "on a variety of different terms without threatening assumptions of male dominance in the society at large" (Novy 61). Whatever they agree on privately, then, will not change or challenge the accepted norms for marital conduct.

Other critics, however, argue against Petruchio's strategic distinction between public and private, claiming that it, and critics' acceptance of it, depend on what political scientists and feminist theorists have called "the myth of the separation of the public and the domestic, of the political from the personal" (Okin 130; cf. Bamber 34 and MacKinnon 194). The play itself blurs the distinction between public and private. We see Katharine and Petruchio alone only in 2.1; we never see Katharine by herself; and when she complains, she always has an audience besides or other than Petruchio. Far from drawing a line between household and common-wealth, in her final speech Katharine explains the ideal relationship be-tween husband and wife by comparing it to the relationship between ruler and subject; this scene suggests that "her domestication is complete only when it is made public" (Slights 188).

The permeable boundary between public and private was most often redrawn to protect the husband's authority and rights — as when wives were enjoined not to complain about or scold their husbands in public.[26] The breaching of the border tended to protect wives, as when neighbors scrutinized or complained about brawling and unquietness. As one histo-rian explains, "the women most vulnerable to domestic violence were those cut off from the community — usually women of gentry status" (Amussen, "Violence and Domestic Violence" 81). Therefore, if, as Maguire argues, "the attempt to negotiate a compromise between personal and public iden-tity is not a problem exclusive to women" (Maguire 157), men and women

---

[26] Wives were often advised to keep their grievances to themselves. In Snawsel's *A Looking Glass*, for instance, Eulalie praises the quiet endurance of a wife who, after "being beaten and abused" by her husband, hides in "her secret closet." When her husband discovers her there, sobbing and "digesting her grief," he asks "Why sittest thou here sighing, and sobbing, and crying like a child?" She asks, "Is it not better to do thus, here to bewail my grief where nobody hears nor sees, than to run and cry out in the streets, and to exclaim on you, as others do on their husbands?" The husband is so impressed by this that he never hits her again (Snawsel D8–D8v).

entered into these negotiations on very different terms. For, as the scenes in Petruchio's house reveal, the private is a sphere in which Petruchio is distinctly more powerful than is Katharine.

Within the household, Katharine is one of Petruchio's possessions: "She is my goods, my chattels; she is my house, / My household stuff" (3.2.219–20).[27] Although Katharine brings property to the marriage and earns more money for Petruchio in the wager scene, she does not control property once she is married. In accord with the laws and customs governing married women's property, all she has is her husband's — as Petruchio reminds her in the tailor scene — while everything Petruchio has is his own (see T. E., *The Law's Resolutions of Women's Rights*, p. 197). Furthermore, that it is Petruchio who describes this agreement underscores his monopoly of self-expression in the play. He has soliloquies in which he explains his motives and intentions; Katharine does not. He speaks more than twice as many lines as she does (564 to her 207; see Kahn 115–16). Petruchio thus controls the resources of the stage as well as Katharine's access to food and clothing. Katharine's baffling silences are the dramatic enactment of the process by which she, like all married women, becomes a "feme covert," that is, one who is absorbed into, or subsumed by, her husband. Marriage made husband and wife one person in the eyes of the law; that person was the husband. He had legal rights and privileges, which he was expected to exercise on behalf of both members of the couple; he also had legal responsibility for his wife. Even legal writers acknowledged that one result of the husband's subsumption of his wife could be that the wife might fear she had become "either none or no more than half a person" (T. E., *Law's Resolutions*, p. 198). As Curtis says of the newly married Katharine: she "knows not which way to stand, to look, to speak, / And sits as one new risen from a dream" (4.1.154–55). Legally, such a partial person had only a limited ability to exercise agency — that is, to act independently, to be held accountable for those actions, to consent, or to enter into contracts.

Linking Katharine's silences to the ambiguous status of the "feme covert" offers one way of thinking about those silences, which complicate efforts to see Katharine as a fully developed character who thinks, feels, and chooses. The play provides no evidence that Katharine is a party to the bargain Petruchio describes; she says nothing. Indeed, Petruchio seems to use the supposed bargain to dismiss whatever Katharine might say or do in the scene. Katharine's silence in this scene raises other questions. Does Katharine agree to marry Petruchio? If so, why? What are her alternatives?

---

[27] Marcus argues that this depiction of the wife as "a private possession of the husband to be tucked away at home was, in England at least, only beginning to emerge as the most desirable family model for haut bourgeois households" (Marcus 187).

We see two very different kinds of love or mating (Hibbard 19–20) but no real alternative to marriage for Katharine, Bianca, or the widow. After all, the play's principal locations are the houses of Katharine's and Bianca's father, husbands, and suitors. Katharine may well be jealous of Bianca's success on the marriage market and does not want to remain a spinster. According to one critic, "her fierce unhappiness and forwardness arise not from the independence of rebellion or even of eccentricity, but from deprivation"; "what she wants is marriage" (Mikesell 152). For instance, Katharine complains to her father that his preference for Bianca will prevent her from getting married herself:

> Nay, now I see
> She is your treasure, she must have a husband;
> I must dance barefoot on her wedding day,
> And for your love to her lead apes in hell.
> Talk not to me. I will go sit and weep
> Till I can find occasion of revenge.   (2.1.31–36)

Katharine also emphasizes her shame when she thinks Petruchio has stood her up.

> Now must the world point at poor Katharine
> And say, "Lo, there is mad Petruchio's wife,
> If it would please him come and marry her!"   (3.2.18–20)

Given Renaissance marriage customs, Katharine might be unmarriageable (because she is considered already betrothed) if Petruchio does not arrive for the wedding; she would thus be, in the words of one critic, "condemned to a life of frustrated spinsterhood" (Ranald 125). Petruchio furthers his taming by making Katharine grateful to him simply for showing up (Ranald 125).

Historians' work on the options and status of unmarried women helps to place in context the absence of alternatives to marriage in *The Taming of the Shrew*. While there were certainly unmarried women in sixteenth- and seventeenth-century England, these women did not have many social and economic options. After England became a Protestant (rather than a Catholic) country with the Reformation in the mid sixteenth century, religious vocations and convent life no longer offered an alternative to marriage. Those who remained unmarried often attained not independence but even greater dependence; an unmarried woman's status was "ambiguous and hence inferior" (Slater 90). She was "a perennial supplicant" (Slater 85), dependent on the head of the household that took her in and desperate to stay in his good graces. *The Taming of the Shrew* depicts a world in which unmarried gentlewomen could not find paid work to support themselves and in which it was not acceptable or possible for such women to live on their own or with one another.[28] The choice they faced was not independence or marriage, but marriage or dependence on a man other than a husband — a father, a brother, a brother-in-law, or in the case of poorer women, a master. Given that "the conditions of the single life were such that even a poor match was preferable to having no husband at all," a woman like Katharine did not need to love her suitor to want to marry him; economic and social need, rather than desire, might have motivated her (Slater 84).

But we can only speculate about Katharine's motives; the text of the play does not make them clear. Although Katharine articulates her rage and humiliation when Petruchio does not come to the wedding, she has no lines at the end of act 3, scene 2 — after the wedding, and after Petruchio has refused to attend the wedding feast and Katharine has defied him. Petruchio's lines provide what could be stage directions for Katharine: "Nay, look not big, nor stamp, nor stare, nor fret; / I will be master of what is mine own" (3.2.217–18). But she says nothing, even as Petruchio launches into his notorious "She is my goods, my chattels" speech (3.2.219–21). By what means does Petruchio get Katharine to go with him, despite her earlier resistance?

Other versions of the play attempt to fill in the gap created by Katharine's silence; these versions allow Katharine to consent to the marriage and to assert her confidence that she is a "match" for her husband. In *A Pleasant Conceited History, Called The Taming of a Shrew* (1594), Katharine "turns aside and speaks":

> But yet I will consent and marry him
> For I, methinks, have lived too long a maid,
> And match him, too, or else his manhood's good. (B3)

In David Garrick's eighteenth-century *Catharine and Petruchio*, an adaptation of Shakespeare's play "with alterations and additions," Catharine responds to Petruchio's impudence in claiming that they will marry the next day by saying, as an aside: "I'll marry my revenge, but I will tame him" (7). In this version Catharine also has a soliloquy at the end of act 1. Responding to her father's earlier remark that Bianca and all their friends will attend the wedding, she says (directly to the audience):

> Why yes. Sister Bianca now shall see
> The poor abandoned Catharine, as she calls me,
> Can hold her head as high, and be as proud,

---

[28] Those women who headed their own households were more likely to be widows than spinsters (Laurence 55–56). See also Stone 382–85.

And make her husband stoop onto her lure,
As she, or e'er a wife in Padua.
As double as my portion be my scorn;
Look to your seat, Petruchio, or I throw you.
Catharine shall tame this haggard — or if she fails,
Shall tie her tongue up, and pare down her nails. (8)[29]

Here Catharine not only consents but also brings her own taming agenda to the marriage.

Achieving the Marital Ideal: Sun and Moon

In Shakespeare's *The Taming of the Shrew*, Katharine's self-assertions after her marriage are few, brief, and unsuccessful; her eloquent articulation of her anger, adulthood, and autonomy in 4.3 (73–80) is her last. The pivotal moment in the taming process — Petruchio's converting Katharine from the outspoken, violent, resistant "shrew" of the first few acts to the "conformable household Kate" of the last scene — occurs in 4.5. Neither hunger nor weariness tames Katharine (directly). The arena of struggle turns out not to be the material domestic world, in which Petruchio has the power to withhold the "household stuff" of clothing, food, and bedding from Katharine. Instead, Petruchio's control over material resources empowers him in an even more important terrain of struggle — language and its capacity to create meaning and shape perceptions (Newman 44; Fineman).

The couple's final conflict begins in a dispute about time. When Katharine disagrees with Petruchio about what time it is, he bursts out angrily:

Look what I speak, or do, or think to do,
You are still crossing it. — Sirs, let't alone.
I will not go today, and ere I do
It shall be what o'clock I say it is. (4.3.184–87)

As Hortensio comments in an aside, "this gallant will command the sun" (4.3.188). Two scenes later, Petruchio demonstrates that he can indeed "command the sun," at least in relation to his wife. On the road to Baptista's house Katharine and Petruchio begin to quarrel over whether it is night or day, whether they see the moon in the sky or the sun. Petruchio insists that: "It shall be moon, or star, or what I list, / Or ere I journey to your father's house. / . . . . / Evermore crossed and crossed, nothing but

[29] Thompson also discusses these passages from *A Shrew* and Garrick's adaptation (19; cf. 18–24).

crossed!" (4.5.7–8, 10). Katharine finally submits when Hortensio reminds her of the consequences of resistance: "Say as he says, or we shall never go" (11). Hortensio presents concession on Katharine's part as the only hope for peace and for moving forward — the play's metaphor for happy marriage. If spouses are stalled in contention, they cannot go anywhere. As Dod and Cleaver explain in their popular seventeenth-century book on domestic life, "if [the wife] will make against [her husband], and seek to have her own ways, there will be doing and undoing. Things will go backward, the house will come to ruin" (Dod and Cleaver F3v). Presented with these alternatives, Katharine chooses to move forward:

> Forward, I pray, since we have come so far,
> And be it moon, or sun, or what you please;
> An if you please to call it a rush candle,
> Henceforth I vow it shall be so for me. (4.5.12–15)

Katharine even goes the game one farther, elaborating on the identification of the old man as a young woman, and blaming her "mistake" on the sun.[30] "And the moon changes even as your mind. / What you will have it named, even that it is, / And so it shall be so for Katharine" (20–22).[31] Hortensio announces Petruchio the victor in a contest that has been simultaneously marital and martial: "Petruchio, go thy ways. The field is won" (23).

The relationship between the sun and the moon was often used to explain the ideal relationship between husband and wife. The analogy helped to explain how the wife could have authority over her servants and children, yet remain subordinate to her husband. Just as the moon reflected the sun's light, "The Wife in her Husband's absence shines in the family, like the fair *Moon* among the lesser stars: but when he comes in, it will be her modesty to contract, and withdraw herself" (Griffith Y3v). When a wife governs the household, she does so "with the consent and reference of her husband's will, taking all her light (as the Moon is said from the Sun, so she) from her husband, for government and authority, as his Lieutenant under him; and so wisely disposing all to his honor accordingly" (S. B., *Counsel to the Husband* D3v–D4). This analogy between husband and wife, sun and moon, corresponds to the assumption that the wife should act as a mirror to her husband, reflecting his moods. Her husband's "face must be her daily looking glass, wherein she ought to be always prying, to see when

---

[30] Richard Burt argues that "Petruchio and Kate become emotionally closer whenever Petruchio enables Kate to redirect the aggression he directs at her at another victim" (Burt 299). In Burt's view this dynamic is especially clear in this scene with the old man as victim, although many critics insist that the scene is free of aggression and coercion.

[31] That Katharine refers to herself in the third person here suggests an emerging gap between how Katharine views herself and how she acts in relation to Petruchio (Quilligan 218, 220).

he is merry, when sad, when content, and when discontent, whereto she must always frame her countenance" (Tilney, lines 1316–20).[32] In 4.5, Katharine begins to mirror her husband's moods and perceptions, to govern her conduct with an eye to his inclinations, to say as he says. It is hardly accidental that they establish this relationship as person and mirror, source of light and authority versus reflection through a debate about the sun and the moon. In discussing the sun and the moon, they become them.

Critics differ markedly in their interpretations of this scene. Some see it as a turning point toward mutuality, reciprocity, and shared playfulness. In Novy's view, for instance, Katharine here "seems more like a partner in the game rather than an object used in it" (Novy 54). Although she submits as a wife, "as a player in the game she is now a full and skillful partner. Most important, she is helping to create her own role as an obedient spouse, and the process of creation gives her pleasure" (Leggatt 59). "Kate is tamed not by Petruchio's whip but by the discovery of her own imagination" (Bean 72; cf. Andresen-Thom 141). With dexterity and wit Katharine participates in Petruchio's game (although, as Burt points out, the couple's "playfulness" is built through shared cruelty toward Vincentio). She again accommodates her husband in the next scene; witnessing the "counterfeit supposes" surrounding Bianca's marriage, Katharine and Petruchio unite as the amused witnesses of others' discomfiture. But whatever "mutuality" the two achieve does not replace their struggles for dominance. When Katharine requests that they "follow, to see the end of this ado" (5.1.114), Petruchio first requires that she overcome her shame in kissing "in the midst of the street" (115). As usual, he threatens that they'll return home if she doesn't comply. In this exchange their compromise reached in 4.5 enables Petruchio to dominate with less struggle.

That Petruchio continues to test and coerce Katharine suggests why many critics see the Sun and Moon scene as one in which Katharine submits not playfully and with pleasure, but wearily, even fearfully (Garner; Kahn; Newman). If Katharine and Petruchio are equal partners in the game, why does Petruchio set the terms, define reality, determine whether the couple will move forward or return home? For many readers and viewers Katharine's motives and thoughts are a greater mystery in this scene than ever before. Why does she choose to submit at this point? What does

---

[32] On such descriptions of wives as reflections, see Dolan, "Gender, Moral Agency and Dramatic Form" 206–07; Ezell 40; and Fineman 152–53. Ezell argues that "the point of these examples is adaptability; it is not that the wife has no mind of her own, but that she deliberately alters it if necessary to conform with her husband's situation. He, of course, being the Good Husband, attempts likewise to oblige her" (40). When Petruchio acts like a shrew, he inverts this convention by holding a mirror up to Katharine (Perret 232).

that submission mean to her? How does it feel? Must we assume that Katharine's feelings correspond to her actions — that she joyously submits — or can we imagine some silent resistance or internal reservation?

Endings and Alternatives

Such questions point to the controversy that surrounds the last scene of the play, and, especially, Katharine's lengthy speech. Is this speech sincere or ironic? Should we take Katharine at her word? Or should we imagine a gap between what she says and what she means? As many critics have argued, the speech is a paradox, the performance itself contradicting the content. "Though the speech pleads subordination, as a speech — a lengthy, ambitious verbal performance before an audience — it allows the speaker to dominate that audience" (Kahn 116; cf. Newman 48). In it we see "a woman dominating a scene by giving advice to other women" (Wayne, "Refashioning the Shrew" 172); Katharine "holds the center stage while preaching humility" (Novy 59). In submission Katharine finds permission and opportunity to speak publicly and authoritatively. Her sermon on wifely subordination is both her "longest utterance and the longest in the play" (Kahn 115). Evidently, Katharine is licensed to speak when she supports, rather than resists, traditional gender roles and hierarchical relations between spouses (Mikesell 160). When she speaks on command, and when she says as Petruchio says, he deems her speech virtuous and laudable.[33]

Yet the other characters do not all agree in evaluating Katharine's speech. To Petruchio, Katharine's willingness not only to obey but to perform that obedience, means "peace . . . and love, and quiet life, / An awful rule, and right supremacy, / And, to be short, what not that's sweet and happy" (112–14). The widow, however, finds Katharine's willingness to throw her cap under Petruchio's foot "a silly pass" (5.2.128); Bianca calls it "a foolish duty" (129). The widow and Bianca are also reluctant to bear witness to Katharine's concluding speech. Obviously, wives view Katharine's conduct differently than husbands do. As one critic points out, "men alone celebrate Kate's reformation" (Burt 303).

---

[33] On this speech as a "command performance," see Bean 74; Burt 299. It reminds us that women's speech was not always prohibited; under certain circumstances it was not only permitted but praised. For instance, William Heale explains that although "the nimbleness of women's tongues" sometimes results in "their husbands' disturbance," women's busy tongues can also do their husbands good "in merchandizing for their profit, in refreshing their wearied spirits, ofttimes in entertaining their friends with courteous compliment" (Heale Fv–F2). See also Snawsel's *A Looking Glass*, p. 187.

The men lay wagers on their wives designed to set the women in competition with one another; they also use the staged conflict among their wives to compete among themselves. Marriage thus becomes one important arena in which men can assert dominance, raise their social status, and prove their manhood (see Boose, *"The Taming of the Shrew"* 214; and Burt 303). Through the wager the men compete with one another as they would in any other gentlemanly sport, such as hunting or hawking (see p. 304); but, since the wager concerns their ability to dominate their wives, the power struggles between men and women are more visible than those among men. Their bet reveals that it has been Katharine's job all along to make Petruchio a winner, to enable him to "lord" it not only over her, but over other men.

If marriage helps to displace the conflicts among male characters, it amplifies the conflicts among female characters that we have seen from the start of the play. Unique as "the only Shakespearean comic heroine without a female friend at any point in the play" (Novy 60), the "reformed" Katharine is as much or more at odds with other women as she was when she bound and beat her sister. She is encouraged to be so. When she and the widow exchange insults, Petruchio and Hortensio make this fight into a spectacle and sport: "To her, Kate!"; "To her, widow!" (5.2.33–34). In the last scene, at Petruchio's command, Katharine fetches Bianca and the widow; it is possible to present her dragging them in since Petruchio urges her to "swinge me them soundly forth unto their husbands" should they refuse to come (5.2.108). For doing so, Katharine is rewarded with the chance to feel better than others. Katharine, who was found wanting in relation to her desirable sister, who was the extreme example of the unmarriageable woman, now regains social value and respect by putting down other women as "froward and unable worms" (5.23.173).

In her last speech Katharine describes the appropriate relation between husband and wife as a hierarchical one similar to that between ruler and subject. The husband is the wife's "lord," "king," "governor," "head," and "sovereign": "Such duty as the subject owes the prince, / Even such a woman oweth to her husband" (5.2.159–60). Analogies between commonwealth and household, political and domestic, were widely used. (See, for instance, Dod and Cleaver's *A Godly Form of Household Government,* p. 204). They emphasized the obedience of dependents, such as wives and servants, and the far-reaching consequences of disobedience. For a subordinate to "seek for rule, supremacy, and sway" (167) is to commit treason, that is, a crime against domestic authority parallel to any threat to, betrayal of, or assault on the monarch and his or her government. Katharine's description of a disobedient wife as "a foul contending rebel / And graceless traitor to her loving lord" (163–64) is not simply a matter of rhetoric; it also refers to legal practice. Killing one's husband or master was petty treason; legal statutes carefully distinguished it from other forms of murder. For women the punishment for petty treason was not hanging — the usual punishment for murder — but burning at the stake, which was also the punishment for women who had committed high treason.

The analogy between household and commonwealth goes beyond assigning enormous power to the husband, father, and master, and enjoining the obedience and loyalty of dependents. It also suggests that the head of the household must rule responsibly and must protect and provide for his dependents. Some critics point to the reciprocal and balanced duties Katharine describes. Yet Katharine emphasizes the necessity of obedience much more than the responsibilities of rule. Furthermore, her claim that the husband labors to support his wife bears no resemblance to what we have seen in the play. Petruchio does not work; indeed, he improves his financial status by marrying Katharine. Although Katharine contrasts the wife, who lies "warm at home, secure and safe" to the husband who must "watch the night in storms, the day in cold," the play we have just seen complicates these neatly divided, gendered spheres (see the section "Women's Work: Gender and the Division of Labor," pp. 206–18). Petruchio's sphere of action is the household: he "watches the night" only in order to keep his wife awake. At home, his wife is not warm, secure, and safe, but hungry, tired, and angry.

In her speech Katharine describes how she herself moved from foul contending rebel to dutiful wife. Again, while her speech echoes the most conventional wisdom about marriage, wifely duties, and femininity, it does not exactly match up with what we have seen.

> My mind hath been as big as one of yours,
> My heart as great, my reason haply more,
> To bandy word for word and frown for frown;
> But now I see our lances are but straws,
> Our strength as weak, our weakness past compare,
> That seeming to be most which we indeed least are. (5.2.174–79)

The whole taming process of the first four acts is compressed in the space between Katharine's three-line description of how she "hath been" and her assertion of her present state: "But now I see."

The speech ends with a dramatic gesture of subordination in which Katharine either places her hand under her husband's foot or offers to do so.

> Then vail your stomachs, for it is no boot,
> And place your hands below your husband's foot,

In token of which duty, if he please,
My hand is ready; may it do him ease.   (5.2.180–83)

Boose has shown that the play borrows this gesture from a wedding ritual. After the husband presented his bride with a wedding ring and promised her his worldly goods, she was to fall prostrate at his feet and kiss his foot; he would then "raise her up into her new status as wife" (Boose, *"Taming of the Shrew"* 195). Representing part of the wedding liturgy, this moment between Katharine and Petruchio corrects and completes their earlier parodic wedding ceremony (3.2). Yet by the time that *The Taming of the Shrew* was produced, this part of the ritual had been officially prohibited for about forty years. To resurrect it for this moment either marks Petruchio and Katharine's union as obviously anachronistic or endows it with the nostalgic prestige of a recently lost custom.

Few modern critics read either Katharine's final speech or this last enactment of subjection "straight" — that is, few argue that Petruchio has tamed Katharine and that she submits willingly. Critics have always had trouble with the ending; even those who have enjoyed and admired it have been reluctant to admit it. Those who insist that the ending is happy and that the play is a romantic comedy tend to downplay Katharine's subordination, seeing her as ironic or playful rather than "sincere." According to such interpretations, which have informed and been informed by a long theatrical tradition, Katharine's final speech should be considered "more as a performance than as an expression of sincere belief" (Novy 58). In Sam Taylor's 1929 film, for instance, Mary Pickford went so far as to wink broadly at the audience. But if Katharine delivers her speech ironically, if she parodies wifely subordination even as she performs it, is Petruchio in on the joke or not? Does Katharine's irony demonstrate her resistance to Petruchio or her complicity with him? Critics disagree. Some argue that Katharine goes so far in her insistence on women's subordination that she offers a critique of Petruchio's goals and desires. Through mimicry she offers the assembled husbands an extreme version of their fantasy wife, their ideal marriage, their own dominance — a vision that they either recognize as unattainable or reject as too crudely hierarchical, too blatantly oppressive (Boose, "Scolding Brides" 179). As farcical as the couple's earlier sparring, Katharine's final sequence of actions — treading on her cap, winning the wager, preaching a homily, and placing her hand beneath Petruchio's foot — "completes the fantasy of male dominance, but also mocks it as mere fantasy" (Kahn 116).

While some see Katharine's irony as a gauge of the lingering antagonism between her and Petruchio, others see it as a means by which she allies herself with Petruchio against or in contrast to the other couples. In this view both Petruchio and Katharine are performers who caricature and parody their roles as they assume them: "Just as Petruchio exaggerates his superiority over his servants in order to tame his wife, so Kate exaggerates her dependence on her husband in order to prove herself his equal in parodic performance" (Wayne, "Refashioning the Shrew" 173). From this perspective Katharine not only wins the wager for Petruchio but also proves herself to be his equal in "a celebration of reciprocity" (Neely 30). According to the most positive interpretations, Petruchio has not tamed or disciplined Katharine but healed and transformed her into a wife and partner. He has converted "Kate's opposition to romantic affection" (Neely 28). In doing so, he has also transformed the play, which "rises from farce to romantic comedy to the exact extent that Kate, in discovering love through the discovery of her own identity, becomes something more than the fabliau stereotype of the shrew turned household drudge" (Bean 66).

In contrast, those critics who do see the final scene as proof of successful taming often have trouble with the play as a romantic comedy; they consider it, instead, a problem play. From this perspective whether we read Katharine's speech as sincere or ironic does not matter because it is clearly not "her" speech (Garner 116). It is rather a speech written by a man, delivered by a boy, and addressed largely to men. Since, in this speech, Katharine reverses all she has said in her eloquent moments of resistance, the play silences Katharine at the same time that it gives her its longest speech (Boose, "Scolding Brides" 179; cf. Quilligan 230). Although the play entertains us with Katharine's raucous resistance to her father and to her husband, it does so only to contain that resistance. The play shows that even the most outspoken, insubordinate, assertive woman can be tamed (Burt 307; Fineman 138).

However one interprets Katharine's controversial final speech, she does not have the last word. Once she offers to place her hand beneath her husband's foot, she does not speak again (Hodgdon 541). She and Petruchio kiss, then depart for bed and the deferred consummation toward which the whole taming process has built. The play concludes with the exchange between Hortensio and Lucentio evaluating what they have just seen. Although Hortensio announces a resounding victory for Petruchio — "thou hast tamed a curst shrew" (5.2.192) — Lucentio muses: " 'Tis a wonder, by your leave, she will be tamed so" (193). By closing on this expression of amazement, the play leaves open to question the extent and duration of Petruchio's success.

The folio edition of *The Taming of the Shrew* has not had the last word, either. As was mentioned above, many productions use the last scene from

A Shrew, returning to Christopher Sly and his assessment of the play he (and we) have seen. From 1754 to 1844 David Garrick's adaptation of the play was the only version performed (see chapter 1, "Alternative Endings," p. 143). Sam Taylor's 1929 film — the first film version of a Shakespeare play — was strongly influenced by Garrick's adaptation, borrowing the lines Garrick provides for Katharine (discussed above).

Furthermore, John Fletcher wrote a sequel to the play, called *The Woman's Prize or The Tamer Tamed* (1611). This play suggests that not all Shakespeare's contemporaries assumed that Petruchio had triumphed decisively. In Fletcher's play, which focuses on Petruchio's second marriage to the indomitable Maria, Petruchio remembers his marriage to Katharine as an endless conflict:

Had I not ev'ry morning a rare breakfast,
Mixed with a learnèd lecture of ill language,
Louder than Tom o'Lincoln? And at dinner,
A diet of the same dish? Was there evening
That e'er passed over us, without "thou knave,"
Or "thou whore," for digestion? (3.3.157–62)

His servant Tranio explains that Petruchio's

bare remembrance of his first wife

. . . .

Will make him start in's sleep, and very often
Cry out for cudgels, colstaves, anything;
Hiding his breeches, out of fear her ghost
Should walk, and wear 'em yet. (1.1.31; 33–36)

Both these speeches dwell on the most conventional characteristics of the shrew, depicting Katharine as a bossy nag who never gave up her struggle to wear the breeches; they also suggest that her behavior provoked violence, so that even after her death Petruchio cries out for weapons in his sleep.

Pursuing Katharine and Petruchio past Shakespeare's enigmatic conclusion, Fletcher depicts Petruchio's misery in those two locations at which he asserted his conjugal authority in *The Taming of the Shrew* — the table (where they dine on quarrels) and the bed (in which his wife still opposes him in nightmares). Fletcher depicts Petruchio as more overtly violent than we find him in *The Taming of the Shrew,* yet as frustrated, harried, and bitter. In qualifying Petruchio's victory, Fletcher does not substitute Katharine as the victor. For one thing, Petruchio's and Tranio's sketches of the marriage suggest that both spouses were miserable. Furthermore, Petruchio's second wife, Maria, describes Katharine as "a fool" who "took a scurvy course; let her be named / 'Mongst those that wish for things, but dare not do 'em (1.2.141–43). For Maria, who consistently asserts her desires and needs, conspires with other women, and participates fully in negotiations with her husband for a marriage on her own terms, Katharine's capitulation — even if compromised by small, daily insubordinations — is despicable.

Characters in *The Woman's Prize* depict the marriage of Katharine and Petruchio as one in which neither spouse managed to dominate the other; the result was misery for both. The play at first seems to turn the conclusion of *The Taming of the Shrew* upside down, substituting female dominance for male dominance, a female tamer for a male one. But the play retreats from endorsing this inversion, as Maria ultimately negotiates a compromise with her husband. In doing so, the play suggests an alternative to the struggle for mastery in which there is a winner and a loser. Depicting Katharine and Petruchio's marriage as a fruitless struggle between equals, *The Woman's Prize* suggests that Maria and Petruchio will achieve a less contentious, more fulfilling equality.

Besides varied interpretations of *The Taming of the Shrew* and alternative endings to the story, there are other stories entirely. In the selection from Thomas Harman's *A Caveat for Common Cursitors* (1568) on page 319, Harman describes how a group of women conspire to tame an unfaithful husband. This story not only reverses the usual structure of tamer-husband and shrew-wife but also takes the taming outside the household, substituting a community of collaborating women for the lone tamer. There were also stories of untameable shrews like the one excerpted from Thomas Heywood's *A Curtain Lecture* (1637) on page 325. To uncover these other possibilities, we must look beyond Shakespeare's play, beyond the stage, beyond those texts celebrated as literary and widely available in textbooks and anthologies to the ballads once sung in the streets, the sermons delivered from pulpits, the works of advice read aloud in homes or consulted in times of trouble. This book brings these once popular works out of research libraries and into classrooms where they can again provoke discussion.

PART ONE

—→✦←—

WILLIAM SHAKESPEARE
The Taming of the Shrew

Edited by David Bevington

The Taming of the Shrew

———————————————— ⤜ ————————————————

[DRAMATIS PERSONAE

CHRISTOPHER SLY, *a tinker and beggar,* ⎤ *Persons*
HOSTESS *of an alehouse,* ⎟ *in the*
A LORD, ⎟ *Induction*
A PAGE, SERVANTS, HUNTSMEN, PLAYERS, ⎦

BAPTISTA, *a rich gentleman of Padua*
KATHARINA, *the shrew, also called Katharine and Kate, Baptista's elder
    daughter*
BIANCA, *Baptista's younger daughter*

PETRUCHIO, *a gentleman of Verona, suitor to Katharina*
GRUMIO, *Petruchio's servant*
CURTIS, NATHANIEL, PHILIP, JOSEPH, NICHOLAS, PETER, *and other servants
    of Petruchio*

GREMIO, *elderly suitor to Bianca*
HORTENSIO, *suitor to Bianca*
LUCENTIO, *son of Vincentio, in love with Bianca*
TRANIO, *Lucentio's servant*

BIONDELLO, *Lucentio's servant*
VINCENTIO, *a gentleman of Pisa*
A PEDANT (*or Merchant*) *of Mantua*
A WIDOW, *courted by Hortensio*

A TAILOR
A HABERDASHER
AN OFFICER
Other Servants of Baptista and Lucentio

SCENE: *Padua, and Petruchio's country house in Italy; the Induction is located in the countryside and at a Lord's house in England*]

INDUCTION, SCENE I°

Enter Beggar (Christopher Sly) and Hostess.

SLY: I'll feeze you,° in faith.
HOSTESS: A pair of stocks,° you rogue!
SLY: You're a baggage.° The Slys are no rogues. Look in the chronicles;
we came in with Richard° Conqueror.
Therefore *paucas pallabris,*° let the world slide. Sessa!°   5
HOSTESS: You will not pay for the glasses you have burst?
SLY: No, not a denier.° Go by, Saint Jeronimy,° go to thy cold bed and
warm thee.°
HOSTESS: I know my remedy; I must go fetch the thirdborough.°
                                                    [*Exit*]
SLY: Third,° or fourth, or fifth borough, I'll answer him by law.° I'll not   10
budge an inch, boy. Let him come, and kindly.°   *Falls asleep.*

Wind° *horns* [*within*]. *Enter a Lord from hunting, with his train.*

LORD:
Huntsman, I charge thee, tender° well my hounds.

Induction, Scene 1. **Location:** Before an alehouse and, subsequently, before the Lord's house nearby. (See lines 72, 132.)   1. **feeze you:** i.e., fix you, get even with you.   2. **A . . . stocks:** i.e., I'll have you put in the stocks.   3. **baggage:** contemptible woman or prostitute. 4. **Richard:** Sly's mistake for "William."   5. *paucas pallabris:* i.e., *pocas palabras,* "few words." (Spanish.)   **Sessa:** of doubtful meaning; perhaps "be quiet," "cease," or "let it go." 7. **denier:** French copper coin of little value.   **Go . . . Jeronimy:** Sly's variation of an often-quoted line from Kyd's *The Spanish Tragedy,* urging caution.   7–8. **go . . . thee:** (Perhaps a proverb; see *King Lear,* 3.4. 46–47.)   9. **thirdborough** constable.   10. **Third:** Sly shows his ignorance; the *third* in "thirdborough" derives from the Old English word *frith,* "peace." **by law:** in the law courts.   11. **kindly:** welcome. (Said ironically.)   s.d. **Wind:** blow. 12. **tender:** care for.

Breathe Merriman°—the poor cur is embossed°—
And couple° Clowder with the deep-mouthed brach.°
Sawst thou not, boy, how Silver made it good° 15
At the hedge corner, in the coldest fault?°
I would not lose the dog for twenty pound.

FIRST HUNTSMAN:

Why, Bellman is as good as he, my lord.
He cried upon it at the merest loss,°
And twice today picked out the dullest scent. 20
Trust me, I take him for the better dog.

LORD:

Thou art a fool. If Echo were as fleet,
I would esteem him worth a dozen such.
But sup them well° and look unto them all.
Tomorrow I intend to hunt again. 25

FIRST HUNTSMAN: I will, my lord.

LORD [seeing Sly]:

What's here? One dead, or drunk? See, doth he breathe?

SECOND HUNTSMAN [examining Sly]:

He breathes, my lord. Were he not warmed with ale,
This were a bed but cold to sleep so soundly.

LORD:

O monstrous beast, how like a swine he lies! 30
Grim death, how foul and loathsome is thine image!°
Sirs, I will practice on° this drunken man.
What think you, if he were conveyed to bed,
Wrapped in sweet° clothes, rings put upon his fingers,
A most delicious banquet° by his bed, 35
And brave° attendants near him when he wakes,
Would not the beggar then forget himself?

FIRST HUNTSMAN:

Believe me, lord, I think he cannot choose.°

---

13. **Breathe Merriman:** give the dog Merriman time to recover its breath.   **embossed:** foaming at the mouth from exhaustion.   14. **couple:** leash together.   **deep-mouthed brach:** bitch hound with the deep baying voice.   15. **made it good:** i.e., picked up the lost scent.   16. **in the coldest fault:** when the scent was lost by a *fault* or break in the scent.   19. **cried . . . loss:** bayed to signal his recovery of the scent after it had been completely lost.   24. **sup them well:** feed them a good supper.   31. **image:** likeness (since sleep was regarded as a likeness of death).   32. **practice on:** play a joke on.   34. **sweet:** perfumed.   35. **banquet:** light repast. 36. **brave:** finely arrayed.   38. **cannot choose:** is bound to.

SECOND HUNTSMAN:
  It would seem strange unto him when he waked.
LORD:
  Even as a flattering dream or worthless fancy.°   40
  Then take him up, and manage well the jest.
  Carry him gently to my fairest chamber,
  And hang it round with all my wanton pictures.
  Balm° his foul head in warm distillèd waters,
  And burn sweet wood to make the lodging sweet.   45
  Procure me music ready when he wakes,
  To make a dulcet° and a heavenly sound.
  And if he chance to speak, be ready straight,°
  And with a low submissive reverence°
  Say, "What is it your honor will command?"   50
  Let one attend him with a silver basin
  Full of rosewater and bestrewed with flowers;
  Another bear the ewer,° the third a diaper,°
  And say, "Will 't please your lordship cool your hands?"
  Someone be ready with a costly suit,   55
  And ask him what apparel he will wear;
  Another tell him of his hounds and horse,°
  And that his lady mourns at his disease.°
  Persuade him that he hath been lunatic,
  And when he says he is,° say that he dreams,   60
  For he is nothing but a mighty lord.
  This do, and do it kindly,° gentle° sirs.
  It will be pastime passing° excellent,
  If it be husbanded with modesty.°
FIRST HUNTSMAN:
  My lord, I warrant you we will play our part   65
  As° he shall think by° our true diligence
  He is no less than what we say he is.
LORD:
  Take him up gently, and to bed with him,

---

40. fancy: flight of imagination. 44. Balm: bathe, anoint. 47. dulcet: melodious.
48. straight: at once. 49. reverence: bow. 53. ewer: jug, pitcher. diaper: towel.
57. horse: horses. 58. disease: i.e., mental derangement. 60. when . . . is: i.e., when he says
he must be mad indeed. (The *is* is stressed.) 62. kindly: naturally (and thus persuasively).
gentle: kind. 63. passing: surpassingly. 64. husbanded with modesty: managed with decorum. 66. As: so that. by: as a result of.

And each one to his office° when he wakes.

                    [Some bear out Sly.] Sound trumpets [within].

Sirrah,° go see what trumpet 'tis that sounds.   70

                             [Exit a Servingman.]

Belike° some noble gentleman that means,
Traveling some journey, to repose him here.

Enter [a] Servingman.

How now? Who is it?

SERVINGMAN: An 't° please your honor, players
That offer service to your lordship.

Enter Players.

LORD:

Bid them come near.—Now, fellows, you are welcome.   75
PLAYERS: We thank your honor.
LORD:

Do you intend to stay with me tonight?
FIRST PLAYER:

So please° your lordship to accept our duty.°
LORD:

With all my heart. This fellow I remember
Since once he played a farmer's eldest son.—   80
'Twas where you wooed the gentlewoman so well.
I have forgot your name, but sure that part
Was aptly fitted and naturally performed.
SECOND PLAYER:

I think 'twas Soto that your honor means.
LORD:

'Tis very true. Thou didst it excellent.   85
Well, you are come to me in happy° time,
The rather for° I have some sport in hand
Wherein your cunning° can assist me much.
There is a lord will hear you play tonight.
But I am doubtful° of your modesties,°   90

---

69. **office:** duty. 70. **Sirrah:** (Usual form of address to inferiors.) 71. **Belike:** perhaps.
73. **An't:** if it. 78. **So please:** if it please. **duty:** expression of respect. 86. **happy:**
opportune. 87. **The rather for:** the more so since. 88. **cunning:** professional skill.
90. **doubtful:** apprehensive. **modesties:** discretion, self-control.

Lest, overeyeing of° his odd behavior—
For yet his honor never heard a play—
You break into some merry passion°
And so offend him; for I tell you, sirs,
If you should smile, he grows impatient.   95

FIRST PLAYER:
Fear not, my lord, we can contain ourselves
Were he the veriest antic° in the world.

LORD [to a Servingman]:
Go, sirrah, take them to the buttery,°
And give them friendly welcome every one.
Let them want° nothing that my house affords.   100

Exit one with the Players.

Sirrah, go you to Barthol'mew° my page,
And see him dressed in all suits° like a lady.
That done, conduct him to the drunkard's chamber,
And call him "madam," do him obeisance.°
Tell him° from me, as he will° win my love,   105
He bear himself with honorable action
Such as he hath observed in noble ladies
Unto their lords by them accomplishèd.°
Such duty to the drunkard let him do
With soft low tongue and lowly courtesy,   110
And say, "What is 't your honor will command,
Wherein your lady and your humble wife
May show her duty and make known her love?"
And then with kind embracements, tempting kisses,
And with declining head into his bosom,°   115
Bid him shed tears, as being overjoyed
To see her noble lord restored to health,
Who for this seven years hath esteemèd him°
No better than a poor and loathsome beggar.
And if the boy have not a woman's gift   120

---

91. **overeyeing of:** witnessing.   93. **merry passion:** outburst of laughter.   97. **veriest antic:** oddest buffoon or eccentric.   98. **buttery:** pantry, or a room for storing liquor (in butts) and other provisions.   100. **want:** lack.   101. **Barthol'mew:** pronounced "Bartlemy."   102. **in all suits:** in every detail (with a pun on *suits* of clothes).   104. **do him obeisance:** show him dutiful respect.   105. **him:** i.e., the page Bartholomew.   **as he will:** if he wishes to.   108. **by them accomplishèd:** performed by the ladies.   115. **with . . . bosom:** bowing his head down onto his chest.   118. **him:** himself.

To rain a shower of commanded tears,
An onion will do well for such a shift,°
Which in a napkin° being close° conveyed
Shall in despite° enforce a watery eye.
See this dispatched with all the haste thou canst.
Anon° I'll give thee more instructions.   125

                                                            Exit a Servingman.

I know the boy will well usurp° the grace,
Voice, gait, and action of a gentlewoman.
I long to hear him call the drunkard husband,
And how° my men will stay themselves from laughter   130
When they do homage to this simple peasant.
I'll in° to counsel them. Haply my presence
May well abate the overmerry spleen°
Which otherwise would grow into extremes.

                                                            [*Exeunt.*]

INDUCTION, SCENE II°

Enter aloft° the drunkard [Sly], with attendants; some with apparel, basin, and ewer and other appurtenances; and Lord.

SLY: For God's sake, a pot of small° ale.
FIRST SERVINGMAN: Will 't please your lordship drink a cup of sack?°
SECOND SERVINGMAN: Will 't please your honor taste of these conserves?°
THIRD SERVINGMAN: What raiment will your honor wear today?
SLY: I am Christophero Sly. Call not me "honor" nor "lordship." I   5
ne'er drank sack in my life; and if you give me any conserves, give me
conserves of beef.° Ne'er ask me what raiment I'll wear, for I have not
more doublets° than backs, no more stockings than legs, nor no more
shoes than feet—nay, sometimes more feet than shoes, or such shoes as°
my toes look through the overleather.°   10
LORD:
Heaven cease this idle° humor° in your honor!

122. shift: purpose.   123. napkin: handkerchief.   close: secretly.   124. in despite: i.e., notwithstanding a natural inclination to laugh rather than cry.   126. Anon: soon.   127. usurp:
assume.   130. And how: i.e., and to see how.   132. I'll in: I'll go in.   133. spleen: mood; the
spleen was the supposed seat of laughter and anger.   Induction, Scene II. Location: A bed-
chamber in the Lord's house.   s.d. aloft: i.e., in the gallery over the rear facade of the
stage.   1. small: weak (and therefore cheap).   2. sack: sweet Spanish wine (suited for a gentleman to drink).   3. conserves: candied fruit.   7. conserves of beef: preserved (salted)
beef.   8. doublets: men's jackets.   9. as: that.   10. overleather: upper leather of the shoe.
11. idle: vain, foolish.   humor: whim, fancy.

O, THAT A MIGHTY MAN OF SUCH DESCENT,   Of such possessions and so
high esteem,
SHOULD BE INFUSÈD WITH SO FOUL A SPIRIT!
SLY: What, would you make me mad? Am not I Christopher Sly, old Sly's   15
son of Burton-heath,° by birth a peddler, by education a cardmaker,° by
transmutation a bearherd,° and now by present profession a tinker?°Ask
Marian Hacket, the fat alewife° of Wincot,° if she know me not. If she
say I am not fourteen pence on the score° for sheer° ale, score me up for°
the lyingest knave in Christendom. What, I am not bestraught:° here's—   20
THIRD SERVINGMAN:
O, this it is that makes your lady mourn!
SECOND SERVINGMAN:
O, this is it that makes your servants droop!
LORD:
Hence comes it that your kindred shuns your house,
As° beaten hence by your strange lunacy.
O noble lord, bethink thee of thy birth.   25
Call home thy ancient° thoughts from banishment,
And banish hence these abject lowly dreams.
Look how thy servants do attend on thee,
Each in his office ready at thy beck.°
Wilt thou have music? Hark, Apollo° plays,   *Music.* 30
And twenty cagèd nightingales do sing.
Or wilt thou sleep? We'll have thee to a couch,
Softer and sweeter than the lustful bed
On purpose trimmed up for Semiramis.°
Say thou wilt walk; we will bestrew° the ground.   35
Or wilt thou ride? Thy horses shall be trapped,°
Their harness studded all with gold and pearl.
Dost thou love hawking? Thou hast hawks will soar

---

16. **Burton-heath:** perhaps Barton-on-the-Heath, about sixteen miles from Stratford, the
home of Shakespeare's aunt.   **cardmaker:** maker of cards or combs used to prepare wool for
spinning.   17. **bearherd:** keeper of a performing bear.   **tinker:** pot mender.   18. **alewife:**
woman who keeps an alehouse.   **Wincot:** small village about four miles from Stratford. (The
parish register shows that there were Hackets living there in 1591.)   19. **on the score:** in debt
(since such reckonings were originally notched or scored on a stick).   **sheer:** nothing but.
score me up for: reckon me to be.   20. **bestraught:** distracted.   24. **As:** as if.   26. **ancient:**
former.   29. **beck:** nod.   30. **Apollo:** i.e., as god of music.   34. **Semiramis:** legendary
queen of Assyria, famous for her voluptuousness.   35. **bestrew:** i.e., scatter rushes on.
36. **trapped:** adorned.

Above the morning lark. Or wilt thou hunt?
Thy hounds shall make the welkin° answer them   40
And fetch shrill echoes from the hollow earth.

FIRST SERVINGMAN:
Say thou wilt course,° thy greyhounds are as swift
As breathèd° stags, ay, fleeter than the roe.°

SECOND SERVINGMAN:
Dost thou love pictures? We will fetch thee straight
Adonis° painted by a running brook,   45
And Cytherea° all in sedges° hid,
Which seem to move and wanton° with her breath,
Even as the waving sedges play wi' th' wind.

LORD:
We'll show thee Io° as she was a maid,
And how she was beguilèd and surprised,   50
As° lively painted as the deed was done.

THIRD SERVINGMAN:
Or Daphne° roaming through a thorny wood,
Scratching her legs that one shall swear she bleeds,
And at that sight shall sad Apollo weep,
So workmanly° the blood and tears are drawn.   55

LORD:
Thou art a lord, and nothing but a lord.
Thou hast a lady far more beautiful
Than any woman in this waning° age.

FIRST SERVINGMAN:
And till the tears that she hath shed for thee
Like envious° floods o'errun her lovely face,   60
She was the fairest creature in the world;
And yet° she is inferior to none.

SLY:
Am I a lord? And have I such a lady?

---

40. **welkin:** sky, heavens.   42. **course:** hunt the hare.   43. **breathèd:** in good physical condition, with good wind.   **roe:** small, swift deer.   45. **Adonis:** a young huntsman with whom Venus is vainly in love. (See Ovid's *Metamorphoses*, Book X, and Shakespeare's poem *Venus and Adonis.*)   46. **Cytherea:** one of the names for Venus (because of her association with the island of Cythera).   **sedges:** grassy marsh plants.   47. **wanton:** play seductively.   49. **Io:** a woman who, according to Ovid, was seduced by Jove concealed in a mist and afterwards transformed into a heifer.   51. **As:** as if.   52. **Daphne:** a wood nymph beloved by Apollo, changed by Diana into a laurel tree to preserve her from Apollo's assault (*Metamorphoses*, Book I).   55. **workmanly:** skillfully.   58. **waning:** degenerate.   60. **envious:** spiteful.   62. **yet:** even today.

Or do I dream? Or have I dreamed till now?
I do not sleep: I see, I hear, I speak,   65
I smell sweet savors, and I feel soft things.
Upon my life, I am a lord indeed,
And not a tinker nor Christopher Sly.
Well, bring our lady hither to our sight,
And once again a pot o' the smallest ale.   70

SECOND SERVINGMAN:
Will 't please your mightiness to wash your hands?
O, how we joy to see your wit° restored!
O, that once more you knew but° what you are!
These fifteen years you have been in a dream,
Or when you waked, so waked as if you slept.   75

SLY:
These fifteen years! By my fay,° a goodly nap.
But did I never speak of° all that time?

FIRST SERVINGMAN:
O, yes, my lord, but very idle words;
For though you lay here in this goodly chamber,
Yet would you say ye were beaten out of door,   80
And rail upon the hostess of the house,°
And say you would present° her at the leet°
Because she brought stone jugs and no sealed quarts.°
Sometimes you would call out for Cicely Hacket.

SLY:
Ay, the woman's maid of the house.   85

THIRD SERVINGMAN:
Why, sir, you know no house, nor no such maid,
Nor no such men as you have reckoned up,
As Stephen Sly, and old John Naps of Greet,°
And Peter Turf, and Henry Pimpernel,
And twenty more such names and men as these,   90
Which never were, nor no man ever saw.

SLY:
Now Lord be thankèd for my good amends!°

---

72. **wit:** mental faculties, senses.   73. **knew but:** only knew.   76. **fay:** faith.   77. **of:** during.   81. **house:** tavern.   82. **present:** bring accusation against.   **leet:** manorial court.
83. **sealed quarts:** quart containers officially stamped as a guarantee of that capacity.
88. **Stephen . . . Greet:** A Stephen Sly lived in Stratford during Shakespeare's day. *Greet* is a
Gloucestershire hamlet not far from Stratford. The Folio reading, "Greece," is an easy mis-
reading if Shakespeare wrote "Greete."   92. **amends:** recovery.

ALL:
Amen.

Enter [the Page as a] lady, with Attendants.

SLY:
I thank thee. Thou shalt not lose by it.

PAGE:
How fares my noble lord?

SLY:
Marry,° I fare well,°
For here is cheer enough. Where is my wife? 95

PAGE:
Here, noble lord. What is thy will with her?

SLY:
Are you my wife, and will not call me husband?
My men should call me "lord"; I am your goodman.°

PAGE:
My husband and my lord, my lord and husband,
I am your wife in all obedience. 100

SLY:
I know it well—What must I call her?

LORD: Madam.
SLY: Al'ce madam, or Joan madam?

LORD:
Madam, and nothing else. So lords call ladies.

SLY:
Madam wife, they say that I have dreamed
And slept above some fifteen year or more. 105

PAGE:
Ay, and the time seems thirty unto me,
Being all this time abandoned° from your bed.

SLY:
'Tis much. Servants, leave me and her alone.
Madam, undress you and come now to bed.

PAGE:
Thrice-noble lord, let me entreat of you 110
To pardon me yet for a night or two,

---

94. **Marry:** a mild oath, derived from "by Mary."   **fare well:** (1) am fine (2) have plenty of good *cheer* (line 95), refreshment.   98. **goodman:** a homely term for "husband." 107. **abandoned:** banished.

Or, if not so, until the sun be set.
For your physicians have expressly charged,
In peril to incur your former malady,
That I should yet absent me from your bed.   115
I hope this reason stands for my excuse.
SLY: Ay, it stands° so that I may hardly tarry so long. But I would be
loath to fall into my dreams again. I will therefore tarry in despite of the
flesh and the blood.

Enter a [Servingman as] messenger.

SERVINGMAN:
Your honor's players, hearing your amendment,   120
Are come to play a pleasant comedy,
For so your doctors hold it very meet,°
Seeing too much sadness hath congealed your blood,
And melancholy is the nurse of frenzy.
Therefore they thought it good you hear a play   125
And frame your mind to mirth and merriment,
Which bars a thousand harms and lengthens life.
SLY:
Marry, I will let them play it.° Is not a comonty° a
Christmas gambold° or a tumbling-trick?
PAGE:
No, my good lord, it is more pleasing stuff.   130
SLY: What, household stuff?°
PAGE: It is a kind of history.°
SLY: Well, we'll see 't. Come, madam wife, sit by my side and let the
world slip; we shall ne'er be younger.

[They sit over the stage.°] Flourish.

ACT 1, SCENE 1°

Enter Lucentio and his man, Tranio.

LUCENTIO:
Tranio, since for the great desire I had

117. **stands:** is the case (with bawdy pun).   122. **meet:** suitable.   128–29. **Marry . . . play it:**
Sly speaks now with imperial authority and condescension, unless the Folio punctuation
should be amended to "Marry, I will. Let them play it."   128–29. **comonty, gambold:** (Sly's
words for *comedy* and *gambol.*)   131. **household stuff:** i.e., domestic doings.   132. **history:**
story.   s.d. **They sit over the stage:** (Possibly the Lord and some servingmen exeunt here or
at line 108. At I.I. 240 ff., a servingman, the Page, and Sly speak, while the Lord is no longer
heard from.)   **Act I, Scene I. Location:** Padua. A street before Baptista's house.

To see fair Padua, nursery of arts,°
I am arrived fore° fruitful Lombardy,
The pleasant garden of great Italy,
And by my father's love and leave am armed
With his good will and thy good company,   5
My trusty servant, well approved° in all,
Here let us breathe° and haply institute°
A course of learning and ingenious° studies.
Pisa, renownèd for grave citizens,
Gave me my being, and my father first°—   10
A merchant of great traffic° through the world,
Vincentio, come of° the Bentivolii.
Vincentio's son, brought up in Florence,
It shall become to serve all hopes conceived
To deck his fortune with his virtuous deeds.°   15
And therefore, Tranio, for the time° I study,
Virtue and that part of philosophy
Will I apply° that treats of° happiness
By virtue specially to be achieved.
Tell me thy mind, for I have Pisa left   20
And am to Padua come as he that leaves
A shallow plash° to plunge him in the deep,
And with satiety seeks to quench his thirst.

TRANIO:

Mi perdonate,° gentle master mine.   25
I am in all affected° as yourself,
Glad that you thus continue your resolve
To suck the sweets of sweet philosophy.
Only, good master, while we do admire
This virtue and this moral discipline,   30

---

2. **Padua . . . arts:** (Padua's was one of the most renowned of universities during Shakespeare's time.) 3. **am arrived fore:** have arrived at, or at the gates of, before. (Padua is not in Lombardy, but imprecise maps may have allowed Shakespeare to think of Lombardy as comprising all of northern Italy.) 7. **approved:** tested and proved trustworthy. 8. **breathe:** pause, settle down. **haply institute:** perhaps begin. 9. **ingenious:** i.e., "ingenuous," liberal, befitting a wellborn person. 11. **first:** i.e., before me. 12. **of great traffic:** involved in extensive trade. 13. **come of:** descended from. 14–16. **Vincentio's . . . deeds:** It will befit Vincentio's son, brought up in Florence, to fulfill all the hopes entertained for him by his friends and relatives by adding virtuous deeds to what fortune has bestowed on him. 17. **for the time:** while. 19. **apply:** study. **treats of:** discusses, concerns. 23. **plash:** pool. 25. *Mi perdonate:* pardon me. 26. **affected:** disposed.

Let's be no stoics nor no stocks,° I pray,
Or so devote° to Aristotle's checks°
As° Ovid° be an outcast quite abjured.
Balk logic° with acquaintance° that you have,
And practice rhetoric in your common talk;°   35
Music and poesy use to quicken° you;
The mathematics and the metaphysics,
Fall to them as you find your stomach° serves you.
No profit grows where is no pleasure ta'en.
In brief, sir, study what you most affect.°   40
LUCENTIO:
Gramercies,° Tranio, well dost thou advise.
If, Biondello,° thou wert come ashore,°
We could at once put us in readiness
And take a lodging fit to entertain
Such friends as time in Padua shall beget.   45
But stay awhile, what company is this?
TRANIO:
Master, some show to welcome us to town.

Enter Baptista with his two daughters, Katharina and Bianca; Gremio, a panta-
loon;° [and] Hortensio, suitor to Bianca. Lucentio [and] Tranio stand by.

BAPTISTA:
Gentlemen, importune me no farther,
For how I firmly am resolved you know:
That is, not to bestow my youngest daughter   50
Before I have a husband for the elder.
If either of you both love Katharina,
Because I know you well and love you well,
Leave shall you have to court her at your pleasure.
GREMIO:
To cart° her rather. She's too rough for me.   55
There, there, Hortensio, will you any wife?

31. **stocks:** persons devoid of feeling, like wooden posts (with a play on stoics). 32. **devote:** devoted. **checks:** restraints. 33. **As:** so that. **Ovid:** Latin love poet (used here to typify amorous light entertainment, as contrasted with the constraining philosophic study of Aristotle). 34. **Balk logic:** argue, bandy words. **acquaintance:** acquaintances. 35. **common talk:** ordinary conversation. 36. **quicken:** refresh. 38. **stomach:** inclination, appetite. 40. **affect:** find pleasant. 41. **Gramercies:** many thanks. 42. **Biondello:** Lucentio apostrophizes his absent servant. **come ashore:** Padua, though inland, is given a harbor by Shakespeare, unless he is thinking of the canals that crossed northern Italy in the sixteenth century. **s.d. pantaloon:** foolish old man, a stock character in Italian comedy. 55. **cart:** carry in a cart through the streets by way of punishment or public exposure (with a play on *court*).

KATHARINA [*to Baptista*]:
I pray you, sir, is it your will
To make a stale° of me amongst these mates?°
HORTENSIO:
"Mates," maid? How mean you that? No mates for you,
Unless you were of gentler, milder mold.   60
KATHARINA:
I' faith, sir, you shall never need to fear;
Iwis° it° is not halfway to her° heart.
But if it were, doubt not her care should be
To comb your noddle° with a three-legged stool,
And paint° your face, and use you like a fool.   65
HORTENSIO:
From all such devils, good Lord deliver us!
GREMIO: And me too, good Lord!
TRANIO [*aside to Lucentio*]:
Husht, master, here's some good pastime toward.°
That wench is stark mad or wonderful froward.°
LUCENTIO [*aside to Tranio*]:
But in other's silence do I see   70
Maid's mild behavior and sobriety.
Peace, Tranio!
TRANIO [*aside to Lucentio*]:
Well said, master. Mum, and gaze your fill.
BAPTISTA:
Gentlemen, that I may soon make good
What I have said—Bianca, get you in.   75
And let it not displease thee, good Bianca,
For I will love thee ne'er the less, my girl.
KATHARINA: A pretty peat!° It is best
Put finger in the eye,° an she knew why.°
BIANCA:
Sister, content you in my discontent—   80
Sir, to your pleasure° humbly I subscribe.°
My books and instruments shall be my company,
On them to look and practice by myself.

---

58. **stale:** laughingstock (with a play on the meaning "harlot," since a harlot might well be carted).   **mates:** rude fellows. (But Hortensio takes the word in the sense of "husband.")
62. **Iwis:** indeed.   **it:** i.e., marriage.   **her:** i.e., my, Kate's.   64. **comb your noddle:** rake your head.   65. **paint:** i.e., make red with scratches.   68. **toward:** in prospect.   69. **wonderful froward:** incredibly perverse.   78. **peat:** darling, pet.   79. **Put...eye:** i.e., weep.   81. **an she knew why:** if she could think of an excuse.   81 **pleasure:** will.   **subscribe:** submit.

LUCENTIO [*aside to Tranio*]:
Hark, Tranio, thou mayst hear Minerva° speak.
HORTENSIO:
Signor Baptista, will you be so strange?°   85
Sorry am I that our good will effects°
Bianca's grief.
GREMIO: Why will you mew° her up,
Signor Baptista, for this fiend of hell,
And make her bear the penance of her° tongue?
BAPTISTA:
Gentlemen, content ye. I am resolved.   90
Go in, Bianca.   [*Exit Bianca.*]
And for° I know she taketh most delight
In music, instruments, and poetry,
Schoolmasters will I keep within my house
Fit to instruct her youth. If you, Hortensio,   95
Or, Signor Gremio, you know any such,
Prefer° them hither; for to cunning° men
I will be very kind, and liberal
To mine own children in good bringing up.
And so farewell.—Katharina, you may stay,   100
For I have more to commune° with Bianca.   *Exit.*
KATHARINA:
Why, and I trust I may go too, may I not?
What, shall I be appointed hours,°
As though, belike,° I knew not what to take,
And what to leave? Ha!   *Exit.* 105
GREMIO: You may go to the devil's dam.° Your gifts° are so good, here's
none will hold° you.—Their love° is not so great, Hortensio, but we
may blow our nails together° and fast it fairly out.° Our cake's dough on
both sides.° Farewell. Yet, for the love I bear my sweet Bianca, if I can
by any means light on° a fit man to teach her that wherein she delights,   110
I will wish° him to her father.

---

84. **Minerva:** goddess of wisdom.   85. **strange:** distant, estranged.   86. **effects:** causes.
87. **mew:** coop (as one would a falcon).   89. **her . . . her:** i.e., Bianca . . . Katharina's.
92. **for:** because.   97. **Prefer:** recommend.   **cunning:** skillful, learned.   101. **commune:** discuss.   103. **appointed hours:** given a timetable.   104. **belike:** perhaps.   106. **dam:**
mother.   **gifts:** endowments. (Said ironically.)   107. **hold:** detain.   **Their love:** i.e., the love
of women.   108. **blow . . . together:** i.e., twiddle our thumbs, wait patiently.   **fast . . . out:**
abstain as best we can.   108–09. **Our cake's dough on both sides:** i.e., we're both out of luck,
getting nowhere.   110. **light on:** come upon.   111. **wish:** commend.

HORTENSIO: So will I, Signor Gremio. But a word, I pray. Though the nature of our quarrel yet never brooked parle,° know now, upon advice,° it toucheth° us both, that we may yet again have access to our fair mistress and be happy rivals in Bianca's love, to labor and effect one 115 thing specially.
GREMIO: What's that, I pray?
HORTENSIO: Marry, sir, to get a husband for her sister.
GREMIO: A husband? A devil.
HORTENSIO: I say a husband. 120
GREMIO: I say a devil. Think'st thou, Hortensio, though her father be very rich, any man is so very a° fool to be married to hell?
HORTENSIO: Tush, Gremio, though it pass° your patience and mine to endure her loud alarums,° why, man, there be good fellows in the world, an° a man could light on them, would take her with all faults, and 125 money enough.
GREMIO: I cannot tell.° But I had as lief° take her dowry with this condition: to be whipped at the high cross° every morning.
HORTENSIO: Faith, as you say, there's small choice in rotten apples. But come, since this bar in law° makes us friends, it shall be so far forth 130 friendly maintained till by helping Baptista's eldest daughter to a husband we set his youngest free for a husband, and then have to 't° afresh. Sweet Bianca! Happy man be his dole!° He that runs fastest gets the ring.° How say you, Signor Gremio?
GREMIO: I am agreed, and would I had given him the best horse in Padua 135 to begin his wooing that would thoroughly woo her, wed her, and bed her and rid the house of her! Come on. *Exeunt ambo.° Manent°*
                                                                        Tranio and Lucentio
TRANIO:
I pray, sir, tell me, is it possible
That love should of a sudden take such hold?
LUCENTIO:
O Tranio, till I found it to be true, 140
I never thought it possible or likely.

113. **brooked parle:** tolerated conference. **advice:** reflection. 114. **toucheth:** concerns. 122. **very a:** utterly a. 123. **pass:** exceed. 124. **alarums:** i.e., loud, startling noises (in military terms, a call to arms). 125. **an:** if. 127. **cannot tell:** i.e., I don't know about that, don't know what to say. **had as lief:** would as willingly. 128. **high cross:** cross set on a pedestal in a marketplace or center of a town. 130. **bar in law:** legal impediment, i.e., Baptista's refusal to receive suitors for Bianca. 132. **have to 't:** renew combat. 133. **Happy . . . dole:** i.e., may happiness be the reward of him that wins. (Proverbial.) 133–34. **the ring:** (An allusion to the sport of riding at the ring, with quibble on "wedding ring" and also sexual sense, "vulvar ring.") s.d. *ambo:* both. *Manent:* they remain onstage.

But see, while idly I stood looking on,
I found the effect of love in idleness,°
And now in plainness do confess to thee,
That art to me as secret° and as dear   145
As Anna° to the Queen of Carthage was,
Tranio, I burn, I pine, I perish, Tranio,
If I achieve not this young modest girl.
Counsel me, Tranio, for I know thou canst;
Assist me Tranio, for I know thou wilt.   150

TRANIO:
Master, it is no time to chide you now.
Affection is not rated° from the heart.
If love have touched you, naught remains but so,
"Redime te captum quam queas minimo."°

LUCENTIO:
Gramercies,° lad. Go forward. This contents: 155
The rest will comfort, for thy counsel's sound.

TRANIO:
Master, you looked so longly° on the maid,
Perhaps you marked° not what's the pith° of all.

LUCENTIO:
O, yes, I saw sweet beauty in her face,
Such as the daughter of Agenor° had,   160
That made great Jove to humble him° to her hand,
When with his knees he kissed° the Cretan strand.

TRANIO:
Saw you no more? Marked you not how her sister
Began to scold and raise up such a storm
That mortal ears might hardly endure the din?   165

LUCENTIO:
Tranio, I saw her coral lips to move,
And with her breath she did perfume the air.
Sacred and sweet was all I saw in her.

---

143. **love in idleness:** i.e., lust bred by idleness, with a pun on *love-in-idleness*, the flower hearts-ease or pansy, to which was attributed magical power in love. (See *A Midsummer Night's Dream*, 2.1.168.) 145. **secret:** trusted, intimate. 146. **Anna:** confidante of her sister Dido, Queen of Carthage, beloved of Aeneas. 152. **rated:** driven away by chiding. 154. *Redime...minimo:* buy yourself out of bondage for as little as you can. (From Terence's *Eunuchus* as quoted in William Lilly's *Latin Grammar*.) 155. **Gramercies:** thanks. 157. **so longly:** for such a long time; perhaps, also, so longingly. 158. **marked:** noted. **pith:** core, essence. 160. **daughter of Agenor:** Europa, beloved of Jove, who took the form of a bull in order to abduct her. 161. **him:** himself. 162. **kissed:** i.e., knelt on.

TRANIO [*aside*]:
Nay, then, 'tis time to stir him from his trance.—
I pray, awake, sir. If you love the maid,   170
Bend thoughts and wits to achieve her. Thus it stands:
Her elder sister is so curst° and shrewd°
That till the father rid his hands of her,
Master, your love must live a maid at home,
And therefore has he closely mewed her up,   175
Because° she will not be annoyed with° suitors.
LUCENTIO:
Ah, Tranio, what a cruel father's he!
But art thou not advised° he took some care
To get her cunning schoolmasters to instruct her?
TRANIO:
Ay, marry, am I, sir; and now 'tis plotted.   180
LUCENTIO:
I have it, Tranio.
TRANIO: Master, for my hand,°
Both our inventions° meet and jump° in one.
LUCENTIO:
Tell me thine first.
TRANIO: You will be schoolmaster
And undertake the teaching of the maid:
That's your device.
LUCENTIO: It is. May it be done?   185
TRANIO:
Not possible; for who shall bear your part
And be in Padua here Vincentio's son,
Keep house° and ply his book,° welcome his friends,
Visit his countrymen, and banquet them?
LUCENTIO:
Basta,° content thee, for I have it full.°   190
We have not yet been seen in any house,
Nor can we be distinguished by our faces
For man or master. Then it follows thus:
Thou shalt be master, Tranio, in my stead,

---

172. **curst**: shrewish.   **shrewd**: ill-natured.   176. **Because**: so that.   **annoyed with**: troubled by.   178. **advised**: aware.   181. **for my hand**: for my part, i.e., it's my guess.   182. **inventions**: plans.   **jump**: tally, agree.   188. **Keep house**: entertain, receive guests.   **ply his book**: pursue his studies.   190. *Basta:* enough.   **full**: i.e., fully thought out.

Keep house, and port,° and servants, as I should.   195
I will some other be, some Florentine,
Some Neapolitan, or meaner° man of Pisa.
'Tis hatched and shall be so. Tranio, at once
Uncase thee.° Take my colored° hat and cloak.
When Biondello comes, he waits on thee,   200
But I will charm° him first to keep his tongue.

TRANIO: So had you need.
In brief, sir, sith° it your pleasure is,
And I am tied to be obedient—
For so your father charged me at our parting,   205
"Be serviceable to my son," quoth he,
Although I think 'twas in another sense—
I am content to be Lucentio,
Because so well I love Lucentio.

                                          [*They exchange clothes.*]

LUCENTIO:
Tranio, be so, because Lucentio loves.   210
And let me be a slave t' achieve that maid
Whose sudden sight° hath thralled my wounded eye.

Enter Biondello.

Here comes the rogue.—Sirrah, where have you been?

BIONDELLO:
Where have I been? Nay, how now, where are you?
Master, has my fellow Tranio stol'n your clothes?   215
Or you stol'n his? Or both? Pray, what's the news?

LUCENTIO:
Sirrah, come hither. 'Tis no time to jest,
And therefore frame° your manners to the time.
Your fellow Tranio here, to save my life,
Puts my apparel and my countenance° on,   220
And I for my escape have put on his;
For in a quarrel since I came ashore,
I killed a man, and fear I was descried.°
Wait you on him, I charge you, as becomes,°

---

195. port: state, style of living.   **197. meaner:** of a lower social class.   **199. Uncase thee:** remove your outer garments.   **colored:** (as opposed to blue generally worn by servants; see 4.1.64).   **201. charm:** i.e., persuade.   **203. sith:** since.   **212. Whose sudden sight:** the sudden sight of whom.   **217. frame:** adapt, suit.   **220. countenance:** bearing, manner. **223. descried:** observed.   **224. as becomes:** as is suitable.

While I make way from hence to save my life.   225
You understand me?
BIONDELLO: I, sir?°—Ne'er a whit.°
LUCENTIO:
And not a jot of Tranio in your mouth.
Tranio is changed into Lucentio.
BIONDELLO:
The better for him. Would I were so, too!
TRANIO:
So could I, faith, boy, to have the next wish after,   230
That Lucentio indeed had Baptista's youngest daughter.
But, sirrah, not for my sake, but your master's, I advise
You use your manners discreetly in all kind of companies.
When I am alone, why, then I am Tranio,
But in all places else your master Lucentio.   235
LUCENTIO: Tranio, let's go.
One thing more rests,° that thyself execute:
To make one among these wooers. If thou ask me why,
Sufficeth° my reasons are both good and weighty.   *Exeunt.*

The presenters° above speak.

FIRST SERVINGMAN:
My lord, you nod. You do not mind° the play.   240
SLY:
Yes, by Saint Anne, do I. A good matter, surely.
Comes there any more of it?
PAGE [*as lady*]:   My lord, 'tis but begun.
SLY: 'Tis a very excellent piece of work, madam lady.
Would 'twere done!   *They sit and mark.°*   245

ACT I, SCENE II°

Enter Petruchio and his man, Grumio.

PETRUCHIO:
Verona, for a while I take my leave

226. I, sir: Lucentio may hear this as "Ay, sir."   Ne'er a whit: not in the least.   237. rests: remains to be done.   239. Sufficeth: it suffices that.   s.d. presenters: characters of the Induction, whose role it is to "present" the play proper.   240. mind: attend to.   245. s.d. mark: observe.   ACT I, SCENE II. Location: Padua. Before Hortensio's house.

To see my friends in Padua, but of all°
My best belovèd and approvèd friend,
Hortensio; and I trow° this is his house.
Here, sirrah Grumio, knock, I say.   5
GRUMIO: Knock, sir? Whom should I knock? Is there any man has re-
bused° your worship?
PETRUCHIO: Villain,° I say, knock me° here soundly.
GRUMIO: Knock you here, sir? Why, sir, what am I, sir, that I should
knock you here, sir?   10
PETRUCHIO:
Villain, I say, knock me at this gate,°
And rap me well, or I'll knock your knave's pate.
GRUMIO:
My master is grown quarrelsome. I should knock you first,
And then I know after who comes by the worst.°
PETRUCHIO: Will it not be?°   15
Faith, sirrah, an you'll not knock, I'll ring it.°
I'll try how you can sol fa and sing it.°   *He wrings him by the ears.*
GRUMIO:
Help, masters,° help! My master is mad.
PETRUCHIO:
Now knock when I bid you, sirrah villain.

Enter Hortensio.

HORTENSIO: How now, what's the matter? My old friend Grumio and my   20
good friend Petruchio? How do you all° at Verona?
PETRUCHIO:
Signor Hortensio, come you to part the fray?
Con tutto il cuore ben trovato,° may I say.
HORTENSIO:
Alla nostra casa ben venuto,
Molto onorato signor mio Petruchio.° —   25
Rise, Grumio, rise. We will compound° this quarrel.

---

2. of all: above all.   4. trow: believe.   6–7. rebused: (A blunder for "abused.")   8. Villain:
i.e., wretch. (A term of abuse.)   me: i.e., for me. (But Grumio, perhaps intentionally,
misunderstands.)   11. gate: door.   13–14. I should . . . worst: i.e., you're asking me to hit
you—and I know who then will get the worst of it.   15. Will it not be? i.e., aren't you going
to do what I said?   16. ring it: sound loudly, using a circular knocker or a bell (with a pun on
wring).   17. I'll . . . sing it: i.e., I'll make you cry out, howl. (To *sol fa* is to sing a scale.)
18. masters: i.e., sirs. (Addressed to the audience.)   21. How do you all: how are you and your
family.   23. Con . . . trovato: with all my heart, well met.   24–25. Alla . . . Petruchio: welcome to our house, my much honored Petruchio. (Italian.)   26. compound: settle.

GRUMIO: Nay, 'tis no matter, sir, what he 'leges° in Latin. If this be not
a lawful cause for me to leave his service! Look you, sir: he bid me knock
him and rap him soundly, sir. Well, was it fit for a servant to use his
master so, being perhaps, for aught I see, two-and-thirty, a pip° out?°   30
Whom would to God I had well knocked at first,
Then had not Grumio come by the worst.
PETRUCHIO:
A senseless villain! Good Hortensio,
I bade the rascal knock upon your gate,
And could not get him for my heart° to do it.   35
GRUMIO: Knock at the gate? O heavens! Spake you not these words plain,
"Sirrah, knock me here, rap me here, knock me well, and knock me
soundly"? And come you now with° "knocking at the gate"?
PETRUCHIO:
Sirrah, begone, or talk not, I advise you.
HORTENSIO:
Petruchio, patience. I am Grumio's pledge.°
Why, this's° a heavy chance° twixt him and you,   40
Your ancient,° trusty, pleasant° servant Grumio.
And tell me now, sweet friend, what happy gale
Blows you to Padua here from old Verona?
PETRUCHIO:
Such wind as scatters young men through the world
To seek their fortunes farther than at home,   45
Where small experience grows. But in a few,°
Signor Hortensio, thus it stands with me:
Antonio, my father, is deceased,
And I have thrust myself into this maze,
Happily° to wive and thrive as best I may.   50
Crowns in my purse I have, and goods at home,
And so am come abroad to see the world.
HORTENSIO:
Petruchio, shall I then come roundly° to thee
And wish thee to a shrewd,° ill-favored° wife?   55

---

27. 'leges: alleges.   30. two . . . out: i.e., drunk, or not quite right in the head. (Derived from
the card game called *one-and-thirty*.)   pip: a spot on a playing card. (Hence, a *pip out* means
"off by one," or "one in excess of thirty-one.")   35. for my heart: i.e., for my life.   38. come
you now with: do you now come along with.   40. pledge: surety.   41. this's: this is.   heavy
chance: sad occurrence.   42. ancient: long-standing.   pleasant: merry.   47. in a few: in
short.   51. Happily: with good luck. (*Happily* and *haply* were not always distinguished.)
54. come roundly: speak plainly.   55. shrewd: shrewish.   ill-favored: ill-natured. (? Kate is
not "ugly," the usual meaning of this term; see line 80.)

Thou'dst thank me but a little for my counsel.
And yet I'll promise thee she shall be rich,
And very rich. But thou'rt too much my friend,
And I'll not wish thee to her.

PETRUCHIO:
Signor Hortensio, twixt such friends as we   60
Few words suffice. And therefore, if thou know
One rich enough to be Petruchio's wife —
As wealth is burden° of my wooing dance —
Be she as foul° as was Florentius' love,°
As old as Sibyl,° and as curst and shrewd   65
As Socrates' Xanthippe,° or a worse,
She moves° me not, or not removes, at least,
Affection's edge° in me, were she as rough
As are the swelling Adriatic seas.
I come to wive it wealthily in Padua;   70
If wealthily, then happily in Padua.

GRUMIO: Nay, look you, sir, he tells you flatly what his mind° is. Why,
give him gold enough and marry him to a puppet or an aglet-baby,° or
an old trot° with ne'er a tooth in her head, though she have as many
diseases as two-and-fifty horses. Why, nothing comes amiss, so° money   75
comes withal.°

HORTENSIO:
Petruchio, since we are stepped thus far in,
I will continue that I broached° in jest.
I can, Petruchio, help thee to a wife
With wealth enough, and young and beauteous,   80
Brought up as best becomes a gentlewoman.
Her only fault, and that is faults enough,
Is that she is intolerable° curst
And shrewd, and froward,° so beyond all measure

---

63. **burden:** undersong, i.e., basis.   64. **foul:** ugly.   **Florentius' love:** (An allusion to John Gower's version in *Confessio Amantis* of the fairy tale of the knight who promises to marry an ugly old woman if she solves the riddle he must answer. After the fulfillment of all promises, she becomes young and beautiful. Another version of this story is Chaucer's "Tale of the Wife of Bath," from *The Canterbury Tales*.)   65. **Sibyl:** prophetess of Cumae, to whom Apollo gave as many years of life as she held grains of sand in her hand.   66. **Xanthippe:** the philosopher's notoriously shrewish wife.   67. **moves:** affects, disturbs (setting up wordplay on *removes*). 68. **Affection's edge:** the keen edge of desire.   72. **mind:** intention.   73. **aglet-baby:** small figure carved on the tag of a lace.   74. **trot:** hag.   75. **so:** provided.   76. **withal:** with it. 78. **that I broached:** what I began.   83. **intolerable:** intolerably.   84. **shrewd, and froward:** ill-natured and refractory.

That, were my state° far worser than it is,   85
I would not wed her for a mine of gold.
PETRUCHIO:
Hortensio, peace! Thou know'st not gold's effect.
Tell me her father's name and 'tis enough;
For I will board° her, though she chide as loud
As thunder when the clouds in autumn crack.°   90
HORTENSIO:
Her father is Baptista Minola,
An affable and courteous gentleman.
Her name is Katharina Minola,
Renowned in Padua for her scolding tongue.
PETRUCHIO:
I know her father, though I know not her,   95
And he knew my deceasèd father well.
I will not sleep, Hortensio, till I see her;
And therefore let me be thus bold with you
To give you over° at this first encounter,
Unless you will accompany me thither.   100
GRUMIO [to Hortensio]:   I pray you, sir, let him go while the humor° lasts.
O'° my word, an° she knew him as well as I do, she would think
scolding would do little good upon him. She may perhaps call him half
a score knaves or so. Why, that's nothing; an he begin once, he'll rail in
his rope tricks.° I'll tell you what, sir: an she stand° him but a little, he   105
will throw a figure° in her face and so disfigure her with it that she shall
have no more eyes to see withal than a cat. You know him not, sir.
HORTENSIO:
Tarry, Petruchio, I must go with thee,
For in Baptista's keep° my treasure is.
He hath the jewel of my life in hold,°   110
His youngest daughter, beautiful Bianca,
And her withholds from me and other more,°
Suitors to her and rivals in my love,
Supposing it a thing impossible,

---

85. state: estate. 89. board: accost, woo. (A metaphor from naval warfare.) 90. crack:
make an explosive noise. 99. give you over: leave you. 101. humor: whim. 102. O': on.
an: if. 105. rope tricks: perhaps Grumio's version of "rope-rhetorics," i.e., scolding in outrageous terms (?) or tricks worthy of hanging (?). stand: withstand. 106. figure: figure of
speech. 109. keep: keeping (with suggestion of "fortified place," where one would store a
treasure). 110. hold: confinement (with a similar pun on "stronghold"). 112. other more:
others besides me.

For those defects I have before rehearsed,° 115
That ever Katharina will be wooed.
Therefore this order° hath Baptista ta'en,
That none shall have access unto Bianca
Till Katharine the curst have got a husband.
GRUMIO: Katharine the curst! 120
A title for a maid of all titles the worst.
HORTENSIO:
Now shall my friend Petruchio do me grace,°
And offer me disguised in sober robes
To old Baptista as a schoolmaster
Well seen° in music, to instruct Bianca, 125
That so I may by this device at least
Have leave and leisure to make love to° her,
And unsuspected court her by herself.

Enter Gremio [with a paper], and Lucentio disguised [as a schoolmaster].

GRUMIO: Here's no knavery!° See, to beguile the old folks, how the young
folks lay their heads together! Master, master, look about you. Who goes 130
there, ha?
HORTENSIO:
Peace, Grumio, it is the rival of my love.
Petruchio, stand by awhile.   *[They stand aside.]*
GRUMIO *[aside]*:
A proper stripling° and an amorous!
GREMIO *[to Lucentio]*:
O, very well, I have perused the note.° 135
Hark you, sir, I'll have them very fairly bound —
All books of love, see° that at any hand° —
And see you read no other lectures° to her.
You understand me. Over and besides
Signor Baptista's liberality, 140
I'll mend° it with a largess.° Take your paper too,
                              [giving Lucentio the note]

---

115. **rehearsed:** related, described. 117. **this order:** these measures. 122. **grace:** a favor.
125. **seen:** skilled. 127. **make love to:** woo. 129. **Here's no knavery:** (Said sarcastically.)
134. **proper stripling:** handsome young fellow. (Said ironically, in reference to Gremio.)
135. **note:** evidently, a list of books for Bianca's tutoring. 137. **see:** see to. **at any hand:** in
any case. 138. **read ... lectures:** teach no other lessons. 141. **mend:** improve, increase.
largess: gift of money.

And let me have them° very well perfumed,
For she is sweeter than perfume itself
To whom they go to. What will you read to her?
LUCENTIO:
Whate'er I read to her, I'll plead for you   145
As for my patron, stand you so assured,
As firmly as° yourself were still in place° —
Yea, and perhaps with more successful words
Than you, unless you were a scholar, sir.
GREMIO:
O this learning, what a thing it is!   150
GRUMIO [aside]:
O this woodcock,° what an ass it is!
PETRUCHIO: Peace, sirrah!
HORTENSIO [coming forward]:
Grumio, mum! — God save you, Signor Gremio.
GREMIO:
And you are well met,° Signor Hortensio.
Trow° you whither I am going? To Baptista Minola.   155
I promised to inquire carefully
About a schoolmaster for the fair Bianca,
And by good fortune I have lighted well
On this young man, for learning and behavior
Fit for her turn,° well read in poetry   160
And other books — good ones, I warrant ye.
HORTENSIO:
'Tis well. And I have met a gentleman
Hath° promised me to help me to° another,
A fine musician to instruct our mistress.
So shall I no whit be behind in duty   165
To fair Bianca, so beloved of me.
GREMIO:
Beloved of me, and that my deeds shall prove.
GRUMIO [aside]:   And that his bags° shall prove.

---

142. **them:** i.e., the books.   147. **as:** as if.   **still in place:** present all the time.
151. **woodcock:** a bird easily caught; proverbially stupid.   154. **you are well met:** i.e., how opportune to meet you just now.   155. **Trow:** know.   160. **Fit for her turn:** suited to her needs (something that is true in more ways than Gremio realizes).   163. **Hath:** who has.
help me to: help me to obtain.   168. **bags:** moneybags.

HORTENSIO:
Gremio, 'tis now no time to vent° our love.
Listen to me, and if you speak me fair,°   170
I'll tell you news indifferent° good for either.
Here is a gentleman whom by chance I met,
Upon agreement from us to his liking,°
Will undertake to woo curst Katharine,
Yea, and to marry her, if her dowry please.   175
GREMIO: So said, so done, is well.°
Hortensio, have you told him all her faults?
PETRUCHIO:
I know she is an irksome brawling scold.
If that be all, masters, I hear no harm.
GREMIO:
No, sayst me so, friend? What countryman?   180
PETRUCHIO:
Born in Verona, old Antonio's son.
My father dead, his fortune lives for me,
And I do hope good days and long to see.
GREMIO:
O sir, such a life with such a wife were° strange.
But if you have a stomach,° to 't, i' God's name.   185
You shall have me assisting you in all.
But will you woo this wildcat?
PETRUCHIO: Will I live?
GRUMIO:
Will he woo her? Ay, or I'll hang her.
PETRUCHIO:
Why came I hither but to that intent?
Think you a little din can daunt mine ears?   190
Have I not in my time heard lions roar?
Have I not heard the sea, puffed up with winds,
Rage like an angry boar chafèd with sweat?
Have I not heard great ordnance° in the field,°
And heaven's artillery thunder in the skies?   195

169. vent: express.   170. speak me fair: deal with me civilly, courteously.   171. indifferent:
equally.   173. Upon . . . liking: who, if we agree to terms satisfactory to him. (In lines 205–206,
we learn that Bianca's suitors will bear his charge of wooing.)   176. So . . . is well: i.e., that's all
very well, when his deeds match his words (which may not be soon).   184. were: would
be.   185. a stomach: an appetite, inclination.   194. ordnance: artillery.   field: battlefield.

Have I not in a pitchèd battle heard
Loud 'larums,° neighing steeds, and trumpets' clang?
And do you tell me of a woman's tongue,
That gives not half so great a blow to hear
As will a chestnut in a farmer's fire?   200
Tush, tush! Fear boys with bugs.°

GRUMIO: For he fears none.

GREMIO: Hortensio, hark.
This gentleman is happily° arrived,
My mind presumes, for his own good and ours.

HORTENSIO:
I promised we would be contributors   205
And bear his charge° of wooing, whatsoe'er.

GREMIO:
And so we will, provided that he win her.

GRUMIO:
I would I were as sure of a good dinner.

Enter Tranio, brave° [as Lucentio], and Biondello.

TRANIO:
Gentlemen, God save you. If I may be bold,
Tell me, I beseech you, which is the readiest way   210
To the house of Signor Baptista Minola?

BIONDELLO: He that has the two fair daughters, is't he you mean?

TRANIO: Even he,° Biondello.

GREMIO:
Hark you, sir, you mean not her to —

TRANIO:
Perhaps him and her,° sir. What have you to do?°   215

PETRUCHIO:
Not her that chides, sir, at any hand,° I pray.

TRANIO:
I love no chiders, sir. Biondello, let's away.

LUCENTIO [*aside*]:
Well begun, Tranio.

HORTENSIO: Sir, a word ere you go.
Are you a suitor to the maid you talk of, yea or no?

---

197. **'larums:** calls to arms.   201. **Fear . . . bugs:** frighten children with bugbears, bogeymen.
203. **happily:** fortunately, just when needed.   206. **charge:** expense.   **s.d. brave:** elegantly
dressed.   213. **Even he:** yes, precisely, he.   215. **him and her:** i.e., both Baptista Minola and
his daughter.   **What . . . do:** what's that to you?   216. **at any hand:** on any account.

TRANIO:
   An if I be, sir, is it any offense?   220
GREMIO:
   No, if without more words you will get you hence.
TRANIO:
   Why sir, I pray, are not the streets as free
   For me as for you?
GREMIO: But so is not she.
TRANIO:
   For what reason, I beseech you?
GREMIO: For this reason, if you'll know,   225
   That she's the choice° love of Signor Gremio.
HORTENSIO:
   That she's the chosen of Signor Hortensio.
TRANIO:
   Softly, my masters! If you be gentlemen,
   Do me this right: hear me with patience.
   Baptista is a noble gentleman,   230
   To whom my father is not all° unknown;
   And were his daughter fairer than she is,
   She may more suitors have, and me for one.
   Fair Leda's daughter° had a thousand wooers;
   Then well one more may fair Bianca have,   235
   And so she shall. Lucentio shall make one,
   Though° Paris° came in hope to speed alone.°
GREMIO:
   What, this gentleman will out-talk us all!
LUCENTIO:
   Sir, give him head. I know he'll prove a jade.°
PETRUCHIO:
   Hortensio, to what end are all these words?   240
HORTENSIO [to Tranio]:
   Sir, let me be so bold as ask° you,
   Did you yet ever see Baptista's daughter?
TRANIO:
   No, sir, but hear I do that he hath two,

226. choice: (1) chosen, (2) excellent. 231. all: entirely. 234. Leda's daughter: Helen of
Troy. 237. Though: even if. Paris: Trojan prince who abducted Helen from her husband,
Menelaus. speed alone: succeed above all others. 239. prove a jade: tire like an ill-
conditioned horse. 241. as ask: as to ask.

The one as famous for a scolding tongue
As is the other for beauteous modesty.   245
PETRUCHIO:
Sir, sir, the first's for me. Let her go by.°
GREMIO:
Yea, leave that labor to great Hercules,
And let it be more than Alcides' twelve.°
PETRUCHIO:
Sir, understand you this of me,° in sooth:°
The youngest daughter, whom you hearken for,°   250
Her father keeps from all access of suitors,
And will not promise her to any man
Until the elder sister first be wed.
The younger then is free, and not before.
TRANIO:
If it be so, sir, that you are the man
Must stead° us all, and me amongst the rest;   255
And if you break the ice and do this feat,
Achieve the elder, set the younger free
For our access, whose hap° shall be to have her
Will not so graceless be to be ingrate.°   260
HORTENSIO:
Sir, you say well, and well you do conceive.°
And since you do profess to be a suitor,
You must, as we do, gratify° this gentleman,
To whom we all rest generally beholding.°
TRANIO:
Sir, I shall not be slack. In sign whereof,   265
Please ye we may contrive° this afternoon,
And quaff carouses° to our mistress' health,
And do as adversaries° do in law —
Strive mightily, but eat and drink as friends.
GRUMIO, BIONDELLO:
O excellent motion!° Fellows, let's be gone.   270

---

246. Let her go by: pass over her.   **248. let . . . twelve:** admit that it would exceed the twelve labors of Hercules (called *Alcides* because he was the reputed grandson of Alcaeus).   **249. of me:** from me.   **sooth:** truth.   **250. hearken for:** lie in wait for, seek to win.   **256. Must stead:** who must help.   **259. whose hap:** he whose good fortune.   **260. to be ingrate:** as to be ungrateful.   **261. conceive:** understand.   **263. gratify:** reward, requite.   **264. beholding:** beholden, indebted.   **266. contrive:** spend, pass (time).   **267. quaff carouses:** drink toasts.   **268. adversaries:** opposing lawyers.   **270. motion:** suggestion.

HORTENSIO:
The motion's good indeed, and be it so.
Petruchio, I shall be your *ben venuto.*°   *Exeunt.*

ACT II, SCENE I°

Enter Katharina and Bianca [with her hands tied].

BIANCA:
Good Sister, wrong me not, nor wrong yourself,
To make a bondmaid and a slave of me.
That I disdain. But for these other goods,°
Unbind° my hands, I'll pull them off myself,
Yea, all my raiment, to my petticoat,   5
Or what you will command me will I do,
So well I know my duty to my elders.
KATHARINA:
Of all thy suitors here I charge thee tell
Whom thou lov'st best. See thou dissemble not.
BIANCA:
Believe me, sister, of all the men alive   10
I never yet beheld that special face
Which I could fancy more than any other.
KATHARINA:
Minion,° thou liest. Is 't not Hortensio?
BIANCA:
If you affect° him, sister, here I swear
I'll plead for you myself but you shall have him.°   15
KATHARINA:
O, then belike° you fancy riches more:
You will have Gremio to keep you fair.°
BIANCA:
Is it for him you do envy me so?
Nay, then, you jest, and now I well perceive

---

272. *ben venuto:* welcome, i.e., host. ACT II, SCENE I. Location: Padua. Baptista's
house. 3. **goods:** possessions. 4. **Unbind:** if you will unbind. 13. **Minion:**
hussy. 14. **affect:** love. 15. **but you shall have him:** if necessary for you to win him.
16. **belike:** perhaps. 17. **fair:** resplendent with finery.

You have but jested with me all this while.   20
I prithee, sister Kate, untie my hands.
KATHARINA (*strikes her*):
If that be jest, then all the rest was so.

Enter Baptista.

BAPTISTA:
Why, how now, dame, whence grows this insolence? —
Bianca, stand aside. Poor girl, she weeps.
Go ply thy needle, meddle not with° her. —   25
For shame, thou hilding° of a devilish spirit,
Why dost thou wrong her that did ne'er wrong thee?
When did she cross° thee with a bitter word?
KATHARINA:
Her silence flouts° me, and I'll be revenged.   *[She] flies after Bianca.*
BAPTISTA:
What, in my sight? Bianca, get thee in.   *Exit [Bianca].*   30
KATHARINA:
What, will you not suffer me?° Nay, now I see
She is your treasure, she must have a husband;
I must dance barefoot on her wedding day,
And for your love to her lead apes in hell.°
Talk not to me. I will go sit and weep   35
Till I can find occasion of revenge.   *[Exit.]*
BAPTISTA:
Was ever gentleman thus grieved as I?
But who comes here?

Enter Gremio, Lucentio [as a schoolmaster] in the habit° of a mean° man, Petruchio, with [Hortensio as a musician, and] Tranio [as Lucentio] with his boy [Biondello] bearing a lute and books.

GREMIO: Good morrow, neighbor Baptista.
BAPTISTA: Good morrow, neighbor Gremio. God save you, gentlemen.   40
PETRUCHIO:
And you, good sir. Pray, have you not a daughter
Called Katharina, fair and virtuous?

---

25. **meddle not with**: have nothing to do with.   26. **hilding**: vicious (hence worthless) beast.   28. **cross**: contradict, thwart.   29. **flouts**: mocks, insults.   31. **suffer me**: let me have my own way.   33–34. **dance ... day, lead ... hell**: popularly supposed to be the fate of old maids.   s.d. **habit**: dress.   **mean**: of low social station. (Said here of a schoolmaster.)

BAPTISTA:
I have a daughter, sir, called Katharina.
GREMIO:
You are too blunt. Go to it orderly.°
PETRUCHIO:
You wrong me, Signor Gremio; give me leave.° —   45
I am a gentleman of Verona, sir,
That, hearing of her beauty and her wit,
Her affability and bashful modesty,
Her wondrous qualities and mild behavior,
Am bold to show myself a forward guest   50
Within your house, to make mine eye the witness
Of that report which I so oft have heard.
And, for an entrance° to my entertainment,°
I do present you with a man of mine,   [*presenting Hortensio*]
Cunning° in music and the mathematics,   55
To instruct her fully in those sciences,°
Whereof I know she is not ignorant.
Accept of° him, or else you do me wrong.
His name is Litio, born in Mantua.
BAPTISTA:
You're welcome, sir, and he, for your good sake.   60
But for° my daughter Katharine, this I know,
She is not for your turn, the more my grief.
PETRUCHIO:
I see you do not mean to part with her,
Or else you like not of° my company.
BAPTISTA:
Mistake me not, I speak but as I find.   65
Whence are you, sir? What may I call your name?
PETRUCHIO:
Petruchio is my name, Antonio's son,
A man well known throughout all Italy.
BAPTISTA:
I know° him well. You are welcome for his sake.

---

44. orderly: in a properly orderly manner.   45. give me leave: excuse me.   53. entrance: entrance fee.   entertainment: reception.   55. Cunning: skillful.   56. sciences: subjects, branches of knowledge.   58. Accept of: accept.   61. for: as for.   64. like not of: do not like.   69. know: know of. (See also line 101.)

GREMIO:

    Saving° your tale, Petruchio, I pray,   70
    Let us that are poor petitioners speak too.
    Bacare!° You are marvelous forward.

PETRUCHIO:

    O, pardon me, Signor Gremio, I would fain° be doing.°

GREMIO: I doubt it not, sir, but you will curse your wooing. — Neighbors, this is a gift very grateful,° I am sure of it. [*To Baptista.*] To express the like kindness, myself, that have been more kindly beholding to you than any, freely give unto you this young scholar [*presenting Lucentio*], that hath been long studying at Rheims, as cunning in Greek, Latin, and other languages, as the other in music and mathematics. His name is Cambio.° Pray, accept his service.   80

BAPTISTA: A thousand thanks, Signor Gremio. Welcome, good Cambio. [*To Tranio.*] But, gentle sir, methinks you walk like a stranger.° May I be so bold to know the cause of your coming?

TRANIO:

    Pardon me, sir, the boldness is mine own,
    That, being a stranger in this city here,
    Do make myself a suitor to your daughter,   85
    Unto Bianca, fair and virtuous.
    Nor is your firm resolve unknown to me
    In the preferment of° the eldest sister.
    This liberty is all that I request,
    That, upon knowledge of° my parentage,   90
    I may have welcome 'mongst the rest that woo,
    And free access and favor° as the rest.
    And toward the education of your daughters
    I here bestow a simple instrument,
    And this small packet of Greek and Latin books.   95
    If you accept them, then their worth is great.

                  [*Biondello brings forward the lute and books.*]

BAPTISTA:

    Lucentio is your name?° Of whence, I pray?

---

70. **Saving:** with all due respect for.   72. *Bacare:* stand back.   73. **fain:** gladly.   **doing:** getting on with the business (with sexual suggestion).   75. **grateful:** pleasing.   80. **Cambio:** In Italian, appropriately, the word means "change" or "exchange."   82. **walk like a stranger:** keep your distance, stand apart.   89. **In the preferment of:** in the precedence you give to.   91. **upon knowledge of:** when you know about.   93. **favor:** leave, permission.   98. **Lucentio . . . name:** Baptista may have learned this information from a note accompanying the books and lute.

TRANIO:
Of Pisa, sir, son to Vincentio.

BAPTISTA:
A mighty man of Pisa. By report   100
I know him well. You are very welcome, sir.
[*To Hortensio.*] Take you the lute, [*to Lucentio*] and you the set of books;
You shall go see your pupils presently.°
Holla, within!

Enter a Servant.

                  Sirrah, lead these gentlemen
To my daughters, and tell them both   105
These are their tutors. Bid them use them well.
            [*Exit Servant, with Lucentio and Hortensio.*]
We will go walk a little in the orchard,°
And then to dinner. You are passing° welcome,
And so I pray you all to think yourselves.

PETRUCHIO:
Signor Baptista, my business asketh haste,   110
And every day I cannot come to woo.
You knew my father well, and in him me,
Left solely heir to all his lands and goods,
Which I have bettered rather than decreased.
Then tell me, if I get your daughter's love,   115
What dowry shall I have with her to wife?

BAPTISTA:
After my death the one half of my lands,
And in possession° twenty thousand crowns.

PETRUCHIO:
And for° that dowry I'll assure her of
Her widowhood,° be it that she° survive me,   120
In all my lands and leases whatsoever.
Let specialties° be therefore drawn between us,
That covenants may be kept on either hand.

BAPTISTA:
Ay, when the special thing is well obtained,
That is, her love; for that is all in all.   125

---

103. presently: immediately.   107. orchard: garden.   108. passing: exceedingly.   118. in
possession: in immediate possession.   119. for: in exchange for.   120. widowhood: i.e., widow's share of the estate.   be it that she: if she should.   122. specialties: terms of contract.

PETRUCHIO:

Why, that is nothing, for I tell you, Father,°
I am as peremptory as she proud-minded;
And where two raging fires meet together,
They do consume the thing that feeds their fury.
Though little fire grows great with little wind,   130
Yet extreme gusts will blow out fire and all.
So I° to her, and so she yields to me,
For I am rough and woo not like a babe.

BAPTISTA:

Well mayst thou woo, and happy be thy speed!°
But be thou armed for some unhappy words.   135

PETRUCHIO:

Ay, to the proof,° as mountains are for winds,
That shakes° not, though they blow perpetually.

Enter Hortensio [as Litio], with his head broke.°

BAPTISTA:

How now, my friend, why dost thou look so pale?

HORTENSIO:

For fear, I promise° you, if I look pale.

BAPTISTA:

What, will my daughter prove a good musician?   140

HORTENSIO:

I think she'll sooner prove a soldier.°
Iron may hold with° her, but never lutes.

BAPTISTA:

Why then, thou can'st not break° her to the lute?

HORTENSIO:

Why, no, for she hath broke that lute to me.
I did but tell her she mistook her frets,°   145
And bowed her hand to teach her fingering,
When, with a most impatient devilish spirit,
"Frets, call you these?" quoth she, "I'll fume with them."

126. **Father:** father-in-law.   132. **So I:** i.e., so I behave, like an extreme gust of wind.
134. **happy be thy speed:** may it turn out well for you.   136. **to the proof:** i.e., in armor, proof
against her shrewishness.   137. **shakes:** shake.   **s.d. broke:** with a bleeding cut. (Hortensio
usually appears on stage with his head emerging through a broken lute.)   139. **promise:** assure.   141. **prove a soldier:** (1) turn out to be a good soldier, (2) put a soldier to the test.
142. **hold with:** hold out against.   143. **break:** train (with pun in next line).   145. **frets:** ridges
or bars on the fingerboard of the lute. (But Kate puns on the sense of "fume," "be indignant.")

And with that word she struck me on the head,
And through the instrument my pate made way;   150
And there I stood amazèd° for a while,
As on a pillory,° looking through the lute,
While she did call me rascal fiddler
And twangling Jack,° with twenty such vile terms,
As had she studied to misuse me so.°   155

PETRUCHIO:
Now, by the world, it is a lusty° wench!
I love her ten times more than e'er I did.
O, how I long to have some chat with her!

BAPTISTA [*to Hortensio*]:
Well, go with me, and be not so discomfited.
Proceed in practice° with my younger daughter;   160
She's apt to learn and thankful for good turns. —
Signor Petruchio, will you go with us,
Or shall I send my daughter Kate to you?

PETRUCHIO:
I pray you, do.   *Exeunt. Manet° Petruchio.*
            I'll attend her here,
And woo her with some spirit when she comes.   165
Say that she rail, why then I'll tell her plain
She sings as sweetly as a nightingale.
Say that she frown, I'll say she looks as clear°
As morning roses newly washed with dew.
Say she be mute and will not speak a word,   170
Then I'll commend her volubility
And say she uttereth piercing° eloquence.
If she do bid me pack,° I'll give her thanks,
As though she bid me stay by her a week.
If she deny° to wed, I'll crave the day°   175
When I shall ask the banns° and when be married.
But here she comes; and now, Petruchio speak.

Enter Katharina.

Good morrow, Kate, for that's your name, I hear.

151. **amazèd:** bewildered.   152. **As on a pillory:** as if with my head in a wooden collar used as punishment.   154. **Jack:** knave.   155. **As . . . so:** as if she had planned how to abuse me so.   156. **lusty:** lively.   160. **practice:** instruction.   164. **s.d.** *Manet:* he remains onstage. 168. **clear:** serene.   172. **piercing:** moving.   173. **pack:** begone.   175. **deny:** refuse.   **crave the day:** ask her to name the day.   176. **ask the banns:** have a reading of the required announcement in church of a forthcoming marriage.

KATHARINA:

Well have you heard, but something hard° of hearing.
They call me Katharine that do talk of me. 180

PETRUCHIO:

You lie, in faith, for you are called plain Kate,
And bonny Kate, and sometimes Kate the curst;
But Kate, the prettiest Kate in Christendom,
Kate of Kate Hall, my superdainty Kate,
For dainties are all Kates,° and therefore, Kate, 185
Take this of me,° Kate of my consolation:°
Hearing thy mildness praised in every town,
Thy virtues spoke of, and thy beauty sounded,°
Yet not so deeply as to thee belongs,
Myself am moved° to woo thee for my wife. 190

KATHARINA:

Moved? In good time!° Let him that moved you hither
Remove you hence. I knew you at the first
You were a movable.

PETRUCHIO: Why, what's a movable?°

KATHARINA:

A joint stool.°

PETRUCHIO: Thou hast hit it. Come, sit on me.

KATHARINA:

Asses are made to bear,° and so are you. 195

PETRUCHIO:

Women are made to bear, and so are you.

KATHARINA:

No such jade° as you, if me you mean.

PETRUCHIO:

Alas, good Kate, I will not burden thee,
For knowing° thee to be but young and light.°

---

179. heard, hard: (pronounced nearly alike.)   185. all Kates: (with a quibble on "cates," con-
fections, delicacies).   186. of me: from me. consolation: comfort.   188. sounded: proclaimed (with a quibble on "plumbed," as indicated by *deeply* in the next line).   190. moved:
impelled (followed by wordplay on the more literal meaning of *move* and *remove*).   191. In
good time: forsooth, indeed.   193. movable: (1) one easily changed or dissuaded, (2) an article
of furniture.   194. A joint stool: a well-fitted stool made by an expert craftsman.   195. bear:
carry (with puns in the following lines suggesting "bear children" and "support a man during
sexual intercourse").   197. jade: an ill-conditioned horse.   199. For knowing: because I
know.   light: (1) of delicate stature, (2) lascivious, (3) lacking a *burden* (see previous line) in the
musical sense of lacking a bass undersong or accompaniment, (4) elusive (in the following line).

KATHARINA:
Too light for such a swain° as you to catch,   200
And yet as heavy as my weight should be.
PETRUCHIO:
Should be? Should — buzz!°
KATHARINA: Well ta'en, and like a buzzard.
PETRUCHIO:
O slow-winged turtle, shall a buzzard take thee?
KATHARINA:
Ay, for a turtle, as he takes a buzzard.°
PETRUCHIO:
Come, come, you wasp,° i' faith you are too angry.   205
KATHARINA:
If I be waspish, best beware my sting.
PETRUCHIO:
My remedy is then to pluck it out.
KATHARINA:
. Ay, if the fool could find it where it lies.
PETRUCHIO:
Who knows not where a wasp does wear his sting?
In his tail.   210
KATHARINA: In his tongue.
PETRUCHIO: Whose tongue?
KATHARINA:
Yours, if you talk of tales,° and so farewell.
PETRUCHIO:
What, with my tongue in your tail? Nay, come again.
Good Kate, I am a gentleman —
KATHARINA: That I'll try.   *She strikes him.*   215
PETRUCHIO:
I swear I'll cuff you if you strike again.
KATHARINA: So may you lose your arms.
If you strike me, you are no gentleman,
And if no gentleman, why then no arms.°

200. **swain:** young rustic in love.   202. **Should . . . buzz:** Petruchio puns on *be* and "bee," and uses *buzz* in perhaps three senses: (1) an interjection of impatience or contempt, (2) a bee's sound, (3) rumor being buzzed about, to which, he implies, Kate had better listen.   204. **buzzard:** (1) figuratively, a fool, (2) in the next line, an inferior kind of hawk, fit only to overtake a slow-winged *turtle* or turtledove, as Petruchio might overtake Kate, (3) a buzzing insect, caught by a turtledove.   205. **wasp:** i.e., waspish, scolding woman (but suggested by *buzzard*, buzzing insect).   213. **talk of tales:** i.e., idly tell stories (with pun on "tail").   219. **no arms:** no coat of arms (with pun on *arms* as limbs of the body).

PETRUCHIO:

    A herald, Kate? O, put me in thy books!°   220

KATHARINA: What is your crest,° a coxcomb?

PETRUCHIO:

    A combless cock,° so° Kate will be my hen.

KATHARINA:

    No cock of mine. You crow too like a craven.°

PETRUCHIO:

    Nay, come, Kate, come. You must not look so sour.

KATHARINA:

    It is my fashion when I see a crab.°   225

PETRUCHIO:

    Why, here's no crab, and therefore look not sour.

KATHARINA: There is, there is.

PETRUCHIO:

    Then show it me.

KATHARINA: Had I a glass, I would.

PETRUCHIO: What, you mean my face?

KATHARINA: Well aimed of° such a young° one.   230

PETRUCHIO:

    Now, by Saint George, I am too young for you.

KATHARINA:

    Yet you are withered.

PETRUCHIO: 'Tis with cares.

KATHARINA: I care not.

PETRUCHIO:

    Nay, hear you, Kate. In sooth, you scape° not so.

KATHARINA:

    I chafe° you if I tarry. Let me go.

PETRUCHIO:

    No, not a whit. I find you passing° gentle.   235

    'Twas told me you were rough, and coy,° and sullen,

    And now I find report a very° liar,

---

220. **books:** (1) books of heraldry, heraldic registers, (2) grace, favor.   **221. crest:** (1) armorial device, (2) a rooster's comb, setting up the joke on *coxcomb*, the cap of the court fool.   **222. A combless cock:** i.e., a gentle rooster (but with sexual suggestion).   **so:** provided that.   **223. a craven:** a cock that is not "game" or willing to fight.   **225. crab:** crab apple.   **230. aimed of:** guessed for.   **young:** i.e., inexperienced. (But Petruchio picks up the word in the sense of "strong.")   **233. scape:** escape.   **234. chafe:** annoy (but suggesting also "excite").   **235. passing:** very. (Also in line 238.)   **236. coy:** disdainful.   **237. a very:** an utter.

For thou art pleasant,° gamesome,° passing courteous,
But slow° in speech, yet sweet as springtime flowers.
Thou canst not frown, thou canst not look askance,°   240
Nor bite the lip, as angry wenches will,
Nor hast thou pleasure to be cross in talk;°
But thou with mildness entertain'st° thy wooers,
With gentle conference,° soft and affable.
Why does the world report that Kate doth limp?   245
O sland'rous world! Kate like the hazel twig
Is straight and slender, and as brown in hue
As hazelnuts, and sweeter than the kernels.
O, let me see thee walk. Thou dost not halt.°

KATHARINA:
Go, fool, and whom thou keep'st command.°   250

PETRUCHIO:
Did ever Dian° so become° a grove
As Kate this chamber with her princely gait?
O, be thou Dian, and let her be Kate.
And then let Kate be chaste and Dian sportful!°

KATHARINA:
Where did you study° all this goodly speech?   255

PETRUCHIO:
It is extempore, from my mother wit.°

KATHARINA:
A witty mother! Witless else her son.°

PETRUCHIO: Am I not wise?

KATHARINA: Yes, keep you warm.°

PETRUCHIO:
Marry, so I mean, sweet Katharine, in thy bed.   260
And therefore, setting all this chat aside,
Thus in plain terms: your father hath consented
That you shall be my wife; your dowry 'greed on;
And will you, nill you,° I will marry you.

---

238. pleasant: merry. **gamesome:** playful, spirited. **239. But slow:** never anything but slow. **240. askance:** scornfully. **242. cross in talk:** always contradicting. **243. entertain'st:** receive. **244. conference:** conversation. **249. halt:** limp. **250. whom thou keep'st command:** i.e., order about those whom you employ, your servants, not me. **251. Dian:** Diana, goddess of the hunt and chastity. **become:** adorn. **254. sportful:** amorous. **255. study:** memorize. **256. mother wit:** native intelligence. **257. Witless . . . son:** i.e., without the intelligence inherited from her, he would have none at all. **258–59. wise . . . warm:** an allusion to the proverbial phrase "enough wit to keep oneself warm." **264. will you, nill you:** whether you're willing or not.

Now, Kate, I am a husband for your turn,°   265
For by this light, whereby I see thy beauty —
Thy beauty that doth make me like thee well —
Thou must be married to no man but me.

Enter Baptista, Gremio, [and] Tranio [as Lucentio].

For I am he am born to tame you, Kate,
And bring you from a wild Kate° to a Kate   270
Conformable° as other household Kates.
Here comes your father. Never make denial;
I must and will have Katharine to my wife.

BAPTISTA:
Now, Signor Petruchio, how speed° you with my daughter?
PETRUCHIO:
How but well, sir, how but well?   275
It were impossible I should speed amiss.
BAPTISTA:
Why, how now, daughter Katharine, in your dumps?°
KATHARINA:
Call you me daughter? Now, I promise° you,
You have showed a tender fatherly regard,
To wish me wed to one half-lunatic,   280
A madcap ruffian and a swearing Jack,°
That thinks with oaths to face° the matter out.
PETRUCHIO:
Father, 'tis thus: yourself and all the world
That talked of her have talked amiss of her.
If she be curst, it is for policy,°   285
For she's not froward,° but modest as the dove.
She is not hot, but temperate as the morn.
For patience she will prove a second Grissel,°
And Roman Lucrece° for her chastity.
And to conclude, we have 'greed so well together   290
That upon Sunday is the wedding day.

265. **for your turn:** to suit you.   270. **wild Kate:** (with a quibble on "wildcat").
271. **Conformable:** compliant.   274. **speed:** fare, get on.   277. **in your dumps:** in low spirits.
278. **promise:** assure.   281. **Jack:** ill-mannered fellow.   282. **face:** brazen.   285. **policy:** cunning, ulterior motive.   286. **froward:** willful, perverse.   288. **Grissel:** patient Griselda, the epitome of wifely patience and devotion (whose story was told by Chaucer in "The Clerk's Tale" of *The Canterbury Tales* and earlier by Boccaccio and Petrarch).   289. **Roman Lucrece:** Lucretia, a Roman lady who took her own life after her chastity had been violated by the Tarquin prince, Sextus. (Shakespeare tells the story in *The Rape of Lucrece.*)

KATHARINA:
I'll see thee hanged on Sunday first.
GREMIO: Hark, Petruchio, she says she'll see thee hanged first.
TRANIO:
Is this your speeding?° Nay then, good night our part!°
PETRUCHIO:
Be patient, gentlemen, I choose her for myself.   295
If she and I be pleased, what's that to you?
'Tis bargained twixt us twain, being alone,
That she shall still be curst in company.
I tell you, 'tis incredible to believe
How much she loves me. O, the kindest Kate!   300
She hung about my neck, and kiss on kiss
She vied° so fast, protesting oath on oath,
That in a twink she won me to her love.
O, you are novices! 'Tis a world° to see
How tame, when men and women are alone,   305
A meacock° wretch can make the curstest shrew. —
Give me thy hand, Kate. I will unto Venice
To buy apparel gainst° the wedding day —
Provide the feast, Father, and bid the guests.
I will be sure my Katharine shall be fine.°   310
BAPTISTA:
I know not what to say. But give me your hands.
God send you joy, Petruchio! 'Tis a match.
GREMIO, TRANIO:
Amen, say we. We will be witnesses.
PETRUCHIO:
Father, and wife, and gentlemen, adieu.
I will to Venice. Sunday comes apace.   315
We will have rings, and things, and fine array;
And kiss me,° Kate. We will be married o' Sunday.

Exeunt Petruchio and Katharine [separately].

GREMIO:
Was ever match clapped up° so suddenly?

---

294. speeding: success. good night our part: good-bye to what we hoped to get. 302. vied: went me one better, kiss for kiss. 304. a world: worth a whole world. 305. meacock: cowardly. 308. gainst: in anticipation of. 310. fine: elegantly dressed. 317. kiss me: Petruchio probably kisses her. 318. clapped up: settled (by a shaking of hands).

BAPTISTA:
Faith, gentlemen, now I play a merchant's part,
And venture madly on a desperate mart.° 320
TRANIO:
'Twas a commodity lay fretting° by you;
'Twill bring you gain, or perish on the seas.
BAPTISTA:
The gain I seek is quiet in the match.
GREMIO:
No doubt but he hath got a quiet catch.°
But now, Baptista, to your younger daughter. 325
Now is the day we long have lookèd for.
I am your neighbor, and was suitor first.
TRANIO:
And I am one that love Bianca more
Than words can witness, or your thoughts can guess.
GREMIO:
Youngling, thou canst not love so dear as I. 330
TRANIO:
Graybeard, thy love doth freeze.
GREMIO: But thine doth fry.
Skipper,° stand back. 'Tis age that nourisheth.
TRANIO:
But youth in ladies' eyes that flourisheth.
BAPTISTA:
Content you, gentlemen, I will compound° this strife.
'Tis deeds° must win the prize, and he of both° 335
That can assure my daughter greatest dower°
Shall have my Bianca's love.
Say, Signor Gremio, what can you assure her?
GREMIO:
First, as you know, my house within the city
Is richly furnishèd with plate° and gold 340
Basins and ewers to lave° her dainty hands;

---

320. **desperate mart**: risky venture.   321. **lay fretting**: i.e., which lay in storage being destroyed by moths, weevils, or spoilage (with a pun on "chafing").   324. **quiet catch**: said ironically; Gremio is sure that Kate will be anything but quiet.   332. **Skipper**: flighty fellow. 334. **compound**: settle.   335. **deeds**: (1) actions, (2) legal deeds.   **he of both**: the one of you two.   336. **dower**: portion of a husband's estate settled on his wife in his will. (Also at line 382 and 4.4.45.)   340. **plate**: silver utensils.   341. **lave**: wash.

My hangings° all of Tyrian° tapestry;
In ivory coffers I have stuffed my crowns;°
In cypress chests my arras counterpoints,°
Costly apparel, tents,° and canopies,   345
Fine line, Turkey° cushions bossed° with pearl,
Valance° of Venice gold in needlework,
Pewter and brass, and all things that belongs
To house or housekeeping. Then at my farm
I have a hundred milch kine to the pail,°   350
Sixscore fat oxen standing in my stalls,
And all things answerable to° this portion.
Myself am struck° in years, I must confess,
And if I die tomorrow, this is hers,
If whilst I live she will be only mine.   355

TRANIO:
That "only" came well in. Sir, list to me:
I am my father's heir and only son.
If I may have your daughter to my wife,
I'll leave her houses three or four as good,
Within rich Pisa walls, as any one   360
Old Signor Gremio has in Padua,
Besides two thousand ducats° by the year
Of° fruitful land, all which shall be her jointure.°
What, have I pinched you, Signor Gremio?

GREMIO:
Two thousand ducats by the year of land!   365
[Aside.] My land amounts not to so much in all. —
That she shall have, besides an argosy°
That now is lying in Marseilles road.°
[To Tranio.] What, have I choked you with an argosy?

TRANIO:
Gremio, 'tis known my father hath no less   370
Than three great argosies, besides two galliases°

---

342. hangings: draperies hung on beds and walls.   Tyrian: dark red or purple.   343. crowns:
five-shilling coins.   344. arras counterpoints: counterpanes of tapestry.   345. tents: bed
curtains.   346. Turkey: Turkish.   bossed: embossed.   347. Valance: fringes of drapery
around the canopy or bed frame.   350. milch kine to the pail: dairy cattle.   352. answerable
to: on the same scale as.   353. struck: advanced.   362. ducats: gold coins.   363. Of: from.
jointure: marriage settlement.   367. argosy: merchant vessel of the largest size.   368. road:
roadstead, harbor.   371. galliases: heavy, low-built vessels.

And twelve tight° galleys. These I will assure her,
And twice as much, whate'er thou off'rest next.
GREMIO:
Nay, I have offered all, I have no more,
And she can have no more than all I have.   375
[*To Baptista.*] If you like me, she shall have me and mine.
TRANIO:
Why then, the maid is mine from all the world,
By your firm promise. Gremio is outvied.°
BAPTISTA:
I must confess your offer is the best;
And, let° your father make her the assurance,   380
She is your own; else, you must pardon me.
If you should die before him, where's her dower?
TRANIO:
That's but a cavil.° He is old, I young.
GREMIO:
And may not young men die, as well as old?
BAPTISTA:
Well, gentlemen, I am thus resolved: 385
On Sunday next, you know
My daughter Katharine is to be married.
Now, on the Sunday following shall Bianca
Be bride [*to Tranio*] to you, if you make this assurance;
If not, to Signor Gremio.   390
And so I take my leave, and thank you both.   *Exit.*
GREMIO:
Adieu, good neighbor. — Now I fear thee not.
Sirrah, young gamester, your father were a fool
To give thee all, and in his waning age
Set foot under thy table.° Tut, a toy!°   395
An old Italian fox is not so kind, my boy.   *Exit.*
TRANIO:
A vengeance on your crafty withered hide!
Yet I have faced it with a card of ten.°
'Tis in my head to do my master good.
I see no reason but supposed Lucentio   400

---

372. **tight:** watertight.   378. **outvied:** outbidden.   380. **let:** provided.   383. **but a cavil:**
merely a frivolous objection.   395. **Set . . . table:** i.e., become a dependent in your household.
a toy: nonsense.   398. **faced . . . ten:** brazened it out with only a ten-spot of cards.

Must get a father, called supposed Vincentio —
And that's a wonder. Fathers commonly
Do get° their children; but in this case of wooing,
A child shall get a sire, if I fail not of my cunning.   *Exit.*

ACT III, SCENE I°

Enter Lucentio [as Cambio], Hortensio [as Litio], and Bianca.

LUCENTIO:
Fiddler, forbear. You grow too forward, sir.
Have you so soon forgot the entertainment
Her sister Katharine welcomed you withal?
HORTENSIO:
But, wrangling pedant, this is
The patroness of heavenly harmony.   5
Then give me leave to have prerogative,°
And when in music we have spent an hour,
Your lecture° shall have leisure for as much.
LUCENTIO:
Preposterous° ass, that never read so far
To know° the cause why music was ordained!   10
Was it not to refresh the mind of man
After his studies or his usual pain?°
Then give me leave to read° philosophy,
And, while I pause, serve in° your harmony.
HORTENSIO:
Sirrah, I will not bear these braves° of thine.   15
BIANCA:
Why, gentlemen, you do me double wrong
To strive for that which resteth in my choice.
I am no breeching scholar° in the schools;
I'll not be tied to hours nor 'pointed times,
But learn my lessons as I please myself.   20
And, to cut off all strife, here sit we down.

---

403. get: beget (with a play on *get*, "obtain," in line 404).   ACT III, SCENE I. Location: The
same.   6. prerogative: precedence.   8. lecture: lesson.   9. Preposterous: inverting the natural order of things, unreasonable.   10. To know: as to know.   12. usual pain: regular
labors.   13. read: teach.   14. serve in: present, serve up.   15. braves: insults.   18. breeching
scholar: i.e., schoolboy liable to be whipped.

[*To Hortensio.*] Take you your instrument, play you the whiles;°
His lecture will be done ere you have tuned.
HORTENSIO:
You'll leave his lecture when I am in tune?
LUCENTIO:
That will be never. Tune your instrument. 25
                        [*Hortensio moves aside and tunes.*]
BIANCA: Where left we last?
LUCENTIO: Here, madam. [*He reads.*]   *"Hic ibat Simois; hic est Sigeia
tellus; Hic steterat Priami regia celsa senis."*°
BIANCA: Conster° them.
LUCENTIO: *"Hic ibat,"* as I told you before, *"Simois,"* I am Lucentio, *"hic* 30
est," son unto Vincentio of Pisa, *"Sigeia tellus,"* disguised thus to get your
love; *"Hic steterat,"* and that Lucentio that comes a-wooing, *"Priami,"* is
my man Tranio, *"regia,"* bearing my port,° *"celsa senis,"* that we might
beguile the old pantaloon.°
HORTENSIO: Madam, my instrument's in tune. 35
BIANCA: Let's hear. [*He plays.*] O fie! The treble jars.
LUCENTIO: Spit in the hole,° man, and tune again.
                              [*Hortensio moves aside.*]
BIANCA: Now let me see if I can conster it: *"Hic ibat Simois,"* I know you
not, *"hic est Sigeia tellus,"* I trust you not; *"Hic steterat Priami,"* take heed
he hear us not, *"regia,"* presume not, *"celsa senis,"* despair not. 40
HORTENSIO:
Madam, 'tis now in tune.   [*He plays again.*]
LUCENTIO: All but the bass.
HORTENSIO:
The bass is right, 'tis the base knave that jars.
[*Aside.*] How fiery and forward our pedant is!
Now, for my life, the knave doth court my love.
Pedascule,° I'll watch you better yet. 45
BIANCA [*to Lucentio*]:
In time I may believe, yet I mistrust.

---

22. the whiles: meantime.   **27–28. Hic . . . senis:** here flowed the river Simois; here is the Sige-
ian land; here stood the lofty palace of old Priam. (Ovid, *Heroides,* [l.33–34.)   **29. Conster:**
construe.   **33. port:** social position, style of living.   **34. pantaloon:** foolish old man, i.e.,
Gremio.   **37. Spit in the hole:** i.e., to make the peg stick.   **45. Pedascule:** a word contemptuously coined by Hortensio, presumably the vocative of an invented Latinism, *pedasculus,* "little
pedant."

LUCENTIO:
Mistrust° it not, for, sure, Aeacides°
Was Ajax, called so from his grandfather.
BIANCA:
I must believe my master; else, I promise you,
I should be arguing still upon that doubt.   50
But let it rest. — Now, Litio, to you:
Good master, take it not unkindly, pray,
That I have been thus pleasant° with you both.
HORTENSIO [to Lucentio]:
You may go walk, and give me leave a while.
My lessons make no music in three parts.   55
LUCENTIO:
Are you so formal,° sir? Well, I must wait.
[Aside.] And watch withal; for but° I be deceived,
Our fine musician groweth amorous.   [He moves aside.]
HORTENSIO:
Madam, before you touch the instrument,
To learn the order° of my fingering,   60
I must begin with rudiments of art,
To teach you gamut° in a briefer sort,
More pleasant, pithy, and effectual
Than hath been taught by any of my trade.
And there it is in writing, fairly drawn.°   [He gives her a paper.] 65
BIANCA:
Why, I am past my gamut long ago.
HORTENSIO:
Yet read the gamut of Hortensio.
BIANCA [reads]:
"Gamut I am, the ground° of all accord,°
A re, to plead Hortensio's passion;
B mi,° Bianca, take him for thy lord,   70

---

47. **Mistrust:** (Lucentio plays upon Bianca's *mistrust* in line 46, in which she expresses scepticism about his secret wooing; his answer seeks to reassure her, while at the same time in
"Litio's" hearing he seems to emphasize the truth of his instruction as he goes on with his lesson
from the *Heroides*. Her reply is ambiguous in the same way.) **Aeacides:** descendant of Aeacus,
king of Aegina, father of Telamon and grandfather of Ajax. 53. **pleasant:** merry. 56. **formal:** precise. 57. **but:** unless. 60. **order:** method. 62. **gamut:** the scale, from the alphabet
name (*gamma*) of the first note plus *ut*, its syllable name, now commonly called *do*. (The *gamut*
of Hortensio begins on G instead of on C.) 65. **drawn:** set out, copied. 68. **ground:** bass
note, foundation. **accord:** harmony. 70. *B mi:* (with a suggestion of "be my").

C fa ut,° that loves with all affection.
D sol re, one clef, two notes° have I;
E la mi,° show pity, or I die."
Call you this gamut? Tut, I like it not.
Old fashions please me best; I am not so nice°   75
To change true rules for odd inventions.

Enter a [Servant as] messenger.

SERVANT:
Mistress, your father prays you leave your books
And help to dress your sister's chamber up.
You know tomorrow is the wedding day.
BIANCA:
Farewell, sweet masters both, I must be gone.
LUCENTIO:
Faith, mistress, then I have no cause to stay.   80
          [Exeunt Bianca, Servant, and Lucentio.]
HORTENSIO:
But I have cause to pry into this pedant.
Methinks he looks as though he were in love.
Yet if thy thoughts, Bianca, be so humble
To cast thy wandering eyes on every stale,°
Seize thee that list.° If once I find thee ranging,°   85
Hortensio will be quit° with thee by changing.°   *Exit.*

ACT III, SCENE II°

Enter Baptista, Gremio, Tranio [as Lucentio], Katharine, Bianca, Lucentio [as Cambio], and others, attendants.

BAPTISTA [*to Tranio*]:
Signor Lucentio, this is the 'pointed day
That Katharine and Petruchio should be married,
And yet we hear not of our son-in-law.

71. *fa ut:* The note C is the fourth note, or *fa*, of a scale based on G but is the first note, *ut,* or *do,* of the more universal major scale based on C. Similarly, D is the fifth note, or *sol,* in the G scale but is the second, or *re,* in the C scale; similarly, with E as sixth and third.   72. **two notes:** hinting at Hortensio's disguise.   73. *E la mi:* (suggesting "Ill am I").   75. **nice:** capricious.   84. **stale:** decoy, bait.   85. **Seize . . . list:** let him who wants you have you.   **ranging:** inconstant. (The metaphor is that of a straying hawk.)   86. **be quit:** get even.   **changing:** loving another.   ACT III, SCENE, II. **Location:** Padua. Before Baptista's house.

What will be said? What mockery will it be,
To want° the bridegroom when the priest attends   5
To speak the ceremonial rites of marriage?
What says Lucentio to this shame of ours?

KATHARINA:

No shame but mine. I must, forsooth, be forced
To give my hand opposed against my heart
Unto a mad-brain rudesby° full of spleen,°   10
Who wooed in haste and means to wed at leisure.
I told you, I, he was a frantic° fool,
Hiding his bitter jests in blunt behavior.
And, to be noted for° a merry man,
He'll woo a thousand, 'point the day of marriage,   15
Make friends, invite, and proclaim the banns,
Yet never means to wed where he hath wooed.
Now must the world point at poor Katharine
And say, "Lo, there is mad Petruchio's wife,
If it would please him come and marry her!"   20

TRANIO:

Patience, good Katharine, and Baptista, too.
Upon my life, Petruchio means but well,
Whatever fortune stays him from his word.°
Though he be blunt, I know him passing wise;
Though he be merry,° yet withal he's honest.   25

KATHARINA:

Would Katharine had never seen him though!   *Exit weeping.*

BAPTISTA:

Go, girl, I cannot blame thee now to weep,
For such an injury would vex a very saint,
Much more a shrew of thy impatient humor.   *Enter Biondello.*

BIONDELLO: Master, master! News, and such old° news as you never   30
heard of!

BAPTISTA: Is it new and old too? How may that be?

BIONDELLO: Why, is it not news to hear of Petruchio's coming?

BAPTISTA: Is he come?

BIONDELLO: Why, no, sir.   35

---

5. want: lack.   10. rudesby: unmannerly fellow.   spleen: i.e., changeable temper.
12. frantic: violently insane.   14. to be noted for: in order to get a reputation as.   23. fortune
... word: accident keeps him from fulfilling his promise.   25. merry: given to joking.
30. old: rare; or perhaps referring to Petruchio's old clothes.

BAPTISTA: What, then?
BIONDELLO: He is coming.
BAPTISTA: When will he be here?
BIONDELLO: When he stands where I am and sees you there.
TRANIO: But say, what to° thine old news? 40
BIONDELLO: Why, Petruchio is coming in a new hat and an old jerkin;°
a pair of old breeches thrice turned;° a pair of boots that have been
candle-cases,° one buckled, another laced; an old rusty sword ta'en out
of the town armory, with a broken hilt, and chapeless;° with two broken
points;° his horse hipped,° with an old mothy saddle and stirrups of no 45
kindred; besides, possessed with the glanders° and like to mose in the
chine,° troubled with the lampass,° infected with the fashions,° full of
windgalls,° sped° with spavins,° rayed° with the yellows,° past cure of
the fives,° stark spoiled with° the staggers,° begnawn with the bots,°
swayed in the back and shoulder-shotten;° near-legged before,° and 50
with a half-cheeked bit° and a headstall° of sheep's leather° which,
being restrained° to keep him from stumbling, hath been often burst
and now repaired with knots; one girth° six times pieced,° and a woman's crupper° of velour,° which hath two letters for her name° fairly set
down in studs, and here and there pierced with packthread.° 55
BAPTISTA: Who comes with him?

---

40. to: about. **41. jerkin:** man's jacket. **42. turned:** i.e., with the material reversed to get more wear. **43. candle-cases:** i.e., discarded boots, used only as a receptacle for candle ends. **44. chapeless:** without the chape, the metal plate or mounting of a scabbard, especially that which covers the point. **45. points:** tagged laces for attaching hose to doublet. **hipped:** lamed in the hip. (Almost all the diseases here named are described in Gervase Markham's *How to Choose, Ride, Train, and Diet both Hunting Horses and Running Horses . . . Also a Discourse of Horsemanship,* probably first published in 1593.) **46. glanders:** contagious disease in horses causing swelling beneath the jaw and mucous discharge from the nostrils. **46–47. mose in the chine:** suffer from glanders. **47. lampass:** a thick, spongy flesh growing over a horse's upper teeth and hindering his eating. **fashions:** i.e., farcins, or farcy, a disease like glanders. **48. windgalls:** soft tumors or swellings generally found on the fetlock joint, so called from having been supposed to contain air. **sped:** far gone. **spavins:** a disease of the hock, marked by a small bony enlargement inside the leg. **rayed:** defiled. **yellows:** jaundice. **49. fives:** avives, a glandular disease causing swelling behind the ear. **stark spoiled with:** completely destroyed by. **staggers:** a disease causing palsylike staggering. **bots:** parasitic worms. **50. shoulder-shotten:** with sprained or dislocated shoulder. **near-legged before:** with knock-kneed forelegs. **51. half-cheeked bit:** one to which the bridle is attached halfway up the cheek or sidepiece and thus not giving sufficient control over the horse. **headstall:** part of the bridle over the head. **sheep's leather:** i.e., of inferior quality; pigskin was used for strongest harness. **52. restrained:** drawn back. **53. girth:** saddle-strap passing under the horse's belly. **pieced:** mended. **54. crupper:** leather loop passing under the horse's tail and fastened to the saddle. **velour:** velvet. **two . . . name:** her initials. **55. packthread:** twine for securing parcels.

BIONDELLO: O, sir, his lackey, for all the world° caparisoned° like the horse; with a linen stock° on one leg and a kersey boot-hose° on the other, gartered with a red and blue list;° an old hat, and the humor of forty fancies° pricked° in 't for° a feather — a monster, a very monster   60
in apparel, and not like a Christian footboy or a gentleman's lackey.

TRANIO:
'Tis some odd humor pricks° him to this fashion;
Yet oftentimes he goes but mean-appareled.

BAPTISTA: I am glad he's come, howsoe'er he comes.

BIONDELLO: Why, sir, he comes not.   65

BAPTISTA: Didst thou not say he comes?

BIONDELLO: Who? That Petruchio came?

BAPTISTA: Ay, that Petruchio came.

BIONDELLO: No, sir, I say his horse comes, with him on his back.

BAPTISTA: Why, that's all one.°   70

BIONDELLO:
Nay, by Saint Jamy,
I hold° you a penny,
A horse and a man
Is more than one,
And yet not many.   75

Enter Petruchio and Grumio.

PETRUCHIO: Come, where be these gallants? Who's at home?

BAPTISTA: You are welcome, sir.

PETRUCHIO: And yet I come not well.°

BAPTISTA: And yet you halt° not.

TRANIO:
Not so well appareled as I wish you were.   80

PETRUCHIO:
Were it° better, I should rush° in thus.
But where is Kate? Where is my lovely bride?
How does my father? Gentles, methinks you frown.
And wherefore gaze this goodly company,

---

57. **for all the world:** in all respects.   **caparisoned:** outfitted.   58. **stock:** stocking.   **kersey boot-hose:** overstocking of coarse material for wearing under boots.   59. **list:** strip of cloth.   59–60. **the humor . . . fancies:** i.e., with a caprice equal to some forty imaginings. 60. **pricked:** pinned.   **for:** in place of.   62. **humor pricks:** whim that spurs.   70. **all one:** the same thing.   72. **hold:** wager.   78. **I come not well:** i.e., I am not made to feel welcome; or, I come admittedly not well appareled.   79. **halt:** limp, move slowly.   81. **Were it:** even if it (my apparel) were.   **rush:** come quickly (referring to *halt not* in line 79).

As if they saw some wondrous monument,°   85
Some comet, or unusual prodigy?°

BAPTISTA:

Why, sir, you know this is your wedding day.
First were we sad, fearing you would not come,
Now sadder that you come so unprovided.°
Fie, doff this habit,° shame to your estate,°   90
An eyesore to our solemn festival!

TRANIO:

And tell us, what occasion of import
Hath all so long detained you from your wife
And sent you hither so unlike yourself?

PETRUCHIO:

Tedious it were to tell, and harsh to hear.
Sufficeth° I am come to keep my word,   95
Though in some part enforcèd to digress,°
Which at more leisure I will so excuse
As you shall well be satisfied withal.
But where is Kate? I stay too long from her.
The morning wears; 'tis time we were at church.   100

TRANIO:

See not your bride in these unreverent robes.
Go to my chamber. Put on clothes of mine.

PETRUCHIO:

Not I, believe me. Thus I'll visit her.

BAPTISTA:

But thus, I trust, you will not marry her.   105

PETRUCHIO:

Good sooth,° even thus. Therefore ha' done with words.
To me she's married, not unto my clothes.
Could I repair what she will wear in me°
As I can change these poor accoutrements,
'Twere well for Kate and better for myself.   110
But what a fool am I to chat with you,
When I should bid good morrow to my bride
And seal the title with a lovely° kiss!   *Exit.*

85. **monument:** portent.   86. **prodigy:** omen.   89. **unprovided:** ill equipped.   90. **habit:**
outfit.   **estate:** position, station.   96. **Sufficeth:** it is enough that.   97. **digress:** i.e., deviate.
106. **Good sooth:** i.e., yes indeed.   108. **Could . . . me:** If I could amend in my character what
she'll have to put up with.   113. **lovely:** loving.

TRANIO:
He hath some meaning in his mad attire.
We will persuade him, be it possible, 115
To put on better ere he go to church.
BAPTISTA:
I'll after him, and see the event° of this.
Exit [with all but Tranio and Lucentio].
TRANIO:
But, sir, to love concerneth us° to add
Her father's liking, which to bring to pass,
As I before imparted to your worship, 120
I am to get a man — whate'er he be
It skills° not much, we'll fit him to our turn —
And he shall be Vincentio of Pisa
And make assurance here in Padua
Of greater sums than I have promisèd. 125
So shall you quietly enjoy your hope
And marry sweet Bianca with consent.
LUCENTIO:
Were it not that my fellow schoolmaster
Doth watch Bianca's steps so narrowly,
'Twere good, methinks, to steal our marriage,° 130
Which once performed, let all the world say no,
I'll keep mine own, despite of all the world.
TRANIO:
That by degrees we mean to look into,
And watch our vantage° in this business.
We'll overreach the graybeard, Gremio, 135
The narrow-prying° father, Minola,
The quaint° musician, amorous Litio,
All for my master's sake, Lucentio. *Enter Gremio.*
Signor Gremio, came you from the church?
GREMIO:
As willingly as e'er I came from school. 140
TRANIO:
And is the bride and bridegroom coming home?

117. **event:** outcome.   118. **concerneth us:** it concerns us, is in our best interest.   122. **skills:** matters.   130. **steal our marriage:** elope.   134. **watch our vantage:** look out for our best opportunity, advantage.   136. **narrow-prying:** suspicious, watchful.   137. **quaint:** skillful.

GREMIO:
> A bridegroom, say you? 'Tis a groom indeed,°
> A grumbling groom, and that the girl shall find.

TRANIO:
> Curster than she? Why, 'tis impossible.

GREMIO:
> Why, he's a devil, a devil, a very fiend.   145

TRANIO:
> Why, she's a devil, a devil, the devil's dam.°

GREMIO:
> Tut, she's a lamb, a dove, a fool to° him.
> I'll tell you, Sir Lucentio. When the priest
> Should ask° if Katharine should be his wife,
> "Ay, by Gog's wouns°," quoth he, and swore so loud   150
> That all amazed the priest let fall the book,
> And as he stooped again to take it up,
> This mad-brained bridegroom took° him such a cuff
> That down fell priest and book, and book and priest.
> "Now take them up," quoth he, "if any list."°   155

TRANIO:
> What said the wench when he rose again?

GREMIO:
> Trembled and shook, forwhy° he stamped and swore
> As if the vicar meant to cozen° him.
> But after many ceremonies done
> He calls for wine. "A health!" quoth he, as if   160
> He had been aboard,° carousing to his mates
> After a storm; quaffed off the muscatel
> And threw the sops° all in the sexton's face,
> Having no other reason
> But that his beard grew thin and hungerly°   165
> And seemed to ask him sops° as he was drinking.
> This done, he took the bride about the neck
> And kissed her lips with such a clamorous smack

---

142. **a groom indeed:** a fine bridegroom he is. (Said ironically, with pun on the sense of "servant," "rough fellow.") 146. **dam:** mother. 147. **a fool to:** i.e., a pitiable weak creature compared with. 149. **Should ask:** came to the point (in the service) where he is directed to ask. 150. **Gog's wouns:** God's (Christ's) wounds. 153. **took:** gave, struck. 155. **list:** choose. 157. **forwhy:** because. 158. **cozen:** cheat. 161. **aboard:** aboard ship. 163. **sops:** cakes or bread soaked in the wine. 165. **hungerly:** hungry looking, having a starved or famished look. 166. **ask him sops:** ask him for the sops.

That at the parting all the church did echo.
And I seeing this came thence for very shame,   170
And after me, I know, the rout° is coming.
Such a mad marriage never was before.   *Music plays.*
Hark, hark! I hear the minstrels play.

Enter Kate, Petruchio, Bianca, Hortensio [as Litio], Baptista, [with Grumio, and train].

PETRUCHIO:
Gentlemen and friends, I thank you for your pains.
I know you think to dine with me today.   175
And have prepared great store of wedding cheer;
But so it is my haste doth call me hence,
And therefore here I mean to take my leave.

BAPTISTA:
Is 't possible you will away tonight?

PETRUCHIO:
I must away today, before night come.   180
Make it no wonder.° If you knew my business,
You would entreat me rather go than stay.
And, honest° company, I thank you all
That have beheld me give away myself
To this most patient, sweet, and virtuous wife.   185
Dine with my father, drink a health to me,
For I must hence; and farewell to you all.

TRANIO:
Let us entreat you stay till after dinner.

PETRUCHIO:
It may not be.

GREMIO: Let me entreat you.

PETRUCHIO:
It cannot be.

KATHARINA: Let me entreat you.   190

PETRUCHIO:
I am content.

KATHARINA: Are you content to stay?

PETRUCHIO:
I am content you shall entreat me stay;
But yet not stay, entreat me how you can.

---

171. **rout:** crowd, wedding party. 181. **Make it no wonder:** don't be amazed at it.
183. **honest:** worthy, kind.

KATHARINA:
  Now, if you love me, stay.
PETRUCHIO: Grumio, my horse.°
GRUMIO: Ay, sir, they be ready. The oats have eaten the horses.°   195
KATHARINA: Nay, then,
  Do what thou canst, I will not go today,
  No, nor tomorrow — not till I please myself.
  The door is open, sir, there lies your way.
  You may be jogging whiles your boots are green.°   200
  For me, I'll not be gone till I please myself.
  'Tis like° you'll prove a jolly,° surly groom,
  That take it on you° at the first so roundly.°
PETRUCHIO:
  O Kate, content thee. Prithee, be not angry.
KATHARINA:
  I will be angry. What hast thou to do?° —   205
  Father, be quiet. He shall stay my leisure.°
GREMIO:
  Ay, marry, sir, now it begins to work.°
KATHARINA:
  Gentlemen, forward to the bridal dinner.
  I see a woman may be made a fool
  If she had not a spirit to resist.   210
PETRUCHIO:
  They shall go forward, Kate, at thy command. —
  Obey the bride, you that attend on her.
  Go to the feast, revel and domineer,°
  Carouse full measure to her maidenhead,
  Be mad and merry, or go hang yourselves.   215
  But for° my bonny Kate, she must with me.
  Nay, look not big,° nor stamp, nor stare, nor fret;
  I will be master of what is mine own.
  She is my goods, my chattels; she is my house,
  My household stuff, my field, my barn,   220

---

194. **horse:** horses.   195. **oats . . . horses:** (A comic inversion.)   200. **be . . . green:** (Proverbial for "getting an early start," with a sarcastic allusion to his unseemly attire.)   **green:** fresh, new.   202. **like:** likely.   **jolly:** arrogant, overbearing.   203. **take it on you:** i.e., throw your weight around.   **roundly:** unceremoniously.   205. **What . . . do:** what business is it of yours?   206. **stay my leisure:** wait until I am ready.   207. **it . . . work:** i.e., things are starting to happen. (The metaphor is perhaps of liquor fermenting.)   213. **domineer:** feast riotously.   216. **for:** as for.   217. **big:** threatening.

My horse, my ox, my ass, my anything;°
And here she stands, touch her whoever dare.
I'll bring mine action° on the proudest he
That stops my way in Padua. — Grumio,
Draw° forth thy weapon. We are beset with thieves.   225
Rescue thy mistress, if thou be a man. —
Fear not, sweet wench, they shall not touch thee, Kate!
I'll buckler° thee against a million.

Exeunt Petruchio, Katharina, [and Grumio].

BAPTISTA:
Nay, let them go — a couple of quiet ones!

GREMIO:
Went they not quickly, I should die with laughing.   230

TRANIO:
Of all mad matches never was the like.

LUCENTIO:
Mistress, what's your opinion of your sister?

BIANCA:
That, being mad herself, she's madly mated.

GREMIO:
I warrant him, Petruchio is Kated.°

BAPTISTA:
Neighbors and friends, though bride and bridegroom wants°   235
For to supply° the places at the table,
You know there wants no junkets° at the feast.
Lucentio, you shall supply the bridegroom's place,
And let Bianca take her sister's room.

TRANIO:
Shall sweet Bianca practice how to bride it?°   240

BAPTISTA:
She shall, Lucentio. Come, gentlemen, let's go.   *Exeunt.*

---

221. ox . . . anything: (This catalogue of a man's possessions is from the Tenth Commandment.) 223. action: (1) lawsuit, (2) attack. 225. Draw: Perhaps Petruchio and Grumio actually draw their swords. 228. buckler: shield, defend. 234. Kated: Gremio's invention for "mated and matched with Kate." 235–36. wants For to supply: are not present to fill. 237. there wants no junkets: there is no lack of sweetmeats. 240. bride it: play the bride.

ACT IV, SCENE I°

Enter Grumio.

GRUMIO: Fie, fie on all tired jades,° on all mad masters, and all foul ways!°
Was ever man so beaten? Was ever man so rayed?° Was ever man so
weary? I am sent before to make a fire, and they are coming after to
warm them. Now, were not I a little pot and soon hot,° my very lips
might freeze to my teeth, my tongue to the roof of my mouth, my heart   5
in my belly, ere I should come by° a fire to thaw me. But I with blowing
the fire shall warm myself; for, considering the weather, a taller° man
than I will take cold. Holla, ho! Curtis!

Enter Curtis.

CURTIS: Who is that calls so coldly?
GRUMIO: A piece of ice. If thou doubt it, thou mayst slide from my   10
shoulder to my heel with no greater a run° but my head and my neck.
A fire, good Curtis!
CURTIS: Is my master and his wife coming, Grumio?
GRUMIO: O, ay, Curtis, ay, and therefore fire, fire! Cast on no water.°
CURTIS: Is she so hot a shrew as she's reported?   15
GRUMIO: She was, good Curtis, before this frost. But, thou know'st, win-
ter tames man, woman, and beast; for it hath tamed my old master and
my new mistress and myself, fellow Curtis.
CURTIS: Away, you three-inch fool!° I am no beast.°
GRUMIO: Am I but three inches? Why, thy horn° is a foot, and so long am   20
I, at the least. But wilt thou make a fire, or shall I complain on thee to
our mistress, whose hand — she being now at hand — thou shalt soon
feel, to thy cold comfort, for being slow in thy hot office?°
CURTIS: I prithee, good Grumio, tell me, how goes the world?
GRUMIO: A cold world, Curtis, in every office but thine, and therefore   25
fire. Do thy duty, and have thy duty,° for my master and mistress are
almost frozen to death.

ACT IV, SCENE I. **Location:** Petruchio's country house. A table is set out, with seats.   1. **jades:**
ill-conditioned horses.   **ways:** roads.   2. **rayed:** dirtied.   4. **a little . . . hot:** proverbial expression for a person of small stature soon angered.   6. **come by:** find.   7. **taller:** (with play
on the meaning "better," "finer").   11. **run:** running start.   14. **Cast . . . water:** alludes to the
round "Scotland's burning," in which the phrase "Fire, fire!" is followed by "Pour on water, pour
on water."   19. **three-inch fool:** another reference to Grumio's size.   **I am no beast:** Curtis
protests being called *fellow* by Grumio, since Grumio in his previous speech has paralleled himself with *beast.*   20. **horn:** i.e., cuckold's horn. (Grumio retorts that he's not too small to cuckold Curtis.)   23. **hot office:** i.e., duty of providing a fire.   26. **have thy duty:** receive your
reward.

CURTIS: There's fire ready, and therefore, good Grumio, the news.

GRUMIO: Why, "Jack boy, ho, boy!"° and as much news as wilt thou.

CURTIS: Come, you are so full of coney-catching.°   30

GRUMIO: Why, therefore fire, for I have caught extreme cold. Where's the
cook? Is supper ready, the house trimmed, rushes° strewed, cobwebs
swept, the servingmen in their new fustian,° the white stockings, and
every officer° his wedding garment on? Be the Jacks° fair within, the
Jills° fair without, the carpets° laid, and everything in order?   35

CURTIS: All ready; and therefore, I pray thee, news.

GRUMIO: First, know my horse is tired, my master and mistress fallen
out.°

CURTIS: How?

GRUMIO: Out of their saddles into the dirt — and thereby hangs a tale.°   40

CURTIS: Let's ha 't,° good Grumio.

GRUMIO: Lend thine ear.

CURTIS: Here.

GRUMIO: There.   [He cuffs Curtis.]

CURTIS: This 'tis to feel a tale, not to hear a tale.   45

GRUMIO: And therefore 'tis called a sensible° tale, and this cuff was but to
knock at your ear and beseech listening. Now I begin: Imprimis,° we
came down a foul° hill, my master riding behind my mistress —

CURTIS: Both of° one horse?

GRUMIO: What's that to thee?   50

CURTIS: Why, a horse.

GRUMIO: Tell thou the tale. But hadst thou not crossed° me, thou
shouldst have heard how her horse fell and she under her horse; thou
shouldst have heard in how miry a place, how she was bemoiled,° how
he left her with the horse upon her, how he beat me because her horse   55
stumbled, how she waded through the dirt to pluck him off me, how he
swore, how she prayed that never prayed before, how I cried, how the
horses ran away, how her bridle was burst, how I lost my crupper, with

29. **Jack . . . boy:** the first line of another round or catch.   30. **coney-catching:** cheating, trickery (with a play on *catch*, "round," in the previous line).   32. **rushes:** used to cover the floor.   33. **fustian:** coarse cloth of cotton and flax.   34. **officer:** household servant.   **Jacks:** (1) servingmen, (2) drinking vessels, usually of leather and hence needing to be clean *within*.   **Jills:** (1) maidservants, (2) "gills," drinking vessels holding a quarter pint, often of metal and hence in need of polishing *without*. (Grumio may joke that the maidservants cannot be expected to be clean *within*.)   35. **carpets:** table covers.   37–38. **fallen out:** quarreling (but with a pun on the literal sense in line 40).   40. **thereby hangs a tale:** there's quite a story to tell about that (but with a risible suggestion of hanging by one's tail).   41. **ha 't:** have it.   46. **sensible:** (1) capable of being felt, (2) showing good sense.   47. **Imprimis:** in the first place.   48. **foul:** muddy.   49. **of:** on.   52. **crossed:** thwarted, interrupted.   54. **bemoiled:** befouled with mire.

many things of worthy° memory, which now shall die in oblivion and
thou return unexperienced to thy grave.   60
CURTIS: By this reckoning he is more shrew than she.
GRUMIO: Ay, and that thou and the proudest of you all shall find when he
comes home. But what° talk I of this? Call forth Nathaniel, Joseph,
Nicholas, Philip, Walter, Sugarsop, and the rest. Let their heads be
sleekly combed, their blue coats° brushed, and their garters of an indif-   65
ferent° knit; let them curtsy with their left legs, and not presume to
touch a hair of my master's horsetail till they kiss their hands. Are they
all ready?
CURTIS: They are.
GRUMIO: Call them forth.   70
CURTIS [calling]: Do you hear, ho? You must meet my master to coun-
tenance° my mistress.
GRUMIO: Why, she hath a face of her own.
CURTIS: Who knows not that?
GRUMIO: Thou, it seems, that calls for company to countenance her.   75
CURTIS: I call them forth to credit° her.

Enter four or five Servingmen.

GRUMIO: Why, she comes to borrow nothing of them.
NATHANIEL: Welcome home, Grumio!
PHILIP: How now, Grumio?
JOSEPH: What, Grumio!   80
NICHOLAS: Fellow Grumio!
NATHANIEL: How now, old lad?
GRUMIO: Welcome, you; how now, you; what, you; fellow, you — and
thus much for greeting. Now, my spruce° companions, is all ready, and
all things neat?   85
NATHANIEL: All things is ready. How near is our master?
GRUMIO: E'en at hand, alighted by this; and therefore be not — Cock's
passion,° silence! I hear my master.

Enter Petruchio and Kate.

PETRUCHIO:
Where be these knaves? What, no man at door

---

59. of worthy: worthy of.   63. what: why.   65. blue coats: usual dress for servingmen.
65–66. indifferent: i.e., well matched and not flamboyant.   71–72. countenance: pay respects
to (with a following pun on the meaning "face").   76. credit: pay respects to (with another
pun following, on "extend financial credit").   84. spruce: lively, trim in appearance.
87–88. Cock's passion: by God's (Christ's) suffering.

To hold my stirrup° nor to take my horse?   90
Where is Nathaniel, Gregory, Philip?
ALL SERVANTS: Here, here, sir, here, sir.
PETRUCHIO:
Here, sir! Here, sir! Here, sir! Here, sir!
You loggerheaded and unpolished grooms!
What, no attendance? No regard? No duty?   95
Where is the foolish knave I sent before?°
GRUMIO:
Here, sir, as foolish as I was before.
PETRUCHIO:
You peasant swain,° you whoreson, malt-horse drudge!°
Did I not bid thee meet me in the park
And bring along these rascal knaves with thee?   100
GRUMIO:
Nathaniel's coat, sir, was not fully made,
And Gabriel's pumps° were all unpinked° i' the heel.
There was no link° to color Peter's hat,
And Walter's dagger was not come from sheathing.°
There were none fine° but Adam, Ralph, and Gregory.   105
The rest were ragged, old, and beggarly.
Yet, as they are, here are they come to meet you.
PETRUCHIO:
Go, rascals, go and fetch my supper in.   *Exeunt Servants.*
[*He sings.*] "Where is the life that late I led?
Where are those° — " Sit down, Kate, and welcome —   110
                                          [*They sit at table.*]
Soud, soud, soud, soud!°

Enter Servants with supper.

Why, when,° I say? — Nay, good sweet Kate, be merry. —
Off with my boots, you rogues! You villains, when?
                           [*A Servant takes off Petruchio's boots.*]

90. **hold my stirrup:** i.e., help me dismount.   96. **before:** ahead (with pun in next line on
"previously").   98. **swain:** rustic.   **whoreson . . . drudge:** worthless plodding work animal,
such as would be used on a treadmill to grind malt.   102. **pumps:** low-cut shoes.   **unpinked:**
lacking in eyelets or in ornamental tracing in the leather.   103. **link:** blacking made from
burnt "links" or torches.   104. **sheathing:** being fitted with a sheath.   105. **fine:** well clothed.
109–10. **Where . . . those:** a fragment of a lost ballad, probably lamenting the man's loss of
freedom in marriage.   111. **Soud:** a nonsense song or expression of impatience, or perhaps
"food!"   112. **when:** an exclamation of impatience.

[*He sings.*] "It was the friar of orders gray,
　　As he forth walkèd on his way° — "
Out,° you rogue! You pluck my foot awry.　　　[*He kicks the Servant.*]　　115
Take that, and mend the plucking of° the other.
Be merry, Kate. — Some water, here. What, ho!

Enter one with water.

Where's my spaniel Troilus? Sirrah, get you hence,
And bid my cousin Ferdinand come hither —　　　[*Exit Servant.*]　　120
One, Kate, that you must kiss and be acquainted with.
Where are my slippers? Shall I have some water?
Come, Kate, and wash, and welcome heartily.
　　　　　　　　　[*A Servant offers water, but spills some.*]
　You whoreson villain, will you let it fall?　　　[*He strikes the Servant.*]
KATHARINA:
　Patience, I pray you, 'twas a fault unwilling.°　　　125
PETRUCHIO:
　A whoreson, beetleheaded,° flap-eared knave! —
Come, Kate, sit down. I know you have a stomach.°
Will you give thanks,° sweet Kate, or else shall I? —
What's this? Mutton?
FIRST SERVANT:　　　　Ay.
PETRUCHIO:　　　　Who brought it?
PETER:　　　　　　　　　　I.
PETRUCHIO:
　'Tis burnt, and so is all the meat.　　　130
What dogs are these? Where is the rascal cook?
How durst you, villains, bring it from the dresser°
And serve it thus to me that love it not?
There, take it to you, trenchers,° cups, and all.
　　　　　　　　　[*He throws the meat, etc., at them.*]

114–15. "It . . . way": a fragment of a lost ballad, probably bawdy.　116. **Out**: exclamation of anger or reproach.　117. **mend the plucking of**: do a better job of pulling off.　125. **unwilling**: not intentional.　126. **beetleheaded**: i.e., blockheaded (since a *beetle* is a pounding tool).　127. **stomach**: appetite (with a suggestion also of "temper").　128. **give thanks**: say grace.　132. **dresser**: one who "dresses" or prepares the food; or, possibly, sideboard.　134. **trenchers**: wooden dishes or plates.

You heedless jolt-heads° and unmannered slaves!   135
What, do you grumble? I'll be with you straight.°   [*They run out.*]
KATHARINA:
I pray you, husband, be not so disquiet.
The meat was well, if you were so contented.°
PETRUCHIO:
I tell thee, Kate, 'twas burnt and dried away,
And I expressly am forbid to touch it;   140
For it engenders choler,° planteth anger,
And better 'twere that both of us did fast,
Since, of ourselves,° ourselves are choleric,
Than feed it with such overroasted flesh.
Be patient. Tomorrow 't shall be mended,   145
And for this night we'll fast for company.°
Come, I will bring thee to thy bridal chamber.   *Exeunt.*

Enter Servants severally.°

NATHANIEL: Peter, didst ever see the like?
PETER: He kills her in her own humor.°

Enter Curtis.

GRUMIO: Where is he?   150
CURTIS: In her chamber,
Making a sermon of continency° to her,
And rails, and swears, and rates,° that° she, poor soul,
Knows not which way to stand, to look, to speak,
And sits as one new risen from a dream.   155
Away, away! For he is coming hither.   [*Exeunt.*]

Enter Petruchio.

PETRUCHIO:
Thus have I politicly° begun my reign,
And 'tis my hope to end successfully.

---

135. **jolt-heads:** blockheads.   136. **with you straight:** after you at once (to get even for
this).   138. **if . . . contented:** if you had chosen to be pleased with it.   141. **choler:** the humor
or bodily fluid, hot and dry in character, that supposedly produced ill temper and was thought
to be aggravated by the eating of roast meat.   143. **of ourselves:** by our natures.   146. **for
company:** as something to do together.   **s.d. severally:** separately.   149. **kills . . . humor:** i.e.,
uses anger to subdue anger in her.   152. **sermon of continency:** lecture on self-restraint.
153. **rates:** scolds.   **that:** so that.   157. **politicly:** with skillful calculation.

My falcon now is sharp° and passing° empty,
And till she stoop° she must not be full-gorged,   160
For then she never looks upon her lure.
Another way I have to man° my haggard,°
To make her come and know her keeper's call:
That is, to watch her,° as we watch these kites°
That bate and beat° and will not be obedient.   165
She ate no meat today, nor none shall eat.
Last night she slept not, nor tonight she shall not.
As with the meat, some undeservèd fault
I'll find about the making of the bed,
And here I'll fling the pillow, there the bolster,   170
This way the coverlet, another way the sheets.
Ay, and amid this hurly° I intend°
That all is done in reverent care of her.
And in conclusion she shall watch° all night,
And if she chance to nod I'll rail and brawl,
And with the clamor keep her still awake.   175
This is a way to kill a wife with kindness;
And thus I'll curb her mad and headstrong humor.°
He that knows better how to tame a shrew,
Now let him speak. 'Tis charity to show.°   *Exit.*   180

ACT IV, SCENE II°

Enter Tranio [as Lucentio] and Hortensio [as Litio].

TRANIO:
Is 't possible, friend Litio, that Mistress Bianca
Doth fancy any other but Lucentio?
I tell you, sir, she bears me fair in hand.°
HORTENSIO:
Sir, to satisfy° you in what I have said,

---

159. **sharp:** hungry. **passing:** very. 160. **stoop:** fly down to the lure. 162. **man:** tame (with a pun on the sense of "assert masculine authority"). **haggard:** wild female hawk; hence, an intractable woman. 164. **watch her:** keep her watching, i.e., awake. **kites:** a kind of hawk (with a pun on *Kate*). 165. **bate and beat:** beat the wings impatiently and flutter away from the hand or perch. 172. **hurly:** commotion. **intend:** pretend. 174. **watch:** stay awake. 178. **humor:** disposition. 180. **'Tis charity to show:** this is to perform an act of Christian benevolence. (On the rhyme with *shrew,* see also the play's final lines.) ACT IV, SCENE II. **Location:** Padua. Before Baptista's house. 3. **bears . . . hand:** gives me encouragement, leads me on. 4. **satisfy:** convince.

Stand by and mark the manner of his teaching.   [*They stand aside.*]   5

Enter Bianca [and Lucentio as Cambio].

LUCENTIO:
Now, mistress, profit you in what you read?°
BIANCA:
What, master, read you? First resolve° me that.
LUCENTIO:
I read that I profess,° *The Art to Love.*°
BIANCA:
And may you prove, sir, master of your art!
LUCENTIO:
While you, sweet dear, prove mistress of my heart!   10
                    [*They move aside and court each other.*]
HORTENSIO [*to Tranio, coming forward*]:
Quick proceeders,° marry! Now, tell me, I pray,
You that durst swear that your mistress Bianca
Loved none in the world so well as Lucentio.
TRANIO:
O despiteful° love! Unconstant womankind!
I tell thee, Litio, this is wonderful.°   15
HORTENSIO:
Mistake no more. I am not Litio,
Nor a musician, as I seem to be,
But one that scorn° to live in this disguise
For such a one° as leaves a gentleman
And makes a god of such a cullion.°   20
Know, sir, that I am called Hortensio.
TRANIO:
Signor Hortensio, I have often heard
Of your entire° affection to Bianca;
And since mine eyes are witness of her lightness,°
I will with you, if you be so contented,   25
Forswear Bianca and her love forever.

---

6. **read:** evidently, both Bianca and "Cambio" carry books.   7. **resolve:** answer.   8. **that I profess:** what I practice.   *The Art to Love:* Ovid's *Ars Amatoria.*   11. **proceeders:** (1) workers, doers, (2) candidates for academic degrees (as suggested by the phrase *master of your art* in line 9).   14. **despiteful:** cruel.   15. **wonderful:** cause for wonder.   18. **scorn:** scorns. 19. **such a one:** i.e., Bianca.   20. **cullion:** base fellow (referring to "Cambio"; literally the word means "testicle").   23. **entire:** sincere.   24. **lightness:** wantonness.

HORTENSIO:

See how they kiss and court! Signor Lucentio,
Here is my hand, and here I firmly vow   [*giving his hand*]
Never to woo her more, but do forswear her,
As one unworthy all the former favors   30
That I have fondly° flattered her withal.

TRANIO:

And here I take the like unfeignèd oath,
Never to marry with her though she would entreat.
Fie on her, see how beastly she doth court him!

HORTENSIO:

Would all the world but he had quite forsworn!°   35
For me, that I may surely keep mine oath,
I will be married to a wealthy widow,
Ere three days pass, which hath as long loved me
As I have loved this proud disdainful haggard.°
And so farewell, Signor Lucentio.   40
Kindness in women, not their beauteous looks,
Shall win my love. And so I take my leave,
In resolution° as I swore before.   [*Exit.*]

TRANIO [*as Lucentio and Bianca come forward again*]:

Mistress Bianca, bless you with such grace
As 'longeth° to a lover's blessèd case!
Nay, I have ta'en you napping,° gentle love,   45
And have forsworn you with Hortensio.

BIANCA:

Tranio, you jest. But have you both forsworn me?

TRANIO:

Mistress, we have.

LUCENTIO: Then we are rid of Litio.

TRANIO:

I' faith, he'll have a lusty° widow now,   50
That shall be wooed and wedded in a day.

BIANCA: God give him joy!

TRANIO: Ay, and he'll tame her.

BIANCA: He says so, Tranio?

---

31. **fondly:** foolishly.   35. **Would . . . forsworn:** i.e., may everyone in the world forsake her except the penniless "Cambio," and may she thus get what she deserves.   39. **haggard:** wild hawk.   43. **In resolution:** determined.   45. **'longeth:** belongs.   46. **ta'en you napping:** i.e., surprised you.   50. **lusty:** merry, lively.

TRANIO:
Faith, he is gone unto the taming-school.   55
BIANCA:
The taming-school! What, is there such a place?
TRANIO:
Ay, mistress, and Petruchio is the master,
That teacheth tricks eleven-and-twenty long°
To tame a shrew and charm her chattering tongue.

Enter Biondello.

BIONDELLO:
O master, master, I have watched so long   60
That I am dog-weary, but at last I spied
An ancient angel° coming down the hill
Will serve the turn.°
TRANIO: What is he, Biondello?
BIONDELLO:
Master, a marcantant,° or a pedant,°
I know not what, but formal in apparel,   65
In gait and countenance surely like a father.
LUCENTIO: And what of him, Tranio?
TRANIO:
If he be credulous and trust my tale,
I'll make him glad to seem Vincentio,
And give assurance to Baptista Minola   70
As if he were the right Vincentio.
Take in your love, and then let me alone.°
                                    [*Exeunt Lucentio and Bianca.*]

Enter a Pedant.

PEDANT:
God save you, sir!
TRANIO: And you sir! You are welcome.
Travel you far on, or are you at the farthest?

---

58. **eleven . . . long:** i.e., right on the money. (Alluding to the card game called "one-and-thirty" referred to at 1.2.30.)   62. **ancient angel:** i.e., fellow of the good old stamp. (Literally, an "angel" or gold coin bearing the stamp of the archangel Michael and thus distinguishable from more recent debased coinage.)   63. **Will ... turn:** who will serve our purposes.   64. **marcantant:** merchant.   **pedant:** schoolmaster (though at lines 90–91 he speaks more like a merchant).   72. **let me alone:** i.e., count on me.

PEDANT:

Sir, at the farthest for a week or two,　　　　　　　　　　75
But then up farther, and as far as Rome,
And so to Tripoli, if God lend me life.

TRANIO:

What countryman, I pray?

PEDANT:　　　　　　　　　　　　Of Mantua.

TRANIO:

Of Mantua, sir? Marry, God forbid!
And come to Padua, careless of your life?　　　　　　　　80

PEDANT:

My life, sir? How, I pray? For that goes hard.°

TRANIO:

'Tis death for anyone in Mantua
To come to Padua. Know you not the cause?
Your ships are stayed° at Venice, and the Duke,
For private quarrel twixt your Duke and him,　　　　　　85
Hath published and proclaimed it openly.
'Tis marvel, but that you are but newly come,
You might have heard it else proclaimed about.

PEDANT:

Alas, sir, it is worse for me than so,°
For I have bills for money by exchange°　　　　　　　　90
From Florence, and must here deliver them.

TRANIO:

Well, sir, to do you courtesy,
This will I do, and this I will advise you —
First, tell me, have you ever been at Pisa?

PEDANT:

Ay, sir, in Pisa have I often been,　　　　　　　　　　95
Pisa renownèd for grave citizens.

TRANIO:

Among them know you one Vincentio?

PEDANT:

I know him not, but I have heard of him;
A merchant of incomparable wealth.

81. goes hard: is serious indeed.　84. stayed: detained.　89. than so: than that.　90. bills
. . . exchange: promissory notes.

TRANIO:

He is my father, sir, and, sooth to say,   100
In count'nance somewhat doth resemble you.

BIONDELLO [*aside*]:   As much as an apple doth an oyster, and all one.°

TRANIO:

To save your life in this extremity,
This favor will I do you for his sake;
And think it not the worst of all your fortunes   105
That you are like to Sir Vincentio.
His name and credit° shall you undertake,
And in my house you shall be friendly lodged.
Look that you take upon you° as you should.
You understand me, sir. So shall you stay   110
Till you have done your business in the city.
If this be courtesy, sir, accept of it.

PEDANT:

O sir, I do, and will repute you° ever
The patron of my life and liberty.

TRANIO:

Then go with me to make the matter good.°   115
This, by the way, I let you understand:
My father is here looked for every day
To pass assurance° of a dower in marriage
Twixt me and one Baptista's daughter here.
In all these circumstances I'll instruct you.   120
Go with me to clothe you as becomes you.   *Exeunt.*

ACT IV, SCENE III°

Enter Katharina and Grumio.

GRUMIO:

No, no, forsooth, I dare not for my life.

KATHARINA:

The more my wrong,° the more his spite appears.
What, did he marry me to famish me?
Beggars that come unto my father's door

---

102. **all one:** no matter.   107. **credit:** reputation.   109. **take upon you:** play your part.
113. **repute you:** regard you as.   115. **make . . . good:** carry out the plan.   118. **assurance:** convey a legal guarantee.   ACT IV, SCENE III. **Location:** Petruchio's house. A table is set out, with seats.   2. **my wrong:** the wrong done to me.

Upon entreaty have a present° alms;   5
If not, elsewhere they meet with charity.
But I, who never knew how to entreat,
Nor never needed that I should entreat,
Am starved for meat,° giddy for lack of sleep,
With oaths kept waking, and with brawling fed.   10
And that which spites me more than all these wants,
He does it under name of perfect love,
As who° should say, if I should sleep or eat
'Twere deadly sickness or else present death.
I prithee, go and get me some repast,   15
I care not what, so° it be wholesome food.
GRUMIO: What say you to a neat's° foot?
KATHARINA:
'Tis passing° good. I prithee, let me have it.
GRUMIO:
I fear it is too choleric a meat.
How say you to a fat tripe finely broiled?   20
KATHARINA:
I like it well. Good Grumio, fetch it me.
GRUMIO:
I cannot tell.° I fear 'tis choleric.
What say you to a piece of beef and mustard?
KATHARINA:
A dish that I do love to feed upon.
GRUMIO:
Ay, but the mustard is too hot a little.   25
KATHARINA:
Why then, the beef, and let the mustard rest.°
GRUMIO:
Nay then, I will not. You shall have the mustard,
Or else you get no beef of Grumio.
KATHARINA:
Then both, or one, or anything thou wilt.
GRUMIO:
Why then, the mustard without the beef.   30

---

5. **present:** immediate (as in line 14).   9. **meat:** food.   13. **As who:** as if one.   16. **so:** so long as.   17. **neat's:** ox's.   18. **passing:** extremely.   22. **I cannot tell:** I don't know what to say.
26. **let . . . rest:** i.e., forget about the mustard.

KATHARINA:

Go, get thee gone, thou false, deluding slave,   [*She*] *beats him.*
That feed'st me with the very name° of meat!
Sorrow on thee and all the pack of you,
That triumph thus upon my misery!
Go, get thee gone, I say.   35

Enter Petruchio and Hortensio with meat.

PETRUCHIO:

How fares my Kate? What, sweeting, all amort?°
HORTENSIO:

Mistress, what cheer?
KATHARINA: Faith, as cold as can be.
PETRUCHIO:

Pluck up thy spirits; look cheerfully upon me.
Here, love, thou seest how diligent I am
To dress° thy meat myself and bring it thee.   40
I am sure, sweet Kate, this kindness merits thanks.
What, not a word? Nay, then thou lov'st it not,
And all my pains is sorted to no proof.°
Here, take away this dish.
KATHARINA: I pray you, let it stand.
PETRUCHIO:

The poorest service is repaid with thanks,   45
And so shall mine before you touch the meat.
KATHARINA: I thank you, sir.
HORTENSIO:

Signor Petruchio, fie, you are to blame.
Come, Mistress Kate, I'll bear you company.   [*They sit at table.*]
PETRUCHIO [*aside to Hortensio*]:

Eat it up all, Hortensio, if thou lovest me. —   50
Much good do it unto thy gentle heart!
Kate, eat apace. And now, my honey love,
Will we return unto thy father's house
And revel it as bravely° as the best,
With silken coats and caps and golden rings,   55
With ruffs, and cuffs, and farthingales,° and things,

32. **the very name:** the mere name.   36. **all amort:** dejected, dispirited.   40. **dress:** prepare.
43. **sorted to no proof:** proved to be to no purpose.   54. **bravely:** splendidly dressed.
56. **farthingales:** hooped petticoats.

With scarves, and fans, and double change of bravery,°
With amber bracelets, beads, and all this knavery.
What, hast thou dined? The tailor stays° thy leisure,
To deck thy body with his ruffling treasure.° 60

Enter Tailor [with a gown].

Come, tailor, let us see these ornaments.
Lay forth the gown.

Enter Haberdasher [with a cap].

What news with you, sir?
HABERDASHER:
Here is the cap your worship did bespeak.°
PETRUCHIO:
Why, this was molded on a porringer° —
A velvet dish. Fie, fie, 'tis lewd° and filthy. 65
Why, 'tis a cockle° or a walnut shell,
A knack, a toy, a trick,° a baby's cap.
Away with it! Come, let me have a bigger.
KATHARINA:
I'll have no bigger. This doth fit the time,°
And gentlewomen wear such caps as these. 70
PETRUCHIO:
When you are gentle,° you shall have one too,
And not till then.
HORTENSIO [*aside*]: That will not be in haste.
KATHARINA:
Why, sir, I trust I may have leave to speak,
And speak I will. I am no child, no babe.
Your betters have endured me say° my mind, 75
And if you cannot, best you stop your ears.
My tongue will tell the anger of my heart,
Or else my heart, concealing it, will break.
And rather than it shall, I will be free
Even to the uttermost, as I please, in words. 80

---

57. **bravery:** finery.   59. **stays:** awaits.   60. **ruffling treasure:** finery trimmed with ruffles.
63. **bespeak:** order.   64. **porringer:** porridge bowl.   65. **lewd:** vile.   66. **cockle:** cockle-
shell.   67. **trick:** trifle.   69. **fit the time:** suit the current fashion.   71. **gentle:** mild. (Petruchio plays on Kate's *gentlewomen*, line 70, i.e., women of high social station.)   75. **endured me
say:** suffered me to say.

PETRUCHIO:
Why, thou sayst true. It is a paltry cap,
A custard-coffin,° a bauble, a silken pie.
I love thee well in that thou lik'st it not.
KATHARINA:
Love me or love me not, I like the cap,
And it I will have, or I will have none.   [*Exit Haberdasher.*]   85
PETRUCHIO:
Thy gown? Why, ay. Come, tailor, let us see't.
O, mercy, God, what masquing° stuff is here?
What's this, a sleeve? 'Tis like a demicannon.°
What, up and down° carved like an apple tart?°
Here's snip, and nip, and cut, and slish and slash,   90
Like to a censer° in a barber's shop.
Why, what i'° devil's name, tailor, call'st thou this?
HORTENSIO [*aside*]:
I see she's like to have neither cap nor gown.
TAILOR:
You bid me make it orderly and well,
According to the fashion and the time.   95
PETRUCHIO:
Marry, and did.° But if you be remembered,°
I did not bid you mar it to the time.
Go hop me over every kennel home,°
For you shall hop without my custom, sir.
I'll none of it. Hence, make your best of it.   100
KATHARINA:
I never saw a better fashioned gown,
More quaint,° more pleasing, nor more commendable.
Belike° you mean to make a puppet of me.
PETRUCHIO:
Why, true, he means to make a puppet of thee.
TAILOR:
She says your worship means to make a puppet of her.   105

---

82. **custard-coffin:** pastry crust for a custard.   87. **masquing:** i.e., suited only for a masque.
88. **demicannon:** large cannon.   89. **up and down:** all over exactly.   **like an apple tart:**
i.e., with slashing or slits like the slits on the crust of fruit tarts, here revealing the brighter
fabric underneath.   91. **censer:** perfuming pan having an ornamental lid.   92. **i':** in (the).
96. **Marry, and did:** indeed I did.   **be remembered:** recollect.   98. **hop . . . home:** hop on
home over every street gutter.   102. **quaint:** elegant.   103. **Belike:** perhaps.

PETRUCHIO:
O, monstrous arrogance! Thou liest, thou thread, thou thimble,
Thou yard, three-quarters, half-yard, quarter, nail!°
Thou flea, thou nit,° thou winter cricket, thou!
Braved° in mine own house with° a skein of thread?
Away, thou rag, thou quantity,° thou remnant,   110
Or I shall so be-mete° thee with thy yard°
As thou shalt think on prating° whilst thou liv'st!
I tell thee, I, that thou hast marred her gown.
TAILOR:
Your worship is deceived. The gown is made
Just as my master had direction.   115
Grumio gave order how it should be done.
GRUMIO: I gave him no order. I gave him the stuff.°
TAILOR:
But how did you desire it should be made?
GRUMIO: Marry, sir, with needle and thread.
TAILOR:
But did you not request to have it cut?   120
GRUMIO: Thou hast faced° many things.
TAILOR: I have.
GRUMIO: Face° not me. Thou hast braved° many men; brave° not me. I
will neither be faced nor braved. I say unto thee, I bid thy master cut out
the gown, but I did not bid him cut it to pieces. Ergo° thou liest.   125
TAILOR: Why, here is the note of the fashion to testify.
                                        [*He displays his bill.*]
PETRUCHIO: Read it.
GRUMIO: The note lies in 's throat° if he say I said so.
TAILOR [*reads*]:   "Imprimis,° a loose-bodied gown° — "
GRUMIO: Master, if ever I said loose-bodied gown, sew me in the skirts of   130
it and beat me to death with a bottom° of brown thread. I said a gown.
PETRUCHIO: Proceed.
TAILOR [*reads*]:   "With a small compassed° cape — "

---

107. **nail:** a measure of length for cloth: 2¼ inches.   108. **nit:** louse egg.   109. **Braved:** defied.   **with:** by.   110. **quantity:** fragment.   111. **be-mete:** measure, i.e., thrash.   **yard:** yard-
stick.   112. **think on prating:** i.e., remember this thrashing and think twice before talking so
again.   117. **stuff:** material.   121. **faced:** trimmed. (But Grumio puns on the meaning
"bullied.")   123. **Face:** bully.   **braved:** dressed finely.   **brave:** defy.   125. **Ergo:** therefore.
128. **lies in 's throat:** i.e., lies utterly.   129. **Imprimis:** first.   **loose-bodied gown:** Grumio
plays on *loose,* "wanton"; a gown fit for a prostitute.   131. **bottom:** i.e., ball or skein. (A weaver's
term for the bobbin.)   133. **compassed:** flared, cut on the bias so as to fall in a circle.

GRUMIO: I confess the cape.

TAILOR [*reads*]:   "With a trunk° sleeve — "   135

GRUMIO: I confess two sleeves.

TAILOR [*reads*]:   "The sleeves curiously° cut."

PETRUCHIO: Ay, there's the villainy.

GRUMIO: Error i' the bill, sir, error i' the bill. I commanded the sleeves
should be cut out and sewed up again, and that I'll prove upon thee,°   140
though thy little finger be armed in a thimble.

TAILOR: This is true that I say. An I had thee in place where,° thou
shouldst know it.

GRUMIO: I am for thee straight.° Take thou the bill,° give me thy mete-
yard,° and spare not me.   145

HORTENSIO: God-a-mercy,° Grumio, then he shall have no odds.°

PETRUCHIO: Well, sir, in brief, the gown is not for me.

GRUMIO: You are i' the right, sir, 'tis for my mistress.

PETRUCHIO: Go, take it up° unto thy master's use.°

GRUMIO [*to the Tailor*]:   Villain, not for thy life! Take up my mistress'   150
gown for thy master's use!

PETRUCHIO: Why sir, what's your conceit° in that?

GRUMIO:

O, sir, the conceit is deeper° than you think for:

Take up my mistress' gown to his master's use!

O, fie, fie, fie!   155

PETRUCHIO [*aside to Hortensio*]:

Hortensio, say thou wilt see the tailor paid.

[*To Tailor.*] Go, take it hence. Begone, and say no more.

HORTENSIO [*aside to the Tailor*]:

Tailor, I'll pay thee for thy gown tomorrow.

Take no unkindness of his hasty words.

Away, I say. Commend me to thy master.   *Exit Tailor.*   160

PETRUCHIO:

Well, come, my Kate. We will unto your father's

Even in these honest, mean habiliments.°

---

135. **trunk:** full, wide.   137. **curiously:** elaborately.   140. **prove upon thee:** prove by fighting
you.   142. **in place where:** in a suitable place.   144. **for thee straight:** ready for you immediately. (Grumio takes *place where* to refer to a place where they can fight, not a court of law.)
bill: (1) the note ordering the gown, (2) a weapon, a halberd.   144–45. **mete-yard:** measuring
stick.   146. **God-a-mercy:** God have mercy. **odds:** advantage.   149. **take it up:** take it
away. **use:** i.e., whatever use he can make of it. (But Grumio deliberately misinterprets both
expressions in a bawdy sense.)   152. **conceit:** idea.   153. **deeper:** more serious (but continuing
the sexual idea of lifting up and using).   162. **honest, mean habiliments:** respectable, plain
clothes.

Our purses shall be proud, our garments poor,
For 'tis the mind that makes the body rich;
And as the sun breaks through the darkest clouds,   165
So honor peereth in° the meanest habit.°
What, is the jay more precious than the lark
Because his feathers are more beautiful?
Or is the adder better than the eel
Because his painted° skin contents the eye?   170
O, no, good Kate; neither art thou the worse
For this poor furniture° and mean array.
If thou account'st it shame, lay it on me.
And therefore frolic; we will hence forthwith,
To feast and sport us at thy father's house.   175
[*To Grumio.*] Go call my men, and let us straight to him;
And bring our horses unto Long Lane end.
There will we mount, and thither walk on foot.
Let's see, I think 'tis now some seven o'clock,
And well we may come there by dinnertime.°   180

KATHARINA:
I dare assure you, sir, 'tis almost two,
And 'twill be suppertime ere you come there.

PETRUCHIO:
It shall be seven ere I go to horse.
Look what° I speak, or do, or think to do,
You are still crossing° it. — Sirs, let 't alone.   185
I will not go today, and ere I do,
It shall be what o'clock I say it is.

HORTENSIO [*aside*]:
Why, so° this gallant will command the sun.

[*Exeunt.*]

ACT IV, SCENE IV°

Enter Tranio [*as Lucentio*], *and the Pedant dressed like Vincentio* [*booted*].°

TRANIO:
Sir, this is the house. Please it you that I call?

---

166. **peereth in:** peeps through. **habit:** attire. 170. **painted:** patterned. 172. **furniture:** furnishings of attire. 180. **dinnertime:** i.e., about noon. 184. **Look what:** whatever. 185. **still crossing:** always contradicting or defying. 188. **so:** at this rate. ACT IV, SCENE IV. Location: Padua. Before Baptista's house. **s.d. booted:** (signifying travel).

PEDANT:
Ay, what else? And but° I be deceived,
Signor Baptista may remember° me,
Near twenty years ago, in Genoa —
TRANIO:
Where we were lodgers at the Pegasus.° —   5
'Tis well; and hold your own° in any case
With such austerity as 'longeth to a father.

Enter Biondello.

PEDANT:
I warrant you. But, sir, here comes your boy.
'Twere good he were schooled.°
TRANIO:
Fear you not him. — Sirrah Biondello,   10
Now do your duty throughly,° I advise you.
Imagine 'twere the right° Vincentio.
BIONDELLO: Tut, fear not me.°
TRANIO:
But has thou done thy errand to Baptista?
BIONDELLO:
I told him that your father was at Venice   15
And that you looked for him this day in Padua.
TRANIO [*giving money*]:
Thou'rt a tall° fellow. Hold thee that to drink.°
Here comes Baptista. Set your countenance,° sir.

Enter Baptista, and Lucentio [as Cambio]. [The] Pedant [stands] bareheaded.

Signor Baptista, you are happily° met.
[*To the Pedant.*] Sir, this is the gentleman I told you of. 20
I pray you, stand good father to me now;
Give me Bianca for my patrimony.
PEDANT: Soft,° son! —
Sir, by your leave, having come to Padua

---

2. **but:** unless.   3. **may remember:** The Pedant is rehearsing what he is to say.   5. **Where . . .
Pegasus:** Tranio is coaching the Pedant in further details of his story.   **the Pegasus:** i.e., an inn,
so named after the famous winged horse of classical myth.   6. **hold your own:** play your
part.   9. **schooled:** i.e., rehearsed in his part.   11. **throughly:** thoroughly.   12. **right:**
real.   13. **fear not me:** don't worry about my doing my part.   17. **tall:** fine.   **Hold . . . drink:**
take that and buy a drink.   18. **Set your countenance:** i.e., put on the expression of an austere
father (line 7).   19. **happily:** fortunately.   23. **Soft:** i.e., steady, take it easy.

To gather in some debts, my son Lucentio   25
Made me acquainted with a weighty cause
Of love between your daughter and himself;
And, for° the good report I hear of you
And for the love he beareth to your daughter
And she to him, to stay him not° too long,   30
I am content, in a good father's care,
To have him matched. And if you please to like°
No worse than I, upon some agreement
Me shall you find ready and willing
With one consent° to have her so bestowed;   35
For curious° I cannot be with you,
Signor Baptista, of whom I hear so well.

BAPTISTA:
Sir, pardon me in what I have to say.
Your plainness and your shortness please me well.
Right true it is your son Lucentio here
Doth love my daughter, and she loveth him,   40
Or both dissemble deeply their affections.
And therefore, if you say no more than this,
That like a father you will deal with him
And pass° my daughter a sufficient dower,
The match is made, and all is done.   45
Your son shall have my daughter with consent.

TRANIO:
I thank you, sir. Where then do you know best
We be affied and such assurance ta'en
As shall with either part's agreement stand?°
                                                           50
BAPTISTA:
Not in my house, Lucentio, for you know
Pitchers have ears, and I have many servants.
Besides, old Gremio is hearkening still,°
And happily° we might be interrupted.

TRANIO:
Then at my lodging, an it like° you.   55

28. for: because of.   30. to stay him not: not to keep him waiting.   32. like: i.e., approve of
the match.   35. With one consent: in unanimity.   36. curious: overly particular.   45. pass:
settle on, give.   48–50. Where . . . stand: where in your view is the best place for us to be
betrothed and for legal assurances to be made that will confirm an agreement satisfactory to both
parties?   53. hearkening still: continually listening.   54. happily: haply, perhaps.   55. an it
like: if it please.

There doth my father lie,° and there this night
We'll pass° the business privately and well.
Send for your daughter by your servant here.

[He indicates Lucentio, and winks at him.]

My boy shall fetch the scrivener° presently.°
The worst is this, that at so slender warning   60
You are like° to have a thin and slender pittance.°

BAPTISTA:
It likes me well. Cambio, hie you home,
And bid Bianca make her ready straight.
And if you will, tell what hath happened:
Lucentio's father is arrived in Padua,   65
And how she's like to be Lucentio's wife.   *[Exit Lucentio.]*

BIONDELLO:
I pray the gods she may with all my heart!

TRANIO:
Dally not with the gods, but get thee gone.   *Exit [Biondello].*
Signor Baptista, shall I lead the way?
Welcome! One mess° is like to be your cheer.°   70
Come, sir, we will better it in Pisa.

BAPTISTA: I follow you.   *Exeunt° [Tranio, Pedant, and Baptista].*

Enter Lucentio [as Cambio] and Biondello.

BIONDELLO: Cambio!
LUCENTIO: What sayst thou, Biondello?
BIONDELLO: You saw my master wink and laugh upon you?   75
LUCENTIO: Biondello, what of that?
BIONDELLO: Faith, nothing; but he's left me here behind to expound the
meaning or moral° of his signs and tokens.
LUCENTIO: I pray thee, moralize° them.
BIONDELLO: Then thus. Baptista is safe,° talking with the deceiving fa-   80
ther of a deceitful son.
LUCENTIO: And what of him?
BIONDELLO: His daughter is to be brought by you to the supper.
LUCENTIO: And then?

56. **lie:** lodge.   57. **pass:** transact.   59. **scrivener:** notary, one to draw up contracts.   **presently:** at once.   61. **like:** likely.   **slender pittance:** i.e., scanty banquet.   70. **mess:** dish.
cheer: entertainment.   72. **s.d.** *Exeunt:* Technically, the cleared stage may mark a new scene,
but the conversation of Lucentio and Biondello suggests that they come creeping back on stage
as the others leave rather than doing the errands Baptista and Tranio bid them.   78. **moral:**
hidden meaning.   79. **moralize:** elucidate.   80. **safe:** i.e., safely out of the way.

BIONDELLO: The old priest of Saint Luke's church is at your command at   85
all hours.
LUCENTIO: And what of all this?
BIONDELLO: I cannot tell, except° they are busied about a counterfeit
assurance.° Take you assurance of her° *cum privilegio ad imprimendum
solum.°* To the church take the priest, clerk, and some sufficient° hon-   90
est witnesses.
If this be not that you look for,° I have no more to say,
But bid Bianca farewell forever and a day.   [*Biondello starts to leave.*]
LUCENTIO: Hear'st thou, Biondello?
BIONDELLO: I cannot tarry. I knew a wench married in an afternoon as   95
she went to the garden for parsley to stuff a rabbit, and so may you, sir.
And so, adieu, sir. My master hath appointed me to go to Saint Luke's,
to bid the priest be ready to come against you come° with your
appendix.°   *Exit.*
LUCENTIO:
I may, and will, if she be so contented.   100
She will be pleased; then wherefore should I doubt?
Hap what hap may, I'll roundly go about her.°
It shall go hard° if Cambio go without her.   *Exit.*

ACT IV, SCENE V°

Enter Petruchio, Kate, [and] Hortensio.

PETRUCHIO:
Come on, i' God's name, once more toward our father's.°
Good Lord, how bright and goodly shines the moon!
KATHARINA:
The moon? The sun. It is not moonlight now.
PETRUCHIO:
I say it is the moon that shines so bright.
KATHARINA:
I know it is the sun that shines so bright.   5

88. **except:** unless. 88–89. **counterfeit assurance:** pretended betrothal agreement.
89. **Take . . . of her:** legalize your claim to her (by marriage). 89–90. *cum . . . solum:* with
exclusive printing rights. (A copyright formula often appearing on the title pages of books, here
jokingly applied to the marriage and to procreation as an act of imprinting.) 90. **sufficient:**
meeting the legal requirement in number and social standing. 92. **that you look for:** what you
are looking for. 98. **against you come:** in anticipation of your arrival. 99. **appendix:** something appended, i.e., the bride (continuing the metaphor of printing). 102. **roundly . . . her:**
set about marrying her in no uncertain terms. 103. **go hard:** be unfortunate (with pun about
erection). **Act iv, Scene v. Location:** A road on the way to Padua. 1. **our father's:** our
father's house.

PETRUCHIO:
Now, by my mother's son, and that's myself,
It shall be moon, or star, or what I list°
Or ere° I journey to your father's house. —
Go on, and fetch our horses back again —
Evermore crossed and crossed, nothing but crossed!   10
HORTENSIO [to Katharina]:
Say as he says, or we shall never go.
KATHARINA:
Forward, I pray, since we have come so far,
And be it moon, or sun, or what you please;
An if you please to call it a rush candle,°
Henceforth I vow it shall be so for me.   15
PETRUCHIO:
I say it is the moon.
KATHARINA: I know it is the moon.
PETRUCHIO:
Nay, then you lie. It is the blessèd sun.
KATHARINA:
Then, God be blessed, it is the blessèd sun.
But sun it is not, when you say it is not,
And the moon changes even as your mind.   20
What you will have it named, even that it is,
And so it shall be so for Katharine.
HORTENSIO:
Petruchio, go thy ways.° The field is won.
PETRUCHIO:
Well, forward, forward. Thus the bowl should run,
And not unluckily against the bias.°   25
But soft! Company is coming here.

Enter Vincentio.

[*To Vincentio.*] Good morrow, gentle mistress. Where away?° —
Tell me, sweet Kate, and tell me truly too,
Hast thou beheld a fresher gentlewoman?
Such war of white and red within her cheeks!   30
What stars do spangle heaven with such beauty

---

7. **list:** please.   8. **Or ere:** before.   14. **a rush candle:** a rush dipped into tallow; hence a very
feeble light.   23. **go thy ways:** i.e., well done, carry on.   25. **against the bias:** off its proper
course. (The *bias* is an off-center weight in a bowling ball enabling the bowler to roll the ball
in an oblique or curving path.)   27. **Where away:** where are you going?

As those two eyes become that heavenly face? —
Fair lovely maid, once more good day to thee. —
Sweet Kate, embrace her for her beauty's sake.

HORTENSIO [*aside*]:

'A° will make the man mad, to make a woman of him.   35

KATHARINA [*embracing Vincentio*]:

Young budding virgin, fair, and fresh, and sweet,
Whither away, or where is thy abode?
Happy the parents of so fair a child!
Happier the man whom° favorable stars
Allots° thee for his lovely bedfellow!   40

PETRUCHIO:

Why, how now, Kate? I hope thou art not mad.
This is a man, old, wrinkled, faded, withered,
And not a maiden, as thou sayst he is.

KATHARINA:

Pardon, old father, my mistaking eyes,
That have been so bedazzled with the sun   45
That everything I look on seemeth green.°
Now I perceive thou art a reverend father.
Pardon, I pray thee, for my mad mistaking.

PETRUCHIO:

Do, good old grandsire, and withal make known
Which way thou travelest — if along with us,   50
We shall be joyful of thy company.

VINCENTIO:

Fair sir, and you, my merry mistress,
That with your strange encounter much amazed me,
My name is called Vincentio, my dwelling Pisa,
And bound I am to Padua, there to visit   55
A son of mine, which long I have not seen.

PETRUCHIO:

What is his name?

VINCENTIO: Lucentio, gentle sir.

PETRUCHIO:

Happily met, the happier for thy son.
And now by law as well as reverend age
I may entitle thee my loving father.
The sister to my wife, this gentlewoman,   60

---

35. '**A:** he.   39. **whom:** to whom.   40. **Allots:** allot.   46. **green:** young and fresh.

Thy son by this° hath married. Wonder not,
Nor be not grieved. She is of good esteem,°
Her dowry wealthy, and of worthy birth;
Besides, so qualified° as may beseem°   65
The spouse of any noble gentleman.
Let me embrace with old Vincentio,
And wander° we to see thy honest son,
Who will of thy arrival be full joyous.   [*He embraces Vincentio.*]

VINCENTIO:
But is this true? Or is it else your pleasure,   70
Like pleasant° travelers, to break a jest°
Upon the company you overtake?

HORTENSIO:
I do assure thee, father, so it is.

PETRUCHIO:
Come, go along, and see the truth hereof,
For our first merriment hath made thee jealous.°   75
                                    Exeunt [all but Hortensio].

HORTENSIO:
Well, Petruchio, this has put me in heart.°
Have to° my widow! And if she be froward,°
Then hast thou taught Hortensio to be untoward.°   *Exit.*

ACT V, SCENE I°

Enter Biondello, Lucentio [no longer disguised], and Bianca. Gremio is out before°
[and stands aside].

BIONDELLO: Softly and swiftly, sir, for the priest is ready.
LUCENTIO: I fly, Biondello. But they may chance to need thee at home;
therefore leave us.
BIONDELLO: Nay, faith, I'll see the church a' your back,° and then come
back to my master's as soon as I can.   5
                        [*Exeunt Lucentio, Bianca, and Biondello.*]

---

62. **by this:** by this time.   63. **esteem:** reputation.   65. **so qualified:** having such qualities.
beseem: befit.   68. **wander:** go (with a suggestion of changing plans).   71. **pleasant:** humorous, jocular.   **break a jest:** play a practical joke.   75. **jealous:** suspicious.   76. **put me in
heart:** encouraged me.   77. **Have to:** i.e., now for.   **froward:** perverse.   78. **untoward:** unmannerly.   **ACT V, SCENE I. Location:** Padua. Before Lucentio's house.   **s.d. out before:** i.e.,
onstage first. (Gremio does not see Biondello, Lucentio, and Bianca as they steal to church, or
else he does not recognize Lucentio in his own person.)   4. **a' your back:** at your back, behind
you. (Biondello first wants to see them in church and safely married.)

GREMIO: I marvel Cambio comes not all this while.

Enter Petruchio, Kate, Vincentio, Grumio, with attendants.

PETRUCHIO:
Sir, here's the door. This is Lucentio's house.
My father's° bears° more toward the marketplace;
Thither must I, and here I leave you, sir.
VINCENTIO:
You shall not choose but° drink before you go.   10
I think I shall command your welcome here,
And by all likelihood some cheer is toward.°   *Knock.*
GREMIO [*advancing*]:   They're busy within. You were best knock louder.

Pedant looks out of the window.°

PEDANT: What's he that knocks as he would beat down the gate?
VINCENTIO: Is Signor Lucentio within, sir?   15
PEDANT: He's within, sir, but not to be spoken withal.°
VINCENTIO: What if a man bring him a hundred pound or two to make
merry withal?
PEDANT: Keep your hundred pounds to yourself. He shall need none, so
long as I live.   20
PETRUCHIO [*to Vincentio*]:   Nay, I told you your son was well beloved in
Padua. — Do you hear, sir? To leave frivolous circumstances,° I pray
you, tell Signor Lucentio that his father is come from Pisa and is here
at the door to speak with him.
PEDANT: Thou liest. His father is come from Padua° and here looking   25
out at the window.
VINCENTIO: Art thou his father?
PEDANT: Ay, sir, so his mother says, if I may believe her.
PETRUCHIO [*to Vincentio*]:   Why, how now, gentleman! Why, this is flat°
knavery, to take upon you another man's name.   30
PEDANT: Lay hands on the villain. I believe 'a means to cozen° somebody
in this city under my countenance.°

Enter Biondello.

8. **father's:** i.e., father-in-law's, Baptista's.   **bears:** lies: (A nautical term.)   10. **You . . . but:**
i.e., I insist that.   12. **cheer is toward:** entertainment is in prospect.   **s.d. window:** i.e., probably the gallery to the rear, over the stage.   16. **withal:** with.   22. **circumstances:** matters.   25. **from Padua:** i.e., from Padua, where we are right now. (Often emended to "from
Mantua," "from Pisa," "to Padua," etc.)   29. **flat:** downright.   31. **cozen:** cheat.   32. **under
my countenance:** by pretending to be me.

BIONDELLO [*aside*]: I have seen them in the church together, God send
'em good shipping!° But who is here? Mine old master Vincentio! Now
we are undone and brought to nothing.   35
VINCENTIO [*seeing Biondello*]: Come hither, crackhemp.°
BIONDELLO: I hope I may choose,° sir.
VINCENTIO: Come hither, you rogue. What, have you forgot me?
BIONDELLO: Forgot you? No, sir. I could not forget you, for I never saw
you before in all my life.   40
VINCENTIO: What, you notorious villain, didst thou never see thy master's
father, Vincentio?
BIONDELLO: What, my old worshipful old master? Yes, marry, sir, see
where he looks out of the window.
VINCENTIO: Is 't so, indeed?   *He beats Biondello.*   45
BIONDELLO: Help, help, help! Here's a madman will murder me. [*Exit.*]
PEDANT: Help, son! Help, Signor Baptista!   [*Exit from the window.*]
PETRUCHIO: Prithee, Kate, let's stand aside and see the end of this con-
troversy.   [*They stand aside.*]

Enter [*below*] *Pedant with servants, Baptista,* [*and*] *Tranio* [*as Lucentio*].

TRANIO: Sir, what are you that offer° to beat my servant?   50
VINCENTIO: What am I, sir? Nay, what are you, sir? O immortal gods! O
fine villain! A silken doublet, a velvet hose, a scarlet cloak, and a copin-
tank° hat! O, I am undone, I am undone! While I play the good
husband° at home, my son and my servant spend all at the university.
TRANIO: How now, what's the matter?   55
BAPTISTA: What, is the man lunatic?
TRANIO: Sir, you seem a sober ancient gentleman by your habit,° but your
words show you a madman. Why, sir, what 'cerns° it you if I wear pearl
and gold? I thank my good father, I am able to maintain° it.
VINCENTIO: Thy father! O villain, he is a sailmaker in Bergamo.   60
BAPTISTA: You mistake, sir, you mistake, sir. Pray, what do you think is
his name?
VINCENTIO: His name! As if I knew not his name! I have brought him up
ever since he was three years old, and his name is Tranio.
PEDANT: Away, away, mad ass! His name is Lucentio, and he is mine   65
only son, and heir to the lands of me, Signor Vincentio.

---

34. **good shipping:** bon voyage, good fortune. 36. **crackhemp:** i.e., rogue likely to end up
being hanged. 37. **choose:** do as I choose. 50. **offer:** dare, presume. 52–53. **copintank:**
high-crowned, sugar-loaf shape. 54. **good husband:** careful provider, manager. 57. **habit:**
clothing. 58. **'cerns:** concerns. 59. **maintain:** afford.

VINCENTIO: Lucentio! O, he hath murdered his master! Lay hold on him,
I charge you, in the Duke's name. O, my son, my son! Tell me, thou
villain, where is my son Lucentio?
TRANIO: Call forth an officer.   70

[Enter an Officer.]

Carry this mad knave to the jail. Father Baptista, I charge you see that
he be forthcoming.°
VINCENTIO: Carry me to the jail?
GREMIO: Stay, officer, he shall not go to prison.
BAPTISTA: Talk not, Signor Gremio. I say he shall go to prison.   75
GREMIO: Take heed, Signor Baptista, lest you be coney-catched° in this
business. I dare swear this is the right Vincentio.
PEDANT: Swear, if thou dar'st.
GREMIO: Nay, I dare not swear it.
TRANIO: Then thou wert best° say that I am not Lucentio.   80
GREMIO: Yes, I know thee to be Signor Lucentio.
BAPTISTA: Away with the dotard! To the jail with him!

Enter Biondello, Lucentio, and Bianca.

VINCENTIO: Thus strangers may be haled° and abused. — O monstrous
villain!
BIONDELLO: O! We are spoiled° and — yonder he is. Deny him, forswear   85
him, or else we are all undone.
*Exeunt Biondello, Tranio, and Pedant, as fast as may be. [Lucentio and Bianca]
kneel.*
LUCENTIO:
Pardon, sweet Father.
VINCENTIO: Lives my sweet son?
BIANCA:
Pardon, dear Father.
BAPTISTA: How hast thou offended?
Where is Lucentio?
LUCENTIO: Here's Lucentio,
Right son to the right Vincentio,   90

---

72. **forthcoming:** ready to stand trial when required.   76. **coney-catched:** tricked.   80. **wert
best:** might as well.   83. **haled:** hauled about, maltreated.   85. **spoiled:** ruined.

That have by marriage made thy daughter mine,
While counterfeit supposes° bleared thine eyne.°

GREMIO:
Here's packing,° with a witness,° to deceive us all!

VINCENTIO:
Where is that damnèd villain Tranio,
That faced and braved° me in this matter so?   95

BAPTISTA:
Why, tell me, is not this my Cambio?

BIANCA:
Cambio is changed° into Lucentio.

LUCENTIO:
Love wrought these miracles. Bianca's love
Made me exchange my state° with Tranio,
While he did bear my countenance° in the town,   100
And happily I have arrivèd at the last
Unto the wishèd haven of my bliss.
What Tranio did, myself enforced him to;
Then pardon him, sweet Father, for my sake.

VINCENTIO: I'll slit the villain's nose, that would have sent me to the jail.   105

BAPTISTA [to Lucentio]: But do you hear, sir? Have you married my
daughter without asking my good will?

VINCENTIO: Fear not, Baptista, we will content you. Go to.° But I will in,
to be revenged for this villainy.   Exit.

BAPTISTA: And I, to sound the depth of this knavery.   Exit.   110

LUCENTIO: Look not pale, Bianca, Thy father will not frown.
                                    Exeunt [Lucentio and Bianca].

GREMIO:
My cake is dough,° but I'll in among the rest,
Out of hope of all but° my share of the feast.   [Exit.]

KATHARINA: Husband, let's follow, to see the end of this ado.

PETRUCHIO: First kiss me, Kate, and we will.   115

KATHARINA: What, in the midst of the street?

PETRUCHIO: What, art thou ashamed of me?

92. **supposes:** suppositions, false appearances (with an allusion to Gascoigne's *Supposes*, an adaptation of *I Suppositi* by Ariosto, from which Shakespeare took the Lucentio-Bianca plot of intrigue). **eyne:** eyes. 93. **packing:** conspiracy. **with a witness:** i.e., and no mistake, with a vengeance. 95. **faced and braved:** stood up to and defied. 97. **Cambio is changed:** a pun. *Cambio* in Italian means "change" or "exchange." 99. **state:** social station. 100. **countenance:** appearance, identity. 108. **Go to:** i.e., don't worry. (An expression of impatience or annoyance.) 112. **My . . . dough:** i.e., I'm out of luck, I failed. 113. **Out . . . but:** having hope for nothing other than.

KATHARINA: No, sir, God forbid, but ashamed to kiss.
PETRUCHIO: Why, then let's home again. [*To Grumio.*] Come, sirrah,
let's away. 120
KATHARINA: Nay, I will give thee a kiss. [*She kisses him.*] Now pray thee,
love, stay.
PETRUCHIO:
Is not this well? Come, my sweet Kate.
Better once° than never, for never too late. *Exeunt.*

Аст v, Scene 11°

*Enter Baptista, Vincentio, Gremio, the Pedant, Lucentio, and Bianca; [Petruchio,
Kate, Hortensio,] Tranio, Biondello, Grumio, and [the] Widow; the servingmen
with Tranio bringing in a banquet.°*

LUCENTIO:
At last, though long,° our jarring notes agree,
And time it is, when raging war is done,
To smile at scapes° and perils overblown.
My fair Bianca, bid my father welcome,
While I with selfsame kindness welcome thine. 5
Brother Petruchio, sister Katharina,
And thou, Hortensio, with thy loving widow,
Feast with° the best, and welcome to my house.
My banquet is to close our stomachs° up
After our great good cheer.° Pray you, sit down, 10
For now we sit to chat as well as eat. [*They sit.*]
PETRUCHIO:
Nothing but sit and sit, and eat and eat!
BASTISTA:
Padua affords this kindness, son Petruchio.
PETRUCHIO:
Padua affords nothing but what is kind.
HORTENSIO:
For both our sakes, I would that word were true. 15

124. **once:** at some time. (Compare with "better late than never.") Аст v, Scene 11. Location: Padua. Lucentio's house. **s.d. banquet:** i.e., dessert. **1. long:** after a long time.
3. scapes: escapes, close calls. **8. with:** upon. **9. stomachs:** appetites (with pun on
"quarrels"). **10. our . . . cheer:** i.e., the wedding feast at Baptista's.

PETRUCHIO:
Now, for my life,° Hortensio fears° his widow.
WIDOW:
Then never trust me if I be afeard.
PETRUCHIO:
You are very sensible,° and yet you miss my sense:
I mean Hortensio is afeard° of you.
WIDOW:
He that is giddy thinks the world turns round. 20
PETRUCHIO:
Roundly° replied.
KATHARINA: Mistress, how mean you that?
WIDOW: Thus I conceive by him.°
PETRUCHIO:
Conceives by me! How likes Hortensio that?
HORTENSIO:
My widow says, thus she conceives° her tale.
PETRUCHIO:
Very well mended. Kiss him for that, good widow. 25
KATHARINA:
"He that is giddy thinks the world turns round":
I pray you, tell me what you meant by that.
WIDOW:
Your husband, being troubled with a shrew,
Measures° my husband's sorrow by his° woe.
And now you know my meaning. 30
KATHARINA:
A very mean° meaning.
WIDOW: Right, I mean you.
KATHARINA:
And I am mean indeed, respecting° you.

16. **for my life:** upon my life.   **fears:** is afraid of. (But the Widow takes the word in the sense of "frightens"; she protests she is not at all *afeard,* frightened, by Hortensio.)   18. **sensible:** (1) sensitive, (2) reasonable.   19. **afeard:** Petruchio takes up the Widow's word and uses it in the sense of "suspicious," fearful she will be untrue.   21. **Roundly:** boldly.   22. **Thus . . . him:** i.e., that's what I think of him, Petruchio. (But Petruchio takes up *conceives* in the sense of "is made pregnant.")   24. **conceives:** intends, interprets (with a possible pun on *tale* and "tail").   29. **Measures:** judges.   **his:** his own.   31. **very mean:** contemptible. (But the Widow takes up *mean* in the sense of "have in mind," and Kate replies in the sense of "moderate in shrewishness.")   32. **respecting:** compared to.

PETRUCHIO: To her,° Kate!
HORTENSIO: To her, widow!
PETRUCHIO:
A hundred marks,° my Kate does put her down.°   35
HORTENSIO: That's my office.
PETRUCHIO:
Spoke like an officer.° Ha'° to thee, lad!   *[He] drinks to Hortensio.*
BAPTISTA:
How likes Gremio these quick-witted folks?
GREMIO:
Believe me, sir, they butt° together well.
BIANCA:
Head, and butt!° An hasty-witted body°   40
Would say your head and butt were head and horn.°
VINCENTIO:
Ay, mistress bride, hath that awakened you?
BIANCA:
Ay, but not frighted me. Therefore I'll sleep again.
PETRUCHIO:
Nay, that you shall not. Since you have begun,
Have at you for° a bitter° jest or two!   45
BIANCA:
Am I your bird? I mean to shift my bush;°
And then pursue me as you draw your bow.
You are welcome all.   *Exit Bianca [with Katharina and the Widow].*
PETRUCHIO:
She hath prevented° me. Here, Signor Tranio,
This bird° you aimed at, though you hit her not.   50
Therefore a health° to all that shot and missed.   *[He offers a toast.]*

---

33. **To her:** a cry used to egg on fighting roosters.   35. **marks:** coins worth thirteen shillings four pence.   **put her down:** overcome her. (But Hortensio takes up the phrase in a bawdy sense.)   37. **officer:** (playing on Hortensio's speaking of his *office* or function).   **Ha':** have, i.e., here's.   39. **butt:** butt heads.   40. **butt:** tail, bottom.   **An hasty-witted body:** a quick-witted person.   41. **head and horn:** (alluding to the familiar joke about cuckold's horns).   45. **Have at you for:** i.e., be on guard against.   **bitter:** sharp.   46. **Am . . . bush:** i.e., if you mean to shoot your barbs at me, I intend to move out of the way, as a bird would fly to another bush (with a possible bawdy double meaning; *bush* can suggest pubic hair).   49. **prevented:** forestalled.   50. **This bird:** i.e., Bianca, whom Tranio courted (*aimed at*) in his disguise as Lucentio.   51. **a health:** a toast.

TRANIO:
O, sir, Lucentio slipped° me like his greyhound,
Which runs himself and catches for his master.
PETRUCHIO:
A good swift° simile, but something currish.°
TRANIO:
'Tis well, sir, that you hunted for yourself.   55
'Tis thought your deer° does hold you at a bay.°
BAPTISTA:
O ho, Petruchio! Tranio hits you now.
LUCENTIO:
I thank thee for that gird,° good Tranio.
HORTENSIO:
Confess, confess, hath he not hit you here?
PETRUCHIO:
'A has a little galled° me, I confess;   60
And as the jest did glance away from° me,
'Tis ten to one it maimed you two outright.
BAPTISTA:
Now, in good sadness,° son Petruchio,
I think thou hast the veriest shrew of all.
PETRUCHIO:
Well, I say no. And therefore for assurance°   65
Let's each one send unto his wife;
And he whose wife is most obedient
To come at first when he doth send for her
Shall win the wager which we will propose.
HORTENSIO:
Content. What's the wager?
LUCENTIO: Twenty crowns.   70
PETRUCHIO: Twenty crowns!
I'll venture so much of° my hawk or hound,
But twenty times so much upon my wife.
LUCENTIO: A hundred then.
HORTENSIO: Content.   75
PETRUCHIO: A match. 'Tis done.

---

52. **slipped:** unleashed.   54. **swift:** (1) quick-witted, (2) concerning swiftness.   **currish:** (1) ig-
noble, (2) concerning dogs.   56. **deer:** (punning on "dear").   **does . . . bay:** turns on you
like a cornered animal and holds you at a distance.   58. **gird:** sharp, biting jest.   60. **galled:**
scratched, chafed.   61. **glance away from:** ricochet off.   63. **sadness:** seriousness.
65. **assurance:** proof.   72. **of:** on.

HORTENSIO: Who shall begin?
LUCENTIO: That will I.
Go, Biondello, bid your mistress come to me.
BIONDELLO: I go. *Exit.* 80
BAPTISTA:
Son, I'll be your half° Bianca comes.
LUCENTIO:
I'll have no halves; I'll bear it all myself.

Enter Biondello.

How now, what news?
BIONDELLO:
Sir, my mistress sends you word
That she is busy and she cannot come. 85
PETRUCHIO:
How? She's busy and she cannot come?
Is that an answer?
GREMIO: Ay, and a kind one too.
Pray God, sir, your wife send you not a worse.
PETRUCHIO: I hope better.
HORTENSIO:
Sirrah Biondello, go and entreat my wife 90
To come to me forthwith. *Exit Biondello.*
PETRUCHIO: Oho, entreat her!
Nay, then she must needs come.
HORTENSIO: I am afraid, sir,
Do what you can, yours will not be entreated.

Enter Biondello.

Now, where's my wife?
BIONDELLO:
She says you have some goodly jest in hand. 95
She will not come. She bids you come to her.
PETRUCHIO:
Worse and worse. She will not come!
O, vile, intolerable, not to be endured!
Sirrah Grumio, go to your mistress.
Say I command her come to me. *Exit [Grumio].* 100

---

81. **be your half:** take half your bet.

HORTENSIO:
I know her answer.
PETRUCHIO: What?
HORTENSIO: She will not.
PETRUCHIO:
The fouler fortune mine, and there an end.°

Enter Katharina.

BAPTISTA:
Now, by my halidom,° here comes Katharina!
KATHARINA:
What is your will, sir, that you send for me?
PETRUCHIO:
Where is your sister, and Hortensio's wife?   105
KATHARINA:
They sit conferring by the parlor fire.
PETRUCHIO:
Go fetch them hither. If they deny to come,
Swinge° me° them soundly forth unto their husbands.
Away, I say, and bring them hither straight.   [*Exit Katharina.*]
LUCENTIO:
Here is a wonder, if you talk of a wonder.   110
HORTENSIO:
And so it is. I wonder what it bodes.
PETRUCHIO:
Marry, peace it bodes, and love, and quiet life,
An awful rule,° and right supremacy,
And, to be short, what not that's sweet and happy.
BAPTISTA:
Now, fair befall thee,° good Petruchio!   115
The wager thou hast won, and I will add
Unto their losses twenty thousand crowns,
Another dowry to another daughter,
For she is changed, as she had never been.°
PETRUCHIO:
Nay, I will win my wager better yet,   120

102. **there an end:** that's that.   103. **by my halidom:** originally an oath by the holy relics, but confused with an oath to the Virgin Mary.   108. **Swinge:** thrash.   **me:** i.e., at my behest. (*Me* is used colloquially.)   113. **awful rule:** authority commanding awe or respect.   115. **fair befall thee:** good luck to you, and congratulations.   119. **as . . . been:** as if she had never existed, i.e., she is totally changed.

And show more sign of her obedience,
Her new-built virtue and obedience.

Enter Kate, Bianca, and [the] Widow.

See where she comes and brings your froward wives
As prisoners to her womanly persuasion. —
Katharine, that cap of yours becomes you not.   125
Off with that bauble. Throw it underfoot.   [*She obeys.*]
WIDOW:
  Lord, let me never have a cause to sigh
  Till I be brought to such a silly pass!°
BIANCA:
  Fie, what a foolish duty call you this?
LUCENTIO:
  I would your duty were as foolish, too.   130
  The wisdom of your duty, fair Bianca,
  Hath cost me a hundred crowns since suppertime.
BIANCA:
  The more fool you, for laying° on my duty.
PETRUCHIO:
  Katharine, I charge thee tell these headstrong women
  What duty they do owe their lords and husbands.   135
WIDOW:
  Come, come, you're mocking. We will have no telling.
PETRUCHIO:
  Come on, I say, and first begin with her.
WIDOW: She shall not.
PETRUCHIO:
  I say she shall — and first begin with her.
KATHARINA:
  Fie, fie! Unknit that threatening, unkind brow,   140
  And dart not scornful glances from those eyes
  To wound thy lord, thy king, thy governor.
  It blots thy beauty as frosts do bite the meads,
  Confounds thy fame° as whirlwinds shake fair buds,
  And in no sense is meet or amiable.   145
  A woman moved° is like a fountain troubled,
  Muddy, ill-seeming, thick, bereft of beauty;

---

128. **pass:** state of affairs.   133. **laying:** wagering.   144. **Confounds thy fame:** ruins your
reputation.   146. **moved:** angry.

And while it is so, none so dry or thirsty°
Will deign to sip or touch one drop of it.
Thy husband is thy lord, thy life, thy keeper,   150
Thy head, thy sovereign; one that cares for thee,
And for thy maintenance commits his body
To painful° labor both by sea and land,
To watch° the night in storms, the day in cold,
Whilst thou liest warm at home, secure and safe;   155
And craves no other tribute at thy hands
But love, fair looks, and true obedience —
Too little payment for so great a debt.
Such duty as the subject owes the prince,
Even such a woman oweth to her husband;   160
And when she is froward, peevish,° sullen, sour,
And not obedient to his honest will,°
What is she but a foul contending rebel
And graceless traitor to her loving lord?
I am ashamed that women are so simple°   165
To offer war where they should kneel for peace,
Or seek for rule, supremacy, and sway,
When they are bound to serve, love, and obey.
Why are our bodies soft, and weak, and smooth,
Unapt to° toil and trouble in the world,   170
But that our soft conditions° and our hearts
Should well agree with our external parts?
Come, come, you froward and unable worms!°
My mind hath been as big° as one of yours,
My heart as great, my reason haply more,   175
To bandy word for word and frown for frown;
But now I see our lances are but straws,
Our strength as weak,° our weakness past compare,
That seeming to be° most which we indeed least are.
Then vail your stomachs,° for it is no boot,°   180
And place your hands below your husband's foot,

---

148. none . . . thirsty: there is no one so thirsty that he.   153. painful: onerous.   154. watch:
stay awake throughout.   161. peevish: obstinate.   162. to his honest will: Kate may suggest that she will be obedient when his will is decent and virtuous, not that his will is
always so.   165. simple: foolish.   170. Unapt to: unfit for.   171. conditions: qualities.
173. unable worms: i.e., poor feeble creatures.   174. big: haughty.   178. as weak: i.e., as weak
as straws.   179. That seeming to be: seeming to be that.   180. vail your stomachs: lower your
pride.   boot: profit, use.

In token of which duty, if he please,
My hand is ready; may it do him ease.°
PETRUCHIO:
Why, there's a wench! Come on, and kiss me, Kate.   [*They kiss.*]
LUCENTIO:
Well, go thy ways,° old lad, for thou shalt ha't.°   185
VINCENTIO:
'Tis a good hearing when children are toward.°
LUCENTIO:
But a harsh hearing when women are froward.
PETRUCHIO: Come, Kate, we'll to bed.
We° three are married, but you two are sped.°
[*To Lucentio.*] 'Twas I won the wager, though you hit the white,°   190
And, being° a winner, God give you good night!
                         Exit Petruchio [*and Katharina*].
HORTENSIO:
Now go thy ways. Thou hast tamed a curst shrew.°
LUCENTIO:
'Tis a wonder, by your leave, she will be tamed so.   [*Exeunt.*]

183. do him ease: give him pleasure.   185. go thy ways: well done.   ha't: have it, the
prize.   186. 'Tis ... toward: i.e., one likes to hear when children are obedient.   189. We ...
sped: i.e., all we three men have taken wives, but you two are done for (*sped*) through disobedient
wives.   190. the white: the center of the target (with quibble on the name of Bianca, which
in Italian means "white")   191. being: since I am.   192. shrew: pronounced "shrow" (and thus
spelled in the Folio). See also 4.1.179 and 5.2.28.

PART TWO

Early Modern Debates

CHAPTER I

Alternative Endings

————————————————————— ≫‹ —————————————————————

I n this section you can contrast the ending of *The Taming of the Shrew* with the endings of two other versions: *A Pleasant Conceited History, Called The Taming of a Shrew* (1594),[1] a play roughly contemporary with Shakespeare's; and *Catharine and Petruchio*, an eighteenth-century adaptation by the actor-dramatist David Garrick. Before the publication of Shakespeare's First Folio in 1623, *The Taming of a Shrew* was the only published version of the play available; between 1754 and 1844 Garrick's adaptation was the only version performed on English and American stages. What counted as "Shakespeare" for readers before 1623, or for audiences between 1754 and 1844, was not what you hold in any contemporary edition of *The Taming of the Shrew*. Furthermore, John Fletcher wrote a sequel to *The Taming of the Shrew* called *The Woman's Prize, or The Tamer Tamed* (1611); and Alexander Pope spliced scenes from *A Shrew*, including the final one, into his edition of Shakespeare's *The Shrew* (1725). Obviously, both Shakespeare's contemporaries and the eighteenth-century editors and actor-managers who helped establish his position as a mainstay of the canon of English literature did not think of the Shakespearean text as

———————————————————

[1] This play will be referred to throughout simply as *The Taming of a Shrew* or as *A Shrew*.

sacrosanct. Instead, they approached that text as fluid, in-process, and available to revision, adaptation, and continuation.

Alternative versions of the play's closing scene reveal that Shakespeare's conclusion is not the only one imaginable. Like films for which different endings are test-marketed, *The Taming of the Shrew* did not, and does not, have a fixed finale. Instead, the story is available with various conclusions, and the dramatic text is open to various interpretations in production, each of which subtly changes the story and hence an audience's reaction and evaluation. But the endings presented here do not exhaust the possibilities; many other endings are imaginable.

→ From *The Taming of a Shrew*   *1594*

Scholars have long debated about the relationship between this play, which was published in a quarto (or small, single-play edition) in 1594, then reprinted in 1596 and 1607, and Shakespeare's *The Taming of the Shrew*, first published in 1623 in the First Folio (the first supposedly complete collection of Shakespeare's plays). *A Shrew* has been variously described as an earlier version of *The Shrew* that Shakespeare used and revised as a source; or as an unauthorized edition of *The Shrew*, reconstructed from actors' (faulty) memories of a production of Shakespeare's play, perhaps with the assistance of a writer. Such a version of a play is sometimes called a "bad quarto."[2] But as a recent editor of *A Shrew* points out, "*A Shrew* is so different from *The Shrew* in so many particulars as to raise the possibility that it was not so much badly copied, as not copied at all" (Holderness 16). Furthermore, "it is, in at least one respect, more complete (and therefore more complex and sophisticated) than the Folio text of *The Shrew*" (Holderness 16). This respect is the Sly-framework, which is closed in the 1594 *A Shrew* but not in the 1623 First Folio *The Shrew*. *A Shrew* and *The Shrew* have also been considered parallel or alternative versions, by two different authors, of an older lost play. All these approaches to the two plays have depended on comparisons, assuming that one must be better or more authentic than the other. Some scholars are urging that we start to think instead about

---

[2] Morris, who subscribes to the "bad quarto" theory, argues that the actor who played Grumio was primarily responsible for the memorial reconstruction of the text that we now call *A Shrew* because he remembers his own part fairly well and "he has a general sense of what others were saying and doing when he was on stage" but "no clear recollection of the sub-plot in which he had no concern" (48). On the relationship between *The Shrew* and *A Shrew*, see Berek; Burns; Greenfield; Holderness 34; Hosley 289–95; Jayne; Marcus; Morris 12–50; Thompson 1–2, 155–56, 160–73; and Wentersdorf.

A Pleasant Conceited History, called the Taming of a Shrew. As It Was Sundry Times Acted by the Right Honorable, the Earl of Pembroke his Servants (London, 1594), F3–G2v.

the two as different plays with their own strengths, as "alternate versions" (Marcus 183; Holderness).

The two plays share a main plot focusing on the taming of an unruly wife; in both, the husband proposes to "bridle and hold back [his] headstrong wife, / With curbs of hunger, ease, and want of sleep" (*A Shrew* D3nD3v). The two plots resemble one another closely, as a recent editor of *The Taming of the Shrew* explains:

> In both plays the husband behaves scandalously at the wedding, starves his wife afterwards, rejects the work of a Haberdasher and a Tailor, and misuses his servants. In both the wife is brought to submission, asserts that the sun is the moon and pretends an old man is a young girl. Each play culminates in a feast at which men wager on their wives' obedience. (Morris 13)

Both plays also include Christopher Sly, a subplot about romantic intrigue, and some similar passages of dialogue. On the other hand, *A Shrew* takes place in Athens, rather than in Padua, and all the characters, except Kate, have different names. The father (Alfonso) has three, rather than two, daughters (Emilia, Kate, and Phylema).

Kate is much less violent in *A Shrew* than in Shakespeare's *The Shrew*. She does not initiate physical violence as she does in *The Shrew;* we do not see her beat her sister, brain her teacher, or hit her suitor. Instead, she seems to learn to use violence from her husband, who, as in *The Shrew*, directs his brutality toward the servants rather than toward her. When the couple arrives at the husband's (Ferando's) house, he rants at his servant: "Come hither, you villain! I'll cut your nose, / You Rogue." The stage directions describe Ferando as beating the servants at three points in this scene and as overturning the table and throwing food (D3). When Kate later beats Ferando's servant, Sander, because he will not give her food — "I tell thee, villain, I'll tear the flesh off / Thy face and eat it [if] thou prates to me thus" (D4v) — she seems to be imitating her husband's conduct.

In *A Shrew* Kate's final speech is distinctly different from the one Katharine delivers in *The Shrew*. In Shakespeare's *The Shrew* Katharine explains the relationship of husband and wife by analogy to the relationship between prince and subject. She depicts a hierarchical relationship in which the wife is subordinate; she also describes separate gendered spheres — the wife safe at home, the husband laboring by sea and land — and justifies them by reference to biological difference: women's "soft," "weak," and "smooth" bodies make them "unapt to toil and trouble in the world." In contrast, Kate's last speech in *A Shrew* argues that "women should submit to men because they are created by God as inferior beings and were moreover responsible for the Fall of man from Paradise" (Thompson 29). Wives should submit to their husbands not because of biological difference, or social roles, or out of love, but because of their own inferiority and sinfulness. This speech reveals how very secular and social is Katharine's sermon on marriage in Shakespeare's *The Shrew*.

A Shrew frames this speech with several layers of commentary, until the play seems like "a nest of boxes" (Marcus 188) in which the meaning continually recedes. Kate's speech is first followed by an exchange between Emilia (Kate's younger sister) and her husband, in which Emilia asserts that it is better for a woman to be a shrew than a sheep. Although her husband has just watched the edifying display of Kate's tameness, he does not oppose his wife. Instead, she seems to have won the quarrel. When *A Shrew* returns to Christopher Sly at the very end, closing the frame begun in the opening scene or induction, it suggests that the whole play has acted as a kind of "taming school"; even Sly has learned "how to tame a shrew." Yet this ending also casts doubt on the school and the lessons learned there, suggesting that shrew taming is a male fantasy rather than a social reality. For Sly, taming his wife is "the best dream / That ever [he] had in [his] life." Many theatrical productions of *The Taming of the Shrew* borrow this concluding scene from *A Shrew*.

The Taming of a Shrew

CAST: A LORD; CHRISTOPHER SLY; ALFONSO; *his daughters* KATE, EMILIA, *and* PHYLEMA; FERANDO, *Kate's husband;* SANDER, *Ferando's servant;* AURELIUS, *Phylema's husband;* VALERIA, *Aurelius' servant;* POLIDOR, *Emilia's husband;* A BOY, *Polidor's servant; and* SIM, *a Tapster.*

Sly sleeps.

LORD:
Who's within there? Come hither, sirs; my Lord's
Asleep again. Go take him easily up,
And put him in his own apparel again,
And lay him in the place where we did find him,
Just underneath the alehouse side below;   5
But see you wake him not in any case.
BOY: It shall be done, my Lord. Come, help to bear him hence.   *Exit.*

Enter Ferando and his servant Sander; Aurelius and his servant Valeria, and Polidor and his boy.

FERANDO:
Come, gentlemen, now that supper's done,
How shall we spend the time till we go to bed?
AURELIUS:
Faith,° if you will, in trial of our wives: 10
Who will come soonest at their husbands' call?

---

10. **Faith:** In faith; a common interjection or oath.

POLIDOR:

Nay, then Ferando he must needs sit out,
For he may call, I think, till he be weary,
Before his wife will come before she list.°

FERANDO:

'Tis well for you that have such gentle wives,   15
Yet in this trial will I not sit out:
It may be Kate will come as soon as yours.

AURELIUS:

My wife comes soonest for a hundred pound.

POLIDOR:

I take it. I'll lay° as much to yours
That my wife comes as soon as I do send.   20

AURELIUS:

How now, Ferando, you dare not lay, belike.°

FERANDO:

Why, true, I dare not lay, indeed.
But how, so little money on so sure a thing?
A hundred pound — why I have laid as much
Upon my dog, in running at a deer.   25
She shall not come so far for such a trifle.
But will you lay five hundred marks with me?
And whose wife soonest comes when he doth call,
And shows herself most loving unto him,
Let him enjoy the wager I have laid.   30
Now what say you? Dare you adventure thus?

POLIDOR:

Ay, were it a thousand pounds, I durst presume
On my wife's love; and I will lay with thee.

Enter Alfonso.

ALFONSO:

How now, sons? What, in conference so hard?
May I, without offense, know whereabouts?°   35

AURELIUS:

Faith, father, a weighty cause about our wives.
Five hundred marks already we have laid,

---

14. **list:** wishes, pleases, chooses.   19. **lay:** Throughout this scene meaning to lay a wager or place a bet.   21. **belike:** by what is likely, by what seems.   35. **whereabouts:** what about.

And he whose wife doth show most love to him,
He must enjoy the wager to himself.

ALFONSO:

Why then, Ferando he is sure to lose. 40
I promise thee, son, thy wife will hardly come,
And therefore I would not wish thee lay so much.

FERANDO:

Tush, father, were it ten times more,
I durst adventure on my lovely Kate;
But if I lose I'll pay, and so shall you. 45

AURELIUS:

Upon mine honor, if I lose I'll pay.

POLIDOR:

And so will I, upon my faith I vow.

FERANDO:

Then sit we down and let us send for them.

ALFONSO:

I promise thee, Ferando, I am afraid thou wilt lose.

AURELIUS:

I'll send for my wife first. Valeria, 50
Go bid your Mistress come to me.

VALERIA:

                  I will, my Lord.   [*Exit Valeria.*]

AURELIUS:

Now for my hundred pound.
Would any lay ten hundred more with me,
I know I should obtain it by her love.

FERANDO:

I pray God you have not laid too much already. 55

AURELIUS:

Trust me, Ferando, I am sure you have,
For you, I dare presume, have lost it all.

Enter Valeria again.

Now, sirrah, what says your mistress?

VALERIA:

She is something busy, but she'll come anon.°

---

59. **anon:** shortly, soon.

FERANDO:

  Why so, did not I tell you this before?   60

  She is "busy" and cannot come.

AURELIUS:

  I pray God your wife send you so good an answer.

  She may be busy, yet she says she'll come.

FERANDO:

  Well, well. Polidor, send you for your wife.

POLIDOR:

  Agreed. Boy, desire your mistress to come hither.   65

BOY:

  I will, sir.   *Exit Boy.*

FERANDO:

        Ay, so so. He "desires" her to come.

ALFONSO:

  Polidor, I dare presume for thee,

  I think thy wife will not deny to come.

  And I do marvel much, Aurelius,

  That your wife came not when you sent for her.   70

Enter the Boy again.

POLIDOR:

  Now, where's your Mistress?

BOY:

  She bade° me tell you that she will not come;

  And° you have any business, you must come to her.

FERANDO:

  Oh, monstrous, intolerable presumption!

  Worse than a blazing star, or snow at midsummer,   75

  Earthquakes or anything unseasonable!

  She will not come, but he must come to her!

POLIDOR:

  Well, sir, I pray you, let's hear what answer your wife will make.

FERANDO:

  Sirrah, command your Mistress to come to me presently.   *Exit Sander.*

AURELIUS:

  I think my wife, for all she did not come,   80

  Will prove most kind. For now I have no fear,

  For I am sure Ferando's wife she will not come.

72. **bade:** commanded.   73. **And:** if.

FERANDO:
The more's the pity; then I must lose.

Enter Kate and Sander.

But I have won! For see, where Kate doth come.

KATE:
Sweet husband, did you send for me?   85

FERANDO:
I did, my love. I sent for thee to come.
Come hither, Kate, what's that upon thy head?

KATE:
Nothing, husband, but my cap, I think.

FERANDO:
Pull it off and tread it under thy feet.
'Tis foolish. I will not have thee wear it.   90

She takes off her cap and treads on it.

POLIDOR:
Oh wonderful metamorphosis!°

AURELIUS:
This is a wonder, almost past belief.

FERANDO:
This is a token of her true love to me.
And yet I'll try her further, you shall see.
Come hither, Kate. Where are thy sisters?   95

KATE:
They be sitting in the bridal chamber.

FERANDO:
Fetch them hither, and if they will not come,
Bring them perforce and make them come with thee.

KATE:
I will.

ALFONSO:
I promise thee, Ferando, I would have sworn   100
Thy wife would ne'er have done so much for thee.

FERANDO:
But you shall see she will do more than this,
For see where she brings her sisters forth by force.

91. **metamorphosis:** transformation.

Enter Kate thrusting Phylema and Emilia before her, to make them come unto their husbands' call.

KATE:

See, husband, I have brought them both.

FERANDO:

'Tis well done, Kate. 105

EMILIA:

Ay, sure, and like a loving peace,° you're worthy
To have great praise for this attempt.

PHYLEMA:

Ay, for making a fool of herself and us.

AURELIUS:

Beshrew thee, Phylema. Thou hast
Lost me a hundred pound tonight, 110
For I did lay that thou wouldst first have come.

POLIDOR:

But thou, Emilia, hast lost me a great deal more.

EMILIA:

You might have kept it better then.
Who bade you lay?

FERANDO:

Now, lovely Kate, before their husbands here, 115
I prithee tell unto these headstrong women,
What duty wives do owe unto their husbands.

KATE:

Then you that live thus by your pampered wills,
Now list to me and mark what I shall say.
Th'eternal power that with His only breath,
Shall cause this end and this beginning frame,° 120
Not in time, nor before time, but with time, confused;°
For all the course of years, of ages, months,
Of seasons temperate, of days and hours,
Are tuned and stopped by measure of His hand. 125
The first world was a form without a form,
A heap confused, a mixture all deformed,
A gulf of gulfs, a body bodiless,

---

106. **peace:** This word, "peace" in the original text, may mean either "peace" or "piece" or may carry connotations of both words.   121. **frame:** make, shape, fashion.   122. **confused:** mixed together, intermingled. This enigmatic line may mean that God does not exist before or in time but is Himself time. All things are present in the mind of God.

Where all the elements were orderless,
Before the great commander of the world,   130
The King of Kings, the glorious God of Heaven,
Who in six days did frame His heavenly work,
And made all things to stand in perfect course.
Then to His image He did make a man,
Old Adam; and from his side asleep,   135
A rib was taken, of which the Lord did make
The woe of man, so termed by Adam then
Woman, for that° by her came sin to us,
And for her sin was Adam doomed to die.
As Sarah to her husband, so should we   140
Obey them, love them, keep and nourish them,
If they by any means do want our helps,
Laying our hands under their feet to tread,
If that by that we might procure their ease.
And for a precedent I'll first begin,   145
And lay my hand under my husband's feet.

She lays her hand under her husband's feet.

FERANDO:
Enough, sweet, the wager thou hast won.
And they, I am sure, cannot deny the same.
ALFONSO:
Ay, Ferando, the wager thou hast won.
And for to show thee how I am pleased in this,   150
A hundred pounds I freely give thee more,
Another dowry for another daughter,
For she is not the same she was before.
FERANDO:
Thanks, sweet father. Gentlemen, goodnight,
For Kate and I will leave you for tonight.   155
'Tis Kate and I am wed, and you are sped.
And so, farewell, for we will to our beds.
                              Exeunt Ferando, Kate, and Sander.
ALFONSO:
Now, Aurelius, what say you to this?

138. **for that**: because.

AURELIUS:

Believe me, father, I rejoice to see
Ferando and his wife so lovingly agree.   160

Exeunt Aurelius, Phylema, Alfonso, and Valeria.

EMILIA:

How now, Polidor, in a dump? What say'st thou man?

POLIDOR:

I say thou art a shrew.

EMILIA:

That's better than a sheep.

POLIDOR:

Well, since 'tis done, let it go. Come, let's in.

Exeunt Polidor and Emilia.

Then enter two bearing Sly in his own apparel again. [They] leave him where they found him, and then go out. Then enter the Tapster.

TAPSTER:

Now that the darksome night is overpast,   165
And dawning day appears in crystal sky,
Now must I haste abroad. But soft, who's this?
What, Sly? Oh, wondrous! Hath he lain here all night?
I'll wake him. I think he's starved by this,
But that his belly was so stuffed with ale.   170
What, how Sly? Awake for shame.

SLY:

Sim°, gi's some more wine. What's, all the players gone?
Am not I a Lord?

TAPSTER:

A Lord with a murrin.° Come, art thou drunken still?

SLY:

Who's this? Tapster, oh Lord, sirrah, I have had   175
The bravest dream tonight that ever thou
Heardst in all thy life.

TAPSTER:

Ay, marry, but you had best get you home,
For your wife will curse you for dreaming here tonight.

SLY:

Will she? I know now how to tame a shrew.   180

---

172. **Sim:** appears to be the Tapster's name (short for Simon).   **gi's:** give us.   174. **murrin:** a hangover or headache.

I dreamed upon it all this night till now,
And thou hast waked me out of the best dream
That ever I had in my life. But I'll to my
Wife presently and tame her too,
And if° she anger me.   185
TAPSTER:
Nay, tarry, Sly, for I'll go home with thee,
And hear the rest that thou hast dreamed tonight.   *Exeunt omnes.*

FINIS.

185. And if: emphatic form of *if;* even if.

➔ **DAVID GARRICK**

From *Catharine and Petruchio*   *1756*

The Taming of the Shrew seems to have been revived in the late 1620s and early
1630s; after this, the play's stage life was shaped by the extraordinary political
and social upheavals of the seventeenth century. With the outbreak of civil war
in England in 1642, stage plays were forbidden by Parliament's order: "Public
Sports do not well agree with Public Calamities, nor Public Stage-plays with
the Seasons of Humiliation" (cited in *Revels History* 4:61). For the next two
decades, which saw the execution of King Charles I and England's experiment
with a nonmonarchial form of government led by Oliver Cromwell (variously
called the interregnum or protectorate), the theatres remained closed.

When Charles I's son, Charles II, was restored to the English throne in
1660, the theatres reopened. But they reopened with a difference. Whereas the
Renaissance theatre presented plays written by men and played by all-male
casts, the Restoration theatre employed actresses to play female (and some
male) parts and produced plays written by women as well as men. Restoration
theatre buildings seem to have been smaller than Renaissance theatres and to
have housed a more select, elite clientele (especially at first). The newly opened
theatres depended on revivals of plays written before 1642; for instance, some
evidence suggests that *The Taming of the Shrew* may have been performed in
1663–64 (Haring-Smith 8–9). But the revived plays were often also adapted; in
other words, their playwrights and directors often cut, rearranged, and added

---

*Catharine and Petruchio. A Comedy in Three Acts. As It Is Performed at the Theatre Royal in
Drury Lane, and at the Theatre in Edinburgh. Altered from Shakespeare's* Taming of the Shrew,
with Alterations and Additions, by David Garrick (Edinburgh, 1756), 26–27.

dialogue, characters, and scenes. The most famous example is the happy ending Nahum Tate provided for his adaptation of *King Lear*. Although some of Shakespeare's plays, such as *Hamlet* and *Othello*, were not adapted, others — such as *The Taming of the Shrew* — were rarely, if ever, performed without substantial revisions.

The various adaptations of *The Taming of the Shrew* were all by actor-dramatists, most of whom intended their versions as starring vehicles for themselves (*Revels History* 5:155). The first adaptation was John Lacy's *Sauny the Scot, or The Taming of the Shrew*, first performed in 1667, published in 1698, and frequently staged well into the eighteenth century (Haring-Smith 10–12). Set in England, the play focuses on Petruchio's servant Grumio, here renamed Sauny and given a heavy Scottish accent. In 1735 James Worsdale turned Lacy's version into a two-act farce, *A Cure for a Scold*. In 1716 two rival theatres, Drury Lane and Lincoln's Inn Fields, presented competing adaptations, both called *The Cobbler of Preston*, one by Charles Johnson and one by Christopher Bullock. Although each version elaborated on the Induction to *The Taming of the Shrew*, the second (Bullock's) was the more successful. Performed seventy-one times between 1716 and 1750, it was published in four editions (Haring-Smith 12–14).

Of all these adaptations, David Garrick's *Catharine and Petruchio*, "altered from Shakespeare's *The Taming of the Shrew*, with alterations and additions," was by far the most important and influential. Garrick was a successful playwright, theatre manager, and, above all, actor. Although Garrick never played Petruchio himself, many prominent actors and actresses performed in *Catharine and Petruchio* in the eighteenth and nineteenth centuries. One actor, John P. Kemble, seems to have initiated the stage tradition in which Petruchio brandishes a whip (see Figure 4); in the promptbook (or annotated script) documenting a 1788 production of *Catharine and Petruchio*, Kemble wrote "whip for Petruchio" in the margin next to Petruchio's entrance in the wedding scene (Haring-Smith 24; Thompson 9). Kemble's acting edition of *Catharine and Petruchio* (1810), which adapted Garrick's adaptation, became the standard acting version throughout the nineteenth century (Haring-Smith 26). In addition to Garrick's 1756 edition, and Kemble's 1810 edition, there were eight more editions published through 1865 (Haring-Smith 255–56). Between 1754 and 1844 Garrick's *Catharine and Petruchio* was the only version of *The Taming of the Shrew* presented on stages in England and America. Performed 234 times from 1754 to 1800, it was the sixth most popular Shakespearean play on the stage during those years.[3]

Garrick conceived *Catharine and Petruchio* as a three-act "afterpiece," a light entertainment intended to follow a full-length play. Reducing Shakespeare's three plots to one, Garrick eliminates the Sly frame, and begins his play after Bianca is already married, with the negotiations between Petruchio and

---

[3] "By contrast, during the fifty years before *Catharine and Petruchio* was staged, there were only 124 performances of all four earlier adaptations of *The Taming of the Shrew* combined" (Haring-Smith 15).

R. *Cruikshank, Del.* G. W. *Bonner, Sc.*

Taming of the Shrew;
OR, KATHARINE AND PETRUCHIO.

Petruchio. There, take it to you, trenchers, cups, and all.

Act II. Scene 2.

FIGURE 4 *Petruchio cracking his whip, from John Kemble's edition of David Garrick's adaptation (1838). Kemble seems to have initiated the stage tradition of having Petruchio wield a whip. The whip is often used to make Petruchio seem dashing and manly, but it also associates him visually with violence — even if he does not flog Katharine.*

Baptista. But the taming plot remains intact. Garrick retains most of Petruchio's speeches that detail his taming strategies, but without Petruchio's proposal to "man" his "haggard," shifting the language of falconry to Catharine instead. Catharine proposes to "make her husband stoop unto her lure" and to "tame this haggard" (Garrick 8).

In the final scene Petruchio announces that his pose as "the lordly husband" has just been "an honest mask" that he can "doff" or "throw off" now that Catharine has been tamed. He promises that there will be no more "rudeness, willfulness, and noise." On the other hand, he delivers the final lines of Catharine's sermon, lamenting how "shameful" it is when women are "so simple" as "to offer war where they should kneel for peace." Garrick drops the part of the final speech that grounds female subjection in biological difference — bodies that are "soft and weak and smooth." He also cuts Katharine's description of her transformation from one whose "mind hath been as big as one of yours" to one who recognizes and accepts her own weakness. In the absence of these lines, it is difficult to know what to make of Catharine's claim that she has been "transformed to stone." Garrick also eliminates Katharine's mention of placing her hand beneath her husband's foot.

Both *The Shrew* and *A Shrew* shift focus away from Katharine and Petruchio after this speech — *The Shrew* with the exchange between Lucentio and Hortensio, *A Shrew* with exchanges between Alfonso and Aurelius, and Emilia and Polidor, and with the return to Christopher Sly. Garrick's version concludes on the husband's statement of the wife's duty. Contrasting with the layered, ambiguous endings in both *The Shrew* and *A Shrew*, it does not qualify or comment.

Catharine and Petruchio

BAPTISTA:
How lik'st thou wedlock? Art not altered, Kate?
CATHARINE:
Indeed I am — I am transformed to stone.
PETRUCHIO:
Changed for the better much; art not, my Kate?
CATHARINE:
So good a master cannot choose but mend° me.
HORTENSIO:
Here is a wonder, if you talk of wonders.
BAPTISTA:
And so it is; I wonder what it bodes!

4. **mend**: improve, restore, amend.

PETRUCHIO:
Marry, peace it bodes, and love, and quiet life,
And awful rule, and right supremacy,
And, to be short, what not, that's sweet and happy.

BIANCA:
Was ever woman's spirit broke so soon?   10
What is the matter, Kate? Hold up thy head,
Nor lose our sex's best prerogative,
To wish and have our will. —

PETRUCHIO:
                              Peace, brawler, peace,
Or I will give the meek Hortensio,
Thy husband there, my taming recipe.   15

BIANCA:
Lord, let me never have a cause to sigh,
Till I be brought to such a silly pass.

PETRUCHIO:
Catharine, I charge thee tell this headstrong woman,
What duty 'tis she owes her lord and husband.

CATHARINE:
Fie, fie, unknit that threatening, unkind brow,   20
Nor dart such scornful glances from those eyes
To wound thy lord, thy king, thy governor.
It blots thy beauty, as frosts bite the meads,
Confounds thy frame, as whirlwinds shake fair buds,
And in no sense is meet or amiable.   25

PETRUCHIO:
Why, well said, Kate.

CATHARINE:
A woman moved, is like a fountain troubled,
Muddy, ill-seeming, thick, bereft of beauty.
And while it is so, none so dry or thirsty
Will deign to sip, or touch a drop of it.   30

BIANCA:
Sister, be quiet. —

PETRUCHIO:
Nay, learn you that lesson. — On, on, I say.

CATHARINE:
Thy husband is thy lord, thy life, thy keeper,
Thy head, thy sov'reign, one that cares for thee,
And for thy maintenance commits his body   35

To painful labor both by sea and land,
To watch the night in storms, the day in cold,
While thou lie'st warm at home, secure and safe;
And craves no other tribute at thy hands,
But love, fair looks, and true obedience —
Too little payment for so great a debt.   40

BAPTISTA:

Now fair befall thee, son Petruchio,
The battle's won, if thou canst keep the field.

PETRUCHIO:

Oh! fear me not.

BAPTISTA:

Then, my now gentle Catharine,   45
Go home with me along, and I will add
Another dowry to another daughter,
For thou art changed as thou hadst never been.

PETRUCHIO:

My fortune is sufficient, here's my wealth:
Kiss me, my Kate, and since thou art become   50
So prudent, kind, and dutiful a wife,
Petruchio here shall doff the lordly husband —
An honest mask, which I throw off with pleasure.
Far hence all rudeness, willfulness, and noise.
And be our future lives one gentle stream   55
Of mutual love, compliance, and regard.

Goes forward with Catharine in his hand.

Such duty as the subject owes the prince,
Even such a woman oweth to her husband;
And when she's peevish, froward,° sullen, sour,
And not obedient to his honest will,   60
What is she but a foul contending rebel
And graceless traitor to her loving lord?
How shameful 'tis when women are so simple
To offer war where they should kneel for peace,
Or seek for rule, supremacy, and sway,   65
Where bound to love, to honor, and obey.   *Exeunt omnes.*

FINIS.

---

59. **froward:** difficult to deal with, hard to please, ungovernable.

CHAPTER 2

Marriage

————————————————— ❯❮ —————————————————

An Ideal and Its Contradictions

Shakespeare's *The Taming of the Shrew* is about marriage. In the Induction
the Lord's elaborate joke on Sly hinges on providing him with a "madam
wife." The play proper begins with Baptista's concerns about marrying off
his two daughters, and the play's two plots follow these daughters' (very
different) courtships and marriages. Unlike many comedies *The Shrew* is as
interested in how couples interact after marriage as it is in their progress to
the altar. The play's final scene presents viewers with three recently married
couples and three models of marriage. The longest and most famous speech
is a homily on marriage, delivered by its tamed shrew.

While the play's interest in marriage is indisputable, how it values the
different marriages it depicts — and the marital advice it offers through
various characters — is not at all clear. Certainly, the play devotes the most
attention to Katharine and Petruchio. But whether it portrays them as
heroes who achieve the best possible union or as caricatures of outdated
ideals is debatable. If their marriage is held up as the "winner," as the wager
scene suggests, is this because it is a stable hierarchy — the husband clearly
the dominant partner and the wife his subordinate — an equal partnership,
or an ever-shifting, constantly renegotiated compromise between these two
overly simple models? While considering the play in the context of other
sixteenth- and seventeenth-century discussions of marriage cannot defin-

itively answer these questions, it can help explain why the play's depiction of marriage is so ambiguous. The questions *The Taming of the Shrew* raises, but cannot answer, were important ones in a period that saw the institution of marriage being redefined and revalued.

In the sixteenth and seventeenth centuries, marriage was not private. Depicting marriage as "a kind of public action" (Gouge 204) motivated by social responsibility rather than by self-interest, many texts insist that the marriage bond was made not just between the husband and wife, or between the couple and God, but among the spouses, their families, their community, and God. As *A Homily of the State of Matrimony* describes, the devil vigilantly watches the couple, hoping to exacerbate any conflicts between them. The other members of the household and the neighbors are also watching. Snawsel's *Looking Glass for Married Folks* suggests that neighbors can intervene in positive ways, helping to reconcile a couple; at the end of that text, which consists of a conversation among neighbors, a husband thanks God and "our good neighbors" (Snawsel H3) for his rejuvenated marriage. But this surveillance also places a burden on the couple. They are accountable to those who watch them and who may find fault with how they conduct themselves at home; they risk shame as well as damnation in marital squabbles. They also have an obligation to set a good example for others; their discord may promote insubordination in their children and servants.

Far from a private issue, marriage was a matter of public significance and debate, intimately intertwined with the religious, political, legal, and social crises and changes reshaping English life. One such dramatic shift was religious: the Reformation in England. In 1536 Henry VIII (king from 1509 to 1547) declared himself supreme head of the Church of England. He thereby divided the English church from its parent, the Roman Catholic church, and substituted himself for the pope as his subjects' spiritual leader. Thereafter, his subjects owed him religious as well as political allegiance. The newly created Church of England, or Anglican church, was a reformed, Protestant church, although it usually sought to define itself against both Catholicism and more radical forms of Protestantism, such as Anabaptism. To enforce this shift from Catholicism to Protestantism and from pope to sovereign as spiritual leader, Henry (and several of his successors) required that subjects swear oaths of allegiance to the sovereign. Attendance at Anglican services was also compulsory.

Henry was motivated by dynastic as well as spiritual concerns: he sought to divorce his wife, Catherine of Aragon, so that he could marry Anne Boleyn and, he hoped, produce a son and heir. But the Roman church could free him to remarry only if it found grounds to annul the existing marriage, that is, to claim that it had never been legitimate. When the church refused to accept Henry's arguments that his marriage should be annulled, he decided to disown its authority altogether. For Henry, then, private life and public policy were closely intertwined.

Besides the personal and political concerns motivating the decisive split, the Reformation in England also built on challenges to Roman Catholic doctrine and practice begun in Germany and Switzerland (with reformers such as Martin Luther and John Calvin, respectively), and in England, as early as the Lollard movement in Geoffrey Chaucer's time (the late fourteenth century). The progress of the Reformation in England was comparatively slow and uneven; for instance, Henry's daughter, Mary Tudor (1553–58), briefly restored Catholicism as the official state religion. But his son, Edward VI (1547–53), and daughter, Elizabeth I (1558–1603), worked to establish the reformed church and to convert subjects to it. Over time, the cumulative reforms dramatically changed English religious belief and practice. The Bible was translated into English so that it was much more widely accessible. *The Book of Common Prayer*, first published in 1549 and 1552, revised prayers and liturgies, including the marriage ceremony. In 1553 a set of forty-two articles or propositions codified official Anglican doctrines; in 1563 these were reissued under Elizabeth without substantial revision as the "Thirty-Nine Articles." Gradually, the focus of worship shifted from sacraments and ceremonies to preaching, from tradition to a more direct relationship between the believer and God.

In England, as elsewhere, reformed beliefs contributed to a reconsideration of marriage. While Catholicism placed a high value on virginity, requiring that its clergy members remain celibate, Protestant reformers argued for the moral prestige and social and spiritual value of marriage; Anglican clergy were allowed to marry. As reformers defended marriage as part of the project of differentiating themselves from Catholicism, they also insisted that it was a serious undertaking with consequences not only for each spouse's body and soul but also for the church and the community. As a result, works defending marriage also offered readers detailed instructions on how to meet the challenges it posed.

Such instruction was offered in sermons, often published after delivery during church services; it was also available in what are now called "conduct books" or "household manuals." Books giving advice on how to conduct one's personal life have a long history, beginning with Xenophon's *Treatise of a Household* (written in the fourth century B.C.; first translated into English in 1532 and reprinted five times by 1573), and including pre-Reformation European texts such as Vives's *Instruction of a Christian Woman* (translated in 1529 and reprinted eight more times in England by

1592) and Castiglione's *Book of the Courtier* (1528; translated into English in 1561). Although scholars point out significant continuities in such books from classical to Christian, and pre- to post-Reformation times (Davies; Todd), books about marriage and domesticity became especially popular and numerous by the late sixteenth century in England. Many of the texts excerpted in this book, such as Dod and Cleaver's *A Godly Form of Household Government*, Whately's *A Bride-Bush*, and Gouge's *Of Domestical Duties*, were popular conduct books.

As many scholars have argued, these books are derivative, borrowing liberally from one another, usually without acknowledgment, and relying heavily on scriptural authority. These books precede modern standards of originality; Shakespeare, too, borrowed from other writers. They cite the Bible constantly, both in the main text, which is often a tissue of biblical quotations, and in the margins, which crowd the pages (see Figure 5). One historian argues that "the similarity of all such treatises is so great that one wonders what moved the different writers to repeat over and over that which had been said so often before" (Powell 128). Another claims that "except for differences of opinion regarding divorce and occasional differences about the subordination of woman, there is far more agreement than divergence of opinion in the treatises throughout the period" (Wright 226). These very repetitions make conduct books valuable sources because it is in the similarities between authors and between works and in the continuities across time that we can best see which ways of imagining and describing private life were most pervasive, which concerns most frequently addressed, which values and standards of conduct most busily inculcated.

By the early seventeenth century, the production of texts prescribing personal conduct seems to have become a small industry. Different people, many of them Protestant clergymen, wrote, translated, compiled, or adapted texts. Although they did not espouse radically new views on marriage and domesticity, the Protestants who wrote these books brought to the discussion of private life an "emphasis, elaboration, and wide distribution" which were, as Rose argues, "completely new" (Rose 119). Many texts, such as those included here, went through multiple editions. In part this was because printing had rapidly established itself as a profitable business, and commercial presses could readily produce texts in large numbers and at relatively reasonable prices; these texts were sold in bookstalls, which were especially abundant in London. With its emphasis on individual Bible study and unmediated access to the scriptures, Protestantism itself may have fostered more widespread literacy and thus helped create more readers for these texts.

In the "spiritualized household" historians have associated with Protestantism, especially in its more radical forms, the father regularly acted as his

Not carnall wisedome.

discretion, and counsell, do prosper in inward & outward goods, and endure long. When we speake of wisedome, we do not meane that this gouernment can be in all points exercised by naturall reason and wisedome: for mans wisedome reacheth but vnto one point, and that the least of that which family-gouernment tendeth vnto.

But learned out of the word.

But the wisedome that we speake of, is not naturall, but fetched from the fountaine of all wisedome, God himselfe: who by his word giueth vnto vs pure light to walke by, not in the Church alone, nor in publike societie of men onely, but euen within the secret of our owne walles, and towards such as be abiding vnder the same roofe. And if we desire to walke with

Gen.5.24.
Psal.119.3.
Wisedome is great wealth.
Without wisedome whatsoeuer a man ta- keth in hand, turneth to his owne hurt.

God as *Enoch* did, we must set vp this light for our selues to liue by at home: For *then we do no iniquitie, when we walke in his way.* Where no wisedome is vsed in gouerning families, there all enormities are to be found, as wofull breaches betweene man and wife, gracelesnesse and vnthriftinesse of chil- dren, lewdnesse of seruants, and foule escapes. And where carnall pollicie ruleth, and not the wisedome which is from aboue, there all that is done, tendeth to the ease, pleasure, and profite of this life, wherein it is fitter for bruite beasts then for men to seeke their felicitie.

Now that there is a good kind of gouerning of a familie, which they who follow wisely, may be

be said to gouerne well, appeareth out of the first Epistle to *Timothie* 3. verse. 4, 5. *One that guideth his house well.* &c. And after: *He that knoweth not to gouerne his owne house,&c.* Where- by it is euident, that there is a way of ordering the family aright, and there is no misgouerning of it.

Wife and thil- full gouern- ment of a house is found out by Prudence, Science, and conserued by Experience.

To set downe this good gouernment exact- ly, is a hard matter. Here onely we will note some things which do appertaine vnto that go- uernment which we speake of. And to do it more orderly, we must consider, that (as may also be ga- thered out of that place of *Timothie*) there are two sorts in euery perfect familie.
$$\left\{\begin{array}{l}1. \text{ The Gouernours.}\\2. \text{ Those that must be ruled.}\end{array}\right.$$
And these two sorts haue speciall duties be- longing to them, the one towards the other: in the carefull performance whereof, from the one to the other, consisteth the *good gouernment of a familie.*

The first sort haue authori- ty in the fami- lie:

The gouernours of a family, be such as haue authoritie in the familie by Gods ordinance, as the father and mother, maister and mistrisse.

who must vse their authori- tie,

To whom as God hath giuen authoritie ouer their children and seruants, so he would haue them to vse it to the wise gouernment of them, not onely for their owne priuate profit, or credit, or pleasure, but also for the good of those whom they are to gouerne: for by a wise go- uernment

FIGURE 5. *Facsimile of pages from John Dod and Robert Cleaver,* A Godly Form of Household Government (*London, 1621*). *These two pages indicate a fairly typical use of marginal glosses. Besides explaining the main text (*much as footnotes do today*), they help a reader to skim the work or to find a passage of particular interest (*as headings might do*). Glosses also sum up the point of a passage and help a reader follow the points of a complicated argument. Often, marginal glosses direct a reader to other places in the book that might be of interest.*

family's spiritual head. Besides leading his wife, children, and servants in prayer, he read to them from the Bible. He may well also have read from conduct books, thus spreading instructions to those who were poor or illiterate. Since the male head of the household was most likely to have the reading skills and disposable income with which to buy books, he is the most likely person to have introduced them into the household, although others might also have done so. Furthermore, conduct books particularly promote the householder's interests; they dwell on his authority (although assuming that it had limits) and reinforce the subordination of his dependents, enjoining their obedience.

Conduct books generally address four topics: (1) religious and secular justifications of marriage; (2) the steps necessary to contract a binding marriage; (3) the relationship between husband and wife; and (4) household government and child rearing (Powell 101–02). The combination of a wedding mass and a feast with which Katharine and Petruchio and the couple in *A Merry Jest* celebrate their marriages was becoming the most accepted way of finalizing marriage; but it was not the only means of marrying, especially when the Protestant re-evaluation of marriage had made it a contract rather than a sacrament. As one historian explains:

> All that was necessary under canon law was a public declaration (a spousal or marriage contract) made in the present tense before witnesses that a man and woman considered themselves married. A couple might also state in the future tense that they intended subsequently to get married, but this was not irrevocable unless they had sexual intercourse.   (Laurence 42)

Over time, procedures for contracting marriage became more standardized, and, as Protestantism took root, marriage was accepted as an honorable vocation. Conduct books then shifted their attention to the social and domestic aspects of marriage and away from legal, ceremonial, or theological issues (Powell 123).

Marital advice was particularly important because those in unhappy marriages had few options. Unlike some other Protestant countries, England did not pursue the concept of marriage as a contract rather than a sacrament to its logical conclusion — that spouses should be able to terminate a contract that no longer met their needs; England did not make divorce readily available. Spouses could achieve a legal separation from an ecclesiastical court, but this would not enable them to marry again. A marriage could be annulled, thus enabling the partners to remarry; but there were very few grounds for annulment, and it rendered any children from the marriage illegitimate. By the end of the seventeenth century the wealthy might seek a divorce by Act of Parliament, but such divorces were costly and rare. Desertion was an unofficial, and frequently used, alternative (Stone 37–41). Despite these limited options, most texts about marriage and domestic life do not present divorce, of whatever kind, as a possibility. One character in Snawsel's text warns a disgruntled wife: "You are married now unto your husband, what manner of man soever he be; you have no liberty to change him for another, or cast him off" (p. 189); those who are unhappily married are "of necessity compelled to live together, which yet cannot be in quiet together" (p. 174). Spousal patience is thus born of

necessity: "No man would be pestered with a woman of a shrewd disposition that should enforce him to fighting, if, with a dash of his pen, he
might turn her packing" (see Whately, p. 225).

All three texts that follow, *A Homily of the State of Matrimony*, Robert
Snawsel's *A Looking Glass for Married Folks*, and T. E.'s *The Law's Resolutions
of Women's Rights*, seek to help couples avoid or negotiate conflict. This conflict is assumed to come largely from inside the couple, from each spouse's
"desire to rule" and "stubborn will and self-love" (p. 173). As a character in
Snawsel's text explains, couples are reluctant to make peace because of

> the stoutness of their hearts, which being proud and stiff, will not stoop one
> to another, which breedeth heart-burnings betwixt them, and inward grudg-
> ing and murmuring one at another. And therefore these cursed seeds of dis-
> sention and discord, being cast once into the heart by the Devil, will spring
> up not only to roots, but trees, and will hardly or never be helped, if at the
> first they be not speedily plucked up by the roots. (Snawsel C6v–C7)

Just as this description of marital discord depends on an agricultural image,
the work of resolving conflict and making peace is described as tilling a
rocky field (*Homily*), or taming an animal (Snawsel). In both images, one
partner is acting upon the other. In *A Homily* this responsibility rests with
the husband; in Snawsel's *Looking Glass* it rests with the wife. More often,
though, texts stress the strenuous labor of learning to work as partners in
marriage: spouses must "knit their minds together" and learn to draw a
yoke "in one concord of heart and mind" (*Homily*, pp. 173, 183).

As these various images suggest, the texts do not consistently assign responsibility for achieving marital harmony and domestic order to one partner
or the other. This inconsistency points to some of the central areas of contradiction and controversy regarding marriage. Historian Lawrence Stone
has argued that the expectation of spouses' becoming companions replaced
that of husbandly domination of the marriage and household. According to
Stone, as marriage came to be viewed as a contract, both spouses took up
roles as equal parties to that contract; during courtship, their parents consulted their wishes; after marriage, they operated as equals. Other historians
have questioned Stone's thesis and suggested that the hierarchical model
coexisted alongside the companionate model, producing conflicts even in the
content of the advice offered (Rose ch. 3; Wayne, Introduction to Tilney;
and Wrightson ch. 4). For instance, works from the period as different as a
sermon and a legal reference book reminded their readers that both models
could be found in the creation account in Genesis.

While it was widely accepted that households were both hierarchical and
patriarchal, with the father-husband-master the governor over all his sub-

ordinates, the status of the wife — who is sometimes positioned with the husband as a "joint governor" or companion and sometimes with the children and servants as a subordinate — complicates discussions of domestic authority and order. Consider, for instance, the complex balancing act between obeying and commanding that *A Homily of the State of Matrimony* dictates for wives: "To obey is another thing than to control or command, which yet they may do to their children, and to their family; but as for their husbands, them must they obey, and cease from commanding, and perform subjection" (*Homily*, p. 176). The wife's complex, contradictory status is especially clear in T. E.'s discussion of her legal status. But the invariable recourse to Genesis in discussions of marriage blurs the distinction between legal, social, and moral or religious approaches to marriage and its subordination of women. On these topics, as T. E. explains, the law "shaketh hand[s] with Divinity." To varying degrees, all of the texts below assume that women's subordination is natural and divinely ordained, or at least inevitable and impossible to change. (See Figure 6 for a depiction of the wife as simultaneously her husband's equal in stature and his subordinate.)

Texts prescribing domestic conduct are didactic — they attempt to reform and teach readers. We might expect, therefore, that they would be univocal — speaking from a stable, unified position of moral certainty and authority. Yet these texts often contradict themselves, articulating and endorsing seemingly opposed ideals. While authors (and readers) may not have been aware of these contradictions, some authors did consciously choose to build various voices and perspectives into their texts, thus drawing on the resources of drama to enliven their texts and engage readers. *A Homily of the State of Matrimony* addresses both husband and wife, imagining objections that each might voice: "But peradventure thou wilt object"; "But peradventure she will say." Note that in these phrases, the homilist addresses the husband in the second person ("you"), but the wife is addressed in the third ("she"). While the homily provides a script for a wife's apology, thus attempting to put submissive words in a woman's mouth, it also provides a script for what Sarah *might* have said had she articulated her annoyance with her husband Abraham: "Thus might she have said; but Sarah neither said nor thought such words, but she kept herself in silence in all things" (p. 179). Here the homily imagines the kinds of things that women should *not* say, while simultaneously censuring and reproducing women's scolding.[1] The homily also tries to imaginemarried women's suf-

---

[1] In this, "A Homily" resembles the many volumes collecting speeches supposedly delivered by shrewish wives. See the excerpt from Thomas Heywood's *A Curtain Lecture*, page 324, in this book.

The Husband is the Wiues hed Eph 5. 23
The Woman is the Glory of the Man 1 Cor. 11. 7

FIGURE 6. *This frontispiece from John Wing's* The Crown Conjugal *(London, 1632) brings together the two dominant models of marriage — as a partnership between equals, and as a hierarchical relationship. On the one hand, the spouses stand side by side and hand in hand. The tall, wide wife takes up as much or more space than her husband; yet his robe and crown indicate that he is the superior, the king of his domestic castle. Similarly, the biblical verse at the top of the image indicates love and mutuality; that at the bottom emphasizes that the husband is the wife's head.*

fering: "Truth it is, that they must [e]specially feel the grief and pains of their matrimony, in that they relinquish the liberty of their own rule, in the pain of their travailing, in the bringing up of their children. In which offices they be in great perils, and be grieved with great afflictions, which they might be without, if they lived out of matrimony" (p. 177). Similarly, Snawsel's *A Looking Glass* allows Xanthippe to articulate her anger and unhappiness; indeed, Snawsel's text weaves together various voices in a contentious conversation about marriage which reads very much like the script for a play.

✦ A Homily of the State of Matrimony   *1623*

The Anglican church produced two official compilations of sermons. The first, *Certain Sermons, or Homilies, Appointed by the King's Majesty, to be Declared and Read, by All Parsons, Vicars, or Curates Every Sunday in Their Churches,* first published in 1547, was composed by Bishop Edmond Bonner, Archbishop Thomas Cranmer, and Nicholas Harpsfield. It had gone through thirty-nine printings by 1640. The second, *The Second Tome of Homilies, of Such Matters as Were Promised and Entitled in the Former Part of Homilies,* in which the homily on matrimony appeared, was first published in 1563 (see Figure 7). Composed by Archbishop Matthew Parker, Bishop James Pilkington, Richard Taverner, and others, under the editorship of Bishop John Jewel, it was printed twenty-two times by 1640.

By gathering together sermons composed by powerful figures in the newly established Anglican church, these books disseminated versions of orthodox Anglican views to every church in the kingdom. Like ballads the sermons were widely circulated and readily accessible, even to the illiterate and poor. Any churchgoer could consult the books, which were placed in all churches, next to the Bible and *The Book of Common Prayer* (which records Anglican liturgies and prayers). At each parish church a sermon was preached every Sunday; although some ministers wrote their own sermons, many simply performed those available in the books of homilies.[2] Furthermore, regular attendance at Anglican services was obligatory; those who refused to attend, such as Protestant dissenters or Catholics, could be fined or even imprisoned. As a result, most English persons would have heard these sermons at least once. For instance, a bride and groom at whose wedding the homily on matrimony was preached

---

[2] See Klein's helpful introduction to her edition of "A Homily."

"A Homily of the State of Matrimony" in *The Second Tome of Homilies* (London, 1623), 239–48.

¶ An Homely of the state of Matrimonie.

He worde of Almyghtie God doeth testifie and declare, whence the originall begynnyng of Matrimonie commeth, and why it is ordeyned. It is instituted of God, to thintent that man and woman should lyue lawfully in a perpetuall frendly felowship, to bryng foorth fruite, and to auoyde fornication. By whiche meanes, a good conscience myght be preserued on both parties, in bridlyng the corrupt inclinations of the fleshe, within the limittes of honestie. For God hath straightly forbydden all whordome & vncleannesse, and hath from time to time, taken greuous punishmentes of this inordinate lust, as all stories and ages hath declared. Furthermore, it is also ordeyned, that the Churche of God and his kyngdome, myght by this kynde of lyfe, be conserued and enlarged, not onely in that God geueth chyldren by his blessyng: but also in that they be brought vp by the parentes godly, in the knowledge of Gods worde, that this the knowledge of God and true religion, myght be delyuered by succession from one to another, that finally, many myght enioy that euerlastyng immortalitie. Wherefore, forasmuch as Matrimonie serueth aswell to auoyde sinne & offence, as to encrease the kingdome of God: You, as all other which enter that state, must acknowledge this benefite of God, with pure and thankfull myndes,

for

FIGURE 7. *First page from the first edition of* A Homily of the State of Matrimony, *from* The Second Tome of Homilies *(1563). Notice the differences between the spelling and typeface in this version and that on page 172.*

might have heard it before at another wedding; in its discussions of conflicts and connections that could emerge only after years of marriage, the sermon also seems to address married couples in the congregation.

Since the homilies were revised and republished, even the official Anglican position they articulated was dynamic rather than static. And, as we will see, individual homilies sometimes contradicted either themselves or other homilies. Furthermore, many adherents of the reformed or Protestant religion dissented from Anglican doctrines and practices. Therefore, while "A Homily of the State of Matrimony" articulates the most widely available and accepted view of marriage, it was not the only view available in sixteenth- and seventeenth-century England. However dominant this view was, it was also unstable, internally divided, and contested.

From its beginning, "A Homily of the State of Matrimony" presents marriage in simultaneously positive and negative terms. Marriage serves three purposes: it provides friendship between the spouses and enables them to reproduce; but it also helps them to control their sexual appetites, to "bridle the corrupt inclinations of the flesh within the limits of honesty." Marriage is thus valuable both for what it enables the spouses to embrace and for what it enables them to avoid. Presenting marriage as a serious, even dangerous, undertaking, the homily does not emphasize pleasure or happiness as reasons to marry. It presents marriage as, at best, an opportunity to "bear Christ's cross," that is, to achieve salvation through suffering.

Throughout the homily, marriage is presented as a perilous adventure with high stakes. Husband and wife risk shame, community censure, and damnation; but they do so for the promise of salvation, honor, contentment, and profit. "For this state of life will be more honorable and comfortable than our houses, than servants, than money, than lands and possessions, than all things that can be told" (p. 183) — if, that is, it is well managed. The threats to marriage come from both inside and outside the household. The homily first warns against the devil's vigilance: "For the devil will assay to attempt all things to interrupt and hinder your hearts and godly purpose, if you will give him any entry" (p. 173); as a result of the devil's interference, "how few matrimonies there be without chidings, brawlings, tauntings, repentings, bitter cursings, and fightings" (p. 173). The marriage is also threatened from within by each spouse's "desire to rule."

Since there is no way out of an unhappy marriage, spouses are urged to arm themselves against these dangers by praying diligently. Constructing marriage as an epic struggle, the homily yet insists that the spouses must not struggle against one another, but rather join together to fight their enemy, the devil. In its discussions of domestic violence, the homily reveals not only its own contradictions, but those inherent in Protestant concepts of marriage. The homily urges husbands not to beat their wives, yet it comforts battered wives with the promise of "a great reward" from God if they endure their suffering patiently:

For if we be bound to hold out our left cheek to strangers, which will smite us on the right cheek, how much more ought we to suffer an extreme and unkind husband! But yet I mean not that a man should beat his wife. God forbid that, for that is the greatest shame that can be, not so much for her that is beaten, as to him that doth the deed. (p. 180)

While the homily attempts to redefine masculinity as nonviolent, it yet offers wives no recourse to beatings except prayer and patience. While the homily deplores husbands' use of violence, it concedes that they might beat their wives anyway. Clearly, the ideal of the politic, patient, "gentle" husband was not the norm in practice.

Yet, the homily does not depict wives as patient sufferers and husbands as intolerant brutes. Rather, it suggests that marriage tests the patience of both spouses; it offers both the opportunity to strive together toward shared goals: social respectability, peace and quiet, eternal reward. The story about Socrates ("a certain strange philosopher") and his notoriously shrewish wife Xanthippe emphasizes the husband's patience; the lengthy story about Abraham and Sarah demonstrates the forbearance of both the good wife and the good husband. Taken together, these stories offer classical and scriptural precedents for the English couple struggling to conquer the frustrations of marriage and to tame their own rebellious wills.

A Homily of the State of Matrimony

The word of Almighty God doth testify and declare whence the original beginning of matrimony cometh, and why it is ordained. It is instituted by God, to the intent that man and woman should live lawfully in a perpetual friendship, to bring forth fruit, and to avoid fornication, by which means a good conscience might be preserved on both parties in bridling the corrupt inclinations of the flesh within the limits of honesty. For God hath straitly forbidden all whoredom and uncleanness, and hath from time to time taken grievous punishment of this inordinate lust, as all stories and ages have declared. Furthermore, it is also ordained that the church of God and His kingdom might by this kind of life be conserved and enlarged, not only in that God giveth children by His blessing, but also in that they be brought up by the parents godly, in the knowledge of God's word, that thus the knowledge of God and true religion might be delivered by succession from one to another, that finally many might enjoy that everlasting immortality. Wherefore, for as much as matrimony serveth us as well to avoid sin and offense as to increase the kingdom of God, you, as all other which enter the state, must acknowledge this benefit of God, with pure and thankful minds; for that he hath so ruled your hearts that you follow not the example of the wicked world, who set their delight in filthiness of sin, but both of you stand in the fear of God and abhor all filthiness. For that is surely the singular gift of God, where the common example of the world declareth how the devil hath their hearts bound and entangled in divers° snares so that they in their wifeless state run into open abominations, without any grudge of their conscience. Which sort of men that live so desperately and filthy° — what damnation tarrieth for them! Saint Paul describeth it to them, saying: "Neither whoremongers, neither adulterers, shall inherit the kingdom of God" (1 Corinthians 6). This horrible judgment of God you be escaped through His mercy, if so be that you live inseparately,° according to God's ordinance.

But yet I would not have you careless, without watching. For the devil will assay to attempt all things to interrupt and hinder your hearts and godly purpose, if you will give him any entry. For he will either labor to break this godly knot once begun betwixt you, or else at the least he will labor to encumber it with divers griefs and displeasures.

And this is [his]° principal craft, to work dissension of hearts of the one from the other; that whereas now there is pleasant and sweet love betwixt you, he will in the stead thereof bring in most bitter and unpleasant discord. And surely that same adversary of ours doth, as it were from above, assault man's nature and condition. For this folly is ever from our tender age grown up with us, to have a desire to rule, to think highly of ourself, so that none thinketh it meet° to give place to another. That wicked vice of stubborn will and self-love is more meet to break and to dissever the love of heart, than to preserve concord.

Wherefore married persons must apply their minds in most earnest wise to concord, and must crave continually of God the help of his Holy Spirit, so to rule their hearts and to knit their minds together, that they be not dissevered by any division of discord. This necessity of prayer must be oft in the practice and using of married persons, that ofttimes the one should pray for the other, lest hate and debate do arise betwixt them. And because few do consider this thing, but more few° do perform it, I say, to pray diligently, we see how wonderful[ly] the devil deludeth and scorneth this state, how few matrimonies there be without chidings, brawlings, tauntings, repentings, bitter cursings, and fightings. Which things whosoever

---

divers: different, not alike.   filthy: filthily.   inseparately: inseparably; without division or discord.   [his]: The 1623 edition prints "the" here, but earlier editions print "his."   meet: suitable, appropriate, acceptable.   more few: even fewer.

doth commit, they do not consider that it is the instigation of the ghostly°
enemy, who taketh great delight therein; for else they would with all
earnest endeavor strive against these mischiefs, not only with prayer, but
also with all possible diligence.

Yea, they would not give place to the provocation of wrath, which
stirreth them either to such rough and sharp words, or stripes,° which is
surely compassed by the devil, whose temptation, if it be followed, must
needs begin and weave the web of all miseries and sorrows. For this is most
certainly true, that of such beginnings must needs ensue the breach of true
concord in heart, whereby all love must needs shortly be banished. Then
can it not be but a miserable thing to behold, that yet they are of necessity
compelled to live together, which yet cannot be in quiet together. And this
is most customable° everywhere to be seen. But what is the cause thereof?
Forsooth, because they will not consider the crafty trains° of the devil, and
therefore give not themselves to pray to God, that He [God] would vouch-
safe to repress his [the devil's] power. Moreover, they do not consider how
they promote the purpose of the devil, in that they follow the wrath of their
hearts while they threat[en] one another, while they in their folly turn all
upside down, while they will never give over their right, as they esteem it,
yea, while many times they will not give over the wrong part indeed. Learn
thou, therefore, if thou desirest to be void of all these miseries, if thou
desirest to live peaceably and comfortably in wedlock, how to make thy
earnest prayer to God, that He would govern both your hearts by the Holy
Spirit, to restrain the devil's power, whereby your concord may remain
perpetually.

But to this prayer must be joined a singular diligence, whereof Saint
Peter giveth this precept, saying: "You husbands, deal with your wives
according to knowledge, giving honor to the wife as unto the weaker vessel,
and as unto them that are heirs also of the grace of life, that your prayers
be not hindered" (1 Peter 3). This precept doth particularly pertain to the
husband: for he ought to be the leader and author of love, in cherishing and
increasing concord, which then shall take place if he will use moderation
and not tyranny, and if he yield something to the woman. For the woman
is a weak creature, not endued° with like strength and constancy of mind;
therefore, they [women] be the sooner disquieted, and they be the more
prone to all weak affections and dispositions of mind, more than men be;
and lighter they be, and more vain in their fantasies and opinions. These

ghostly: spiritual.   stripes: blows, strokes, or lashes, especially marks left by a whip or other
object.   customable: customary; usual.   trains: schemes to deceive or entrap; snares, traps, or
lures.   endued: endowed or invested with.

things must be considered of° the man, that he be not too stiff, so that he ought to wink at some things, and must gently expound all things, and to forbear.

Howbeit, the common sort of men doth judge that such moderation should not become a man. For they say that it is a token of womanish cowardness and therefore they think that it is a man's part to fume in anger, to fight with fist and staff. Howbeit, howsoever they imagine, undoubtedly Saint Peter doth better judge what should be seeming to a man, and what he should most reasonably perform. For he saith reasoning should be used, and not fighting. Yea, he saith more, that the woman ought to have a certain honor attributed to her; that is to say, she must be spared and borne with, the rather for that she is the weaker vessel, of a frail heart, inconstant, and with a word soon stirred to wrath. And therefore, considering these her frailties, she is to be the rather spared. By this means, thou shalt not only nourish concord, but shall have her heart in thy power and will. For honest natures will sooner be retained to do their duties rather by gentle words than by stripes. But he which will do all things with extremity and severity, and doth use always rigor in words and stripes, what will that avail in the conclusion? Verily nothing, but that he thereby setteth forward the devil's work. He banisheth away concord, charity, and sweet amity, and bringeth in dissension, hatred, and irksomeness, the greatest griefs that can be in the mutual love and fellowship of man's life.

Beyond all this, it bringeth another evil therewith, for it is the destruction and interruption of prayer. For in the time that the mind is occupied with dissension and discord, there can be no true prayer used. For the Lord's Prayer hath not only a respect to particular persons, but to the whole universal, in the which we openly pronounce that we will forgive them which have offended against us, even as we ask forgiveness of our sins of God. Which thing, how can it be done rightly, when their hearts be at dissension? How can they pray each for other, when they be at hate betwixt themselves? Now, if the aid of prayer be taken away, by what means can they sustain themselves in any comfort? For they cannot otherwise either resist the devil, or yet have their hearts staid in stable comfort in all perils and necessities, but by prayer. Thus all discommodities, as well worldly as ghostly, follow this froward testiness,° and cumbrous° fierceness in manners, which be more meet for brute beasts than for reasonable creatures. Saint Peter doth not allow these things, but the devil desireth them gladly. Wherefore, take the more heed. And yet a man may be a man, although he

---

of: by. **froward:** perverse, difficult to deal with, hard to please. **testiness:** irritability, crankiness. **cumbrous:** causing distress, trouble, or annoyance.

doth not use such extremity, yea, although he should dissemble° some things in his wife's manners. And this is the part of a Christian man which both pleaseth God and serveth also in good use to the comfort of their marriage state.

Now as concerning the wife's duty: what shall become her? Shall she abuse the gentleness and humanity of her husband, and, at her pleasure, turn all things upside down? No, surely, for that is far repugnant against God's commandment. For thus doth Saint Peter preach to them: "You wives, be you in subjection to obey your own husbands" (1 Peter 3). To obey is another thing than to control or command, which yet they may do to their children, and to their family; but as for their husbands, them must they obey, and cease from commanding, and perform subjection. For this surely doth nourish concord very much: when the wife is ready at hand to her husband's commandment; when she will apply herself to his will; when she endeavoreth herself to seek his contentation,° and to do him pleasure; when she will eschew all things that might offend him. For thus will most truly be verified the saying of the poet [Euripides]: "A good wife by obeying her husband shall bear the rule, so that he shall have a delight and a gladness the sooner at all times to return home to her." But, on the contrary part, when the wives be stubborn, froward, and malapert,° their husbands are compelled thereby to abhor and flee from their own houses, even as they should have battle with their enemies.

Howbeit, it can scantly° be, but that some offenses shall sometime chance betwixt them. For no man doth live without fault, [e]specially for that° the woman is the more frail party. Therefore let them beware that they stand not in their faults and willfulness; but rather let them acknowledge their follies, and say: "My husband, so it is, that by my anger I was compelled to do this or that. Forgive it me, and hereafter I will take better heed." Thus ought the wom[e]n more readily to do, the more they be ready to offend. And they shall not do this only to avoid strife and debate, but rather in the respect of the commandment of God, as Saint Paul expresseth it in this form of words: "Let women be subject to their husbands, as to the Lord; for the husband is the head of the woman, as Christ is the head of the church" (Ephesians 5). Here you understand that God hath commanded that you should acknowledge the authority of the husband, and refer to him the honor of obedience. And Saint Peter saith in that place before rehearsed, that "holy matrons did in former time deck themselves not with gold and silver, but in putting their whole hope in God, and in

---

dissemble: to pretend not to see or notice, to ignore. contentation: contentment. malapert: presumptuous, impudent, saucy. scantly: scarcely, hardly. for that: because.

obeying their husbands, as Sarah obeyed Abraham, calling him Lord; whose daughters you be," saith he, "if you follow her example" (1 Peter 3). This sentence is very meet for women to print in their remembrance.

Truth it is, that they must [e]specially feel the grief and pains of their matrimony, in that they relinquish the liberty of their own rule, in the pain of their travailing,° in the bringing up of their children. In which offices they be in great perils, and be grieved with great afflictions, which they might be without, if they lived out of matrimony. But Saint Peter saith that this is the chief ornament of holy matrons, in that they set their hope and trust in God; that is to say, in that they refused not from marriage for the business° thereof, for the [griefs]° and perils thereof, but committed all such adventures to God, in most sure trust of help, after that they have called upon his aid. Oh, woman, do thou the like, and so shalt thou be most excellently beautified before God and all his angels and saints; and thou needest not to seek further for doing any better works. For obey thy husband, take regard of his requests, and give heed unto him to perceive what he requireth of thee, and so shalt thou honor God and live peaceably in thy house. And beyond all this, God shall follow thee with his benediction, that all things shall well prosper both to thee and to thy husband, as the psalm saith: "Blessed is the man which feareth God, and walketh in his ways; thou shalt have the fruit of thine own hands; happy shalt thou be, and well it shall go with thee. Thy wife shall be as a vine plentifully spreading about thy house. Thy children shall be as the young springs of the olives about thy table. Lo, thus shall that man be blessed," saith David, "that feareth the Lord."

This let the wife have ever in mind, the rather admonished thereto by the apparel of her head, whereby is signified, that she is under covert or obedience of her husband.° And as that apparel is of nature so appointed to declare her subjection, so biddeth Saint Paul that all other of her raiment should express both shamefacedness° and sobriety.° For if it be not lawful for the woman to have her head bare, but to bear thereon the sign of her power wheresoever she goeth, more is it required that she declare the thing that is meant thereby. And therefore these ancient women of the old world called their husbands lords, and showed them reverence in obeying them.

But peradventure she will say that those men loved their wives indeed. I know that well enough, and bear it well in mind. But when I do admonish

---

travailing: laboring to give birth. business: anxiety, care, distress. [griefs]: The 1623 edition prints "gifts" here, but all other editions print "grief" or "griefs," which makes more sense in this context. covert . . . husband: See the discussion of "coverture" in the headnote to T. E., *The Law's Resolutions of Women's Rights* (p. 193). shamefacedness: modesty, bashfulness, or shyness. sobriety: seriousness, gravity.

you of your duties, then call not to consideration what their [your husbands'] duties be. For when we ourselves do teach our children to obey us as their parents, or when we reform our servants and tell them that they should obey their masters, not only at the eye but as the Lord,° if they should tell us again our duties, we should not think it well done. For when we be admonished of our duties and faults, we ought not then to seek what other men's duties be. For though a man had a companion in his fault, yet should he not thereby be without his fault.

But this must be only looked on:° by what means thou mayest make thyself without blame. For Adam did lay the blame upon the woman, and she turned it unto the serpent; but yet neither of them was thus excused. And therefore bring not such excuses to me at this time, but apply all thy diligence to hear thine obedience to thine husband. For when I take in hand to admonish thy husband to love thee and to cherish thee, yet will I not cease to set out the law that is appointed for the woman, as well as I would require of the man what is written for his law. Go thou, therefore, about such things as becometh thee only, and show thyself tractable to thy husband. Or rather, if thou wilt obey thy husband for God's precept,° then allege such things as be in his duty to do, but perform thou diligently those things which the law-maker hath charged thee to do. For thus is it most reasonable to obey God, if thou wilt not suffer thyself to transgress his law. He that loveth his friend seemeth to do no great thing; but he that honoreth [him] that is hurtful and hateful to him — this man is worthy most commendation.

Even so think you: if thou canst suffer an extreme husband, thou shalt have a great reward therefore. But if thou lovest him only because he is gentle and courteous, what reward will God give thee therefore? Yet I speak not these things that I would wish the husbands to be sharp towards their wives; but I exhort the women that they would patiently bear the sharpness of their husbands. For when either parts do their best to perform their duties the one to the other, then followeth thereon great profit to their neighbors for their example's sake. For when the woman is ready to suffer a sharp husband, and the man will not extremely entreat his stubborn and troublesome wife, then be all things in quiet, as in a most sure haven.

Even thus was it done in old time, that everyone did their own duty and office, and was not busy to require the duty of their neighbors. Consider,

---

eye . . . Lord: Masters expect obedience from servants not only when they can be seen ("at the eye") but always, not only in their actions but in their thoughts and consciences ("as the Lord"). **this must be only looked on:** this must be your primary concern. **precept:** command, order, mandate.

I pray thee, that Abraham took to him his brother's son; his wife did not blame him therefore. He commanded him to go with him a long journey; she did not gainsay° it, but obeyed his precept. Again, after all those great miseries, labors, and pains of that journey, when Abraham was made as lord over all, yet did he give place to Lot of his superiority; which matter Sarah took so little to grief that she never once suffered her tongue to speak such words as the common manner of women is wont to do in these days, when they see their husbands in such rooms° to be made underlings and to be put under their youngers.° Then they upbraid° them with cumbrous talk, and call them fools, dastards,° and cowards for so doing. But Sarah was so far from speaking any such thing that it came never into her mind and thought so to say, but [she] allowed the wisdom and will of her husband. Yea, besides all this, after the said Lot had thus his will, and left to his uncle the less portion of land, he chanceth to fall into extreme peril; which chance, when it came to the knowledge of this said patriarch, he incontinently° put all his men in harness,° and prepared himself, with all his family and friends, against the host of the Persians. In which case, Sarah did not counsel him to the contrary, nor did say, as then might have been said, "My husband, whither goest thou so unadvisedly? Why runnest thou thus on head?° Why dost thou offer thyself to so great perils, and art thus ready to jeopard[ize] thine own life, and to [im]peril the lives of all thine, for such a man as hath done thee such wrong? At the least way, if thou regardest not thyself, yet have compassion on me, which for thy love have forsaken my kindred and my country, and have the want both of my friends and kinsfolks, and am thus come into so far countries with thee. Have pity on me, and make me not here a widow, to cast me into such cares and troubles." Thus might she have said; but Sarah neither said nor thought such words, but she kept herself in silence in all things.

Furthermore, all that time when she was barren, and took no pains as other women did by bringing forth fruit in his house, what did he [Abraham]? He complained not to his wife, but to Almighty God. And consider how either of them did their duties as became them; for neither did he despise Sarah because she was barren, nor never did cast it in her teeth. Consider again how Abraham expelled the handmaid out of the house when she [Sarah] required it. So that by this I may truly prove that the one

---

gainsay: contradict, oppose, or hinder. in such rooms: in the position. and to be put . . . youngers: Note the assumption here that wives are heavily invested in their husbands' social status, which determines their own. The author assumes that women cannot bear to see their husbands "made underlings." upbraid: reproach, find fault with. dastards: slow-witted, cowardly persons—those who meanly or basely shrink from danger. incontinently: imme- diately. put . . . in harness: armed, equipped, prepared for battle. on head: headlong.

was pleased and contented with the other in all things. But yet set not your eyes only on this matter, but look further what was done before this: that Hagar used her mistress [Sarah] despitefully,° and that Abraham himself was somewhat provoked against her; which must needs be an intolerable matter and a painful to a freehearted woman and a chaste.

Let not, therefore, the woman be too busy to call for the duty of her husband, where she should be ready to perform her own; for that is not worthy any great commendations. And even so again, let not the man only consider what belongeth to the woman, and to stand too earnestly gazing thereon; for that is not his part or duty. But, as I have said, let either party be ready and willing to perform that which belongeth [e]specially to themselves. For if we be bound to hold out our left cheek to strangers, which will smite us on the right cheek, how much more ought we to suffer an extreme and unkind husband? But yet I mean not that a man should beat his wife. God forbid that, for that is the greatest shame that can be, not so much to her that is beaten, as to him that doth the deed. But if by such fortune thou chancest upon such a husband, take it not too heavily, but suppose thou that thereby is laid up no small reward hereafter, and in this lifetime, no small commendation to thee, if thou canst be quiet.

But yet to you that be men, thus I speak: let there be none so grievous fault to compel you to beat your wives. But what say I? Your wives? No, it is not to be borne with that an honest man should lay hands on his maid-servant to beat her. Wherefore, if it be a great shame for a man to beat his bond-servant, much more rebuke it is to lay violent hands upon his free-woman. And this thing be well understood by the laws which the paynims° have made, which doth discharge her any longer to dwell with such a husband, as unworthy to have any further company with her that doth smite her. For it is an extreme point, thus so vilely to entreat her like a slave that is fellow to thee of thy life, and so joined unto thee beforetime in the necessary matters of thy living. And therefore a man may well liken such a man (if he may be called a man rather than a wild beast) to a killer of his father or his mother. And whereas we be commanded to forsake our father and mother for our wives' sake, and yet thereby do work them none injury but do fulfill the law of God, how can it not appear, then, to be a point of extreme madness to entreat her despitefully, for whose sake God hath commanded thee to leave parents? Yea, who can suffer such despite? Who can worthily express the inconvenience that [it] is to see what weepings and wailings be made in the open streets, when neighbors run together

---

despitefully: contemptuously, insolently. Abraham had a child by Sarah's servant, Hagar.
paynims: pagans or heathens, here meaning pre-Christians.

to the house of so unruly a husband, as to a bedlam-man,° who goeth about to overturn all that he hath at home? Who would not think that it were better for such a man to wish the ground to open and swallow him in, than once ever after to be seen in the market?

But, peradventure,° thou wilt object that the woman provoketh thee to this point. But consider thou again that the woman is a frail vessel, and thou art therefore made the ruler and head over her, to bear the weakness of her in this her subjection. And therefore study thou to declare the honest commendation of thine authority, which thou canst no way better do than to forbear to urge her in her weakness and subjection. For even as the king appeareth so much the more noble, the more excellent and noble he maketh his officers and lieutenants, whom if he should dishonor and despise the authority of their dignity, he should deprive himself of a great part of his own honor; even so, if thou dost despise her that is set in the next room° beside thee, thou dost much derogate° and decay the excellency and virtue of thine own authority. Recount all these things in thy mind, and be gentle and quiet. Understand that God hath given thee children with her, and [thou] art made a father, and by such reason appease thyself.

Dost thou not see the husbandmen,° what diligence they use to till that ground which once they have taken to farm, though it be never so full of faults? As, for an example, though it be dry, though it bringeth forth weeds, though the soil cannot bear too much wet, yet he tilleth it, and so winneth fruit thereof. Even, in like manner, if thou wouldst use like diligence to instruct and order the mind of thy spouse, if thou wouldst diligently apply thyself to weed out by little and little the noisome° weeds of uncomely manners out of her mind, with wholesome precepts, it could not be, but [that] in time thou shouldst feel the pleasant fruit thereof to both your comforts. Therefore, that this thing chance not so, perform this thing that I do here counsel thee: whensoever any displeasant matter riseth at home, if thy wife hath done aught amiss, comfort her and increase not the heaviness. For though thou shouldst be grieved with never so many things, yet shalt thou find nothing more grievous than to want the benevolence of thy wife at home. What offense soever thou canst name, yet shalt thou find none more intolerable than to be at debate with thy wife. And for this cause most of all oughtst thou to have this love in reverence. And if reason moveth thee to bear any burden at any other men's hands, much more at thy wife's. For if she be

---

bedlam-man: a lunatic or madman; one who should be in an asylum, such as Bethlehem hospital in London (popularly known as Bedlam). **peradventure:** possibly, perhaps. **room:** place, position. **derogate:** lessen, detract from, disparage. **husbandmen:** farmers. **noisome:** harmful, noxious.

poor, upbraid her not; if she be simple, taunt her not, but be the more courteous; for she is thy body, and made one flesh with thee.

But thou, peradventure, wilt say that she is a wrathful woman, a drunkard, and beastly, without wit and reason. For this cause bewail° her the
more. Chafe not in anger, but pray unto Almighty God. Let her be admonished and helped with good counsel, and do thou thy best endeavor
that she may be delivered of all these affections. But if thou shouldst beat
her, thou shalt increase her evil affections; for frowardness and sharpness is
not amended with frowardness, but with softness and gentleness. Furthermore, consider what reward thou shalt have at God's hand. For where thou
mightst beat her, and yet for the respect of the fear of God thou wilt abstain
and bear patiently her great offenses, the rather in respect of that law,
which forbiddeth that a man should cast out his wife, what fault soever she
be [en]cumbered with, thou shalt have a very great reward. And before the
receipt of that reward, thou shalt feel many commodities.° For by this
means she shall be made the more obedient, and thou for her sake shalt be
made the more meek.

It is written in a story of a certain strange° philosopher, which had a
cursed wife, a froward, and a drunkard, when he was asked for what
consideration he did so bear her evil manners, he made answer: "By this
means," said he, "I have at home a schoolmaster, and an example how I
should behave myself abroad. For I shall," saith he, "be the more quiet with
others, being thus daily exercised and taught in the forbearing of her."
Surely it is a shame that paynims should be wiser than we; we, I say, that
be commanded to resemble angels, or rather God himself, through meekness. And for the love of virtue, this said philosopher Socrates would not
expel his wife out of his house. Yea, some say that he did therefore marry
his wife to learn this virtue by that occasion.

Wherefore, seeing many men be far behind the wisdom of this man, my
counsel is that first and before all things a man do his best endeavor to get
him a good wife, endued with all honesty and virtue. But if it so chance that
he is deceived, that he hath chosen such a wife as is neither good nor
tolerable, then let the husband follow this philosopher, and let him instruct
his wife in every condition, and never lay these matters to sight.°

For the merchantman, except he first be at composition° with his factor°

---

bewail: lament, mourn.   commodities: conveniences, comforts.   strange: foreign, alien.
never . . . sight: never notice these matters or bring them up; that is, the husband should ignore
his wife and his own unhappiness, as Socrates did.   except . . . composition: Unless he has first
settled his debts or accounts; unless he has come to an agreement.   factor: agent, deputy, or
representative. Specifically, one who buys or sells for another person in exchange for a com-
mission.

to use his inter[af]fairs° quietly, he will neither stir his ship to sail, nor yet will lay hands upon his merchandise. Even so, let us do all things that we may have the fellowship of our wives, which is the factor of all our doings at home, in great quiet and rest. And by these means all things shall prosper quietly, and so shall we pass through the dangers of the troublous sea of this world. For this state of life will be more honorable and comfortable than our houses, than servants, than money, than lands and possessions, than all things that can be told. As all these, with sedition and discord, can never work us any comfort, so shall all things turn to our commodity and pleasure, if we draw this yoke in one concord of heart and mind.

Whereupon, do your best endeavor that after this sort you use your matrimony, and so shall you be armed on every side. You have escaped the snares of the devil, and the unlawful lusts of the flesh; you have the quietness of conscience by this institution of matrimony, ordained by God. Therefore, use oft prayer to Him, that He would be present by you, that He would continue concord and charity betwixt you. Do the best you can of your parts,° to [ac]custom yourselves to softness and meekness, and bear well in worth such oversights as chance.° And thus shall your conversation be most pleasant and comfortable.

And although — which can no otherwise be — some adversities shall follow, and otherwhiles° now one discommodity, now another shall appear, yet, in this common trouble and adversity, lift up both your hands unto heaven; call upon the help and assistance of God, the author of your marriage; and surely the promise of relief is at hand. For Christ affirmeth in his gospel: "Where two or three be gathered together in my name, and be agreed, what matter soever they pray for, it shall be granted them of my heavenly Father." Why therefore shouldst thou be afraid of the danger, where thou hast so ready a promise, and so nigh° a help? Furthermore, you must understand how necessary it is for Christian folk to bear Christ's cross; for else we shall never feel how comfortable God's help is unto us. Therefore, give thanks to God for his great benefit, in that you have taken upon you this state of wedlock; and pray you instantly that Almighty God may luckily defend and maintain you therein, that neither you be overcome with any temptations, nor with any adversity. But, before all things, take good heed that you give no occasion to the devil to let° and hinder your prayers by discord and dissension. For there is no stronger defense and stay in all our life than is prayer, in the which we may call for the help of God, and obtain it; whereby we may win his blessing, his grace, his defense and

---

interaffairs: a business transaction between two parties.   of your parts: given your abilities.
chance: happen.   otherwhiles: sometimes.   nigh: near, accessible.   let: prevent.

protection, so to continue therein to a better life to come; which grant us He that died for us all, to whom be all honor and praise, forever and ever. Amen.

→ ROBERT SNAWSEL

From *A Looking Glass for Married Folks* *1610*

In an "Epistle to the Reader" with which he begins his book, Snawsel explains that he took it upon himself to seek a remedy for the discord between husbands and wives. Snawsel attributes this discord to no more than ignorance, yet suggests that its consequences are profound:

> many have lived ignorantly, and so of necessity wickedly and discontentedly together, to the dishonor of God, the offense and evil example of others, the loss of their credits, the wasting of their goods, the corrupting of their children and servants; and finally to the consuming of their own bodies; yea, many to the destroying of their souls forevermore. (A3v)

Snawsel proposes to rectify this ignorance, and thereby prevent disaster, by writing a book about how spouses, particularly wives, should conduct themselves. His claim that "there was no book extant of this subject in English" (A3v) can hardly be true. Numerous sermons and treatises on marriage already existed.

In fact, Snawsel's own text translates and expands a Latin dialogue called *Conjugium* or "Marriage" (1523) by Desiderius Erasmus, a Dutch Renaissance humanist. Snawsel acknowledges this debt, and explains that, since Erasmus's dialogue had already been published in an (anonymous) English translation as *A Merry Dialogue, Declaring the Properties of Shrewd Shrews, and Honest Wives* (1557), he will offer more than a translation.[3] While Erasmus's dialogue occurs between two women, Snawsel adds two other women, a husband, and some discussion of husbands' duties. Snawsel was also concerned that readers "might attain to all that which [Erasmus] counselleth there, and yet

---

[3] Hosley argues that Erasmus's *A Merry Dialogue* was a source for *The Taming of the Shrew* (172–74). See also Wayne, Introduction to Tilney 29–32.

Robert Snawsel, *A Looking Glass for Married Folks, Wherein They May Plainly See Their Deformities; and also How to Behave Themselves One to Another, and Both of Them Towards God. Set Forth Dialogue-Wise for . . . Plainness's Sake* (London, 1610), C–C3, Dv–D5v. There is also an inside title which differs slightly from that on the title page. It is "A Looking Glass for Married Folks, or A Profitable Conference, Between Four Women and One Man, Touching Their Behaviors toward God and Their Husbands, and What They Ought to Be; and also the Duty of Husbands, toward Their Wives."

be damned." Therefore, he "added thereunto the substance of faith and repentance" (A4v). The text that resulted was published in 1610, 1619, and 1631. Although Erasmus's dialogue was available considerably earlier than Snawsel's adaptation and therefore might have been known to Shakespeare, I have chosen to include Snawsel's later elaboration on Erasmus because, by including more voices, Snawsel offers a more noisy and contentious dramatization of debates over marriage. Erasmus provided the dramatic scenario — a conversation between an honest wife and a shrew in the course of which the shrew comes to see the error of her ways; but Snawsel's characters are so fully developed, and their conversation is so animated that this "dialogue" is almost indistinguishable from a playscript. As Wayne has argued, "the dialogue form, whether in a colloquy or transposed to the drama, was especially appropriate for exploring a subject that was being revised and contested as it had never been before" (Wayne, Introduction to Tilney 38). Snawsel's *A Looking Glass for Married Folks* also demonstrates both the influence of early humanists, such as Erasmus, on later Protestant approaches to marriage, and the shifting emphases in post-Reformation writings; for instance, Snawsel adds to Erasmus the expectation that spouses should be partners who strive together toward mutual "faith and repentance." Finally, looking at the later text helps us see the enduring popularity of stories about the reform of unruly wives. A dialogue first written in Latin, and thus for learned readers, in 1523, finds an even wider audience in English a century later.

In Snawsel's version, the most active interlocutors are Erasmus's original pair: Eulalie, whose name identifies her as "well-spoken," and Xanthippe, a scold; Margery, a character Snawsel introduces, and whom he identifies as "a proud malapert" (a presumptuous or impudent person), often bursts into the conversation. Like Erasmus's dialogue, Snawsel's text attempts to imagine a possibility we do not see in *The Taming of the Shrew* — a conversation among women which men do not stage, enter, or witness. As you read these passages, you might try to imagine a conversation among Bianca, the widow, and Katharine after the last scene of *The Taming of the Shrew*. Obviously, the women's voices in *A Looking Glass for Married Folks* are no more authentic than are the female characters' voices in *The Taming of the Shrew*. These are still voices created by a male author; it can even be argued that Snawsel represents female privacy in part for the prurient or voyeuristic pleasure of male readers (Fleming). The women's conversation also works to convince wives who scold and fight to stop doing so; that is, its purpose is to reform a "terrible mannish woman" who insists on reminding her husband that he has "met and meddled with his match." But while we cannot take Snawsel's text as evidence of what married women really thought and felt, or how they might have talked to one another when alone, we can read it as evidence of how — and why — women's voices and conversations were imagined and represented.

Whatever else the text accomplishes, it presents the complex status of women's speech during this period. For if women are simply supposed to be silent, then texts like Snawsel's, which are woven almost entirely from their voices, could not exist. On the one hand, Snawsel presents the conventional indictment of shrewish, or scolding and nagging, speech. By naming the recalcitrant wife Xanthippe, Snawsel, like Erasmus before him, links her to the prototypical shrew, the wife of Socrates. In *The Taming of the Shrew*, for instance, Petruchio promises Hortensio that even if Katharine were "as curst and shrewd / As Socrates' Xanthippe" he would still court and wed her (1.2.60–70); "A Homily of the State of Matrimony" (p. 172) and *A Juniper Lecture* also retell the story of Socrates and Xanthippe. On the other hand, in her efforts to turn Xanthippe from a shrew into a good wife, Eulalie, whose very name focuses on her speech, dominates the text with her preaching, as Katharine dominates the stage in her final sermon on marriage in *The Taming of the Shrew*. In telling the history of her own transformation into a good wife, Eulalie explains that she prayed to God that he "would set a watch before my lips, lest I should offend in my tongue." She does this because she realizes the power of her speech not only to do harm, but to do good:

> though my tongue be one of the least members of my body, yet if it were not rightly used, I might offend the most by it; I might much displease my husband, and hurt my neighbors, and destroy my own body and soul forever. . . . And on the other side, if my tongue were rightly ordered, I might much glorify God, beautify his Gospel, and adorn my Christian profession; speak in the behalf, and for the credit of my husband, and for the good of my neighbors; and therefore I prayed unto God, that he would open the door of my mouth, and give me utterance and wisdom, that when I speak, my words might be directed by his Spirit, to put life and power into them, and season them with wisdom, and to make them forcible,[4] gracious, and savory[5] in the ears of the hearers. So that to conclude, always after I would be careful what, and when to speak, the manner how, and to whom, yielding that reverence to my husband, that is due to him. (C5–C5v)

Eulalie's remarks suggest that the many efforts to control women's speech in this period assumed not that women's speech was worthless or trivial but, instead, that it was powerful, sometimes dangerous. Eulalie's goal is not to silence herself, but to govern her speech; through speech, rather than silence, she reforms her husband, redeems her marriage, and teaches Xanthippe, thus the reader, how to be a good wife.

To the extent that *A Looking Glass* has a plot, that plot revolves around the education of Xanthippe. This shrew, though, is tamed not by her husband, but by another woman. Furthermore, Eulalie instructs and reforms Xanthippe by

---

[4] **forcible:** forceful, strong, convincing.
[5] **savory:** agreeable, pleasing.

narrating how she tamed her own husband. In this text taming is not what husbands do to wives, but rather what wives do to husbands. Rather than waste her time in violent, yet ultimately pointless, resistance, Xanthippe should learn to tame her husband "by gentle handling" (E). Since Xanthippe had the patience to teach her parrot to speak, "doth it seem irksome and tedious unto you to take some pains to make your husband a good man?" (E5). Eulalie continues: "You have heard how great pains men take to break their horses, and what curious means and devices they use to tame Lions, Bulls, and Elephants:[6] and shall we think much to take a little pains to have good husbands?" (E5). Suggesting that wifely obedience is a performance, and that submission is an effective, if somewhat duplicitous, means of gaining control in a marriage, Eulalie argues that the wife can best achieve happiness by convincing her husband of his importance and of her own obedience. The methods for doing so are familiar from *The Taming of the Shrew*: the wife should mirror her husband's moods, refrain from public complaint, and suffer silently and privately. Despite its emphasis on taming husbands as if they were animals, the text assumes that it is women who must compromise, women who must change. The text concludes with Xanthippe and Ben-Ezer happily reconciled; yet, while both have been instructed, it is Xanthippe's new humility that Eulalie, and the text, struggle most earnestly to achieve.

A Looking Glass for Married Folks

[The women have been discussing their desire to dress fashionably. Xanthippe complains that her husband is too cheap to allow her to do so; she also complains that he is often drunk, and a disgusting bedfellow. In the discussion that follows, she describes the current state of her relationship to her husband.]

MARGERY: But do you rattle him up° at his coming home?

XANTHIPPE: Yes, I handle him as he deserves; I make him know that I have a tongue in my head.

MARGERY: And what saith he again?

XANTHIPPE: At the first, he is as loud as I, thinking to bear me down with great words.

MARGERY: But do you never fall from scolding to scuffling?

XANTHIPPE: Once we were fallen out so far, that a little more would have made us fight outright. He got up a great cudgel, and shaked it at me, threatening me with thundering speeches.

---

[6] At this point in Erasmus's *A Merry Dialogue* Xanthippe interjects, "Such a beast have I at home" (255).

rattle him up: scold or yell at him loudly.

EULALIE: Oh, lamentable living between man and wife!

MARGERY: Wast thou not afraid then, Xanthippe?

XANTHIPPE: Afraid? No! On the other side, I took up the trivet;° and if
he had but touched me with a finger, he should well have seen and felt,
that I would have laid about me lustily with both my hands.

MARGERY: I promise you, I commend you for your manly courage; you
had got a new kind of target° when you had the trivet; you did but lack
your distaff° instead of a javelin.°

XANTHIPPE: I would have made him have known that he had met and
meddled with his match.

EULALIE: Oh, neighbor, this should not be so.

XANTHIPPE: What tell you me of it? If he will not use me as his wife, I
will not entreat him as my husband.

EULALIE: But Paul, as I said before, teacheth, that wives should be in
subjection to their husbands with all reverence, and not to be check-
mates with them; and Peter sets down Sarah for an example to women,
who called her husband "lord."°

MARGERY: We have heard of these things before as well as you. But the
same Paul, I trow,° teacheth, that husbands should love their wives, as
Christ did his Church.

XANTHIPPE: Well, let him first do his duty, and then I will do mine.

EULALIE: But yet when the case stands thus, I think it is the wife's part
to yield first to her husband.

XANTHIPPE: Husband! . . . Marry, in good time, if he be a husband that
makes no more account of me than of his kitchen girl.

MARGERY: But, in kindness, Xanthippe, tell me: did he, when you stood
so stoutly to him, leave off to threaten you blows?

XANTHIPPE: Did he? Yes! And it was best for him, too, I trow, or else,
as I am an honest woman, I swear to you I would have belabored my
fellow well and soundly.

EULALIE: Oh, terrible mannish woman! I did not think that thou hadst
been of such a peremptory spirit. Thou dost not remember that he hath
power over thee, and that thou shouldst let thy desire be subject to thy
husband's.

---

trivet: a stand for a pot or kettle, often standing on three legs.   target: shield.   distaff: a staff
used for winding wool for spinning, that is, a tool traditionally associated with women's domestic work.   javelin: a light spear, that is, a weapon traditionally associated with men's military exploits.   Peter . . . "lord": Note that Eulalie cites the same passages discussed in *A
Homily of the State of Matrimony* (p. 177).   trow: trust.

MARGERY: It was well done, Xanthippe! Hold him out still at stave's° end. Yield him not an inch, lest he take an ell.° Let him not crow over thee.

EULALIE: You need not give her such wicked counsel. What, will you have all the world to exclaim on our sex, and cry out upon womankind?

MARGERY: Why, none but men will speak against us; and if they do, we can give them two words for one in the hottest manner.

EULALIE: Methought you said your husband left his threatening. Methinks, then, Xanthippe, in all equity and conscience, you should cease your scolding.

XANTHIPPE: I mind not to leave it yet.

MARGERY: What does he, I pray thee, whilst thou art scolding?

XANTHIPPE: What? Sometimes he sleeps, slug as he is; sometimes he falls a-laughing; sometimes he takes his fiddle, which hath scarce three strings, and thereon he strikes with his fiddling stick as loud as he can, that he may therewith drown the noise of me.

MARGERY: I am sure this behavior of his angers thee to the heart.

XANTHIPPE: It grieves me indeed to the very guts, and I so chafe sometimes that I can hardly hold my hands.

EULALIE: I pray you, good neighbor, hold your tongue, and give me leave to speak my mind a little to you.

XANTHIPPE: Say on heartily, and speak your pleasure.

EULALIE: You shall be as bold with me when you please; methinks we two for old acquaintance sake should be very bold and familiar one with another.

XANTHIPPE: You say true. For truly we have been playfellows from our cradles; and of all that ever I had, there was none that ever I loved better than you.

EULALIE: Well then, this I say in love that I have towards you still, and my request is even as you love me, to hearken unto me. You are married now unto your husband, what manner of man soever he be; you have no liberty to change him for another, or cast him off. In old time, indeed, when couples could not agree, divorcement was permitted and appointed as an extreme remedy, but now that is quite abolished. Ben-Ezer must be your husband, and you, Xanthippe, his wife, till one of you die.

XANTHIPPE: A vengeance on them, whosoever they be, that have taken away that law and liberty from us.

---

stave: a stick, especially a heavy one that might be used as a weapon. **ell:** a measure of length; forty-five inches in England.

[Eulalie points out that it is Christ's pleasure that it should be so, but Xanthippe cannot believe this. If a wife cannot exchange one husband for another, Xanthippe wonders whether she can transform the husband she is stuck with into a new man. Eulalie assures her that she can, and that she herself has done so. Below, Eulalie describes how she reformed her once contentious marriage.]

EULALIE: When he [her husband] looked at any time very sad, and there were no fit time to speak to him, I would not then laugh and dally with him, and play the tomboy, as many women are wont to do in such a case. But I put upon me a sad countenance also, and looked heavily. For even as a looking glass, if it be a good one, doth show the countenance of him that glasses himself° in it, so it beseems an honest wife to frame herself to her husband's affection, and not to be merry when he is melancholy, nor jocund when he is sad, much less fleer° when he is angry. And if at any time he were stirred, I would either pacify him with gentle speech, or give way to his wrath, till it were somewhat allayed. Or else I would keep silence, till there were fit time for clearing myself, or advising him with reverence and discretion. This course also I took: if at any time he came drunken home, I would not then for anything have give[n] him a foul word, but I would cause his bed to be made very soft and easy, that he might sleep the better, and by fair speeches get him to it.

MARGERY: Here are fetters for the legs, and yokes for the necks of women! Must they crouch in this manner to their currish and swinish husbands? If I had such a one, as he behaved himself like a swine, so I would use him like a beast.

EULALIE: I had thought we had been rid of your company.

MARGERY: I stood behind, and heard you so long, that I could no longer hold my peace. Are you a woman, and make them such dishclouts and slaves to their husbands? Came you of a woman, that you should give them no prerogative, but make them altogether underlings?

EULALIE: I pray you be patient. I have not spoke nor counselled anything but what I have done myself. And I have done nothing but that which is warranted by the word of God.

MARGERY: I hope the word of God doth show men their duties to wives, as well as the wives toward their husbands.

EULALIE: It is so; but first we must show the one, before we can do the other.

---

glasses himself: looks at himself in the mirror. **fleer:** sneer, grimace, mock or laugh at, ridicule.

MARGERY: You should have begun with the men first.

EULALIE: It might haply have been somewhat tedious, and women mostly are so fickle, and will find themselves so many things to do, and are so soon weary of hearing and reading any good thing, that they would scarce stay to hear the beginning of their duty. Therefore, I thought best to begin with them first.

MARGERY: Trust me, you are a small friend to your own sex.

EULALIE: More than you are to your own self. For you are ignorant and careless of that good which you might have by your husband, if you would be loving and submissive to him.

MARGERY: Tell not me of the good which I may have by my submission. For this is the truth of it, I care not though he heard me: I never mean to have my neck brought under his girdle, but I will rather make him buckle and bend unto me, or else he shall have an unquiet life.

EULALIE: It is true, indeed, that many such as you are will have their husbands bend and crouch unto them. But how seemly or warrantable° this is, let everyone judge. It is neither for the woman's credit nor profit, when the stream runs with violence this way. What a horrible sin is it, that the woman should usurp the man's authority, and the poor man dares not do anything, but what his wife will? And as she saith, so it must be, or else the house will not hold her, neither will she look upon him without lumping° and louring.° And if any describe the ugliness of her countenance in the time of her anger, she will scarce be friends with them. Oh therefore, oh therefore, that these masterly dames would but glass themselves, that they might see their rugged brows, their fiery eyes, pouting mouths, their black and poisoned tongues, which utter horrible blasphemies both against God and men, especially against their husbands, whom they should love most dearly. So here is the cause why many men think it their greatest wisdom to possess their souls in patience, and to pass by many grievances in our sex. Only this is the refuge of those that are godly, to comfort themselves in the Lord their God. Therefore, well saith Solomon: "It is better to live in the wilderness with a dinner of green herbs, than to have a stalled ox, or to live in a wide house with a contentious woman."

MARGERY: I will be sworn, if there were but three or four more here, if they were of my mind, we would teach you how to defame and shame us in this manner.

---

warrantable: permissible, praiseworthy, agreeable.   lumping: looking sulky or disagreeable. louring: frowning, scowling.

EULALIE: You defame and shame yourselves. I only show what shrews are, and those that will neither be ruled by God nor their husbands. As he that toucheth not pitch shall not be defiled, so she that is not of this stock and lineage is not blamed.

XANTHIPPE: Let her alone, good Eulalie, and tell me how did you after your husband was in bed.

EULALIE: When his stomach was emptied, and he [had] come to himself, when he was not stirred in his affections, nor troubled with other actions, but he and I alone, either in bed, or in some convenient place, I would gently admonish him, or rather entreat him, that he would have a care of the health of his body, and to avoid that sin, to be overcome with drink; telling him of such young men, yea, gallant gentlemen as he knew, who got surfeits° by so overcharging their stomachs. Also, with weeping eyes I would entreat him to have a care of his estate and credit, children and servants, lest the one should be undone by his spending their portions, and the other by following his unseemly course of life. This was the manner of my proceeding with him, seasoning my speeches in the best manner, that they might not be distasted but digested of him. Also sometimes I was wont to use a preface, and make him promise me that he would have patience with me, if I, a simple woman, should put him in mind of something that might tend to his credit or welfare any way. And when I had told him my mind, I would break off that talk, and fall into some other more delightful to him. For, gossip° Xanthippe, I may say to you that this is the weakness of us women, that when we have begun to speak, we are so talkative and full of words, that we wot° not when to leave.°

XANTHIPPE: It is the pleasure of men indeed so to say of us, who have no better sport than to speak of and report our infirmities. But say on, I pray you.

EULALIE: I had also a special care of this, that I would not find fault with my husband for anything, in anybody's presence, nor complain of him abroad. A matter is soon amended that is but between two, and not blazed abroad. But if the matter be of such a nature that it cannot well be holpen° by the wife's counsel, it is a seemlier course that the wife make complaint to her husband's parents, or some of his kindred, rather than to her own; and also that she moderate her complaint and temper

---

got surfeits: made themselves sick through overindulgence.   **gossip:** friend. A *gossip* was originally a godmother at the christening of a baby or a female friend of the mother invited to be present at the birth. It then came to mean simply a friend, as here. It could also mean a person who delights in idle talk of the kind that we still call "gossip," thus associating plentiful but inconsequential speech not only with women but with women's friendships. **wot:** know.   **leave:** leave off, stop.   **holpen:** helped.

her speech so that she may seem not to hate her husband's person, but only his ill conditions. Neither let her blab out all, that . . . when her husband comes to hear of it by his friends, that she hath spoken of his faults with the least, he may be forced to acknowledge his wife's courtesy and kind dealing, and say, as Saul did of David, "She is more righteous than I."

XANTHIPPE: She had need be an Academic, and brought up in their schools and University, that should skill° to do this as you have set down.

EULALIE: By this means, we shall draw our husbands to show us the like kindness.

XANTHIPPE: There are some husbands, whom no gentle entreaty will do any good.

EULALIE: Truly I think there are few or none such. But say there be. First of all, as I have said before, the husband must be borne, endured, and dwelled with, though never so wretched and wicked, even a devil incarnate. Therefore, it is far better to bear with one like ourselves, or that may be bettered by our courteous carriage, than one that will be [made] worse everyday than other, by our overthwart and crabbed behavior.

skill: understand, know how.

The "Feme Covert": Married Women's Legal Status

In *The Taming of the Shrew* marriage negotiations and property settlements occur between men. Men bargain over women; women are not officially parties to the contracts. Although Bianca maneuvers to attain her own choice, the play is most interested in Katharine and Petruchio, whose marriage seems to be contracted between father and groom rather than bride and groom. Once Petruchio and Katharine marry, Petruchio monopolizes the couple's material resources (food, domestic space, clothing, money), and can restrict his wife's access even to subsistence. It is further assumed by everyone in the play except Katharine herself that Petruchio has the right, even the responsibility, to "tame" her; at the end of the play the other male characters warmly congratulate him for his success. Petruchio is also a more fully developed character than Katharine is. He has more lines; he addresses the audience directly several times, whereas we never see Katharine alone; and his self-justifying speeches are balanced against her puzzling silences and unexplained reversals.

This dramatic situation, in which the husband monopolizes resources and dominates the stage, has its parallel in the legal relation between husband and wife during this period. At marriage, husband and wife became one legal agent — the husband — by means of the husband's "subsumption" of his wife into himself (Laslett 20). In this process the wife became a "feme covert," meaning that she was "veiled, as it were, clouded and overshadowed" (T. E. I7). This phenomenon, then, enacted legally the figural understanding of marriage as a process by which husband and wife became "one flesh." An unmarried woman (or "feme sole") had approximately the same legal rights and responsibilities as a man; she could own and sell property, bequeath her property by will, make contracts, sue and be sued (Greenberg 172). But through marriage a woman conferred many of these rights and responsibilities onto her husband, who exercised them for her; she could not regain them except as a widow. In practice, this had various consequences. If a married woman wished to bring a suit for injury, she had to do so jointly with her husband; anyone who wished to sue her had also to sue her husband (Greenberg 173–74). A married woman was not liable for most misdemeanors she might commit; instead, her husband, as the corporate legal agent representing them both, would be held accountable for her actions.

The wife emerged from coverture into full legal responsibility when her husband ("her stern, her *primus motor*, without whom she cannot do much at home, and less abroad") died or deserted her, or when she committed a serious crime on her own. "In matters criminal and capital causes, a Feme covert shall answer without her husband" (T. E. O6v, O7v); that is, a married woman was individually accountable for any felonies she committed alone. As Belsey explains, "women became capable while and only while they had no husbands, but were always accountable" (153).

Rather than efface all married women's legal rights, coverture led in practice to curious contradictions. A woman could appear in court as her husband's attorney, but a married woman could not be a plaintiff in a lawsuit about her own property or about her own business, even if she ran that business with her husband's consent (Hogrefe 99; Greenberg 173). Similarly, although a married woman could not usually make a will without her husband's consent, she could act as his executor for even the largest estates (Hogrefe 99–100).

While a woman lost certain property rights through marriage, she gained others. She might receive a marriage settlement or "jointure" at the time of marriage; this property she would hold jointly with her husband while he lived, but it would be promised to her if she were widowed. After her husband's death, the jointure became the wife's property absolutely, and she could bequeath it to others as she chose. Although only some women received a jointure, every wife was entitled to her "dower" at her husband's death; this was one-third of his personal property if he died without a will but with an heir; one-half if he died without an heir. A wife held her dower for her life but could not bequeath it to anyone else. Her husband could not deprive her of her right to dower in his will, nor could he convey it to someone else except with her consent. The wife could, however, lose her dower if her husband committed treason or if she eloped with another man (Greenberg 174; Hogrefe 100–03; Kermode and Walker 191–92; Laurence, ch. 15). Her husband might also leave her additional money or property in his will.

→ T. E.

From *The Law's Resolutions of Women's Rights* *1632*

In *The Law's Resolutions of Women's Rights*, a reference work for women pieced together out of various legal treatises, the compiler, known only as T. E., begins at the very beginning, with Creation.[7] He lets the two distinct versions of the creation story and their different implications stand side by side. First, he explains that God created man and woman simultaneously, granting them "joint sovereignty" over the other creatures. Then he describes the creation of woman after and out of man. In this version woman is not a joint sovereign but "a help and companion," whom Adam names as he names the other creatures. In these two juxtaposed narratives we can see one source of the enduring tension between incompatible models for marriage: either an equal partnership or a hierarchical relation. T. E. explicitly links the idea of Eve in the second Creation account, as bone of Adam's bones and flesh of his flesh, to married women's subsequent legal status as "either none or no more than half a person." Yet he also acknowledges the corporate legal personhood of husband and wife as a "fiction of Law," a fiction to which there are exceptions in both theory and practice. Unable to leave Genesis yet, T. E. offers one more explanation for married women's limited legal rights. Like Kate in her final speech in *The Taming of a Shrew*, he depicts women's subjection as a punishment for Eve's transgression; yet he challenges the etymology for "woman" as the "woe of man" that Kate uses in *A Shrew*. Claiming that the Law "shaketh hands with Divinity," he begins his treatise with the claim that law is grounded in an in-

[7] The title page explains that this text was compiled by "I. L." but revised by "T. E." "T. E." is commonly referred to as the author.

T. E., *The Law's Resolutions of Women's Rights, or The Law's Provision for Women* (London, 1632), Book 1, B2–B3v; Book 3, K–Kv. Each book is paginated separately.

evitable, divinely ordained gender hierarchy, and thus, that neither the law nor that hierarchy can be challenged or changed.

Acknowledging that women may be frustrated by their strictly circumscribed legal rights, T. E. suggests that they find their own unofficial ways of getting around the limitations: "I know no remedy, though some women can shift it well enough" (p. 198). In pursuing their desire within the constraints of marriage — which seems, at least theoretically, to cancel them as persons — married women are represented as "shifting it," as managing a demanding, repressive situation by bending, if not breaking, the rules. Married women are thus "covert" both in that they are subsumed by their husbands and in that they are stealthy, sly maneuverers within that subsumption.

In a passage lifted almost verbatim from Sir Thomas Smith's *De Republica Anglorum: The Manner of Government or Policy of the Realm of England* (London, 1583), T. E. describes at length how women can maximize their authority and options, and manage their husbands.

> Though our law may seem somewhat rigorous towards wives, yet for the most part, they can handle their husbands so well and doucely [sweetly], specially when they be sick, that where the law gives them nothing, their husbands at their death of their good will give them all, and few there be that be not either made sole or chief executor of the husband's last will and testament, having for the most part the government of the children and their portions. (T. E. Rv)

Thus even this encyclopedia of women's rights assumes a disparity between legal theory and practice; it also acknowledges, perhaps even encourages, women's ingenious ways of asserting themselves within an unchangeable subsumption. This strategy resembles that depicted in ballads about bossy women and marriages turned upside down. As Joy Wiltenburg points out, this message

> is a two-edged sword, offering women the satisfaction of feeling in control — and of exercising some control at the level of individual interaction — and discouraging them from seeking to disturb the hierarchy itself. [Women] are also encouraged to view their de facto power as a sort of inside joke: men's pretensions are debunked, but in the process female power is defined as comic. (Wiltenburg 101)

Wiltenburg's insight into the comic nature of the strategy that T. E. calls "shifting it" points toward the relationship between an encyclopedia of women's rights and a comedy such as *The Taming of the Shrew*. Just as some productions have Katharine wink broadly as she delivers her sermon on wifely submission and some critics see her submission as strategic, this seemingly sober, didactic work by T. E. offers married women unofficial possibilities. Illegible on the surface of legal theory or of Katharine's speech, they must be read between the lines.

The Law's Resolutions of Women's Rights

BOOK I

Section 2. The Creation of Man and Woman

God, the first day when he created the World, made the matter of it, separating light from darkness. The second day, he placed the firmament,° which he called Heaven, betwixt the waters above the firmament and the waters under the firmament. The third day, he segregated the waters under the firmament into one place, calling the waters Seas and the dry land Earth, which he commanded to bring forth fructifying herbs, plants, and trees. The fourth day, he made the Sun, the Moon, and the Stars in the firmament to be for signs, seasons, days, and years, and to give light upon the earth. The fifth day, he made by his Word the fishes of the sea, whales, and every feathered fowl of the air, commanding them to increase. The sixth day, he made cattle, creeping things, the beasts of the earth. And now, having made all things that should be needful for them, he created Man; Male and Female made he them, bidding them multiply and replenish the earth, and take joint sovereignty over the fishes of the sea, the fowls of the air, and over all beasts moving upon the earth (Genesis 1).

In the second chapter, Moses declareth and expresseth the Creation of Woman, which word in good sense signifieth not the woe of Man, as some affirm, but with Man. For so in our hasty pronouncing we turn the preposition "with" to "woe" or "we," oftentimes. And so she was ordained to be with Man as a help and a companion, because God saw it was not good that Man should be alone. Then when God brought Woman to Man to be named by him, he found straightway that she was bone of his bones, flesh of his flesh, giving her a name, testifying she was taken out of Man. And he pronounced that for her sake Man should leave Father and Mother and adhere to his Wife which should be with him one.

Now Man and Woman Are One

Now because Adam hath so pronounced that man and wife shall be but one flesh, and our Law is that if a feoffment° be made jointly to John at Stile and to Thomas Noke and his wife of three acres of land that Thomas and his wife get no more but one acre and a half, *quia una persona;°* and a writ of conspiracy doth not lie against one only, and that is the reason . . . a writ

---

firmament: the sky or heavens.   feoffment: an endowment or transfer of land, often with some conditions.   *quia una persona:* because they are one person (at law).

of conspiracy doth not lie against baron and feme,° for they are but one person. And by this a married women perhaps may either doubt whether she be either none or no more than half a person. But let her be of good cheer. Though for the near conjunction which is between man and wife, and to tie them to a perfect love, agreement, and adherence, they be by intent and wise fiction of Law, one person, yet in nature and in some other cases by the Law of God and Man, they remain divers.° For as Adam's punishment was several° from Eve's, so in criminal and other special causes our Law argues them several persons. . . . Seeing therefore I list° not to doubt with Plato whether women be reasonable or unreasonable creatures, I may not doubt but every woman is a temporal person, though no woman can be a spiritual vicar.

[Here follows a paragraph discussing how hermaphrodites fit into this creation account, and what their legal status might be.]

Section 3. The Punishment of Adam's Sin

Return a little to Genesis, in the third Chapter whereof is declared our first parents' transgression in eating the forbidden fruit, for which Adam, Eve, the serpent first, and lastly, the earth itself, is cursed. And besides the participation of Adam's punishment, which was subjection to mortality, exiled from the garden of Eden, enjoined to labor, Eve, because she had helped to seduce her husband, hath inflicted on her an especial bane.° "In sorrow shalt thou bring forth thy children; thy desires shall be subject to thy husband, and he shall rule over thee."

See here the reason of that which I touched before, that women have no voice in Parliament; they make no laws; they consent to none; they abrogate none. All of them are understood either married or to be married, and their desires subject to their husband. I know no remedy, though some women can shift it well enough. The Common Law here shaketh hand[s] with Divinity.

BOOK 3

Section 8. That Which the Husband Hath Is His Own

But the prerogative of the husband is best discerned in his dominion over all extern° things in which the wife by combination° divesteth herself of propriety° in some sort, and casteth it upon her governor. For here practice

---

baron and feme: husband and wife. If one spouse is indicted for conspiracy, the other is also assumed to be implicated. This is the reason that a woman lost her dower if her husband was convicted of treason; she was assumed to have been complicit. **divers:** different, not alike. **several:** separate. **list:** choose, desire. **bane:** curse, woe, undesirable fate. **extern:** external. **combination:** marriage. **propriety:** property.

everywhere agrees with the Theoric of Law, and forcing necessity submits women to the affection thereof. Whatsoever the husband had before coverture either in goods or lands, it is absolutely his own; the wife hath therein no seisin° at all. If anything when he is married be given him, he taketh it by himself distinctly to himself.

If a man have right and title to enter into lands, and the tenant enfeoff° the baron and feme, the wife taketh nothing. . . . The very goods which a man giveth to his wife are still his own. Her chain, her bracelets, her apparel, are all the goodman's goods. . . . A wife how gallant soever she be, glistereth but in the riches of her husband, as the moon hath no light, but it is the sun's. Yea, and her Phoebe borroweth sometime her own proper light from Phoebus.°

Section 9. That Which the Wife Hath Is the Husband's

For thus it is: if before marriage, the woman were possessed of horses, neat,° sheep, corn, wool, money, plate,° and jewels, all manner of moveable substance is presently by conjunction° the husband's to sell, keep, or bequeath if he die. And though he bequeath them not, yet are they the husband's executor's and not the wife's which brought them to her husband.

---

seisin: possession, claim to ownership.   enfeoff: give or transfer land, often with some conditions.   Phoebus: a name for Apollo, the sun god. Phoebe is a female form of that name.   neat: an ox or bullock, cow or heifer.   plate: silver or gold dishes or utensils, or coins or bullion.   conjunction: marriage.

CHAPTER 3

The Household: Authority and Violence

―――――――――――――――――⟩⟨――――――――――――――――――

The Household

In sixteenth- and seventeenth-century England, as in the fictional world depicted in Shakespeare's *The Taming of the Shrew*, social life was organized around households. Households were not only buildings — the places in which people lived and worked in relation to others — but also communities. In these communities the good of the individual and the good of the whole were assumed to be the same; they were governments in miniature, in which some ruled and others served. In *The Taming of the Shrew* Katharine moves from her father's house to her husband's house; these are the play's two main locations. The play does not offer any alternative arena of action not owned and run by men.

The taming plot itself is also Katharine's journey from one household to the other (and back again). Petruchio tames in greatest earnest once he reaches his own household, where he controls Katharine's access to basic sustenance and commands a staff of servants. Katharine's last speech gestures toward other arenas of action for men — who risk discomfort and danger "by sea and land" in order to support their wives who lie "warm at home" — but in the staged action, men and women alike take all their risks and fight all their battles at home. In its busy cast of servants, the play also reminds us that the inhabitants of the sixteenth- and seventeenth-century household extended beyond the married couple and their children to include guests, relatives, and servants. Besides those servants who lived in the house — preparing and serving food, cleaning, pulling off muddy boots, and so on — there were frequent visitors such as tailors, tutors, and music teachers.

Households were usually presided over by men. Although few women ran households, they could wield some power, impose discipline, manage resources, and contribute valued, skilled work in households. Not many people lived alone; most were attached to a household, where they both lived and worked. Laws that discouraged vagrancy and made poverty a crime reinforced the household as the basic social unit and punished those who were "masterless" and unattached.

The household was considered a small model of the larger society, a seminary that prepared children and servants for their roles in public life. Intimately connected to, rather than separate from, public, political life, the household was understood as the foundation of social order; disorder in the household led to disorder in the society at large. It was also the most basic unit of production and the most important work site for women. As a result, the stakes of governing a household were high. Household governors had to control and discipline their subordinates (wives, children, and servants), using violence when necessary to assert and maintain their authority. Since few laws existed to regulate the master's use of his power, prescriptive texts such as conduct books and sermons intervened to convince men to exercise *self*-control. While these texts sketch out a broad area of domestic authority and power for men who head households, they also insist on the limits of this authority as well as the responsibility that must accompany and constrain it.

→ JOHN DOD and ROBERT CLEAVER

From *A Godly Form of Household Government* 1621

The contents of this book were "first gathered by R.C." (of uncertain identity but possibly Robert Cleaver) and later "newly perused, amended, and augmented by John Dod and Robert Cleaver," as the title page of later editions explains. Although Dod and Cleaver are now widely referred to as the authors, this process demonstrates the collaboration through which books about personal conduct were produced. Who is the author of *A Godly Form of Household Government?* The unidentified "R.C.," who "gathered" it, Dod and Cleaver,

---

John Dod and Robert Cleaver, *A Godly Form of Household Government: For the Ordering of Private Families According to the Direction of God's Word* (London, 1621), A7, A8–B, L6v–L7.

who "perused, amended, and augmented" it, or both? Was it written, or, as these verbs suggest, assembled? Issues of authorship are further complicated by the fact that many domestic conduct books borrowed from and repeated one another, blurring distinctions between one author's perspective and another's, one book and another. Whatever process produced it, however, *A Godly Form of Household Government* was one of the most popular conduct books published in this period. In various forms it was published twice in 1598 and seven more times up to 1630.

Of the various names on the title page, it is easiest to find information about John Dod, a clergyman who held an office in the Church of England. After frequent warnings Dod was suspended from his post in 1604 for nonconformity (departures from orthodox Anglican doctrine). Dod's career, in its crudest outlines, reveals the intolerance of the Anglican church, the conflicts over doctrine and practice in which dissenters from the church engaged, and the serious consequences of these conflicts. In the course of the seventeenth century, these conflicts had further-reaching reverberations. Attempts to reform and "purify" the church in England contributed to tensions among Parliament, the king, and his court; these tensions, in turn, helped fuel the civil war that broke out in 1642. Dissenters from the Anglican church, now commonly called Puritans, also emigrated to the colonies in America.

The excerpts from *A Godly Form of Household Government* presented below demonstrate the "analogical" habit of thought in sixteenth- and seventeenth-century England.[1] Emphasizing parallels, equivalencies, or correspondences, analogies were used to explain one thing in reference or relation to another. For instance, in the passages included here, the household and its government are explained by analogy to the commonwealth or, according to the *Oxford English Dictionary*, "the whole body of people constituting a nation or state, the body politic." According to this analogy, the household *is* a little commonwealth; its inhabitants are divided into governors and those who must be ruled (or subjects). Both household and commonwealth are assumed to be not only hierarchical but also patriarchal — the ultimate authority in the household is the husband, father, and master. Servants and children are the subordinates or subjects who must be "held in by the bridle of government." The wife is both a governor, with authority over servants and children, and her husband's subordinate. Even as a governor she acts as her husband's "fellow-helper" (B2): "the husband, without any exception, is master over all the house, and hath more to do in his house with his own domestical affairs, than the magistrate. The wife is ruler over all other things, but yet under her husband" (p. 206). Gesturing toward a distinct sphere of domestic authority for women and assigning duties and responsibilities to all members of the little household commonwealth, Dod and Cleaver suggest that domestic relations were reciprocal

---

[1] On the analogical habit of thought, see Amussen, *Ordered Society*, and Orlin, *Private Matters*, ch. 2.

and interdependent rather than rigidly divided between dominance and submission. They also suggest that masters had obligations to, as well as authority over, their dependents. The "chief-governor" should be neither "lordly" (or tyrannical) nor overly familiar. He also had to earn and scrupulously maintain his authority: "He that knoweth not to govern, deserveth not to reign."

Although this analogy assumes that a hierarchical, largely patriarchal organization is natural, inevitable, and immutable, the history of the seventeenth century suggests otherwise. As manifested most dramatically in the beheading of the monarch (Charles I) in 1649, seventeenth-century Englishmen were in the process of questioning and destabilizing hierarchical structures of governance. Certainly, male householders were more likely to defend their own rights to disobey and dethrone their king than to defend the rights of their wives and servants to rebel. But the urgent repetition of the analogy between household and commonwealth does not prove that patriarchal governance, in household or in commonwealth, was stable or unquestioned. For example, note how hard Dod and Cleaver work to justify hierarchy. What does it mean to claim that "nothing [is] more unequal than that every man should be like equal"? Note also how Dod and Cleaver bring together the two distinct justifications of wifely subordination that we saw in Katharine's closing speeches in *The Taming of the Shrew* and *The Taming of a Shrew*. As in *The Shrew*, in which Katharine describes a husband as a "governor" and "sovereign," they justify domestic hierarchy by analogy to political life. As in *A Shrew* and T. E.'s *Law's Resolutions of Women's Rights*, they justify the wife's subordination through reference to Genesis. God created humans as the lords over all creatures but also made Eve the helper to her husband. Even in Genesis, they claim, the wife was both a fellow-governor and her husband's subordinate.

Pervading sixteenth- and seventeenth-century texts, from *The Taming of the Shrew* to conduct books and sermons to legal theory, the analogy between household and commonwealth confers public significance on private actions. Rose argues that the late sixteenth and early seventeenth century was "a particular historical moment when private life was beginning to be assigned as much dignity and significance as public life and to be related analogously, rather than hierarchically, to public affairs" (Rose 98); through analogy, then, the household was positioned as a separate but equal sphere. Blurring the distinction between public and private, the analogy raises the stakes of domestic conduct. In particular, it places enormous weight on the obedience of the subjects in the household — the wife, servants, and children — whose disobedience was often construed as threatening political as well as domestic order. For instance, the possibility that a wife or servant might kill the head of the household was so disturbing that the crime had a special legal status. In legal statutes after 1352 (25 Edward 3), killing one's husband or master, defined as petty treason, was carefully distinguished from other forms of murder and pronounced analogous to high treason — any threat to or assault on the monarch and his or her government. While a man who killed his wife or servant was accused of murder, "if any servant kill his master, any woman kill her husband, or any secular or religious person kill his prelate to whom he owes obedience, this is treason" (Rastall 460.b). Petty treason, like high treason, was thus a crime against authority and hierarchy, that is, a crime of the governed against the governor, of the low against the high. This legal construction of husband-murder as petty treason informs Katharine's description in *The Shrew* of a disobedient wife as a "foul contending rebel and graceless traitor"; similarly, clergyman John Wing reminds his readers that "an undutiful wife is a home-rebel, a house-traitor" (297). Women convicted of petty treason were sentenced to the same punishment as those convicted of high treason: they were burned at the stake. In contrast, women convicted of murder were hanged. In legal theory, if not always in practice, the punishment of female petty traitors collapsed the distinction between the two kinds of treason: for women these capital offenses were not only analogous but virtually the same.

From *A Godly Form of Household Government*

A household is, as it were, a little commonwealth, by the good government whereof God's glory may be advanced and the commonwealth which standeth of several families benefited, and all that live in that family receive much comfort and commodity.°

. . . .

To set down this good government exactly is a hard matter. Here only we will note some things which do appertain unto that government which we speak of. And to do it more orderly, that it may be the better understood, we must consider, that . . . there are two sorts in every perfect family:

1. The Governors;
2. Those that must be ruled.

And these two sorts have special duties belonging to them, the one towards the other, in the careful performance whereof, from the one to the other, consisteth the good government of a family.

The governors of a family be such as have authority in the family by God's ordinance, as the father and mother, master and mistress.

To whom as God hath given authority over their children and servants, so he would have them to use it to the wise government of them, not only

---

commodity: convenience. This the first sentence of the text proper, after the dedicatory epistle with which the volume opens.

for their own private profit, credit, or pleasure, but also for the good of those whom they are to govern. For by a wise government, much good cometh to the parties governed. If masters, then, or parents do not govern, but let servants and children do as they list, they do not only disobey God, and disadvantage themselves, but also hurt those whom they should rule. For whenas any have such liberty to do as they list,° it maketh them grow out of order, to the provoking of God's displeasure, and curse against themselves; whereas, if they had been held in by the bridle of government, they might be brought to walk so as the blessing of God might follow them in their courses.

All government of a family must be in comeliness° or decency, that is, it must be such as is meet and convenient both for the governor and for the persons governed. And therefore it is impossible for a man to understand how to govern the commonwealth that doth not know to rule his own house, or order his own person. So that he that knoweth not to govern, deserveth not to reign.

Lordliness is unmeet in a household government, and yet familiarity with such as are under government breedeth contempt. Again, for the persons governed, all in the family are not to be governed alike. There is one rule to govern the wife by, another for children, another for servants; one rule for young ones, another for old folks.

The government of a family tendeth unto two things [e]specially. First, Christian holiness; and secondly, the things of this life. By the first, God is glorified; by the second, this present life is sustained in such sort as God seeth good for us.

. . . .

For as in a city there is nothing more unequal than that every man should be like equal, so it is not convenient that in one house every man should be like and equal together. There is no equality in that city where the private man is equal with the magistrate, the people with the senate, or the servant with the master, but rather a confusion of all offices and authority.

The husband and the wife are Lords of the house, for unto them the Lord said: "Be you Lords over the fish of the sea, and over the fowl of the heaven, and over every beast that moveth upon the earth" (Genesis 1.28). And the selfsame Creator said that "the woman should be a helper unto the man" (Genesis 2.18). Therefore, the husband, without any exception, is

---

list: choose, desire. comeliness: suitableness, seemliness, propriety.

master over all the house, and hath more to do in his house with his own domestical affairs, than the magistrate.° The wife is ruler over all other things, but yet under her husband. There are certain things in the house that only do appertain to the authority of the husband, wherewith it were a reproach for the wife, without the consent of her husband, to meddle: as to receive strangers or to marry her daughter.° But there are other things in which the husband giveth over his right unto his wife: as to rule and govern her maidens;° to see to those things that belong unto the kitchen and to housewifery, and to their household stuff. Other mean things, as to buy and sell certain necessary things, may be ordered after the wit, wisdom, and fidelity of the woman.

It cannot well be rehearsed how many virtues and profits the mutual concord and love of man and wife doth bring to great things both at home and abroad, nor how many losses and incommodities do grow of the dissension and discord between them. For the household, when their master and mistress or dame are at debate, can no otherwise be in quiet and at rest than a city where rulers agree not. But when it seeth them in concord and quietness, then it rejoiceth, trusting that they will be even so unto them, as it perceiveth them to be among themselves.

Women's Work: Gender and the Division of Labor

Katharine's final speech in *The Taming of the Shrew* describes spheres of activity divided by gender — the wife warm at home, and the husband braving storms and cold "by sea and land." She suggests that the wife is idle (she *"lies* . . . at home, secure and safe"*) while the husband "commits his body to painful labor"; she does not depict the household as a place where women work. In the rest of the play the domestic work that we see — cooking and serving food, for instance — is done by servants. The husband disrupts that work, messing up the bed and throwing food, but neither spouse does it.

Yet the gendered division of spheres that Katharine describes was part of a gendered division of labor, whose logic was that women worked in the home, while men worked outside it: "The duty of the husband is to get goods, and of the wife to gather them together and save them. The duty of the husband is to travel abroad to seek a living; and the wife's duty is to

---

hath more . . . magistrate: that is, the master has more authority in his own house than does the magistrate.   marry her daughter: arrange the marriage of her daughter.   maidens: maidservants and/or unmarried daughters.

keep the house" (Dod and Cleaver L3v–L4; see also Tilney 120). These duties reveal how spouses' roles are defined through their relations to the "house"; these relations survive in the words we use to describe a "*hus*band," originally a peasant who owned his own house and land, later the male owner and head of a household; and a "*house*wife," the woman who manages or directs the affairs of her household. These words have come to refer particularly to the marital relation between the man and woman, but they originate in issues of property and ownership, paid and unpaid labor. The husband owns and rules the house, but the housewife runs it. The two ballads presented below, "A Woman's Work Is Never Done" (1629) and "The Woman to the Plow, and the Man to the Hen-Roost; or A Fine Way to Cure a Cot-Quean" (1629), elaborate on these duties and offer a particularly vivid picture of the work that women might have done in the home.

"A Woman's Work Is Never Done" catalogues the various duties that a woman without servants, but with several small children, might have done. The housewife's duties include cooking, cleaning, and child care (including breastfeeding, which is described as painful, ceaseless, and wearisome). In this ballad the woman's job largely consists of responding to others' needs and demands; her work, which has no set limit and for which she receives neither credit nor compliments (let alone wages) is presented as unrewarding and joyless. But her work is also presented as crucial to the family. As Ezell argues, prescriptive texts depict "the Good Wife's labor . . . as different in kind from her husband's, but not less valued" (38). This is especially true in "The Woman to the Plow, and the Man to the Hen-Roost," which demonstrates that women's work inside the house participated in a larger economy and was defined in contrast to men's work. Women's work also extends outside the house. In this ballad the wife's jobs include milking cows and minding fowl; she might also have sold extra milk and eggs, along with the cheese and butter she made, at market. "The Woman to the Plow" depicts a housewife as engaged in skilled, productive labor that might profit the family as well as help them feed themselves. Although the ballad insists that women are "naturally" better at some jobs than are men, and vice versa, it also suggests that the wife can cross the boundary between home and marketplace, inner and outer. The ballad depicts a couple who live and work on a small farm. A couple who lived in London and owned a shop might have a different roster of duties, differently divided; under those circumstances the wife might help mind the shop in addition to her housekeeping duties.

Some women also did paid work outside the home. The work available to them was usually related to the kinds they did in their own houses. They might work as servants in other people's houses or on farms; they might serve as midwives, nurses, or wet nurses (that is, they might breastfeed other women's children); they might prepare and serve food and drink, or make cloth and clothing. Women might also make money by taking in lodgers or through casual, occasional prostitution (Laurence 128–30).

Even wealthy women who could afford servants worked in the home. Dod and Cleaver explain that the mistress of the house "must be able to direct and prescribe what and how in every business. Where she hath little skill, by reason of her education, she must be careful by conferring and marking [observing closely] to learn skill. . . . She is to deal in such things, that she may be able to direct her servants and to find them out when they have done amiss" (Dod and Cleaver F4v). Dod and Cleaver insist that the mistress should never think that she is above any kind of work and should never be idle: "Though nice Dames think it an unseemly thing for them to soil their hands about any household matters (and therefore if they do anything, it is but pricking of a clout [that is, needlework]), yet the virtuous woman" does whatever job needs doing (Dod and Cleaver F6; cf. Gataker D3).

WHAT IS A BALLAD?

Like plays and sermons, ballads, or printed song sheets, were accessible to a wide range of people: men and women, masters and servants, literate and illiterate, Londoners and villagers. Sung in the streets by those who hawked them, they mediated between oral and written culture; printed on one side of a single sheet of paper, and thus cheap and portable, widely circulated in printed form and by memory, they could be consumed by those with neither spending money nor reading skills. Ballad sheets include the lyrics in rhymed stanzas and, often, crude illustrations which may or may not be relevant to the ballad's subject. Often "recycled," these illustrations appear on many different ballads (see Figure 8 on p. 214). The tune is indicated only by reference to another song ("to the tune of . . .") with which readers were assumed to be familiar. Ballads were published by specialist printers who distributed them through their own networks or peddlers. Besides working the streets of London, these peddlers traveled the countryside. The fact that so many of these texts survive is evidence in itself that they were mass-produced and widely distributed.

The purchasers of ballads were most probably the middling or industrious sort, the London craftsmen, tradesmen, and merchants and their households, who "possessed both literacy and disposable income, however modest," as well as some members of the upper classes (Wiltenburg 39). Heads of household were not the only ones with the money to buy texts or the ability to read them. Even wage laborers might have thought of them as an affordable luxury, occasionally "worth the price of a few drinks" (Wiltenburg 30). Purchasing power would not have restricted which hands could hold or eyes could see printed ballads, since they were routinely passed around or affixed to walls. Furthermore, some women, servants, and laborers might have been able to read ballads; reading ability, a much more common skill than writing, was spread unevenly throughout all but the most impoverished classes. Black-letter type, in which many of the texts discussed here were printed, was more widely legible than other kinds of type or, certainly, handwriting (see Figure 7 on page 170 for an example of black-letter type; Figures 8 and 10 on pages 214 and 248–49 for facsimiles of ballad sheets).[2]

Nor did literacy wholly determine access. Many who could not read might still hear ballads sung on the street by their sellers and learn them by heart; or someone else might read a ballad to them or recite it (roughly!) from memory. During this transmission process, those who disseminated songs and stories must also have changed them. Although this process, by its very nature, leaves few traces, we can assume that the surviving texts offer only one of the versions in circulation and that textual reception was a dynamic, interactive process. The elite may also have formed part of the audience for ballads; indeed, many ballads survive because relatively learned, wealthy people such as Samuel Pepys chose to collect them.

✈ "A Woman's Work Is Never Done"   *1629*

In looking for the evidence a ballad can provide about women's domestic work, we should also consider the voice speaking therein. Does the ballad endorse this voice or comment on it in any way? Although "A Woman's Work Is Never Done" is about the experience of a married woman, it is addressed to "maids"; the last stanza casts it as a warning to maidens about what they can expect from marriage. The ballad claims to be in a woman's voice, although the voice is recounted by an "I" whose identity we do not know. How seriously should we take this as an insight into women's experience, perspective, inner thoughts, and feelings? Participating in a long tradition of female complaints, ballads like this one "attribute to women a high degree of self-consciousness, a weighing of their life's pattern against other possible patterns instead of a stolid acceptance

---

[2] On literacy, see Cressy and Thomas. On ballads I have found Wiltenburg ch. 3 especially helpful.

"A Woman's Work Is Never Done" (London, c. 1629, 1650s).

of their lot" (Wiltenburg 50). Yet, while they "attribute" self-consciousness to women, such ballads may not accurately describe what women thought and felt. Like the women's voices in *The Taming of the Shrew* or Snawsel's *A Looking Glass,* these voices are mediated, invented, perhaps ventriloquized — written by men yet placed in women's mouths. But we cannot be sure even of this. While we know something about Shakespeare and Snawsel, and we also know that a boy actor played the part of Katharine, we do not know who wrote "A Woman's Work Is Never Done," or what difference it might have made if a male or a female singer gave it voice.

"*A Woman's Work Is Never Done*"

Here is a song for maids to sing,
Both in the winter and in the spring.
It is such a pretty conceited thing,
Which will much pleasure to them bring.
Maids may sit still, go, or run,
But a woman's work is never done.

*To a delicate Northern tune: "A Woman's Work
Is Never Done," or "The Beds Making"*

As I was wand'ring on the way,
I heard a married woman say
That she had lived a solid° life
Ever since the time that she was made a wife.
"For why,"° quoth she, "my labor is hard,   5
And all my pleasures are debarred.°
Both morning, evening, night and noon,
I'm sure a woman's work is never done.

"And now," quoth she, "I will relate
The manner of my woeful fate,   10
And how myself I do bestow,°
As all my neighbors well do know.
And therein all that will it hear,
Unto my song I pray awhile give ear.
I'll make it plainly to appear right soon,   15
How that a woman's work is never done.

---

3. **solid:** filled up, as in packed with activities; also, serious rather than pleasurable.   5. **For why:** because.   6. **debarred:** prohibited, forbidden.   11. **bestow:** employ.

"For when that I rise up early in the morn,
Before that I my head with dressings adorn,
I sweep and cleanse the house, as need doth require,
Or, if that it be cold, I make a fire.   20
Then my husband's breakfast I must dress,
To fill his belly with some wholesome mess.
Perhaps thereof I eat a little, or none,
But I'm sure a woman's work is never done.

"Next thing that I in order do,   25
My children must be looked unto.
Then I take them from their naked beds,
To put on their clothes and comb their heads.
And then, what hap soever do betide,
Their breakfast straight I must provide.   30
'Bread!' cries my daughter and 'Drink!' my son;
And thus a woman's work is never done.

"And when that I have filled their bellies full,
Some of them I pack away to school,
All save one sucking child, that at my breast   35
Doth gnaw and bite, and sorely me molest.
But when I have laid him down to sleep,
I am constrained the house to keep,
For then the pottage-pot° I must hang on;
And thus a woman's work is never done.   40

"And when my pottage-pot is ready to boil,°
I must be careful all the while.
And for to scum° the pot is my desire,
Or else all the fat will run i' th' fire.
But when th'leven o'clock bell it doth chime,   45
Then I know 't is near upon dinnertime.
To lay the tablecloth I then do run,
And thus a woman's work is never done.

---

39. **pottage-pot:** a kettle for cooking pottage (soup or stew) or porridge, that is, large quantities that need to be cooked for a long time. **hang on:** hang the pot on a hook over the fire. 41. **boil:** The ballad says "hoil" here. This is either a misprint for "boil," or, as the editor of *The Roxburghe Ballads* suggests, it means "to expel, or boil over." 43. **scum:** skim. The speaker does not want the pot to overflow or "run in the fire."

"When dinnertime is gone and over-past,
My husband he runs out o'th'doors in haste.   50
He scarce gives me a kiss for all that I
Have dealt and done to him so lovingly,
Which sometimes grieves me to the heart,
To see him so clownishly depart.
But to my first discourse let me go on,   55
To show a woman's work is never done.

"There's never a day, from morn to night,
But I with work am tired quite.
For when the game with me is at the best,
I hardly in a day take one hour's rest.   60
Sometimes I knit, and sometimes I spin,
Sometimes I wash, and sometimes I do wring,
Sometimes I sit, and sew by myself alone,
And thus a woman's work is never done.

"In making of the beds such pains I take,   65
Until my back, and sides, and arms do ache.
And yet my husband deals so cruelly,
That he but seldom comes to comfort me.
And then at night, when the clock strikes nine,
My husband he will say, ' 'tis supper time.'   70
Then presently he must be waited upon.
And thus a woman's work is never done.

"When supper's ended to bed we must go —
You all do know 'tis fitting it should be so!
Then do I think to settle all things right,   75
In hope that I shall take some rest by night.
The biggest of my children together I lay,
And place them by degrees so well as I may.
But yet there is a thing to be thought upon;
For why? A woman's work is never done.   80

"Then if my husband turns me to the wall,
Then my sucking child will cry and brawl.
Six or seven times for the breast 'twill cry,
And then, I pray you judge, what rest take I?

And if at any time asleep I be,   85
Perchance my husband wakes, and then wakes me.
Then he does that to me which I cannot shun,
Yet I could wish that work were oftener done.

"All you merry girls that hear this ditty,
Both in the country and in the city,   90
Take good notice of my lines I pray,
And make the use of the time you may.
You see that maids live more merrier lives,
Than do the best of married wives.
And thus to end my song as I begun: 95
You know a woman's work is never done."

FINIS.

→ "The Woman to the Plow, and the Man to the Hen-Roost"
1629

While "A Woman's Work Is Never Done" presents a housewife's complaint or lament, perhaps with some sarcasm, this ballad allies itself with the comic tradition of inversion. In this tradition humor springs from the overturning of expectations, the reversal of roles, and the incongruities when spouses do one another's work. The world turned upside down in the ballad is chaotic, its role reversals resulting in destroyed property (the wife ruins the field and kills the horse), wasted energy (the husband churns air, and the wife scatters seed), loss of profit, and physical injury (the baby's nose is broken, and the husband is kicked in the head by a cow). While the wife causes the most damage to property, the husband causes the most injury to persons. Although some of the losses cannot be recouped, the ballad still presents the reversal of roles as comic and, ultimately, instructive. But it is not clear what the spouses learn. What might "hose-and-doublet housewifery" be, and how does this reversal — with its disastrous results — cure it? Given that "cot-quean" can mean either "a coarse, vulgar, scolding woman" or a man who "busies himself unduly or meddles with matters belonging to the housewife's province" (OED), how are the events of the ballad a "cure for a cot-quean"?

"The Woman to the Plow and the Man to the Hen-Roost; or A Fine Way to Cure a Cot-Quean" (London, 1629).

The Woman to the Plow
AND
The Man to the Hen-Roost:
O R, a fine way to cure a Cot-Quean,
The Tune is, *I have for all good wives a Song.*

BOth Men and Women listen well,
A merry Jest I will you tell,
Betwixt a Good man and his Wife,
Who bred the other day at strife:
He told her for her huswifery,
And bid so und fault as well as he,
With him I his work without the doors,
Quoth he, a pox on all such whores,
With you and I cannot agree,
Let's change our work, content, quoth she,
My Wheel and Distaff here take thou,
And I will drive the Cart and Plow.
This was concluded twixt them both,
To Cart and Plow the good-wife goeth,
The goodman he at home both tarry,
To see that nothing both miscarry,
An apron he before him put,
Judge was not this a handsome fut,
He sweeps the House, he makes the Cheese
He gropes the Hens the ducks & Geese,
He Brews and Bakes as well as he ran,
But not as it should be done, poor man!
And did make his Cheese one day,
Two Piggs their Bellies broke with whey,

Nothing that he in hand did take,
Did come to good, once he did Bake,
And burnt the Bread as black as a sack
Another time he went to Rock
The Cradle, an it threw the Child o'th floor
And broke his Nose, and put it sore.
He went to milk one Evening tide,
A Skittish Cow on the wrong side,
His pail was full of milk God wot,
She kickt and spilt it every jot,
Besides that he gave him a blow o'th face
Which was scant well in six weeks space,
Thus was he served, and yet so well
And more mischances yet befell,
Before his apron he'd leave off,
Thus all his Neighbours did him scoff,
Now list and mark one pretty jest,
I will make you laugh above all the rest,
As he to churn his Butter went,
One Morning with a good intent,
The Cot-quean fool he surely meant,
For he had quite forgot the Cream,
He Churn'd all day, with all his might,
And yet he could get no Butter at night.

TWere strange indeed for me to utter
That without Cream he should make
Now having show'd his huswifery, (butter
Who did all things thus untowardly,
Unto the good-wife I'le turn my Rhime,
And tell you how she spent her time,
She us'd to drive the Cart and Plow,
But do't well she knew not how,
She made so many banks i'th ground,
He been better held given five pound,
That she had neither shan't in hand,
So sorely she did spoil the Land,
As she did go to Sow likewise,
She made a Feast for Crows and Pies,
She threw away a handful at a place,
And left all bare another space,
At the Harrow he could not rule the place
But did one Land, and left two bare,
And shortly after once more
As she came home with a Load of Hay,
She overthrew it nay and worse,
She broke the Cart and kill'd a Horse,
The good-man that time had ill luck,
He set in the Sow and kill'd a Duck,
And being girded at his heart
For loss on's Duck, his Horse and Cart,
The many turns on both sides him,
His eyes did with salt water run:

Then now, quoth he, full well I see,
The Wheels for he the Plow's for me,
I the intreat, quoth he, good-wife,
To take thy Charge, and all my life
I'le never med'le with huswifery more,
My sins such faults as I did before,
Give me the Cart-whip and the Flail
Take thou the Churn and milking pail,
The good wife she was well content,
And about her huswifery she went,
As to Brewing and to Ditching,
Reaping, Mowing, Lading, Pitching,
He would be rul'd no ling still before,
But after that ne're troubled more,
I Wish all Wives that troubled be,
With Host and Doublet huswifery,
To overt em as this was an old,
When men they work and ne're be chid,
Though she it s intime had some loss,
I hereby she was eas'd of a Cross,
I'le heard of this is a husband-men,
Let Wives alone to grope the Hen,
And medule you with the Horse and Ox,
And keep your Lambs safe from the Fox,
So shall you live Contented lives,
And take sweet pleasure in your Wives.
FINIS.

Printed for J. Wright, J. Clarke, W. Thackeray, and T. Passinger.

◄ FIGURE 8. *Facsimile of "The Woman to the Plow, and the Man to the Hen-Roost; or A Fine Way to Cure a Cot-Quean" (1629). Like many ballads, this one is printed on one side of a single sheet of paper. It could thus be cheaply produced and easily transported by the ballad sellers who carried their stock with them through the streets of London and across the country. It could also be pasted up on a wall. The ballad is also typical in its use of "black-letter" type, which some historians argue was the type that most people in the period found easiest to read. Although the illustrations advise a reader, viewer, or purchaser of the ballad that it is about the relationship between men and women, they otherwise seem unrelated to the ballad's content. The figures pictured are more lavishly dressed than would seem appropriate for a husband and wife hard at work on their farm; the ladies hold fans rather than tools; and the figures pose stiffly rather than engage in the chores that the ballad describes.*

"The Woman to the Plow, and the Man to the Hen-Roost"

The Tune is, "I Have for All Good Wives a Song."

Both Men and Women, listen well,
A merry jest I will you tell,
Betwixt a good-man and his wife,
Who fell the other day at strife.
He chid° her for her housewifery;   5
And she found fault, as well as he,
With him for's work without the doors.
Quoth he, "A pox on all such whores!
Since you and I cannot agree,
Let's change° our work!" "Content!" quoth she.   10
"My wheel and distaff here take thou,
And I will drive the Cart and Plow."

This was concluded 'twixt them both,
To cart and plow the good-wife go'th.
The goodman, he at home doth tarry,   15
To see that nothing doth miscarry.
An apron he before him put.
Judge, was not this a handsome slut?°
He fleets° the milk; he makes the cheese;

5. **chid:** chided, scolded. 10. **change:** exchange. 18. **slut:** kitchen-maid or drudge.
19. **fleets:** skims.

He gropes° the hens, the ducks, and geese.   20
He brews and bakes as well as he can,
But not as it should be done, poor man!
As [he] did make his cheese one day,
Two pigs their bellies broke with whey.

Nothing that he in hand did take   25
Did come to good. Once he did bake,
And burnt the bread as black as a stock.°
Another time, he went to rock
The cradle, and threw the child o'th'floor,
And broke his nose, and hurt it sore.   30
He went to milk, one eveningtide,
A skittish° cow on the wrong side.
His pail was full of milk, God wot,
She kicked and spilt it every jot.
Beside, she hit him a blost° o'th'face   35
Which was scant well in six weeks' space.

Thus was he served, and yet too well,
And more mischances yet befell,
Before his apron he'd leave off,
Though all his neighbors did him scoff.   40
Now list and mark one pretty jest,
'Twill make you laugh above all the rest.
As he to churn his butter went,
One morning with a good intent,
The cot-quean° fool did surely dream,   45
For he had quite forgot the cream.
He churned all day, with all his might,
And yet he could get no butter at night.

'Twere strange, indeed, for me to utter
That without cream he should make butter.   50
Now having showed his housewifery,
Who did all things thus untowardly,

20. **gropes:** looks for eggs.   27. **stock:** a stick of wood, black either because it still has bark on it or because it has been in the fire.   32. **skittish:** apt to start or shy suddenly and without cause.   35. **blost:** blow.   45. **cot-quean:** the housewife of a laborer. This term can also be used to insult either women or men. It can refer to a coarse, vulgar, scolding woman, that is, a woman who is not a "lady" or who usurps male authority; it can also refer to a man who does "women's work."

Unto the goodwife I'll turn my rhyme,
And tell you how she spent her time.
She used to drive the cart and plow,
But do't well she knew not how.   55
She made so many banks° i'th'ground,
He [had] been better [to] have giv'n five pound
That she had never ta'en in hand,
So sorely she did spoil the land.   60

As she did go to sow, likewise,
She made a feast for crows and pies.°
She threw away a handful at a place,
And left all bare another space.
At the harrow° she could not rule the mare,   65
But did one land, and left two bare.
And shortly after, on a day,
As she came home with a load of hay,
She overthrew it, nay and worse,
She broke the cart and killed a horse.   70
The goodman that time had ill luck —
He let in the sow and killed a duck.

And being grievèd at his heart,
For loss on's duck, his horse, and cart,
The many hurts on both sides done,
His eyes did with salt water run: 75
"Then now," quoth he, "full well I see,
The wheel's for her, the plow's for me.
I thee entreat," quoth he, "goodwife,
To take thy charge and, all my life,
I'll never meddle with housewifery more,   80
Nor find such faults as I did before.
Give me the cart-whip and the frail,°
Take thou the churn and milking-pail."

The goodwife, she was well content,   85
And about her housewifery she went.

---

57. **banks:** ridges. 62. **pies:** magpies. 65. **harrow:** a large rake dragged across plowed ground to break up clods of earth, root out weeds, or cover seeds that have been planted. 83. **frail:** a basket used for packing produce.

He to hedging° and to ditching,°
Heaping, mowing, lading, pitching;°
He would be twattling° still before,
But after that ne'er twattled more.   90
I wish all wives that troubled be,
With hose-and-doublet housewifery,
To serve them as this woman did.
Then may they work and ne'er be chid,
Though she i'th'int'rim had some loss,   95
Thereby she was eased of a cross.

Take heed of this, you husbandmen,
Let wives alone grope the hen,
And meddle you with the horse and ox,
And keep your lambs safe from the fox.   100
So shall you live contented lives,
And take sweet pleasure in your wives.

FINIS.

87. **hedging:** constructing hedges or fences. **ditching:** digging or repairing ditches. 88. **heaping:** gathering, accumulating, amassing. **lading:** loading. **pitching:** pitching or throwing hay into piles with a pitchfork. 90. **twattling:** talking idly, chattering, babbling.

Wife Beating

Male heads of household (husbands, fathers, and masters) had the legal right to discipline or "correct" their subordinates. As Hunt argues, "the single most important advantage possessed by male heads of household in early modern England was their virtually absolute right to demand obedience from their subordinates and the corollary right to discipline their subordinates when this obedience was not forthcoming" (Hunt 18). The right to use force to secure obedience and to maintain order was widely assumed, even by those who did not exercise it. As long as a husband did not kill, maim, or seriously endanger his subordinates or disturb his neighbors, he was not accountable for how he treated those in his care. It was not assumed, however, that women had a right to beat their husbands (although women did have the right to correct those beneath them, children and servants); in addition, "relatively few men or women in early modern England thought wives had an absolute right not to be beaten" (Hunt 24).

Domestic violence must be considered within the larger context of a culture in which force was routinely used to punish transgressions (officially and unofficially), to resolve disputes (from pub brawls and duels to war), and to maintain order. "Not only was this a society suffused with personal relationships of dominance and submission but it was one that saw violence as a necessary, if not always optimal, way of maintaining order in any hierarchical relationship" (Hunt 14). Wife beating had an ambiguous status precisely because of the wife's double position as joint governor (and thus the corrector of children and servants) and subordinate (and thus subject to her husband's correction).[3] As William Gouge argues, "God hath not ranked wives among those in the family who are to be corrected" (see p. 226). Those who "are to be corrected" are children and servants; to beat a wife is to treat her like one or the other. In Gouge's view the husband's authority over the wife is not sufficient to justify his beating her: "The small disparity which . . . is betwixt man and wife, permitteth not so high a power in a husband, and so low a servitude in a wife, as for him to beat her" (p. 226). Further, the wife's own authority as "a joint governor of the family" will be compromised if her subordinates see her being beaten: "can they respect her as a mother or a mistress who is under correction as well as they?"

Because violence was so integral a part of both dominance and masculinity, those prescriptive texts, including *A Homily of the State of Matrimony* (p. 169) and conduct books such as those excerpted below, which urged men not to abuse their right to "correct" and discipline their wives, worked to separate masculinity from violence.[4] As *A Homily* insists, "And yet a man may be a man, although he doth not use such extremity (p. 175–76)."

At the same time that sermons and conduct books strove to convince husbands to govern themselves and their fists from within, a network of informal surveillance also discouraged them from abusing their power: ministers preached; neighbors pried and condemned; church courts meted out fines or imposed separations between abusive husbands and battered

---

[3] On the contradictory role of the wife, see Amussen, *Ordered Society* 41–47, 72–85; Belsey ch. 6; Boose, "Scolding Brides" 194; Rose 126–29; and Stone 195–202.

[4] In the ballad "Hold Your Hands, Honest Men!," the wife praises her husband's expertise in "martial discipline" (line 92), but wishes that he would not direct it toward her: "I would not care, / So me he'd spare, / On whom he did use his hands" (115–17). This ballad forms a pair with "Keep a Good Tongue in Your Head," in which a husband laments that his wife cannot rule her tongue (*RB* 3: 237–48). Taken together, the pair of ballads suggests that each spouse has a body part in special need of governance; for the wife it is the tongue, and for the husband the hands. It also links women's loquacity to men's violence, suggesting that each causes the other in a pattern of circular causation. Men beat women because they nag and scold; women complain because men abuse them.

wives. In fact, depositions from hearings in church courts provide evidence that husbands did beat their wives and that neighbors observed domestic conduct and intervened to regulate how a husband meted out "correction." As William Heale reminds his readers, whatever violence "is committed within our own family, is acted (as it were) on an open theatre, where we have store of spectators: our children, our servants, our neighbors, sometimes our nearest kindred, oft-times our dearest friends" (Heale C3v). By scrutinizing men's behavior, this circle of spectators protected women. "For women, embeddedness in a community of friends, neighbors, relatives, and work-mates was the most effective means to counterbalance the overwhelming power of men both in the family and in society" (Hunt 23; cf. Amussen, "Domestic Violence" 81).

While men's authority over their households was broad in scope, it did have limits — even if it was not always clear exactly what these were or who should set and reinforce them. The male authors of conduct books attempt to persuade male readers to govern themselves and to eschew violence as undignified and ineffective. Both the texts represented here were relatively popular. William Whately's *A Bride-Bush, or A Direction for Married Persons* went through three editions: 1617, 1619 (enlarged), and 1623. So did William Gouge's lengthy *Of Domestical Duties: Eight Treatises:* 1622, 1626, and 1634. Both writers were ministers in the Anglican church but with Puritan sympathies (that is, interest in reforms more radical and far-reaching than the Anglican church had embraced). While these sympathies sometimes led them into controversy, they did not prevent them from having successful careers as officeholders. Whately, the vicar of Banbury (in Oxfordshire), had a strong reputation as a preacher. Known as "the Roaring Boy of Banbury," he drew listeners from Oxford to hear his rousing pulpit rhetoric. Gouge served as preacher (or lecturer) and later as rector at Saint Anne's in Blackfriars (London).

Both men's publications got them into trouble with the church and government around the same time. In *A Bride-Bush,* Whately argued that both adultery and desertion automatically annulled a marriage. Since this went against church doctrine, he was summoned for disciplinary action; but he retracted his claims, and the case was dismissed (in 1621). He included a retraction and apology in the second edition of *A Bride-Bush* and also disclaimed his controversial opinion in a subsequent text, *A Care-Cloth, or A Treatise of the Cumbers and Troubles of Marriage* (London, 1624). In 1621 Gouge was imprisoned for nine weeks for supposedly treasonable passages in a book he had edited, Sir Henry Finch's *The World's Great Restauration;* ultimately, he obtained release. Gouge also provoked protests from his female parishioners, who reviled him as "a hater of women" because he insisted vigorously on women's subjection to their husbands (Woodbridge 129–30). That both these ministers got into potentially serious scrapes suggests the perils of publication in a century of profound political, religious, and social upheaval.

Gouge's and Whately's earnest discussions of how to govern a wife — and, especially, how to secure subjection from an insubordinate wife without resorting to force — suggest that Petruchio operates within the limits proposed by moralists: he never strikes Katharine despite provocation. Indeed, Whately might argue that a husband in Petruchio's position would be justified in treating "a woman of base and servile condition in base and servile manner." However, Petruchio employs the more covert means of coercion — the "other forcible means . . . besides beating" — that Gouge and Whately outline. These include restraining a wife's liberty and denying her those things she likes most (Gouge, Whately); and withholding kindness and generosity from her (Whately).

Although both Gouge and Whately use various arguments to discredit wife beating, they do not rely on some that we might most expect to find. They do not argue that the husband has no right to beat his wife or that doing so is unfair, immoral, or illegal. Instead, they maintain that refraining from violence is more dignified, authoritative, and expedient than resorting to it. In their view domestic violence is counterproductive because it promotes rather than subdues resistance. Gouge warns that since a wife has "no ground to be persuaded that her husband hath authority to beat her," his doing so will lead her to "rise against him, over-master him (as many do) and never do any duty aright" (p. 227–28). As Abigail explains in Snawsel's *A Looking Glass*, "the wife would be made more unruly and outrageous by beating" (Snawsel G4). At its most dangerous, this resistance will fester inwardly rather than burst into visibility, thus opening up a gap between "outward subjection" and "inward hatred" (p. 228). This is just the kind of disparity between inner feelings and outward behavior that some readers and viewers of *The Taming of the Shrew* use to explain what happens to Katharine's resistance. According to this view, her resistance does not disappear; it just goes underground.

The argument is also made, in these conduct books and elsewhere, that a husband should not beat his wife because "they two are one flesh." In beating his wife, a husband also beats himself, and "no man but a frantic, furious, desperate wretch will beat himself" (p. 226). But at this point we can begin to see significant differences between Gouge and Whately. For instance, both writers consider medical practice as an analogy for wife beating. Yet Gouge rejects the analogy, while Whately accepts it. Gouge argues that even a surgeon (a "chirurgeon") will not operate on himself.

Rather than accepting the notion that a husband should cause his wife pain in order to cure her, just as he would lance a boil on his own body, Gouge suggests that if a wife is so insubordinate that she must be beaten, the husband should hand her over to an authority who will act as physician to her character, hurting her in order to heal her. Whately, however, accepts the idea that if the husband and wife are one flesh, then under extreme circumstances the husband can use force "to heal his own flesh with a corrosive."

Both writers accept the notion that physical punishment plays an important role in maintaining domestic order. Both also insist that, in the case of the wife, violence should be the absolutely last resort. Yet Gouge suggests that this physical punishment should take place outside of the house and be administered by a magistrate rather than the husband. For him, any violence against a wife should not be "domestic" unless the wife forces her husband to act in self-defense. In contrast, Whately argues that, under certain conditions, "even blows . . . may well stand with the dearest kindnesses of matrimony" (p. 224). Gouge argues that there is no scriptural warrant for wife beating, while Whately claims that Scripture is irrelevant since no wives in Scripture deserved beating. (Similarly, in Gouge's and Becon's discussions of servant beating, below, Scripture is used in the service of opposing arguments.)

→ WILLIAM WHATELY

From *A Bride-Bush* 1623

Chapter 9. Of the Parts and Ends of a Man's Authority

But authority must be exercised as well as preserved. Yea, verily, it cannot be kept unless it be used, being like a sword that will rust and be marred if it lie still in the scabbard without using. Now, that men may understand how to use this precious thing (for authority is one of the richest jewels of the world; it is a model of God's sovereignty, and a little map of his great greatness that is greater than all and the very life and soul of all societies), it is necessary for us to direct them herein, by standing upon three points. First, to show the parts of authority; secondly, the

William Whately, *A Bride-Bush, or A Direction for Married Persons* (London, 1623), P–P3.

end; and thirdly, the manner of using it. So men knowing what, why, how to do in this business shall not want° sufficient information.

Of the parts of authority, first I mean by authority a power of exercising government and dominion over another. And this hath two parts, to guide and to recompense, to direct and to requite. Direction consists in the enjoining and appointing of lawful things to be done, and in the forbidding and prohibiting of things at least indifferent. Recompense is also double, of good and obedient carriage° by commendation and rewards; of evil and disobedient [carriage] by reproofs and punishments.

Commendation is the encouraging of one in well-doing by manifestation of a good liking, in words tending to praise him. Reward is the bestowing of some benefit more than were otherwise due upon him that hath done well, for his further animating therein. Reproof is a charging of a fault upon the offender with words, tending to put him to shame and grief for it. Punishment is the inflicting of some smart or loss or like evil upon the offender that may cause him to be sorry for his fault and to reform it. These are the parts of government; I mean those things which a governor, by virtue of his place, both may and must take upon him to do, and which are so appropriated to the place of a governor that none other may adventure to do them all, unless he will exceed his vocation, sin against God, and wrong the person over whom he so usurpeth.

Now concerning all the former (viz.° commanding, forbidding, commending, rewarding, reproving), it is of all hands° granted that it is lawful for a husband to exercise them all upon his wife. Yea, and for some kind of punishment also, by withdrawing from her the plentiful demonstrations of kindness and fruits of his liberality, and by abridging her of her liberty, and the enjoyment of many things delightful, it is yielded that a husband may inflict the same. But whether he may correct her, yea or no, with blows, because it seemeth too impious in him to do it, and too servile in her to suffer it, that is a question.

For my part, I would be loath to allow a husband the liberty of carrying himself unto his wife as unto his slave. He can but strike and beat his bondwoman; with what face can he come to kiss and embrace the same person whom he hath laid upon with his fist, or with a cudgel? How doth he cherish her as his own flesh, whom he thus opprobriously putteth to grief and smart? Would he use himself so, if himself should offend? Where hath he an example of any godly husband that hath taken up a staff against his wife? Why will he do that which he can never show that any good man

---

want: lack.　**carriage:** conduct, behavior.　**viz.** (short for *videlicet*): that is to say, namely. **of all hands:** on all sides, by everyone.

hath done before him? Is this to err in her love — to smite her on the face, or to fetch blood or blueness of her flesh?

But yet if a wife will put upon herself even servile conditions, if she will abase herself to foolish, childish, slavish behavior, I see not why the rod or staff or wand should not be for the fool's back in this case also. And seeing God hath given the husband authority, and hath nowhere forbidden him the exercise of any part of authority, nor hath abridged him in any parcel thereof, no not by enjoining him any duty that cannot stand together with the exercise of this part of authority, I cannot dare to say but that (if she give just cause after much bearing and forbearing, and trying all other ways, in case of utmost necessity, so that he exceed not measure) he may lance his own arm where it swelleth, and scratch his own hand where it itcheth, though he make it smart after.

It is most intolerable for a man in anger to strike his wife for those weaknesses which are incident even to virtuous women. But if she will rail upon him with most reproachful terms; if she will affront him with bold and impudent resistances; if she will tell him to his teeth that she cares not for him, and that she will do as she lusts° for all him; if she will fly in his face with violence and begin to strike him, or break into any such unwomanly words or behavior; then let him bear awhile, and admonish and exhort and pray. But if still she persists against reproofs and persuasion, if her father be living let him be entreated to fight. If she have none, or he cannot or will not, I think the husband shall not offend in using a fool according to her folly, a child in understanding like a child in years, and a woman of base and servile condition in base and servile manner. For even so should he use himself in like case were he appointed to be a ruler over himself.

And well may he cherish her upon her reformation, though upon extremity of misdemeanor he do chastise. To cherish one's person and plaster their wounds are things nothing incompossible.° Indeed, wrathful corrections seem to make kindnesses indecent, because contraries do not likely issue from the same fountain. But even blows, after patient forbearance, after much waiting for amendment without blows, and so applied that it is apparent a man seeks not to ease his stomach, but to heal his own flesh with a corrosive° when nothing else will do it — even blows I say, with these limitations, may well stand with the dearest kindnesses of matrimony.

'Tis true, that no man in Scripture hath so cudgelled his wife. And why is this? Is it not because no wife in Scripture is read to have offended in such kinds and degrees as might reasonably call for such severity? In those

---

lusts: likes, pleases.   **incompossible:** incompatible, impossible to combine.   **corrosive:** caustic medicine or poultice that eats away putrefying or infected tissue.

former times, God permitted (though not allowed)° a husband for lighter matters than whoredom to put away his wife. No doubt that remedy made it needless to strike. No man would be pestered with a woman of shrewd disposition that should enforce him to fighting if, with a dash of his pen, he might turn her packing. But without all question, if in Scripture we should have read of any woman so insolent as we see some in experience, we may conclude that either divorce should have severed them or else blows should have been used as a sharp medicine for so festered a sore. To conclude, let it be the wisdom of a man to make choice of one that shall not need this rigor rather than to dispute about the lawfulness of using it.

allowed: approved of. Divorce was permitted, but not encouraged.

→ WILLIAM GOUGE

From *Of Domestical Duties: Eight Treatises*   *1634*

TREATISE 4

Section 44. Of Husbands Beating Their Wives

Contrary [to the ideal] are the furious and spiteful actions of many unkind husbands (heads too heady),° whose favors° are buffets, blows, strokes, and stripes, wherein they are worse than the venomous viper. For the viper for his mate's sake casteth out his poison. And wilt not thou, oh, husband, in respect of that near union which is betwixt thee and thy wife, lay aside thy fierceness and cruelty? Many wives by reason of their husbands' fury are in worse case than servants, for:

1. Such as will not give a blow to a servant, care not what load they lay upon their wives.

2. Where servants have but a time and term to be under the tyranny of such furious men, poor wives are tied to them all their life long.

3. Wives cannot have so good remedy by the help of law against cruel husbands as servants may have against cruel masters.

4. Masters have not such opportunity to exercise their cruelty over

heads too heady: too overbearing, rash, impetuous.   favors: gifts given as marks of favor, affection, or esteem.

William Gouge, *Of Domestical Duties: Eight Treatises* (London, 1634), 394–97.

servants as husbands over wives, who are to be continually at board and bed with their husbands.

5. The nearer wives are, and the dearer they ought to be to their husbands, the more grievous must strokes needs be when they are given by a husband's hand, than by a master's.

6. The less power and authority that a husband hath to strike his wife, than a master to strike a servant, the more heavy do his strokes seem to be, and the worse doth the case of a wife seem to be in that respect, than of a servant. Not unfitly, therefore, is such a man (if he may be thought a man rather than a beast) said to be like a father-queller and mother-queller.°

QUESTION: May not then a husband beat his wife?

ANSWER: With submission to better judgments, I think he may not. My reasons are these:

1. There is no warrant throughout the whole Scripture by precept or example for it; which argument, though it be negative, yet for the point in hand it is a forcible argument in two respects. (1) Because the Scripture hath so plentifully and particularly declared the several duties of husbands and wives, and yet hath delivered nothing concerning a husband's striking and beating his wife. (2) Because it hath also plentifully and particularly spoken of all such as are to correct, and of their manner of correction, and of their bearing correction who are to be corrected, and of the use they are to make thereof, and yet not anything at all concerning a husband's punishing, or a wife's bearing in this kind. The Scripture being so silent in this point, we may well infer that God hath not ranked wives among those in the family who are to be corrected.

2. That small disparity which . . . is betwixt man and wife, permitteth not so high a power in a husband, and so low a servitude in a wife, as for him to beat her. Can it be thought reasonable that she who is the man's perpetual bed-fellow, who hath power over his body, who is a joint parent of the children, a joint governor of the family, should be beaten by his hands? What if children or servants should know of it (as they must needs, for how can such a thing be done in the house, and they of the house know it not)? Can they respect her as a mother or a mistress who is under correction as well as they?

3. The near conjunction, and very union that is betwixt man and wife suffereth not such dealing to pass betwixt them. The wife is a man's self: "They two are one flesh" (Ephesians 5.31). No man but a frantic, furious, desperate wretch will beat himself. Two sorts of men are in Scripture noted to cut and lance their own flesh: idolaters, as the Baalites (1 Kings 18), and

queller: killer.

demoniacs, as he that was possessed with a legion of devils (Mark 5.5). Such are they who beat their wives — either blinded in their understanding, or possessed with a devil.

OBJECTION: He that is best in his wits will suffer his body to be pinched, pricked, lanced, and otherwise pained if it be needful and behoveful.°

ANSWER: 1. A man's heart will not suffer him to do any of these himself. There are chirurgeons° whose office it is to do such things. If the chirurgeon himself have need of any such remedy for his own body, he will use the help of another chirurgeon. If the case so stand as a wife must needs be beaten, it is fitter for a husband to refer the matter to a public magistrate (who is as an approved and licensed chirurgeon) and not to do it with his own hands.°

2. Though some parts of the body may be so dealt withall, yet every part may not, as the heart, which the wife is to the man.

3. The comparison holdeth not. For the forenamed pinching, lancing, etc., is no punishment for any fault, as the beating of a wife in question is. There is no question but a man that hath skill may, if need be, open a vein, lance a boil, splinter a broken bone, or disjointed joint in his wife's body, which may be more painful than correction. And herein the comparison holdeth, but not in the other.

OBJECTION: There is as near a conjunction between Christ and his Church, as betwixt man and wife. Yet Christ forbeareth not to correct and punish his Church.

ANSWER: There is a double relation betwixt Christ and the Church. He is a husband unto it, having made it "of his flesh, and of his bones" (Ephesians 5.30), and a supreme Lord over it, having "all power in heaven and earth committed unto him" (Matthew 28.19). In this latter respect, he punisheth, not in the forme[r]. A husband is not such a supreme Lord over his wife. Therefore, Christ's example is no warrant to him.

4. There is no hope of any good to proceed from a husband's beating of his wife. For where the party corrected is persuaded that the party which correcteth hath no authority or right so to do, it [i.e., she] will not be brought patiently to take it, but will resist, and strive if it be possible to get the mastery. Let a stranger strike such a child of years or a servant as will patiently bear many strokes at a parent's or master's hand, [and] they will turn again at that stranger, and endeavor to give him as good as he brings. Now a wife, having no ground to be persuaded that her husband hath

---

behoveful: useful, advantageous.   chirurgeons: surgeons, those who cure diseases and injuries by manual operations rather than by prescribing medicines.   not . . . hands: A public magistrate, such as a justice of the peace, would be a more appropriate person to administer corporal punishment to a wife than her own husband would be.

authority to beat her, what hope is there that she will patiently bear it, and be bettered by it? Or rather, is it not likely that she will, if she can, rise against him, over-master him (as many do) and never do any duty aright? A fault in a wife is not taken away but increased by blows.

OBJECTION: Smart and pain may make her dread her husband, stand in awe of him, and do her duty the better.

ANSWER: Such dread and awe beseems neither the place of a husband to enact it, nor the place of a wife to yield it. Though perforce she may be brought to yield some outward subjection, yet inward hatred of her husband's person may be joined therewith, which is as bad, if not worse than, outward disobedience.

OBJECTION: She may be of so outrageous a disposition as, but by force, she will not be kept in any compass.

ANSWER: 1. It hath been of old time answered that no fault should be so great as to compel a husband to beat his wife.

ANSWER: 2. Other forcible means may be used besides beating by her husband's hands: she may be restrained of liberty, denied such things as she most affecteth, be kept up, as it were, in hold.° And, if no other means will serve the turn, be put over to the magistrate's hands, that if she be of so servile a disposition, as by no other means she will be kept under than by fear and force, by smart and pain, she may fear the magistrate, and feel his hand, rather than her husband's.

OBJECTION: If a wife wax so mannish, or rather mad, as to offer to strike and beat her husband, may he not in that case beat her to make her cease her outrage?

ANSWER: I doubt not but that that good provision which is made in law to preserve a man's life may be applied to this purpose. The law simply condemns all murder. Yet if a man be so assaulted as there is no way to preserve his own life, but by taking away his life that assaults him, it condemneth not him as a murderer, because he did it in defense of himself. So if a husband be set upon by his wife, it is lawful and expedient that he defend himself. And if he can do it no other ways but by striking her, that is not to be reckoned an unlawful beating her.

kept up . . . in hold: shut or locked up, prevented from leaving the house.

Servant Beating

Although the conflict between Katharine and Petruchio has always attracted attention and stirred controversy, critics have paid considerably less attention to the high frequency of violence against servants in the play, or to the fact that Katharine and Petruchio both perpetrate this violence. The play positions violence against servants as an unobjectionable, almost invisible background to the more controversial skirmishes between husband and wife. Petruchio talks about how he will tame Katharine, but not at all about how he handles his servants; Petruchio teaches Katharine not to strike or oppose him, but he is not particularly concerned that she learn not to hit servants. Turning our attention to sixteenth- and seventeenth-century attitudes toward the "correction" of servants can bring the servants in the play into focus, and inform how we think about and evaluate their treatment.

In sixteenth- and seventeenth-century England, so many people, including aristocrats at court, spent some part of their life in service that it was considered a developmental phase more than a permanent social status. As Ann Kussmaul notes: "For most servants, it was a transitional occupation, specific to their transitional status between childhood and adulthood" (Kussmaul 4). Indeed, most adolescents would have had some experience as a servant or apprentice; servants "constituted around 60 percent of the population aged fifteen to twenty-four" (Kussmaul 3) and 13.4 percent of the total population (Laurence 36). Forty percent of children were servants for some part of their lives; 20 percent grew up in houses in which servants were employed (Laurence 36, see also 132–37). Furthermore, by Peter Laslett's calculation, "a quarter, or a third, of all the families in the country contained servants" in the seventeenth century (Laslett 13).

Servants were considered integral members of the families and households that they served. In recompense for their obedience and industry, their master and mistress were supposed to treat them as their own children, especially since many servants joined households at a very young age. Good masters were encouraged to develop a loving bond with their servants, in part because this would insure better service and submission; masters were also expected not to overwork them, to provide sufficient food, clothing, and shelter, and to pay them adequately and punctually. Part of the master's responsibility was vigilant surveillance over servants' souls and characters, as well as their conduct: "The householder must have a diligent and watching eye, that no vice creep into his house" (Becon ZZ2v). The mistress was especially charged to "watch over the manners and behavior of such as be in her house, and to help her husband in spying out evils that are breeding, that by his wisdom they may be prevented or cured" (Dod and Cleaver D6).

The cure of the evils that were spied out by the master's and mistress's watching eyes might well require physical punishment. While husbands were discouraged from beating their wives, as we have seen, masters were licensed, even encouraged, to "correct" their servants. The distinction made between wife beating and servant beating relied on the assumption that servants (like children but unlike wives) were unambiguously subordinate to their masters. As Dod and Cleaver argue: "God hath put the rod of correction in the hands of the Governors of the family, by punishments to save them from destruction which, if the bridle were let loose unto them, they would run into" (D5v); "If any man think fighting unmeet for Christians, or be loath to soil their hands, lest they should get themselves an ill name, let them know . . . that household chastisement is agreeable to God's will, [as] is evident out of the Proverbs" (Dod and Cleaver D4v). In contrast, however, Becon also cites Scripture to demonstrate that, since all souls are equal in God's eyes, there is no justification for beating servants; in Becon's view, Christians distinguish themselves from Turks by refraining from such activity. But even Becon says that the householder may "minister such moderate correction to the offender as shall seem meet to his wisdom." In defining what constitutes "moderate correction," the master is his own arbiter, and therein lies the potential for abuse.

If the master is allowed to wield the rod of correction, so is the mistress. But rules of propriety govern the administration of corporal punishment in the household. Correction was authorized to the extent that it was not random, rash, and enacted in anger, but rather operated within carefully set limits to reinforce hierarchies of gender and class. Dod and Cleaver and Gouge both insist that "it is not comely or beseeming that the wife should take upon her to rule and correct the men-servants; so likewise, it is not comely or meet, that the husband should meddle with the punishing or chastising of the maid-servants" (Dod and Cleaver sig. Aa3v; see also Gouge). But Gouge proposes an exception to this gendered decorum of violence: "If a maid should wax stout and mannish, and turn against her mistress (she being weak, sickly, with child, or otherwise unable to master her maid), the master may and must beat down her stoutness and rebellion" (p. 242). Conduct books outline other rules that masters should follow when correcting their servants. Masters should always punish in response to a particular fault, rather than out of anger; they should be sure that they are punishing the right party and that the punishment suits the crime; they should consider whether the servant's mistake was intentional or accidental; and they should not disgrace the servant in front of others. Inappropriately administered correction might harden a servant, promoting resistance, surliness, and poor work.

In their discussions of masters' roles as disciplinarians, as in their discussions of wife beating, conduct books sought to convince men to use their power responsibly and to moderate their use of violence. Masters' authority was "temporary and circumscribed" (Burnett 56). Yet, as Gouge's discussion of masters' duties makes clear, the only firmly fixed limits were the law and life: masters could not command their servants to break God's law or civil law; in fact, servants were licensed to disobey commands to break either law. Masters also had no right to kill their servants.

Within these limits the difference between moderate correction and brutal abuse was harder to determine. And the potential for abuse was great. In his attempts to delineate the limits of masters' authority, Gouge also catalogues the ways that masters and mistresses can abuse their power and create disorder. He describes mistresses who conspire with their servants to do things "privily without their husbands' consent"; masters and mistresses who have sex with their servants ("give their servants power over their own body");[5] masters who order servants to break the law, or who kill them. Furthermore, laws tended to support rather than limit masters' power, as historian Michael MacDonald explains:

> Maximum, not minimum, wages were established by law. A servant who struck or killed his master was liable to be prosecuted for petty treason, not simply assault or murder. Servants and apprentices who ran away from their masters were tracked down; and if they were caught they might be branded or (for a brief period during the sixteenth century) sold into slavery.
> (MacDonald 88)

Servants who considered themselves to have been abused rather than corrected — which usually meant that they had been badly injured, even permanently disabled — did have some legal recourse. Gouge acknowledges this when he claims that abused wives are at a greater disadvantage than abused servants (p. 225). A servant who was maimed and thereby made unfit for subsequent employment might be cared for by the parish; obviously, parishes sought to limit the number of such cases for which they would become responsible (Burnett 56). Furthermore, "servants who were beaten, raped, or ejected from their jobs before the end of their contracts could appeal to local authorities for redress" (MacDonald 88); indeed, servants frequently sued their employers for mistreatment. However, given that "moderate correction" was not only accepted but condoned, it was very difficult to prove that abuse had occurred. As a result, cases that came to court were those of aggravated brutality, and those for which plaintiffs were

---

[5] Young women servants were especially vulnerable to rape and sexual exploitation, and to conceiving illegitimate children for whom they would bear full responsibility, which might include being dismissed from service.

able to convince other servants to testify as witnesses (MacDonald 88; Smith 152–53).

Especially in Gouge's text, the balance of power described between masters and servants is very similar to that widely assumed to exist between husbands and wives. In the economy of dominance and subordination governing both relationships, the status of each party depends on the other. If the subordinate party asserts mastery — in literature on shrewish women, as we have seen, this is often depicted as wearing the breeches — he or she usurps that privilege from the master of the household, thereby subjugating him. Such inversions were possible — and widely feared — in class as well as gender relations. Gouge warns that if servants are not kept in subjection, they will become masters and be "advanced above their place and degree" and governors will be "dejected below their place and degree," like a scale suddenly thrown off balance. Gouge's description of the balance of power in households offers a reminder that class as well as gender determined who would dominate and who would submit in sixteenth- and seventeenth-century households. His text also reveals that gender and class might sometimes work at cross-purposes; for instance, a mistress had power over her male servants (see Figure 9 for an image of a woman wielding a bundle of rods, commonly used in disciplinary beatings). A wide range of texts, from conduct books to popular, humorous tales of shrew taming, placed the burden on the male head of household (the master, husband, and father) to keep the economy of dominance and submission in balance by asserting, maintaining, but not exceeding his own authority.

→ THOMAS BECON

From *A New Catechism Set Forth Dialogue-Wise in Familiar Talk Between the Father and the Son*   *1560*

Thomas Becon (1512–1567), a Protestant clergyman, was an early and ardent supporter of the Reformation in England. He lived, preached, and wrote about a generation before the other ministers and writers represented in this book (such as John Dod, William Gouge, and William Whately). As a result, he weathered the dilemmas and reversals of the early Reformation. Although Henry VIII initiated the official split between the English church and the church in Rome, zealots such as Becon pushed reform further than Henry was

Thomas Becon, *A New Catechism Set Forth Dialogue-Wise in Familiar Talk Between the Father and the Son* (1560), in *The Works of Thomas Becon*, 3 vols. (London, 1564): 1:Zz3v–Zz4.

Emblem XIV.

Emb.14.   *I.D. Sculp.*

Pueros caſtigo, viroſque.

The

FIGURE 9. *A woman holding rods used for beating. This emblem, from Nathaniel Crouch's* Delights for the Ingenious *(London, 1684), combines an image of what boys fear most (being beaten) with one of what men fear most (women). The caption reads: "I punish both boys and men." Although the poem that accompanies the picture does not claim that women routinely beat boys (who were probably most often disciplined by fathers, masters, and male teachers), the illustration links women to violent punishment.*

ready to go. Many of Becon's books were censured as heretical. Despite the fact that Becon routinely published under a pseudonym, in 1543 he had to recant doctrines he had advocated in print; his books were publicly burned. The reign of Edward VI offered Becon a brief respite; but when Mary Tudor's accession briefly returned the country to Catholicism, Becon was in even greater danger. For seven months in 1553 he was committed to the Tower for seditious preaching; he was evicted from his clerical office for having married; and his books were listed among those heretical works that it was illegal to sell, read, or own. Upon his release from the Tower, he went to live in Strasbourg and did not return to England until Elizabeth's accession and the reinstitution of Protestantism as the national religion. At that time he was restored to his position as rector of a parish in London and as a preacher at Canterbury cathedral. Although his works were controversial — even prohibited — for most of his life, Becon was a prolific and influential writer.

A New Catechism Set Forth Dialogue-Wise in Familiar Talk Between the Father and the Son

Of the Office of Masters or Householders
Toward Their Servants

SON: It is the duty of a godly householder or master not to be rigorous and hasty with their servants, but rather to be gentle and quiet with them. So that if the servants sometime through negligence or oversight leave anything undone or do not things in such order as they ought to do, they quietly and patiently bear with them, exhorting them from henceforth to be more diligent and circumspect in doing their duty. And by no means like a madman fall out with them, curse and lame them, cast dishes and pots at their heads, beat them, put them in danger of their life, etc. This becometh not Christian modesty, nor civil sobriety. It becometh every godly master or householder ever to set before his eyes this saying of the wiseman: "Be not as a Lion in thine own house, destroying the household folks, and oppressing them that are under thee" (Ecclesiasticus 4). Hereto agreeth the saying of Saint Paul: "You masters put away threatenings, knowing that your master also is in heaven, neither is there any respect of persons with him" (Ephesians 6). Again "Masters, do unto your servants that which is just and equal, knowing that you also have a master in heaven" (Colossians 4).

FATHER: Why, is it not lawful for a master to correct his servants that offend, as well by stripes° as by words?

stripes: blows, strokes, or lashes, especially marks left by a whip or other object.

SON: If words may do good, what need stripes? Who offendeth not sometime? If a servant be so negligent or willful that he will not amend his
fault, although many times heretofore admonished and rebuked for the
same, the master may use his discretion in this behalf, and minister such
moderate correction to the offender as shall seem meet° to his wisdom,
this always considered: that measure be observed in all things and that
correction be ministered with discretion and favor. We be bought all
with one price, and we be all inheritors of one glory. Christian men may
not handle their servants as the unfaithful Turks do, which entreat° their
servants as bond-slaves, yea, as beasts without any respect of manhood.

meet: fitting, becoming, proper.   entreat: treat.

→ WILLIAM GOUGE

From *Of Domestical Duties: Eight Treatises*   *1634*

TREATISE 8

Section 4. Of Masters' Maintaining Their Authority

After that masters have chosen good servants, their duty is well to use
them; which, by reason of the difference betwixt masters and servants,
cannot be well done except masters wisely maintain their authority. A
master therefore must be able "well to rule his own house" (1 Timothy 3.4).
This is a duty which the Apostle in particular requireth of a Bishop, who
is master of a house; but it appertaineth in general to all masters of families.
Women, also, who by virtue of their places are mistresses, are commanded
"to guide the house" (1 Timothy 5.14) or to rule and perform the part of a
mistress therein. It was the Centurion's commendation that, having servants under him, he had them at his command (Matthew 8.9).
    1. God's image and authority, which a master carrieth, is thus preserved.
    2. Thus shall a master have much better service done. Not one servant
of a thousand, that is not kept under authority, will do good service.

William Gouge, *Of Domestical Duties: Eight Treatises* (London, 1634), 660–64, 668–72. Biographical information on Gouge is provided in the headnote to the first excerpt from *Of
Domestical Duties* (p. 220–21).

For this end, three things are to be observed:

1. That masters carry themselves worthy of their place, and worthy of that honor which is due to them, which may best be done by making themselves a pattern of such good things as in their places appertain to them. "I and my house will fear the Lord," saith Joshua (Joshua 24.15). He would not only put them to it, but he also would do it; he would go before them. "I will behave myself wisely; I will walk within my house with a perfect heart," saith David (Psalms 101.2).

2. That masters keep their servants in awe and fear. Children must be "kept in subjection" (1 Timothy 3.4); much more servants.

3. That masters do the things which they do in their carriage towards their servants with authority: "Command, forbid, rebuke" (to use the Apostle's phrase) "with all authority" (Titus 2.15). The manner of speech which the Centurion used to his servants ("Go, come, do this") savor[s] of authority (Matthew 8.9). So the Church taking upon her the person of a mistress, useth a word of authority: "I charge you" not to do this (Canticles [Song of Songs] 3.5).

Section 5. Of Masters' Making Their Authority to Be Despised

The aberrations in the defect contrary to the forenamed duty and point of wisdom are many, as:

1. When masters carry themselves basely and abjectly before their servants, being light in their behavior, foolish in their carriage, given to drunkenness, uncleanness, lewd company, and other vices. [Some discussion of Old Testament examples of this follows.]

Mistresses oft lose their authority by conspiring with their servants to go abroad, take away goods, gossip, and do such other like things privily without their husbands' consent. They make themselves thereby slaves to their servants, not daring to do anything which may offend their servants, lest they should discover to their masters such lewd pranks as their mistresses did.

2. When masters are too remiss and sheepish, entreating and praying their servants to do such things as they ought to command and require at their hands. And if it be not done, all their remedy is patience, or else to do it themselves. Howsoever this might be counted meekness and gentleness towards equals and strangers over whom we have no authority, yet towards servants it is too base remissness. Yea, it is a relinquishing of that power which God hath given, and whereof God will take an account.

3. When masters suffer their servants to be their companions, playing, drinking, reveling with them, and saying, as it is in the proverb, "hail fellows met." Thus servants oft take liberty to presume above their master. For men are naturally prone to ambition, and "if an inch be given, they will take an ell."° They who in this kind so far debase themselves as to give their servants power over their own body, do make both themselves and their true lawful bedfellow to be despised. Themselves, in that such servants as are so made one flesh will think to keep in awe such a master or mistress as they have known, through fear of revealing that sin. Their bedfellow, in that such servants will think to be maintained and bolstered up by the master or mistress whom they have so known. On this ground was Sarah despised in the eyes of Hagar, her maid (Genesis 16.3–4).°

4. When masters are overruled by their servants to do any unjust or unlawful thing. As Joash, who by his servants was drawn to idolatry (2 Chronicles 24.17); and Zedekiah, who gave the prophet Jeremiah into his servants' hands, using this base and abject speech; "The King is not he that can do anything against you" (Jeremiah 38.5). Thus will servants soon prove masters. And if they once come to this high pitch to rule, rather than to be ruled, they will quickly prove intolerable. For this is one of the four things noted by the wiseman which "the earth cannot bear," namely, "a servant when he reigneth" (Proverbs 30.22). And this is one of those evils which proceed from rulers, that "servants ride upon horse," that is, are advanced above their place and degree. Whence it followeth that "Governors walk as servants upon the earth"; they are dejected below their place and degree (Ecclesiastes 10.5, 7). It falleth out in this case betwixt servants and masters, as betwixt scales or balances: if the weights that use to lie in one balance to keep it down be taken away, it will suddenly fly up, and so the other balance will be kept down.

Section 6. Of Masters' Too Great Rigor

The contrary in the excess is too great rigor and austerity manifested in look, speech, and actions.

1. In look, when a master cannot cast a good eye on his servant. Jacob was much discountenanced by the countenance of his master (Genesis 31.2,5). Many masters by their continual frowning brows and fiery eyes do much terrify their servants.

---

ell: measurement of length, forty-five inches in England. (Genesis 16.3–4): Sarah's servant Hagar had sex with Sarah's husband, Abraham, and had a child by him (Ishmael). "A Homily of the State of Matrimony" (p. 169) discusses Sarah and Abraham's marriage at length.

2. In speech, when masters cannot give a good word to their servants; but if they be moved never so little, cast upon them all the reproachful names that they can call to mind, little thinking of this fearful doom: "whosoever shall say 'thou fool' shall be in danger of hell fire" (Matthew 5.22).

Thus did Saul manifest a malicious and mischievous mind against Jonathan and David by the foul language he gave (1 Samuel 20–30). Some have such a froward and perverse tongue as they can never speak directly to their servants, but if they command or forbid a thing, they will do it after such a manner as their servant can scarce tell what they mean, and this not only when their servant hath offended them, but in their best mood. So shrewish are others, as their tongues seldom lie still, but they are ever chiding upon every small occasion. Whereby, it cometh to pass that their servants are no more moved with it than the doves and stares° that continually abide in belfries are moved with the ringing of bells. Such bitterness also is mixed with the chidings of many, as they belch out of their black mouths most direful imprecations. What can be said of such tongues, but that they are "set on fire of hell" (James 3.6)? As other aberrations wherein masters are reproved are to be applied to mistresses, so this especially. For mistresses do commonly most offend in shrewishness of speech.

3. In action, when masters are too frequent and too furious strikers, striking their servants on every occasion, not caring how they strike. In these and other like evidences of too much austerity and plain arrogancy, masters forget that they are men. Though for outward order a master be more excellent than a servant, yet as a man he ought to judge himself equal. This extreme can be no good means to maintain authority, but it is a plain abuse thereof. Masters ought so to carry themselves, as their servants may rather reverence than dread them.

Section 7. Of Masters' Commanding Power,
Restrained to Things Lawful

[In a paragraph at the beginning of this section, Gouge lays out his program for the next several sections.]

Within the list° of these two virtues, Justice and Equity, whereunto all the duties which masters owe their servants shall afterward be referred, must the commanding power of masters be bounded.

Justice requireth two things:

1. A restraint of masters' commandments.

2. An execution thereof.

---

stares: starlings.　list: limits, bounds.

The restraint is unto God's law, that a master command nothing against it, but what is agreeable to it. Abshai would fain have had David's warrant to have killed Saul, but David was so far from commanding him to do it as he kept him from it (1 Samuel 26.9).°

Masters are but subordinate ministers under God. They must therefore command nothing against his Law. As a judge, high-sheriff, and all other officers under the king must make the king's law the ground of all those things which they require of the king's subjects, so masters must make God's law the ground of all those things which they require of their servants, who are also the servants of Christ. Besides, to what purpose is it to command that which a servant may and must refuse to do? But in no unlawful thing may he obey.

Section 13. Of the Power of Masters to Correct Their Servants

The second point wherein a master's power consisteth [after commanding] is correction, which may be given by looks, words, or deeds.

By a man's look, his anger and wrath against another is manifested. In Hebrew the same word signifieth a face and wrath because wrath soonest sheweth itself in a man's face. It is noted of Cain, that being "very wroth,° his countenance fell down" (Genesis 4.5). Now the manifestation of a master's wrath against his servant is a correction.

But words, whether of rebuke or threatening, do much more declare the same. This phrase which Solomon useth, "a servant will not be corrected by words" (Proverbs 29.19) showeth that there is a correction by words; and though it be negatively propounded, yet doth it not imply that correction by words is not to be used to a servant, but rather, if thereby he be not moved, that blows must be added thereto, which is a correction by deeds, whereof Christ maketh mention in the parable of those servants that, according to the greatness of their fault, are to be "beaten with many stripes" (Luke 12.47). It is therefore in a master's power to correct his servant with stripes or blows. Which being so, I will show:

1. How far his power herein extendeth.
2. How it is to be ordered.

(**I Samuel 26.9**): Abshai, David's servant, wanted to kill King Saul so that David, secretly anointed king by the prophet Samuel, could take his place. **wroth**: displeased, angry, sorrowful.

Section 14. Of the Restraint of Masters' Power:
That It Reacheth Not to Their Servants' Life

Concerning the extent of a master's power in correcting his servant, this question is to be resolved: whether a master have power for any fault to take away his servant's life?

ANSWER: His power reacheth not so far, as is evident by these reasons:

1. There is no precept, nor approved example, nor any other warrant out of God's Word for it. The Jews had great power over such servants as were strangers: "Of them they might buy bond-men and bond-maids; they might have them for a possession, and take them for an inheritance for their children after them, to be bond-men forever" (Leviticus 25.44–46). They might be put to the most toiling, droiling,° base, and abject works that they had, as drawing water, hewing wood, and the like (Joshua 9.27). But yet their masters had not power over their lives.

2. A master might not dismember his servant. If unawares° he did smite out an eye or tooth of his servant, he must make a recompense, which was to let him go free (Exodus 21.26). Much less, therefore, might he take away his servant's life.

3. If a servant died under his master's hand, when he corrected him, though he intended not willfully to murder him, that master was to be punished (Exodus 21.20). It was not, therefore, lawful for a master wittingly to kill a servant.

4. The power of life is proper to the public magistrate, who doth all things in open public places, that so there may be many witnesses of his just proceeding. If masters had this power, many might privily be put to death, and no man know for what cause, as it is in popish Inquisitions.°

5. The approved laws of men make it willful murder for a master to slay his servant wittingly, though the servant's fault be never so heinous. Neither the authority of the master, nor desert of the servant shall exempt the master that slayeth his servant from the guilt and punishment of felony.

OBJECTION: In ancient times masters had this power.

ANSWER: They never of right had it, though some might exercise it. Among God's people it was never exercised in any age of the world. That liberty which was taken, was among the heathen. And yet, among them, as

---

droiling: having to do with drudgery or slavery.   unawares: unintentionally.   popish Inquisitions: The Inquisition was established in 1235 by Pope Gregory IX to inquire into offenses against the Roman Catholic Church. Since the Inquisition relied on torture to secure confessions and recantations of heretical beliefs and was largely a Continental phenomenon, it came to represent for the post-Reformation English the cruelty and clandestinity that they associated with Catholicism and foreignness.

polities came to be more and more civilly governed, that usurped liberty by the laws of magistrates was much restrained. And when emperors and kings became Christians, it was utterly taken away.

OBJECTION: If a man take an enemy by war, he hath power to kill him.

ANSWER: If in the time of the war he slay him not, but then spare him, and take him as a captive, and make him his servant, though but a bond-slave, he hath not power of his life.

Section 15. Of Masters' Excess in Correcting Servants

Contrary to their just and due power do they who, in their rage, stab their servants, or otherwise make them away; yea, they also, who so unmercifully and unmeasurably beat them with rod, cudgel, or any other thing, as death follow thereupon. For many there be who, having once begun to strike, know not when to cease, but lay on as if they were striking stocks or blocks, and not their own flesh. God foresaw that masters were prone to such cruelty, and therefore set a stint° number of stripes, which none that beat another might exceed (Deuteronomy 25.3).

Among these may be reckoned such desperate masters as in their mood will strike their servants with anything that cometh next to hand, be it heavy, cragged, hard, or sharp, they care not: [They are] "as a madman who casteth fire-brands, arrows, and death" (Proverbs 26.18). These things may endanger a servant's life. If not, they may break his head, or otherwise wound, bruise, and lame him.

It is beyond a master's power by any correction to impair life, health, or strength of his servant, or any way in his body to disable him from doing that which otherwise he might have been able to do.

If masters — no, not for punishment of any sin — may not take away or endanger the life of his servant, what may we think of such masters as, without fault of their servants, cause them to be made away, by putting them upon some desperate attempt, either to maintain their own quarrel, or for some other unjust end? David dealt thus with Uriah, but afterwards he sorely repented this part of injustice (2 Samuel 11.5).° At another time, when three of his servants had fetched him water, which he longed for, with jeopardy of their lives, though in safety they returned, yet his heart smote him for his longing, and he would not drink of that water, because they had ventured their lives to fetch it (2 Samuel 23.15).

But what may we say of such masters as cause their servants for their

---

stint: an allotted or prescribed number. The limit on strokes set in Deuteronomy is forty. (2 Samuel 11.15): Because David was in love with Uriah's wife, Bathsheba, he ordered Uriah into the most dangerous part of a battle, where he was killed. David then married Bathsheba.

sakes to commit felony, murder, treason, rebellion, and such other things as cause the public magistrate to unsheath his sword against them and cut them off? We noted this before to be a grievous fault, in regard of the unlawfulness of the thing. Here further we may note it to be much more heinous in regard of the mischief that followeth thereupon, which is the loss of their servant's life; so as thus they make themselves accessary to a detestable sin, and guilty of the blood of their servant.

Section 16. Of Masters' Ordering That Correction They Give to Their Servants

1. That masters may well order that correction which they give to their servants, difference must be put betwixt the age, sex, disposition, and faults of those whom they correct.°

2. Masters ought not to be so forward to strike such as are grown in years as the younger sort. Years bring understanding, and a rebuke will make one of understanding more sorry for a fault, and more careful to amend it, than blows; smart° more works upon the younger sort. But if, notwithstanding their years, they be stout, and will not regard words, their stoutness must be beaten down with blows. "Smite a scorner," saith the wiseman; and, again, "Judgments are prepared for scorners and stripes for the back of fools" (Proverbs 19.25, 29).

Seeing servants in years are in this case to be corrected, it is further requisite to put a difference betwixt the kind or measure of correction which is given to them and to the younger sort. If they be corrected as children, they may either make a toy of it, or the more disdain at it. "Blueness,° wound[s], and stripes piercing into the inward parts of the belly are a purging medicine against evil" to stout servants of ripe years (Proverbs 20.30).

3. If there be a master and mistress joint-governors over a house, it is fittest for the master to correct men-servants, the mistress maids. "It is a great reproach for a man to beat a maid-servant" (Chrysostom 26); and a man-servant will much disdain to be smitten by a woman. Abraham put his maid over to Sarah [his wife] in such a case (Genesis 16.6). Yet if a maid should wax stout, and mannish, and turn against her mistress (she being weak, sickly, with child, or otherwise unable to master her maid), the master may and must beat down her stoutness and rebellion. So much did the Law of God permit (Exodus 21.20).

---

faults . . . correct: In the margin Gouge directs his reader to his earlier discussion of how parents should order the correction they give to their children. He points out that the advice he offers there "may in many points be here fitly applied." **smart:** pain. **Blueness:** bruising.

4. If servants be of an ingenious disposition, willing and forward to do that which belongeth unto them, sorry when they have committed a fault, and careful to amend their faults, many things may be passed over in them which must be corrected in others. To this may be applied the counsel of the wiseman: "Take no heed to all the words that are spoken" (Ecclesiastes 7.21).

5. Correction must be measured according to the greatness of the fault punished, and the circumstances whereby the fault may justly be aggravated. "The servant that knew his master's will and did it not, shall he be beaten with many stripes; but he that knew not, and did commit things worthy of stripes, shall be beaten with few stripes" (Luke 12.47–48).

Many aberrations are daily committed contrary to every branch of this direction, in that masters and mistresses in exercising this part of their power are carried away with passion, and do that which they do in this kind after their own pleasure. Thus they turn a duty into a sin, and by undue correcting of their servants, provoke God to correct them in his wrath, either here or in the world to come.

CHAPTER 4

Shrews, Taming, and Untamed Shrews

Shrews and Shrew Taming

The Taming of the Shrew participates in a tenacious popular tradition of depicting domestic violence as funny. Since one needs neither money nor literacy to gain access to a ballad, joke, or puppet show, and since ballad sellers, peddlers, and puppeteers disseminated their wares across England, people from every class would have been familiar with this tradition. This tradition usually depicted the inversion of the expected order of gender relations; the woman on top wears the breeches, scolds those who are her social superiors, beats up and bosses her husband, and generally asserts her mastery. Both the domineering wife and her weak husband are ridiculed and censured. Usually, but not always, this inversion is corrected — the woman on top is put down — often through violence. Thus, communal rituals for mocking and correcting domestic disorder, such as parades in which neighbors parodied the conduct of bossy wives and weak husbands (see p. 13) or the cucking of a scold described in a ballad (see p. 292), operated in the same way that stories, songs, and jokes did; they attempted to correct disorder by exposing it in its crudest outlines. Singing songs, repeating stories and jokes, and participating in as well as observing shaming rituals, members of a community produced as well as absorbed these lessons in proper gender relations.

Reactions to the shrew-taming tradition must have varied among husbands and wives, mockers and mocked. Although texts sought "to put pressure on women to dissociate themselves from rebellion and model their behavior on the ideal of submissiveness," some women probably identified with or rooted for unruly behavior (Wiltenburg 125). Even women who complied with the ideals for female conduct may have found some satisfaction in imagining flagrant disregard for those ideals. At a time when, as we have seen, conduct books and sermons discouraged husbands from using the violence to which, nonetheless, they had a legal right, husbands may have relished the spectacle of brutality, especially since violent representations of shrew taming often suggested that it did no permanent harm and, indeed, worked in the interests of domestic peace and order. In these representations violence, whether perpetrated by women or men, does no lasting damage and brings none of the dire consequences threatened in prescriptive literature. Except in the cartoonishly murderous world of *Punch and Judy*, a husband's violence tames his shrewish wife and reasserts his mastery; it does not compromise his authority, harden her heart, or maim or kill her.

Several conventions characterize most comic depictions of shrew taming. One is a remarkable resilience, physical and emotional, in the wife. In *A Merry Jest of a Shrewd and Curst Wife Lapped in Morel's Skin* (p. 254), for instance, the wife not only survives a severe beating without lasting scars or disabilities (her white skin is as "fair and clear" as ever) but also without a grudge. She forgives and forgets, and the reader is expected to do the same. These texts do not consider the possibility that the wife wrapped in morel's skin or the cucked (dunked) scold might not get over it, that she might harbor unspoken resentments. These texts also treat pain very lightly, passing over the woman's suffering; this is especially obvious in *Punch and Judy*, in which we are always aware that Judy is a puppet who cannot feel. By minimizing the woman's emotional and physical pain, and downplaying her motivations for acting as she does, these texts also shy away from making her a fully developed character. Even the language of "taming" suggests that the unruly woman is less than human; she is a "shrew" (a small mammal to which evil powers were attributed), a horse to be bridled, a "haggard" or wild falcon to be mastered.

In all the texts about shrews and shrew taming here, the women instigate the violence or conflict and thus seem to provoke retaliation. Furthermore, the husband's or community's punishments are depicted as a last resort; they are not angry and uncontrolled actions, but rather a conscious strategy for governing the unruly.

Finally, comic depictions of shrew taming and wife beating often depict the husband as coming from a lower class than either his wife or the reader/viewer. Just as Petruchio positioned himself as a "gentle" man by using policy rather than force, husbands who use violence to subdue their wives are often depicted as markedly ungentle, even vulgar (in its meaning of common, low, or coarse). In such representations, "the violence is a plebian activity; people of 'quality' observe it with amusement and approval but are not shown engaging in it themselves. This redefinition of violence against women as a lower-class activity offered respectable audiences a means of distancing themselves from the violence while still enjoying it, and suggests that violent shrew taming was increasingly seen as a forbidden fruit" (Wiltenburg 128). By the eighteenth century "wife beating became, for literate people, a particular mark of the inferiority and animality of the poor" (Hunt 27). This did not mean that domestic violence never occurred among the affluent, elite, and literate. It simply meant that the upper classes distanced themselves from this violence by representing it as "beneath" them.

Some people must also have enjoyed other kinds of stories. *The Taming of the Shrew* is itself an alternative to the most brutal stories of shrew taming, such as *A Merry Jest*. There were texts written by women, which have stronger claims for recording women's voices than any of the texts written by men collected here, however various they may be. Stories also survive in which women tame men successfully and permanently or in which shrews and scolds talk on, indomitable and unrepentant to the last. Such stories (included here in the section on "Untamed Shrews," p. 317) are far less common than those of shrew taming; less widely circulated in the sixteenth and seventeenth centuries, they are also harder to track down now. We must consider the context in which they appeared: the stories by Harman and Heywood reprinted below occur in collections of stories about disorderly or criminal behavior; they seek to entertain readers but also to promote order. Since the authors who tell these stories hardly endorse the "shrewish" conduct they describe, we must be wary of reading these texts as authentic or unmediated accounts of women's empowerment and resistance. But, in their striking difference from the norm (as represented by the first three selections in this chapter), these stories do suggest the possibility that other narrative and social structures were imaginable than those endlessly reproduced in stories of shrew taming.

⤳ "The Cruel Shrew"   *Circa 1600–1650*

In "The Cruel Shrew, or The Patient Man's Woe," from the first half of the seventeenth century, the husband catalogues many of the characteristics of the stereotypical shrew (see Figure 10). As discussed in the Introduction, shrew-ishness was not restricted to excessive or hostile speech. The husband complains repeatedly about his wife's tongue and her noisiness: she bawls, curses, rails, scolds, and snores; but his complaints extend beyond her nagging and verbal abuse. According to him, she is lazy and vain, she gossips and drinks with her friends, and she is physically abusive. Although she beats him with a cudgel and scratches and tears at him, she refuses to submit to any physical retaliation. As in many other ballads about shrews, all these behaviors can be summed up in the cruel shrew's insistence on wearing the breeches. Demanding extreme versions of husbandly prerogatives, the shrew is depicted — entirely from her husband's point of view — as refusing him any rights at all.

Besides depicting the relation between spouses as one of violent, contentious rivalry, the ballad also pits the larger communities of men and women against one another. The speaker addresses an audience of men — "bachelors and married men" — to whom he appeals as jury members who must "give their verdicts" as to which spouse is to blame for this miserable marriage. Although the speaker seems to assume that his male auditors will side with him, he suggests that his wife's "mates," an all-female jury, might decide otherwise. When in conflict with her husband, the wife calls upon her friends "her part to take."

In part because divorce was not readily available, there are few solutions to what the ballad calls the husband's "piteous cause." One solution would be to tame the cruel shrew, but this defeated and patient man does not propose to do so. He might also desert his wife, which would require him to leave his home and his employment and to begin life again elsewhere as a kind of fugitive. Or he could apply for a legal separation, which would not enable him to remarry and would probably require him to support his wife. The ballad does not explore any of these possible solutions, however, presenting the husband's situation as hopeless and irresolvable. The only possible escape the husband imagines is death, although he does not go so far as proposing to murder his wife. First, he expresses his desire that his own "lingering life . . . were at an end." Then, rather than imagine his own wife's death, he imagines a "harmless honest man" who has been fortunate enough to have death "take his wife from of his hand." Perhaps he could trade the dead wife for his own. In accord with wedding vows that joined husband and wife "till death us depart" (or separate), the ballad imagines death as the only

Arthur Halliarg, "The Cruel Shrew, or The Patient Man's Woe" (London, c. 1600–1650).

The Cruell Shrow:

OR,
The Patient Mans VVoe.

Declaring the misery, and the great paine,
By his vnquiet wife he doth dayly sustaine.

To the Tune of *Cuckolds all a rowe,*

Come Batchelers and Maried men,
　and listen to my Song;
And I will shew you plainely then,
　the iniury and wrong
That constantly I doe sustaine,
　by the vnhappy life,
The which does put me to great paine,
　by my vnquiet wife.

Shée neuer linnes her bauling,
　her tongue it is so loud,
But alwaies shee'le be railing,
　and will not be contrould:
For shee the Britches still will weare,
　although it breedes my strife,
If I were now a Batcheler,
　I'de neuer haue a Wife.

Sometime I goe i'the morning,
　about my dayly worke.
My wife she will be snorting,
　and in her bed she'le lurke:
Untill the Chimes doe goe at Eight,
　then she'le beginne to wake;
Her mornings draught well spiced
　to cleare her eyes she'le take. (straight

As soone as shee is out of bed,
　her Looking-glasse shée takes,
So vainely is she dayly led,
　her mornings worke shé makes

In putting on her braue atyre,
　that fine and costly be.
Whilst I worke hard in durt and mire,
　alacke what remedy.

Then she goes forth a Gossiping,
　amongst her owne Comrades.
And then she falls a bowsing,
　with her merry blades:
When I come from my labour hard,
　then shée'le begin to scould,
And calls me Rogue without regard,
　which makes my heart full cold.

When I come home into my house,
　thinking to take my rest:
Then she'le begin me to rouse,
　before she did but iest:
With out you Raskall, you haue béns'
　abroad to meet your Whore:
Then she takes vp a Cudgels end,
　and breaks my head full sore.

When I for quietnesse sake desire,
　my wife for to be still;
She will not grant what I require,
　but swears shee'le haue her will:
Then if I chance to heaue my hand,
　straight way she'le murder cry:
Then iudge all men that here doe stand,
　in what a case am I.

The second Part, To the same Tune.

A And if a friend by chance me call,
to drinke a pot of Beere:
Then she'le begin to curse and brall,
and fight, and scratch, and teare:
And sweares vnto my worship she'le send
me straight without delay,
Or else with the same Cudgels end,
thee will me soundly pay.

And if I chance to sit at meat,
vpon some holy day,
She is so sullen she will not eate,
but byds me curse and away:
She'le pout, and loure, and curse & banne,
this is the weary life
That I doe leade, poore harmelesse man,
with my most dogged wife.

Then is not this a pitteous cause,
Let all men now it trie,
And giue their verdits by the Lawes,
betweene my wife and I,
And iudge the cause, who is to blame,
Ile to their Iudgement stand,
And be contented with the same,
and put thereto my hand.

If I abroad goe any where,
my businesse for to doe,
Then will my wife anone be there,
for to encrease my woe:
Straight may she such a noise will make,
with her most wicked tongue,
That all her mates her part to take,
about me soone will thronge.

Thus am I now tormented still,
with my most cruell wife,
All through her wicked tongue so ill,
I am weary of my life:

I know not truly what to doe,
nor how my selfe to mend;
This lingring life doth bring my woe,
I would twere at an ende.

O that same harmelesse honest man,
whom Death did so befriend,
To take his wife from out his hand,
his sorrowes for to end:
Would change with me to rid my care,
and take my wife aline,
For his dead wife vnto his share,
then I would hope to thriue.

But so it likely will not be,
that is the worst of all,
For to encrease my haply woe,
and for to bring my fall.
My wife is still most froward bent,
such to my lucklesse fate,
There is no man will be content,
with my vnhappy state.

Thus to conclude and make an ende,
of these my Verses rude,
I pray all wiues for to amende,
and with peace to be endude:
Take warning all men by the life,
that I sustained long,
Be carefull how you'le chuse a Wife,
and so Ile ende my Song.

FINIS.

Arthur Halliarg.

London, Printed by M. P, for Henry
Gosson on London Bridge neare
the Gate.

◄ FIGURE 10 *Facsimiles of "The Cruel Shrew, or The Patient Man's Woe" (first half of the seventeenth century). Here, as in most ballads, the only indication of the tune is a reference to another tune, which readers are presumed to know. This ballad is printed on both sides of a single sheet. As the pages are less crammed with type than in Figure 8, it is easier to read. Ballad printers often "recycled" illustrations, drawing, often randomly, from a limited stock of woodcuts. The same woodcuts, such as the very fashionable man and woman pictured here, appeared again and again in different ballads, serving more as ornaments than as depictions of characters and events described in the ballad.*

way out of this unhappy marriage. Sympathizing with the husband and placing all the blame on the wife, the ballad flirts with, but also retreats from, exploring murder as the logical consequence of a husband's anger at his "unquiet" wife.

"The Cruel Shrew"

Declaring the misery, and the great pain,
By his unquiet wife he doth daily sustain.

To the tune of "Cuckolds All A-row"

Come, bachelors and married men,
    and listen to my song,
And I will show you plainly, then,
    the injury and wrong
That constantly I do sustain   5
    by the unhappy life,
The which does put me to great pain,
    by my unquiet wife.

She never lins° her bawling,
    her tongue it is so loud;   10
But always she'll be railing,°
    and will not be controlled.
For she the breeches still will wear,
    although it breeds my strife.
If I were now a bachelor,   15
    I'd never have a wife.

Sometime I go i'the morning
    about my daily work;

---

9. **lins:** ceases.   11. **railing:** uttering abusive language; bantering or jesting.

My wife she will be snorting,°
  and in her bed she'll lurk
Until the chimes do go at eight,   20
  then she'll begin to wake.
Her morning's draught, well-spicèd° straight,
  to clear her eyes she'll take.

As soon as she is out of bed
  her looking-glass she takes,   25
(So vainly is she daily led);
  her morning's work she makes
In putting on her brave attire,
  that fine and costly be,
Whilst I work hard in dirt and mire.   30
  Alack! What remedy?

Then she goes forth a-gossiping
  amongst her own comrades;
And then she falls a-boozing
  with her merry blades.°   35
When I come home from my labor hard,
  then she'll begin to scold,
And calls me rogue, without regard,
  which makes my heart full cold.
                                                              40
When I come home into my house,
  thinking to take my rest,
Then she'll begin me to abuse
  (before she did but jest),
With — "Out, you rascal! you have been
  abroad to meet your whore!"   45
Then she takes up a cudgel's end,
  and breaks my head full sore.

When I, for quietness' sake, desire
  my wife for to be still,
She will not grant what I require,   50
  but swears she'll have her will.
Then if I chance to heave my hand,
  straightway she'll "murder!" cry;
Then judge all men that here do stand,
  in what a case am I.   55

---

19. **snorting**: snoring.   23. **spicèd**: may have our meaning of *spiked* here.   36. **blades**: companions, probably male.

The Second Part

To the Same Tune

And if a friend by chance me call
    to drink a pot of beer,
Then she'll begin to curse and brawl,
    and fight, and scratch, and tear,   60
And swears unto my work she'll send
    me straight, without delay,
Or else, with the same cudgel's end,
    she will me soundly pay.

And if I chance to sit at meat   65
    upon some holy day,
She is so sullen, she will not eat,
    but vex me ever and ay;°
She'll pout, and lour, and curse, and bann.°
    This is the weary life   70
That I do lead, poor harmless man,
    with my most doggèd wife.

Then is not this a piteous cause?
    Let all men now it try,
And give their verdicts, by the laws,   75
    between my wife and I,
And judge the cause, who is to blame.
    I'll to their judgment stand,
And be contented with the same,
    and put thereto my hand.   80

If I abroad go anywhere,
    my business for to do,
Then will my wife anon° be there,
    for to increase my woe.
Straightway she such a noise will make   85
    with her most wicked tongue,
That all her mates, her part to take,
    about me soon will throng.

---

68. ay: always.   69. lour: frown, scowl.   **bann**: curse.   83. anon: at once, soon.

Thus am I now tormented still
   with my most cruel wife;
All through her wicked tongue so ill,   90
   I am weary of my life.
I know not truly what to do,
   nor how my self to mend.
This ling'ring life doth breed my woe;   95
   I would 'twere at an end.

Oh that some harmless honest man,
   whom death did so befriend,
To take his wife from of° his hand,
   his sorrows for to end,
Would change with me, to rid my care,   100
   and take my wife alive
For his dead wife unto his share;°
   then I would hope to thrive.

But so it likely will not be,   105
   (that is the worst of all!)
For, to increase my daily woe,
   and for to breed my fall,
My wife is still most froward° bent —
   such is my luckless fate! —
There is no man will be content   110
   with my unhappy state.

Thus to conclude and make an end
   of these my verses rude,
I pray all wives for to amend,
   and with peace to be endued.°   115
Take warning, all men, by the life
   that I sustainèd long:
Be careful how you'll choose a wife,
   and so I'll end my song.   120

FINIS.

99. **of:** either an intensification of "from" or "off."   103. **unto his share:** in exchange for his dead wife.   109. **froward:** perverse, difficult to deal with, hard to please.   116. **endued:** endowed or invested with.

➔ A Merry Jest of a Shrewd and Curst Wife Lapped in Morel's Skin, for Her Good Behavior *circa 1550*

Although this lengthy ballad was printed only once, and survives in just a few copies, it offers a particularly elaborate and fully developed version of a folktale that circulated orally and was very popular; it is also considered a possible source for Shakespeare's play (Hosley 289). Like *The Taming of the Shrew, A Merry Jest* centers on a family in which there are two sisters, the younger favored by the father and pursued by suitors, the elder shrewish and thus less likely to find a suitor. In *A Merry Jest* once a young man who wishes to court and marry the older, shrewish sister enters the scene, the focus shifts to this couple's negotiations and conflicts before and after marriage. *A Merry Jest* introduces a new character to the dynamics familiar to us from *The Taming of the Shrew.* The young women have a mother as well as a father.[1]

This mother, herself a shrew, has trained her favorite, first-born daughter to insist on her own way and to strive to be the master. While Katharine's anger stems from her frustrated desire for marriage, "the normal female life-trajectory within patriarchy," the daughter here "defies prescriptions for female behavior in her urge to master her husband" (Mikesell 152). As a result, both father and mother predict that their daughter will never submit to her husband; for the father this is an embarrassment, for the mother it is a triumph. While the father warns the young man not to marry his daughter, the mother acts as her daughter's advocate in the marriage negotiations, insisting that the marriage occur only on her daughter's terms. As these early scenes make clear, *A Merry Jest* raises more voices than does *The Taming of the Shrew.* Here, both mother and daughter are active, demanding participants in the marriage negotiations; indeed, they set the agenda.

Despite the fact that the bride in *A Merry Jest* is more a party to her marriage contract than Katharine in *The Taming of the Shrew* seems to be, that contract is presented from the beginning as too excessive and unreasonable in its demands on the husband. Nor is it clear that the husband makes the contract in good faith or feels bound by it: "Even as the cat was wont with the mouse / To play, forsooth even so did he" (lines 491–92). After the marriage the mother ceases to act as the daughter's advocate. She dismisses her daughter's shame and reluctance after her wedding night, making light of the violence that has accompanied the consummation of the marriage. Ultimately, the mother herself seems to be tamed or at least subdued by her son-in-law.

---

[1] In *The Taming of the Shrew* the word *father* appears fifty-four times, more often than in any other Shakespeare play except *King Lear* and *3 Henry VI* (Novy 55–56), but no mother appears or is mentioned.

A Merry Jest of a Shrewd and Curst Wife Lapped in Morel's Skin, for Her Good Behavior (London, c. 1550).

From the beginning the negotiations between the husband and wife in *A Merry Jest* revolve around the class difference between them. The wife's family is wealthy, and her mother offers the suitor substantial money and land; clearly, his primary motive for marrying is financial gain. Mother and daughter also seem to expect that his lower economic and social class will make him more likely to submit to his wife. Whenever the two spouses quarrel, the wife stresses her husband's social inferiority and indebtedness: "What shouldst thou be, were't not for me? / A rag on thine arse thou shouldst not have, / Except my friends had giv'n it thee" (lines 688–690). Because of this, as the wife insists, "Thou art not he that shall rule me" (line 692).

But the wife's class is not so high that she is not expected to work. In the marriage negotiations the mother claims that her daughter will make a good "housewife" — she can card, spin, thresh, fan, and "save." The conflict between the spouses erupts not just over who will be master but also over whether the wife will perform her duties as mistress — whether she will prepare and serve food to her husband and servants. Describing an inversion like that in "The Woman to the Plow, and the Man to the Hen-Roost," *A Merry Jest* depicts domestic disorder as caused by a woman who refuses to feed her servants and fights "as [she] had been a man" (line 710); it celebrates the restoration of order in a final feast at which the wife impresses everyone with her diligence as hostess and her husband presides at the table "like a man" (line 1049). The ballad begins and ends with the same enigmatic image of the couple, who can be seen either as at a stand-off, eying one another warily, or as at peace, exchanging wedding gifts (see Figure 11). Unlike *The Taming of the Shrew, A Merry Jest* goes out of its way to insist that the wife's subservience is not just a public performance, although (as in *The Shrew*) it is a domestication that, paradoxically, is not complete until made public. The wife promises to obey her husband "in presence of people, and eke alone" (line 1010).

The husband's strategy for subduing his wife, which is described once as "taming" her and twice as "charming" her, is markedly more violent than Petruchio's in *The Taming of the Shrew*. While Petruchio's taming culminates in sexual consummation, the taming in *A Merry Jest* begins with the consummation of the marriage, which is also the first instance of violence between the couple. The husband hits his wife as they "dally," and promises not to hit her again as long as she agrees "in all sports to abide my will" (line 516). In this first instance, to which even the bride's mother responds with prurient interest and enjoyment, the couple's wrestling is presented as titillating and the bride's reluctance as silly. The husband's motives, and his tactics, are quite different in the later taming sequence. His violent scheme to subordinate his wife is depicted as an earnest, desperate response to her intolerable conduct. It is also depicted as unbelievably, unbearably bloody. On the one hand, Petruchio is more "gentle," in the various senses of that word, than is the husband in *A Merry Jest*. On the other hand, as one critic remarks, "it does not speak well of a hero that the best thing to be said in his favor is that he neither beats his wife senseless nor wraps her in a salted horsehide" (Woodbridge 207).

FIGURE II A Merry Jest of a Shrewd and Curst Wife Lapped in Morel's Skin, for Her Good Behavior *(London, c. 1550) begins and ends with this image. Because woodcuts were frequently reused, we cannot be sure that the illustration is directly tied to the poem's contents. Since the man and woman appear to be exchanging gifts, this might be an image of betrothal or reconciliation. Would the image have a different meaning at the end of the poem than it does at the beginning? The empty scrolls over each figure's head make the picture seem incomplete. What are the two spouses thinking? What might each say?*

Two critics have found in this tale a domesticated version of medieval romances in which a knight pursues and conquers a dragon; in this "loveless, deromanticized world . . . a man has no dragons to conquer but his wife" (Woodbridge 203). This interpretation suggests that the tale presents the wife as less than human; she is not as fully developed a character as the husband is, and we are not invited to imagine and sympathize with her feelings. In part because she is an obstacle her husband must overcome on his quest for manhood, her suffering is not taken as seriously as his qualms and frustrations. "Like dragons to be conquered in medieval romance or maidens to be deflowered in love stories, the shrew appears in sixteenth- and seventeenth-century narratives as the test obstacle essential for positing the culture's terms for male dominance not only over women but over other men as well" (Boose, *"Taming of the Shrew"* 214). Yet the wife resists more strenuously, vocally, and persistently than does Katharine in *The Taming of the Shrew*. Although *A Merry Jest*, like the folktales to which it is related, locates "audience sympathy securely and exclusively with the beleaguered husband" (Mikesell 150–51), some readers may still find themselves reading against the conventions and rooting for the feisty wife. Like Chaucer's "Wife of Bath's Prologue and Tale," which also combines a shrewish wife and the conventions of medieval romance, *A Merry Jest* raises the question of what women want. Even if it ultimately subdues its two shrews, in raising that question, depicting the rigors of taming, and casting itself as a fantasy, *A Merry Jest* opens up some doubt about the ideal of marital hierarchy and the means by which it is achieved.

A Merry Jest of a Shrewd and Curst Wife Lapped in Morel's Skin, for Her Good Behavior

Listen, friends, and hold you still,
Abide awhile and dwell.
A merry jest tell you I will,
And how that it befell.
As I went walking upon a day,
Among my friends to sport,   5
To a house I took the way,
To rest me for my comfort.

A great feast was kept there then,
And many one was thereat,
With wives and maidens, and many a good man,   10
That made good game and chat.
It befell then at that tide

An honest man was there;
A cursèd dame sat by his side,   15
That often did him dere.°

His wife she was, I tell you plain,
This dame, you may me trow;°
To play the master she would not lain°
And make her husband bow.   20
At every word that she did speak,
To be at peace he was full fain,°
Or else she would take him on the cheek,
Or put him to other pain.

When she did wink, he durst not stir;   25
Nor play wherever he went,
With friend or neighbor to make good cheer,
When she her brows bent.
These folk had two maidens fair and free,
Which were their daughters dear.   30
This is true, believe you me,
Of conditions° was none their peer.

The youngest was meek and gentle, iwis;°
Her father's condition she had.
The eldest her mother's, withouten miss:°   35
Sometime frantic, and sometime mad.
The father had his pleasure in the one alway,
And glad he was her to behold;
The mother in the other, this is no nay,
For in all her curstness she made her bold.   40

And at the last she was, in fay,°
As curst as her mother in word and deed,
Her mischievous pageants sometime to play,
Which caused her father's heart to bleed.
For he was woe and nothing glad,   45
And of her would fain be rid.
He wished to God that some man her had,
But yet to marriage he durst her not bid.

---

16. **dere:** grieve, vex, annoy. 18. **trow:** believe, trust. 19. **lain:** conceal, disguise.
22. **fain:** disposed, inclined, willing. 32. **conditions:** circumstances, wealth and social position; also, as in the next stanza, character, nature. 33. **iwis:** certainly, indeed, truly.
35. **withouten miss:** without doubt. 41. **in fay:** in faith.

Full many there came the youngest to have,
But her father was loath her to forgo; 50
None there came the eldest to crave,
For fear it should turn them to woe.
The father was loath any man to beguile,
For he was true and just withall;
Yet there came one within a while, 55
That her demanded in the hall.

Another there came right soon also,
The youngest to have he would be fain,
Which made the father's heart full woe,
That he and the youngest should part in twain. 60
But the mother was fell,° and might her not see,
Wherefore of her she would have been rid.
The young man full soon she granted pardie;°
Great gold and silver with her she bid,

Saying full soon he would her have. 65
And wedded they were, short tale to make.
The father said, "so God me save,
For heaviness and sorrow I tremble and quake."
Also, his heart was in great care,
How he should bestow the eldest, iwis, 70
Which should make his purse full bare.
Of her he would be rid by heaven's bliss.

As hap was° that this young man should
Desire the eldest withouten fail.
To marriage, he said, full fain he would, 75
That he might her have for his avail.
The father said, with words anon,
"Gold and silver I would thee give
If thou her marry, by sweet Saint John,
But thou shouldst repent it all thy life. 80

"She is conditioned, I tell thee plain,
Most like a fiend, this is no nay.
Her mother doth teach her, withouten lain,
To be master of her husband another day.
If thou shouldst her marry, and with her not gree,° 85

---

61. **fell:** cruel, ruthless, fierce.   63. **pardie:** by God, indeed.   73. **As hap was:** it so happened.   85. **gree:** agree.

Her mother thou shouldst have alway in thy top.°
By night and day that should vex thee,
Which sore would stick then in thy crop.°

"And I could not amend it, by God of might,
For I dare not speak myself for my life;   90
Sometime among, be it wrong or right,
I let her have all for fear of strife.
If I ought say she doth me treat
(Except I let her have her will)
As a child that should be beat.   95
She will me charm; the Devil her kill.

"Another thing thou must understand:
Her mother's good will thou must have also.
If she be thy friend, by sea or by land,
Amiss with thee then can it not go.   100
For she doth her love with all her mind,
And would not see her fare amiss.
If thou to her darling could be kind,
Thou couldst not want, by heaven's bliss.

"If thou to the mother now wilt seek,   105
Behave thyself then like a man,
And show thyself both humble and meek;
But when thou hast her, do what thou can.
Thou wot'st° what I said to thee before;
I counsel thee, mark my words well.   110
It were great pity, thou wert forlore
With such a devilish fiend of hell."

"I care not for that," the young man said.
"If I can get the mother's good will,
I would be glad to have that maid;   115
Methinketh she is withouten evil."
"Alas, good man, I am sorry for thee,
That thou wilt cast thy self away.
Thou art so gentle and so free;
Thou shalt never tame her, I dare well say.   120

"But I have done, I will say no more,
Therefore, farewell, and go thy way.

86. **in thy top:** attacking you from a superior position, coming down on you.   88. **crop:** craw;
it will be hard for you to take.   109. **Thou wot'st:** you know.

Remember what I said to thee before,
And beware of repentance another day."

*How the young man departed from the father, and sought to the mother for to
have the maid to marriage.*

Now is the young man come to the dame,   125
With countenance glad, and manners demure,
Saying to her, "God keep you from blame,
With your dear daughter so fair and pure."
She welcometh again the fair young man,
And bid him "come near, gentle friend."   130
Full courteously he thanked the good dame then,
And thought her words full good and kind.

Then he began, I shall you tell,
Unto the mother thus to say,
With words fair that become him well,   135
For her dear daughter thus to pray,
Saying: "good dame, now, by your leave,
Take it for none evil though I come here.
If you to me good leave would give,
With you right fain would I make good cheer."   140

The dame said: "sit down, awhile abide,
Good cheer anon then will we make.
My daughter shall sit down by thy side;
I know well thou comest only for her sake."
"You say full true, forsooth," said he,   145
"My mind is steadfastly on her set.
To have that maiden fair and free,
I would be fain, if I could her get."

The mother thanked him for his good will,
That he her daughter did so desire,
Saying: "I hope you come for none evil,   150
But in good honesty her to require.
For if you did, I will be plain,
Right soon it should turn you unto grief,
And also your coming I would disdain,
And bid you walk with a wild mischief.   155

"But surely I take you for none of those;
Your conditions show it in no wise.

Wherefore me think you do not gloze,°
Nor I will not counsel you by mine advice.   160
For I love my daughter as my heart,
And loath I were, I will be plain,
To see her suffer pain and smart,
For if I did, my heart were slain.

"If that thou shouldst another day   165
My daughter have, and her good will,
Order her then unto her pay°
As reason requireth, it is good skill.
In women sometime great wisdom is;
And in men full little it is often seen.   170
But she is wise withouten miss;
From a young child up she hath so been.

"Therefore to her thou must audience give
For thine own profit, when she doth speak;
And then shalt thou in quiet live,   175
And much strife thus shalt thou break.
How say'st thou, young man, what is thy mind?
Wouldst thou her have, my daughter dear?
Then to her thou must be kind,
And alway ready to make her good cheer.   180

"For a hundred pounds of money have thou shalt,
Of silver and eke° of gold so round,
With a hundred quarters of corn and malt,
And forty acres of good ground.
If thou wilt live with her like a man,   185
Thou shalt her have, and this will I give,
And ever after while I can,
Be thy good mother as long as I live.

"And I will speak to my daughter for thee,
To know if it be her will also.   190
If she be content, my daughter free,
Then together may you go."
The mother demanded her daughter then,
If that she could find in her mind
With all her heart to love that young man,   195
So that he to her would be kind?

159. **gloze:** deceive, flatter.   167. **pay:** satisfaction, contentment, pleasure.   182. **eke:** also.

She said, "yea, mother, as you will,
So will I do in word and deed.
I trust he cometh for none ill,
Therefore the better may we speed.
But I would have one that hath some good,°   200
As well as I, good reason is.
Methink he is a lusty blood,
But goods there must be withouten miss."

The young man was glad these words to hear,   205
And thanked the mother of her good will,
Beholding the maiden with right mild cheer,
And prayed her heartily to be still,
Saying to her then in this wise:
"Mine heart, my love, my darling dear,   210
Take no displeasure of my enterprise,
That I desire to be your peer.

"I am not rich of gold nor fee,°
Nor of great merchandise, you shall understand.
But a good craft I have, pardie,   215
To get our living in any land.
And in my heart I can well find,
You for to love above all other,
Forevermore to you to be kind,
And never forsake you for none other.   220

"Like a woman I will you use,
And do you honor, as you should do me.
And for your sake all other refuse,
As good reason is it should so be."
"By my troth, but well you say,   225
And methink by your countenance, iwis,
That you should not another day,
For no cause deal with me amiss.

"And in you I hope pleasure to take,
If you would be gentle as you should,
And never none other for your sake,   230
To marry for a thousand pound of gold.
But sometime you must me a little forbear,

---

201. **good:** goods, property.   213. **fee:** portable property, possessions.

For I am hasty, but it is soon done.
In my fume° I do nothing fear,   235
Whatsoever thereof to me become.

"And I cannot refrain me in no wise,
For I have it by nature a part, iwis.
It was wont to be my mother's guise,°
Sometime to be master withouten miss.   240
And so must I, by God, now and then,
Or else I would think it should not be well,
For though you were never so good a man,
Sometime among I will bear the bell.°

"And therefore tell me with words plain,   245
If you can be patient what time it is,
To suffer with me a little pain,
Though that you think I do amiss?
Or else say nay, and make a short end,
And soon we shall asunder depart.   250
Then at your liberty you may hence wend;
Yet I do love you with all my heart."

The young man was glad of her love, in fay,
But loath he was master her for to make,
And bethought him what her father before did say,   255
When he on wooing his journey did take,
And so consented to all her will,
When he advised him° what he should do.
He said: "you may me save or spill,°
For you have my love, sweet heart, and no moe."   260

The mother, hearing this, for the father sent,
Showing to him what was befall;
Wherewith he was right well content,
Of all their promises in general.
Upon this greement they departed then,   265
To prepare all things for the feast.
Glad was the bride and her spouse then,
That they were come to his behest.°

235. **fume:** a fit of anger, an irritable mood.   239. **guise:** manner, way, habit.   244. **bear the bell:** take first place, be the best, win.   258. **When he advised him:** when he reflected on; when he told himself.   259. **spill:** kill, destroy, ruin.   268. **behest:** vow, agreement.

How the bride was married with her father and mother's good will.

The day approached, the time drew near,
That they should be wedded withouten miss.
The bride was glad and made good cheer,   270
For she thought to make great joy and bliss,
As that day to triumph with games and sport,
Among her friends a rule to bear,
And eke with his friends that thither should resort,
Thinking that nobody might be her peer.   275

The bridegroom was glad also, in fay,
As man might be upon the mold.°
And to himself thus gan° he say:
"Now shall I receive a heap of gold,
Of pounds many one, and much goods beside,   280
To rejoice my sorrows, and also my smart.
I know not her peer in this country so wide,
But yet I fear alway her proud heart.

"She is so sib° to the mother, withouten fail,   285
Which hath no peer that I know:
In all mischief she dare assail,
The boldest archer that shooteth in a bow.
But no force, I care not, I wote what I think,
When we be wed and keep house alone,   290
For a small storm I may not shrink
To run to my neighbor to make my moan."

Soon to the church now were they brought,
With all their friends them about,
There to be married as they ought.
And after them followed a full great rout,°   295
With them to offer,° as custom is,
Among good neighbors it is alway seen,
Full richly decked, withouten miss.
And she thought herself most like a queen.   300

Incontinent° when the mass was done,
Homeward forsooth they took the way.
There followeth after them right soon,

278. **upon the mold**: in the world.   279. **gan**: began; thus he began to say.   285. **sib**: akin,
similar.   296. **rout**: crowd.   297. **to offer**: to give worship.   301. **Incontinent**: at once.

Many a tall man and woman full gay;
The fathers and mothers next of all,   305
Unto the bridegroom and bride also,
As to them then it did befall,
With them that tide so for to go.

*How the bride and her friends came from the church, and were of the bridegroom
at their feast honestly served.*

When they came home the boards were spread;
The bride was set at the high dais.   310
Everyone said she had well sped
Of such a fair husband as served her miss.°
The friends sat about her on every side,
Each in their order, a good sight to see;
The bride in the midst, with much pride,   315
Full richly beseen she was, pardie.

The mother was right glad of this sight,
And fast she did her daughter behold,
Thinking it was a pleasant wight.°
But alway her father's heart was cold,   320
When he remembered what might befall
Of this young daughter, that was so bold.
He could nothing be merry at all,
But moaned the young man full many a fold.°

Behold, how often with countenance sad,   325
Saying to himself: "alas, this day!
This young man proveth much worse than mad,
That he hath married this cursèd may.°
Where I have counselled him by heaven's bliss
That he should not meddle in no wise,   330
Lest he repented, withouten miss,
That ever he made this enterprise.

"But seeing it is thus, self do self have,°
He is worse than mad that will him moan;
For I will no more, so God me save,   335
But God send him joy, with my daughter Joan.
She is as curst, I dare well swear,

---

312. **served her miss:** compensated for her weakness, suited her. 319. **wight:** creature.
324. **many a fold:** many times, often. 328. **may:** maid. 333. **self . . . have:** What one does
one must live with; one must accept responsibility for one's own choices and actions.

And as angry, iwis, as ever was wasp.
If he her anger, she will him tear,
And with her nails also him clasp.   340

"What availeth it to say ought now?
The deed is done, no remedy there is.
Good cheer to make, I make God a vow,
Is now the best, withouten miss.
For now is the time it should so be,   345
To make good game and sport, in fay,
In comforting all this company,
That be assembled here this day."

The father and mother were diligent still,
To welcome the friends both more and less.
The young man did also his good will   350
To serve them well at every mess.°
Wherein the mother great pleasure took,
And so did the father eke truly.
The bride gave a friendly look,
Casting on him a wanton eye.   355

Then was the bridegroom rejoicèd sore,
Alway our Lord thanking of his great grace,
Having in mind times many a score,
That his bride showed him such a fair place.
The minstrels played at every board;   360
The people therewith rejoiced right well,
Giving the bridegroom their good word,
And the bride also, that in beauty did excel.

The time passed forth, the dinner was done,
The tables were taken up all.   365
The bridegroom welcomed them every each one,
That were there in the hall.
They thanked him then, and the bride also,
Of their great cheer they had,
And swore great oaths, so mote I go,   370
They were never at feast so glad.

"Now we will remember you ere we depart,
As use and custom doth require."

352. **mess**: course, dish.

He thankèd them with all his heart,   375
So did both dame and sire.
The bride to the table again was set,
To keep countenance then, indeed.
The friends that were together met
Begifted them richly with right good speed.   380

The father and the mother first began,
To order them in this wise.
The bridegroom was set by the bride's side then,
After the country guise.
Then the father the first present brought,   385
And presented them there richly, in fay,
With deeds of his land in a box well-wrought,
And made them his heirs for aye.°

He gave them also of malt and corn
A hundred quarters and more,   390
With sheep and oxen, that bare large horn,
To keep for household store.
And then came the mother, as quick as a bee,
To the bridegroom with words smart,
Saying, "son, so mote I thee,°   395
I must open to thee my heart."

She gave them also both cart and plow,
And bade them alway to do well,
And God should send them good enow,
If they did mark what she did tell.   400
"Before the people in this hall,
I will say and to thee rehearse,
A hundred pound now give thee I shall,
But hearken first unto my verse.

"Thou hast here my daughter dear,   405
A pleasant thing it is.
In all the country I know not her peer,
So have I part of bliss.
For she is wise and fair withall,
And will nothing cast away.   410
I trow there be now none in this hall,
That better can save all thing, in fay.

388. aye: always.   395. so mote I thee: may I thrive.

"Nor better doth know what doth behove
Unto a house or housewifery,
Than she doth, which causeth me to move
This matter to thee so busily.   415
She can card, she can spin,
She can thresh, and she can fan;°
She can help thee good[s] to win,
For to keep thee like a man.   420

"And here is a hundred pound in gold
To set thee up, thy craft to use.
Wherefore, I am plain, I would thou should
In no manner of wise thy self abuse,
To strive with my daughter or her to entreat   425
For anything that she shall do.
Hereafter, my child, therefore, to beat,
It should turn plainly to thy great woe."

"Oh! My dear mother, take no displeasure
Till you have cause what so befall,
But use yourself alway by measure,   430
For other cause none have you shall.
My wife and I full well shall gree,
I trust to God in throne.
She is my love, and ever shall be,
And none but she alone."   435

"Oh! My dear son, thou mak'st me glad,
Which before was full of sorrow.
For my dear daughter, I was full sad,
But now I say, our Lord to borrow,
Thou giv'st me good comfort. Now farewell care.   440
Here is thy hundred pound.
I pray God give thee well to fare,
And keep thee whole and sound."

"I thank you, dear mother," the young man said,
"Of your good gift and daughter dear.   445
Methinks she is the worthiest maid,
In all this land, withouten peer.
I hope to live with her alway

---

418. fan: separate the wheat from the chaff; winnow grain.

So gently, that she shall find,   450
(And you, her mother, I dare well say)
In every season, gentle and kind."

The people standing them to behold,
Regarded the words of the bridegroom then,
And said he answered with words cold,°   455
Which became full well the good young man.
And then they pressed forth each after other,
With gold and silver, and rich gifts eke.
And many a scorn they gave the mother,
But ever they praised the young man meek.   460

To whom he gave thanks with all his might,
As honesty requireth him to do.
He ordered himself alway aright,
Yet they thought all he should have woe;
For he was matchèd so, iwis,   465
That he could not want for sorrow, in fay,
But alway hampered, withouten miss,
Of mother and daughter, forever and aye.

When all was done they gan depart,
And took their leave full friendly though,   470
Thanking each other with all their heart,
And on their way home they gan go.
The father and mother thanked them all,
The bride and bridegroom also, without miss,
Did thank the company in general,   475
Departing from them with joy and bliss.

Then they went home while it was day,
And left the bride and bridegroom there,
And they that did abide there, in good fay,
They made at even° again good cheer.   480
And after supper they did make good sport,
With dancing and springing° as was the use.°
Young people by other there did resort,
To no man's hinder or confuse.°

---

455. **cold:** temperate, dispassionate.   480. **even:** evening time.   482. **springing:** lively dancing, jigging.   **use:** custom.   484. **To no man's hinder or confuse:** to no one's hindrance or
confusion; that is, the festivities were not at anyone's expense.

After that all sports were ended and done,   485
And that the bride should go to bed,
About the hall they dancèd soon,
And suddenly away the bride was led,
To take her rest with her dear spouse,
As reason would it should so be.   490
Even as the cat was wont with the mouse
To play, forsooth even so did he.

The next morning, if that you will hear,
The mother did come to their bedside,
Demanding them what was their cheer;
And the bride began her head to hide,   495
Saying to her, as one ashamed,
"Iwis, dear mother, I would you were gone,
Ere you came here I was not blamed
For being in his arms here all alone."   500

"Mine own dear daughter, be not displeased,
Though I do let° you of your disport.
I would be loath you were diseased,°
But you shall have a caudle° for your comfort.
Awhile I will go and let you alone,   505
Till you be ready for to rise."
And suddenly the mother was from them gone,
To make the caudle after the best wise.

When that the mother departed was,
The[y] dallied together and had good game.   510
He hit her awry: she cried, "alas!
What do you, man? Hold up for shame!"
"I will, sweet wife," then gan he say,
"Fulfill your mind, both loud and still;
But you be able, I swear in fay,   515
In all sports to abide my will."

And they wrestled so long beforn
That this they had for their great mead:°
Both shirt and smock was all to-torn,
That their uprising had no speed.°   520
But yet the mother came again,

---

502. **let:** prevent, distract.   503. **diseased:** made uncomfortable.   504. **caudle:** a comforting,
substantial warm drink, such as a thin porridge or gruel, often given to the sick.
518. **mead:** reward.   520. **no speed:** no success; they could not manage to get out of bed.

And said to her daughter, "how dost thou now?"
"Marry, mother, between us twain,
Our shirts be torn, I make God a vow.

"By God's dear mother," she swore then,   525
"This order with us may not continue.
I will no more lie by this man,
For he doth me brast,° both vein and sinew.
Nay, nay, dear mother, this world goeth on wheels.°
By sweet Saint George, you may me trow,   530
He lieth kicking with his heels,
That he is like to bear me a blow."

"My own dear daughter, if thy smock be asunder,
Another thou shalt have then, by this light.
I pray thee heartily do thou not wonder,   535
For so was I dealt with the first night
That I by thy father lay, by the rood.
And I do thee with words plain:
Methought never night to me so good,
As that same was when I took such pain."   540

"Why, mother, were you then glad
To be thus dealt with as I am now?
Methink[s] my husband worse than mad,
For he doth exceed, I make God a vow.
I could not lie still, nor no rest take,   545
Of all this night, believe you me.
Sometime on my side, and sometime on my back,
He rode and laid me, so mote I thee.

"And from the bed's head unto the bed's feet,
A cloth we had not us for to deck.   550
Neither our coverlet, nor yet our sheet,
That I pray God, the devil him check.
For I am ashamed, my mother dear,
Of this night's rest, by God in throne.
Before our friends I dare not appear.   555
Would to God's passion I had lain alone!"

---

528. **brast:** burst, break, violate, cause to explode from within.   529. **goeth on wheels:** goes its own way.

"Nay, nay dear daughter, be not ashamed,
For here is nothing done amiss.
They be more worthy to be blamed,
That hereof thinketh shame, iwis.
For this is honesty for thee and us all;
And a new smock I will thee fet;°
And eke for thee, my son, I shall
For thy true labor a new shirt get."

And soon of these they were both sped,°
The daughter, and eke the son also.
Full quickly they rose out of their bed,
And with their mother they gan go
Abroad among their friends all,
Which bid them good luck, and eke good grace.
The caudle was ready there in the hall,
With mirth and glee for their solace.

Thus ended the feast with sport and play,
And all their friends, each with other,
Did take their leave and went their way,
From bride and bridegroom, with father and mother,
Which right heartily did thank them though,
So did the bride and bridegroom, eke.
Yet when the friends were all ago,
This young folk abode with the mother all the week.

The father was glad to see them agree,
So was the mother, by heaven['s] queen.
And said each to other, "so mote I thee,
I thought not so well it should have been
Between them twain as it is now.
And therefore alone here shall they bide.
We will leave them all, I make God a vow,
And go to dwell in our house hard beside."°

At short conclusion they went their way,
Leaving their children all that was there,
And came not again of many a day,
For their dear daughter to inquire.
Thus they bode together then.

560

565

570

575

580

585

590

562. **fet:** fetch.   565. **sped:** discharged, taken care of.   588. **hard beside:** nearby.

He set up his shop with haberdash ware,°
As one that would be a thriving man,   595
To get great goods for his welfare.

And after that he took great pain
To order his plows and cattle also.
He kept both boy, and also swain[s],°
That to the cart and plow do go.   600
And some kept neat,° and some kept sheep,
Some did one thing, some did another,
But when they came home to have their meat,
The wife played the devil then, like her mother.

With countenance grim, and words smart,   605
She gave them meat, and bade them brast.°
The poor folk that come from plow and cart,
Of her lewd words they were aghast,
Saying each to other, "what dame is this?
The devil I trow hath brought us here.   610
Our master shall know it, by heaven's bliss,
That we will not serve him another year."

The goodman was forth in the town abroad,
About other things, I you say.
When he came homeward he met with a goad;°   615
One of his carters° was going away,
To whom he said, "Lob, whither goest thou?"
The carter spied his master then,
And said to him, "I make God a vow,
No longer with thy wife abide I can.   620

"Master," he said, "by God's blist,°
Our dame is the devil, thou may'st me believe.
If thou have sought her, thou hast not missed
Of one that full often thee shall grieve.
By God, a man thou canst not have   625
To go to cart, nor yet to plow,
Neither boy, nor yet knave,
By God's dear mother, I make God a vow,

594. haberdash ware: petty merchandise, small wares.   599. swain[s]: male servants or
workers.   601. neat: oxen or bullocks, cows or heifers.   606. bade them brast: commanded
them to burst.   615. goad: a spur or incitement.   616. carters: servants, especially those who
drive carts.   621. blist: bliss.

That will bide with thee day or night.
Our dame is not for us, for she doth curse.   630
When we shall eat or drink with right,
She bans and frowns, that we be all the worse.
We be not used, wherever we wend,°
To be sorely looked on for eating of our meat.
The devil, I trow, us to thee send.   635
God help us a better mistress to get."

"Come on thy way, Lob, and turn again.
Go home with me, and all shall be well.
An ox for my meinie° shall be slain,
And the hide at the market I will sell."   640
Upon this, together home they went.
The goodman was angry in his mind,
But yet to his wife, with good intent,
He said, "sweet heart, you be unkind.

"Entreat our meinie well alway,   645
And give them meat and drink enow,
For they get our living every day,
And theirs also, at cart and plow.
Therefore I would that they should have
Meat and drink to their behoof.   650
For, my sweet wife, so God me save,
You will do so, if you me love."

"Give them what thou wilt, I do not care,
By day or night, man, believe thou me.
Whatever they have, or how they fare,   655
I pray God evil m[o]te they thee.°
And specially that whoreson that doth complain,
I will quit° him once if ever I live.
I will dash the knave upon the brain,
That ever after it shall him grieve."   660

"What! My dear wife, for shame, be still.
This is a pain such words to hear.
We cannot always have our will,
Though that we were a king's peer.
For, to shame a knave, what can they get?°   665

633. **wend:** turn.   639. **meinie:** household, employees.   656. **evil m[o]te they thee:** evil may they thrive.   658. **quit:** repay, get back at.   665. **to shame . . . get:** How can you shame someone who cannot get by on his own? Why would you insult someone who is your social inferior?

Thou art as lewd,° 'fore God, as they,
And therefore shalt thou serve them of meat,
And drink also, from hence alway.

"What! wife, you be to blame,
To speak to me thus in this wise.   670
If we should strive, folk would speak shame,
Therefore be still in mine advice.
I am loath with you to strive,
For aught that you shall do or say.
I swear to Christ, wife, by my life,   675
I had rather take Morel and ride my way

"To seek mine adventure, till your mood be past.
I say to you these manners be not good.
Therefore, I pray you that this be the last
Of your furious anger that seemeth so wood.°   680
What can it avail you me for to grieve,
That loveth you so well as I do mine heart?
By my troth, wife, you may me believe,
Such toys as these be would make us both smart."

"Smart in the twenty feigning devils' name!   685
That list me once well for to see.
I pray God give thee evil shame!
What shouldst thou be, were't not for me?
A rag on thine arse thou shouldst not have,
Except my friends had giv'n it thee.   690
Therefore, I tell thee well, thou drunken knave,
Thou art not he that shall rule me."

"Oh! Good wife cease and let this overpass.
For all your great anger and high words eke,
I am mine own self, even as I was,   695
And to you will be loving, and also meek.
But if you should do thus, as you do begin,
It may not continue no time, iwis.
I would not let,° for kith nor kin,
To make you mend all things that is amiss."   700

"Make me! Marry, out upon the drivel,
Sayest thou that? Wilt thou begin?

666. **lewd:** ignorant, rude, common, vulgar, base.   680. **wood:** insane, out of control.
699. **let:** cease.

I pray God and our Lady that a foul evil
Lighten upon thee and all thy kin.
By God's dear blist, vex me no more,   705
For if thou do thou shalt repent.
I have yet somewhat for thee in store."
And with that a staff in her hand she hent.°

"At him full soon then she let flee,
And whirled about her as it had been a man.   710
Her husband then was fain,° pardie,
To void° her stroke, and go his way then.
"By God's dear mother," then gan she swear,
"From henceforth I will make thee bow.
For I will trim thee in thy gear,   715
Or else I would I were called a sow.

"Fie on all wretches that be like thee,
In word or work both loud and still!
I swear by him that made man free,
Of me thou shalt not have thy will,   720
Now nor never, I tell thee plain.
For I will have gold and riches enow,
When thou shalt go jagged as a simple swain,
With whip in hand at cart and plow."

"Of that, my dear wife, I take no scorn,   725
For many a goodman, with mind and heart,
Hath gone to plow and cart beforn
My time, iwis, with pain and smart,
Which now be rich, and have good at will,
Being at home, and make good cheer.   730
And there they intend to lead their life still,
Till our Lord do send for them here.

"But now I must ride a little way,
Dear wife; I will come right soon again.
Appoint our dinner, I you pray,   735
For I do take on me great pain.
I do my best, I swear by my life,
To order you like a woman, iwis.
And yet it cannot be withouten strife,
Through your lewd tongue, by heaven's bliss."   740

708. **hent:** seized, grabbed.   711. **fain:** content, constrained, obliged.   712. **void:** avoid.

"Ride to the devil, and to his dame;
I would I should thee never see!
I pray to God send thee mickle° shame,
In any place wherever thou be.
Thou wouldst fain the master play,   745
But thou shalt not, by God I make thee sure!
I swear I will thy petticoat pay,°
That long with me thou shalt not endure."

*How the goodman rode his way, till he thought her anger was past; and then
he returned home again.*

The goodman was sorry, and went his way
About his business, as he was used,   750
And to himself thus gan he say:
"Lord God, how was I thus abused!
When I took this wife I was worse than mad,
And yet can I blame myself and none other,
Which maketh me sigh and often be sad,   755
Repenting full sore, by God's dear mother.

"Fie upon goods withouten pleasure!
Between man and wife that cannot agree,
It is a pain far passing measure,
Such strife to see where as love should be.   760
For there was ne'er man, iwis,
So hampered with one wife as I am now,
Wherefore I think, withouten miss,
She shall repent it, I make God a vow.

"Except she turn and change her mind,   765
And eke her conditions everichone,°
She shall find me to her so unkind,
That I shall her coil° both back and bone,
And make her blue and also black,
That she shall groan again for woe.   770
I will make her bones all to crack,
Without that she her conditions forgo.

"I was never so vexed this time beforn,
As I am now of this wife alone.
A vengeance on her that ever she was born!   775

---

743. **mickle:** much.   747. **I . . . pay:** I'll make you pay for this.   766. **everichone:**
everyone.   768. **coil:** beat.

For she maketh me often full woe begone.
And I cannot tell where me to turn,
Nor me to wend, by God in fay,
Which cause me often for to mourn,
Or yet to know what for to say.   780

"I am worse than mad or wood,
And yet I am loath with her to begin.
I fear me I shall never make her good,
Except I do wrap her in black Morel's skin,
That can no more draw at plow nor cart.   785
It shall be too late to call for her kin,
When she beginneth once for to smart,
For little ease thereby she shall win.

"Morel is old, he can labor no more,
Nor do no good, but alway eat.   790
I trow, I have kept him thus long in store,
To work a charm that shall be feat.°
The whoreson is blind and lame also,
Behind and before, he cannot steer.
When he from the stable to the street should go,   795
He falleth down right then in the mire.

"Yet I am loath him for to kill,
For he hath done me good service ere now.
But if my wife fulfill not my will,
I must him flay, by God I trow.   800
But at this point now will I be:
I will be master, as it is reason,
And make her subject unto me,
For she must learn a new lesson.

"Her father did warn me of this beforn,   805
How I should it find in every degree;
But I did take it for half a scorn,
And would not believe him then, pardie.
But now I perceive it very well
He did it for good will, iwis.   810
Wherefore I think that Morel's fell°
Must mend all thing that is amiss.

792. **feat:** fitting, suitable, proper.   811. **fell:** skin or hide.

"Thus he that will not believe his friend,
As her dear father was unto me,
He is worthy for to find   815
Alway great pain and misery.
But I may not choose him to believe,
For the deed doth prove himself, in fay.
Ever she is ready me for to grieve,
And thinks to continue so alway.   820

"But now I will home to prove her mind,
And see what welcome I shall have.
She may be to me so unkind
That she shall repent it, so God me save.
For if I should of her complain,   825
Folk would me mock, and give me scorn,
And say, I were worthy of this pain,
Because it was showed me so well beforn."

How the goodman was welcomed when he returned home again.

The goodman came riding to the gate,
And knockèd as he had been wood.   830
His servant right soon did meet him thereat,
And bid him welcome with right mild mood.
The master said, "what doth my dame now?
Is she as frantic yet as she was?
Then will I tame her, I make God a vow,   835
And make her sing full loud, alas."

"Where art thou, wife? Shall I have any meat?
Or am I not so welcome unto thee,
That at my commandment I shall aught get?
I pray thee heartily soon tell thou me.   840
If thou do not serve me, and that anon,
I shall thee show mine anger, iwis.
I swear by God, and by saint John,
Thy bones will I swaddle,° so have I bliss."

Forth she came, as brim° a boar,   845
And like a dog she rated° him then,
Saying thus: "I set no store
By thee, thou wretch, thou art no man.

844. swaddle: bind up, or beat soundly. 845. brim: fierce. 846. rated: scolded angrily,
drove away (especially a dog).

Get thee hence out of my sight,
For meat nor drink thou get'st none here.   850
I swear to thee, by Mary bright,
Of me thou get'st here no good cheer."

"Well, wife," he said, "thou dost me compel
To do that thing that I were loath.
If I bereave Morel of his old fell,   855
Thou shalt repent it, by the faith now go'th.°
For I see well that it will no better be,
But in it thou must, after the new guise.
It had been better, so mote I thee,
That thou hadst not begun this enterprise."   860

How the goodman caused Morel to be slain, and the hide salted, to lay his wife therein to sleep.

"Now will I begin my wife to tame,
That all the world shall it know.
I would be loath her for to shame,
Though she do not care, you may me trow.
Yet will I her honesty regard,   865
And it preserve, wherever you may.
But Morel, that is in yonder yard,
His hide therefore he must lose, in fay."

And so he commanded anon
To slay old Morel, his great horse,   870
And flay him then, the skin from the bone,
To wrap it about his wife's white corse.°
Also, he commanded of a birchen tree
Rods to be made a good great heap;
And swore by dear God in Trinity,   875
His wife in his cellar should skip and leap.

"The hide must be salted," then he said eke,
"Because I would not have it stink.°
I hope herewith she will be meek,
For this I trow will make her shrink   880
And bow at my pleasure, when I her bid,

---

856. **by the faith now go'th:** by what people now believe.   872. **corse:** corpse, body.   878. I . . . **stink:** By salting the horsehide, the husband preserves it so that it will not stink. But the salt will also burn and sting the wife's open wounds.

And obey my commandments both loud and still.
Or else I will make her body bleed,
And with sharp rods beat her my fill."

Anon with that, to her he gan to call.   885
She bid, "abide, in the devil's name!
I will not come, what so befall.
Sit still with sorrow and mickle shame.
Thou shalt not rule me as pleaseth thee,
I will° well thou know, by God's dear Mother.   890
But thou shalt be ruled alway by me,
And I will be master, and none other."

"Wilt thou be master, dear wife? In fay,
Then must we wrestle for the best game.
If thou it win, then may I say,   895
That I have done myself great shame.
But first I will make thee sweat, good Joan,
Red blood, even to the heels adown,
And lap thee in Morel's skin alone,
That the blood shall be seen even from the crown."   900

"Sayest thou me that, thou wretched knave?
It were better thou hadst me never seen.
I swear to thee, so God me save,
With my nails I will scratch out both thine eyen.
And, therefore, think not to touch me once,   905
For, by the mass, if thou begin that,
Thou shalt be handled for the nonce,
That all thy brains on the ground shall squat."

"Why then, there is no remedy, I see,
But needs I must do even as I thought,   910
Seeing it will none otherwise be.
I will thee not spare, by God that me bought.
For now I am set thee for to charm,
And make thee meek, by God's might;
Or else with rods, while thou art warm,°   915
I shall thee scourge with reason and right:
    Now, good Morel's skin,
    Receive my curst wife in."

890. will: wish.   915. warm: glowing with exertion, dangerous, angry, excited.

How the curst wife in Morel's skin lay,
Because she would not her husband obey.

"Now will I my sweet wife trim°
According as she deserveth to me.
I swear by God and by Saint Sim,   920
With birchen rods well beat shall she be.
And after that in Morel's salt skin
I will her lay, and full fast bind,
That all her friends, and eke her kin,   925
Shall her long seek ere they her find."

Then he her met, and to her gan say,
"How sayest thou, wife, wilt thou be master yet?"
She swore by God's body, and by that day,
And suddenly with her fist she did him hit,   930
And defied him, drivel at every word,
Saying, "precious whoreson, what dost thou think?
I set not by thee a stinking turd.
Thou shalt get of me neither meat nor drink."

"Sayest thou me that, wife?" quoth he then.   935
With that, in his arms he gan her catch.
Straight to the cellar with her he ran,
And fastened the door with lock and latch,
And threw the key down him beside,
Asking her then if she would obey.   940
Then she said, "nay, for all thy pride,"
But she was master, and would abide alway.

"Then," quoth he, "we must make a fray."
And with that her clothes he gan to tear.
"Out upon thee, whoreson!" then she did say.
"Wilt thou rob me of all my gear?   945
It cost thee naught, thou arrant thief."
And quickly she got him by the head.
With that she said, "God give thee a mischief,
And them that fed thee first with bread."   950

They wrestled together thus, they two,
So long that the clothes asunder went,
And to the ground he threw her tho,°

919. **trim:** restore, put right; or to beat, scold. 953. **tho:** then.

That clean from the back her smock he rent.
In every hand, a rod he got,   955
And laid upon her a right good pace,
Asking of her, "what game was that?"
And she cried out, "whoreson, alas! alas!

"What wilt thou do? Wilt thou kill me?
I have made thee a man of naught.   960
Thou shalt repent it, by God's pity,
That ever this deed thou hast ywrought."
"I care not for that, dame," he did say,
"Thou shalt give over, ere we depart,
The mastership all, or all this day   965
I will not cease to make thee smart."

Ever he laid on, and ever she did cry,
"Alas! Alas that ever I was born!
Out upon thee, murderer, I thee defy,
Thou hast my white skin, and my body all to-torn.   970
Leave off betime, I counsel thee."
"Nay, by God, dame, I say not so yet.
I swear to thee, by Mary so free,
We begin but now — this is the first fit.

"Once again we must dance about,   975
And then thou shalt rest in Morel's skin."
He gave her then so many a great clout,
That on the ground the blood was seen.
Within a while, he cried, "new rods, new!"
With that she cried full loud, "alas!"   980
"Dance yet about, dame, thou came not where it grew."°
And suddenly with that in a swoon she was.

He spied that, and up he her hent,
And wrang her hard then by the nose.
With her to Morel's skin straight he went,   985
And therein full fast he did her close.
Within a while she did revive,
Through the gross salt that did her smart.
She thought she should never have gone on live
Out of Morel's skin, so sore is her heart.   990

981. thou came . . . grew: We've only just begun.

When she did spy that therein she lay,
Out of her wit she was full nigh,
And to her husband then did she say,
"How canst thou do this villainy?"
"Nay, how sayest thou? Thou cursèd wife,   995
In this foul skin I will thee keep
During the time of all thy life,
Therein forever to wail and weep."

With that her mood began to sink,
And said, "dear husband, for grace I call.   1000
For I shall never sleep nor wink
Till I get your love, whatso befall.
And I will never to you offend,
In no manner of wise, of all my life,
Nor to do nothing that may pretend   1005
To displease you with my wits five.

"For father nor mother, whatsoever they say,
I will not anger you, by God in throne,
But glad will your commandments obey,
In presence of people, and eke alone."   1010
"Well, on that condition, thou shalt have
Grace, and fair bed to rest thy body in;
But if thou rage more, so God me save,
I will wrap thee again in Morel's skin."

Then he took her out in his arms twain,   1015
And beheld her so piteously with blood arrayed.
"How thinkest thou, wife, shall we again
Have such business more?" to her he said.
She answered, "nay, my husband dear,
While I you know, and you know me,   1020
Your commandments I will, both far and near,
Fulfill alway in every degree."

"Well then, I promise thee, by God, even now,
Between thee and me shall never be strife.
If thou to my commandments quickly bow,   1025
I will thee cherish all the days of my life."
In bed she was laid, and healèd full soon,
As fair and clear as she was beforn.
What he her bid was quickly done,
To be diligent, iwis, she took no scorn.   1030

Then was he glad, and thought in his mind,
"Now have I done myself great good,
And her also, we shall it find,
Though I have shed part of her blood.
For, as methink[s] she will be meek,   1035
Therefore I will her father and mother
Bid to guest now the next week,
And of our neighbors many other."

How the goodman did bid her father and mother to guest and many of his
neighbors, that they might see his wife's patience.

Great pain he made his wife to take
Against the day that they should come.   1040
Of them was none that there did lack,
I dare well say unto my doom.
Yea, father and mother, and neighbors all,
Did thither come to make good cheer.
Soon they were set in general;   1045
The wife was diligent as did appear.

Father and mother was welcome then,
And so were they all, in good fay.
The husband sat there like a man;
The wife did serve them all that day.   1050
The goodman commanded what he would have;
The wife was quick at hand.
"What now!" thought the mother, "this arrant knave
Is master, as I understand.

"What may this mean," then she gan think,   1055
"That my daughter so diligent is?
Now can I neither eat nor drink,
Till I it know, by heaven['s] bliss."
When her daughter came again
To serve at the board, as her husband bade,   1060
The mother stared with her eyen twain,
Even as one that had been mad.

All the folk that at the board sat
Did her behold then, everichone.
The mother from the board her got,   1065
Following her daughter, and that anon,
And in the kitchen she her found,

Saying unto her in this wise:
"Daughter, thou shalt well understand,
I did not teach thee after this guise."   1070

"Ah, good mother! You say full well;
All things with me is not as you ween.°
If you had been in Morel's fell
As well as I, it should be seen."
"In Morel's fell! What devil is that?"   1075
"Marry, mother, I will it you show,
But beware that you come not thereat,
Lest you yourself then do beshrew.°

"Come down now in this cellar so deep,
And Morel's skin there shall you see,   1080
With many a rod that hath made me to weep,
When the blood ran down fast by my knee."
The mother this beheld, and cried out "alas!"
And ran out of the cellar as she had been wood.
She came to the table where the company was,   1085
And said, "out, whoreson! I will see thy heart blood."

"Peace, good mother! Or, so have I bliss,
You must dance else as did my wife,
And in Morel's skin lie, that well salted is,
Which you should repent all the days of your life."   1090
All they that were there held with the young man,
And said he did well in every manner degree.
When dinner was done, they departed all then;
The mother no longer durst there be.

The father abode last, and was full glad,   1095
And gave his children his blessing, iwis,
Saying the young man full well done had,
And merrily departed withouten miss.
This young man was glad you may be sure,
That he had brought his wife to this.   1100
God give us all grace in rest to endure,
And hereafter to come unto his bliss.

Thus was Morel slain out of his skin,
To charm a shrew, so have I bliss.

1072. **ween:** imagine, think.   1078. **beshrew:** pervert, corrupt, abuse.

Forgive the young man, if he did sin,   1105
But I think he did nothing amiss.
He did all thing even for the best,
As was well provèd then.
God save our wives from Morel's nest,
I pray you say all, amen.   1110

Thus endeth the jest of Morel's skin,
Where the curst wife was lappèd in.
Because she was of a shrewd leer,°
Thus was she served in this manner.

FINIS

Quoth Master Charm-her:
He that can charm a shrewd wife
    Better than thus,
Let him come to me, and fetch ten pound,
    And a golden purse.

1113. **leer:** countenance, temper, disposition.

➔ "The Cucking of a Scold"   *circa 1615–1630*

While *A Merry Jest* describes how a husband privately and unofficially disci-
plines his shrewish wife, this ballad describes the formal, public punishment of
a scold by "cucking," or dunking her in water. Unlike "shrew," a term of abuse
with no legal status, "scold" (like "witch") is a legal category, describing a
woman who offends against public order and peace through her speech. Just as
ballads and tales blame shrews for a range of disorderly or aggressive behaviors,
"charges of being a 'common scold' that were likely to bring women to the
cucking-stool usually involved not merely brawling and abuse but also such
offences as indiscriminate slander, tale-bearing, the stirring up of strife, the
deliberate sowing of discord between neighbours, and sometimes also the pur-
suit of quarrels through needless lawsuits and legal chicanery" (Ingram,
" 'Scolding Women' " 68). In this ballad, however, the scold's offense is restricted to insulting speech.

   Although the young woman in this ballad is married, her husband never
appears — as a target of her verbal abuse, or as her governor, punisher, or
protector. Both her transgressive speech and her shaming punishment occur
outside her home. This ballad depicts the woman as a member of her com-

"The Cucking of a Scold" (London, c. 1615–1630).

munity who uses her tongue in her disputes with neighbors and who, by the age of seventeen, already has a reputation as "a famous scold."

Since they had few other resources, women often used their tongues to retaliate against lapses of manners and custom, or infractions against property, as the scold here does. Those they insulted or cursed might respond by accusing them of scolding or witchcraft (which had even more serious consequences for the accused woman). Although the ballad claims that "without mighty wrong, / She [the scold] would not show her skill" (p. 292), it also suggests that the scolding for which she is punished is an excessive response to a minor offense.

The scold's punishment begins with the constable's desire to "revenge / This most outrageous wrong"; since, as constable, he has the power to punish the scold on his own initiative, he imprisons and displays her in "the cage." As one historian explains, "Scolds were sometimes punished in the stocks,[2] by being incarcerated in the town "cage" or, occasionally, by being carted or paraded round the town with basins ringing before them" (Ingram, " 'Scolding Women" 58). When the scold continues to "brawl" in the cage, a justice of the peace intervenes to impose a "just punishment," cucking. By the early seventeenth century, cucking had become the typical punishment for scolds (Ingram, " 'Scolding Women' " 58; on scolds see also Underdown). Ballads like this one may have helped to establish the scold as a legal category of offense, with cucking as the standard punishment (Ingram, " 'Scolding Women' " 59).

Cucking was not the only possible punishment for scolding, however, nor was it a community's first choice. The community might try less violent means of shaming a scold into silence (such as the cage in the ballad). A woman sentenced to cucking might be allowed to pay a fine instead, or she might be warned that cucking would follow a second offense. Also, attempts were made to ensure that the punishment was not excessively severe or fatal. Such caution was necessary since cucking could lead to drowning; the punishment was dangerous and frightening as well as humiliating. Bridles, usually made of metal, either covered the mouth or inserted a prong (or brank) to hold down the tongue; thus, they treated the offending woman as an unruly animal. While some of these bridles survive and other evidence suggests that they were used in the north of England in the seventeenth century, "the scold's bridle had a very brief history and was never used at all in most parts of England" (Ingram, " 'Scolding Women' " 58).

Long viewed as quaint reminders of the "world we have lost," the stool used for cucking (see Figure 12) and the bridle (see Figure 13) are now often considered instruments of torture, evidence of the history of violent corporal punishments rather than that of "merry old England." Emphasizing how brutal and painful bridling could be, Boose, for instance, argues that the bridle is "an instrument of torture, despite the fact — as English legal history is proud to boast — that in England torture was never legal" (Boose, "Scolding Brides"

---

[2] In the stocks the offender was in a sitting position, with her legs in front of her and her ankles secured between two boards with openings that cuffed them; the wrists might also be secured. Like the cage, then, this punishment immobilized and displayed the offender.

196). The very sight of the bridle or cucking stool might be punishment enough for some women. Ingram claims that, often, "in the case of first offenders, the cucking-stool was simply set against the culprit's door as a warning, or the scold was ordered to ride or be carried home in the stool without actually undergoing a ducking" (Ingram, " 'Scolding Women' " 62). This display of the offending woman, like the cage or the parade described in "The Cucking of a Scold," suggests that shame was a crucial part of all punishments of scolds, as it was of many early modern punishments. Since shame entailed exposure to community ridicule and censure, community members were more than witnesses of these punishments; they were crucial participants.

As a result, the punishments of scolds reveal how the history of violence, crime, and punishment and the history of festivity and popular culture intersect. Rather than decide that the cucking stool and the bridle belong in one history or the other, it is most useful to consider them as evidence of both. Which emphasis looms as the most significant depends on which participant you consider — the offending woman at the center of the ceremony, or her community. The quasi-military parade to the pond and the ritual cucking of the scold described in this ballad are clearly a festive occasion for her community, if not for her: "For joy the people skipped." Describing this occasion

FIGURE 12 *A woman on a cucking stool, from T. N. Brushfield,* Chester Archeological and Historic Society Journal *2 (1855–62). The offender would be plunged into the water repeatedly; "The Cucking of a Scold" suggests that this would continue until she ceased speaking up. As in the ballad, a crowd watches.*

through jaunty exaggeration, the ballad creates subsequent occasions for mirth at an assertive woman's discomfiture; each performance — especially if many singers joined in on the chorus — would be another festive occasion at the scold's expense. Of course, some witnesses of these proceedings, or audiences of the ballad, might have dissented from the revelry and objected vocally or silently. But such responses are not recorded.

FIGURE 13 *A woman wearing a scold's bridle, from Ralph Gardiner's* England's Grievance Discovered (*London, 1655*). *A metal tongue suppressor, or "brank," thrusts into the woman's mouth to keep her from talking. To increase her humiliation, she is being led through the town on a leash.*

The only resistance the ballad describes is that of the scold, who protests even after the cucking is underway. As the unwilling star of this pageant, "the famous scold" is made a spectacle — stripped to her undergarment, wreathed with a necklace of cows' tongues. The initial result of her "cucking" is also described in terms of her appearance "like a drowned rat."

Although parades on this scale do not seem to have accompanied cucking as a rule, this ballad does make clear that it is a gala event in which most of the community participates. The ballad also makes the ritual seem excessive and bizarre, at least to a modern reader. If the scold's provocative insults to the constable were an excessive response to a small offense, as the ballad suggests, her punishment seems even more so.

"The Cucking of a Scold"

To the tune of "The Merchant of Emden"

A wedded wife there was,
Iwis, of years but young;
But if you think she wanted wit,
I'll swear she lacked no tongue.
Just seventeen years of age,   5
This woman was — no more;
Yet she would scold with anyone,
From twenty to threescore.°
   The cucking of a scold,
   The cucking of a scold,   10
   Which if you will but stay to hear,
    The cucking of a scold.
As nimble as an eel,
This woman's tongue did wag,
And faster you shall have it run,   15
Than any ambling nag.
But without mighty wrong,
She would not show her skill.
But, if that she were movèd once,
The [sport]° was not so ill.   20
   The cucking, etc.
Each man might quickly know,
Whenas the game begun;
But none could tell you for his life,

---

8. threescore: three times twenty, or sixty years.   **20. [sport]:** This word is illegible in the original text. In his edition of the ballad Rollins suggests "sport."

What time she would have done.   25
She was a famous scold,
A dainty scold in grain,°
A stouter scold was never bred,
Nor born in Turn-gain Lane.°
   The cucking, etc.
Upon a time it chanced,   30
And she did thus alledge,
A neighbor's maid had taken half
Her dishclout° from the hedge.
For which great trespass done,
This wrong for to requite,   35
She scolded very handsomely,
Two days and one whole night.
   The cucking, etc.
Which something° did molest
The neighbors round about.   40
But this was nothing to the fits
That she would thunder out.
But once, the truth to tell,
Worse scolding did she keep,
For waking of her little dog,   45
That in the sun did sleep.
   The cucking, etc.
Six winter days together,
From morning eight o'clock,
Until the evening that each one   50
Their doors began to lock,
She scolded for this wrong,
Which she accounted great,
And unto peace and quietness
No man could her entreat.   55
   The cucking, etc.
So that this little devil,
With her unquiet tongue,
Continually, both far and near,
Molested old and young.   60
But yet soon after this,
She made a greater brawl
Against the constable that did

---

27. **in grain:** by nature, through and through.   29. **Turn-gain Lane:** Turn-again Alley or
Lane was a proverbial expression for a blind alley, a dead end.   34. **dishclout:** dish-
cloth.   40. **something:** somewhat.

But piss against her wall.   65
　　The cucking, etc.
She called him "beastly knave"°
And "filthy jack"° for this;
And said that every cuckold° now
Against her wall must piss.   70
And in most raging sort
She railed at him so long,
He made a vow he would revenge
This most outrageous wrong.
　　The cucking, etc.   75
And first of all behold:
He clapped her in the cage,
Thinking thereby her devilish tongue
He would full well assuage.
But now worse than before   80
She did to brawling fall.
The constable and all the rest
She vilely did miscall.
　　The cucking, etc.
Thus night and day she sent   85
Such brawling from her breast
That ne'er a neighbor in the town
Could take one hour's rest.
Which when the Justice knew,
This judgment then gave he: 90
That she upon a cucking stool
Should justly punished be.
　　The cucking, etc.
Upon three market days,
This penance she should bide;   95
And everything fit for the same
The officers did provide:
A hundred archers good
Did first before her go;
A hundred and five nimble shot   100
Went next unto the row.
　　The cucking, etc.
A hundred armèd men
Did also follow there,

67–68. knave: a male servant, one of low social condition, or a dishonorable, deceitful person; **jack:** a low-born or ill-mannered person, a servant or laborer. Note that both these terms, which link "low" social status with bad manners and lax morals, are class putdowns. **69. cuckold:** a man whose wife is unfaithful.

The which did guard the gallant scold 105
With piercing pikes and spears
And trumpets sounding sweet.
In order with them comes
A company most orderly,
With pleasant fifes and drums. 110
    The cucking, etc.
And forty parrots then,
On sundry perches high,
Were carried eke before the scold,
Most fine and orderly.
And last of all a mighty wisp° 115
Was borne before her face —
The perfect token of a scold,
Well-known in every place.
    The cucking, etc. 120
Then was the scold herself
In a wheel-barrow brought,
Stripped naked to the smock,°
As in that case she ought.
Neats'° tongues about her neck 125
Were hung in open show.
And thus unto the cucking stool
This famous scold did go.
    The cucking, etc.
Then fast within the chair 130
She was most finely bound,
Which made her scold excessively,
And said she should be drowned.
But every time that she
Was in the water dipped, 135
The drums and trumpets sounded brave,
For joy the people skipped.
    The cucking, etc.
Six times when she was ducked
Within the water clear, 140
That like unto a drownèd rat
She did in sight appear.
The Justice thinking then
To send her straight away,
The constable she callèd "knave," 145

---

116. **wisp:** a bunch of hay or straw. This word also refers to a figure made of hay — a "straw man" or invented interlocutor — considered the appropriate audience for a scold's empty speech. 123. **smock:** undergarment, a shift or slip. 125. **Neats':** oxen's or cows'.

And knaved him all the day.
   The cucking, etc.
Upon which words, I wot,
They ducked her straight again
A dozen times o'er head and ears.   150
Yet she would not refrain,
But still reviled them all.
Then to't again they go,
Till she at last held up her hands,
Saying "I'll no more do so."   155
   The cucking, etc.
Then was she brought away.
And after, for her life,
She never durst begin to scold
With either man or wife.   160
And if that every scold
Might have so good a diet,
Then should their neighbors every day
Be sure to live in quiet.
   The cucking of a scold,   165
   The cucking of a scold,
   Which if you will but stay to hear,
   The cucking of a scold.

FINIS

→ From *The Tragical Comedy, or Comical
Tragedy, of Punch and Judy*   *1828*

"Belike you mean to make a puppet of me."
                    Katharine, *The Taming of the Shrew* (4.3.103)
"There *was* a reason for Punch beating his wife — she was a shrew."
                                                    (Speaight 184)

Punch and Judy is a puppet show, usually performed by a single puppetmaster,
or "punchman," using glove-puppets with carved wooden heads. The puppe-
teer holds a "swazzle" (something like a small kazoo) in his mouth to produce
Punch's characteristic squeaking voice. Although Punch himself probably derives from the Italian puppet *pulcinella*, which was introduced into England

John Payne Collier, *The Tragical Comedy, or Comical Tragedy, of Punch and Judy* (London,
1828), 83–89.

after the Restoration (1660), the drama may also have drawn on English popular traditions, particularly the comic representation of the shrew and her tamer. As one historian of English puppetry argues, "the character of Punch, with his droll aggressiveness, was shaped in England; so was the shrewishness of his wife" (Speaight 220–21).

Punch is usually armed with a stick, which he wields in a series of encounters with as many as thirteen other characters, all of whom he beats and most of whom he kills (see Figure 15). Of his antagonists, only Judy is a woman. All versions begin with Punch's conflict with his wife Judy and his murder of their cranky baby; when she strenuously objects to this, Punch murders her. In early versions (such as Collier's below) Judy strikes the first blow (as Katharine strikes the first and only blow between spouses in *Shrew*). (See Figure 14.) In historian George Speaight's view, this marks her as a shrew and justifies Punch's subsequent conduct: "There *was* a reason for Punch beating his wife — she was a shrew" (Speaight 184). Like the many ballads and stories about marital conflict, then, this historian assumes a connection between women's unruly tongues and men's impulsive violence. In this view, shrewishness provokes, and therefore justifies, violence. Speaight further argues that Punch "must have expressed the subconscious desires of many suffering husbands in his audience" (Speaight 192). But if husbands identified with Punch, suffering wives in the audience might have identified with Judy's complaints, her retaliation, and her vows of revenge for her murdered baby.

Some men's identification with Punch cannot alone explain the show's enduring popularity over many centuries, with mixed audiences of men and women, adults and children, wealthy and poor, learned and illiterate, and in locations that range from the street to parlors. Many different kinds of viewers seem to have found something to laugh at and enjoy in the crude conflicts played out by puppets on this tiny stage (Shershow 161–82). *Punch and Judy* began as an attraction at fairs, but by the late eighteenth century had evolved into a traveling street performance operating out of a portable booth stage. In the nineteenth century, perhaps as many as ten punchmen (each working with an assistant) supported themselves on the streets of London. Especially during holiday seasons, they would also be invited into homes for parlor performances. Still found today largely in English seaside resorts in the summer, *Punch and Judy* shows continue to attract a mixed audience of children and adults, men and women, and people of "all sorts of classes" (Mayhew 46). Audiences still delight in the extreme violence of this puppet show; children watching the show especially like to tell on Punch, yelling to Judy that he has killed the baby in her absence.

Obviously, it makes a difference that Punch and Judy are puppets who do not bleed or bruise, whose facial expressions never change, whom we know cannot be hurt. For this reason, *Punch and Judy* offers an extreme version of the farce that some critics find in *The Taming of the Shrew*. According to some definitions, farce, even when performed by human actors rather than puppets,

◄ FIGURE 14 *George Cruikshank's illustrations of* Punch and Judy: A Tragical Comedy *(1828). Judy strikes the first blow in retaliation after Punch kills their baby.*

◄ FIGURE 15 *Here Punch teaches Judy "one little more lesson," beating her to death with his trademark stick. Cruikshank's drawing offers a reminder that, although they are engaged in a fatal struggle, the puppets' stiff postures and blank expressions do not change.*

depicts a world "without pain or conscience"; it "lets us participate without feeling the responsibilities and liabilities that the situation would normally evoke" (Heilman 152). Allowing us to take pleasure in aggressive feelings we would otherwise suppress, farce is "an economical strategy for acknowledging and accepting hostility. But all it does is accept — it does not transform" (Berek 102; see also Garner 109–10). However, not everyone agrees that the conflicts between Katharine and Petruchio, and between the two of them and their servants, can be read as farce. By violently representing farce, *Punch and Judy* highlights the extent to which *The Taming of the Shrew* is, or is not, farcical.

The 1929 film version of *The Taming of the Shrew*, the first "talking picture" of a Shakespeare play, directed by Sam Taylor and starring Mary Pickford and Douglas Fairbanks, begins with a *Punch and Judy* show in which Judy refuses Punch's request for a kiss and beats him soundly. But in this version, as in others, Punch soon gains the upper hand; he beats Judy with a stick, shouting "I'll tame you" until at last she embraces him, exclaiming, "You're wonderful." Taylor thus uses Punch and Judy to shape how viewers will evaluate the rest of the play, especially the interactions between Petruchio and Katharine; but it is interesting to note the changes Taylor makes so that the conflict between the puppet-spouses will not end in murder, and will thus predict the comic resolution in the play proper. In Taylor's version, Judy submits to Punch and thus avoids being beaten to death; she also rewards his abuse with admiration. Punch, then, is the same as always; it is Judy who is different and who bears the burden of transforming tragedy into comedy by means of her abrupt conversion from shrew to good wife.

Unlike plays such as *The Taming of the Shrew, Punch and Judy* has never depended on a written script. Each punchman's show, and each performance of that show, would have been somewhat different. Evidence also suggests that the shows changed over time. Those scripts that survive attempt to capture live, multiple, continuously changing performances. The first transcription was made in 1828. A publisher commissioned George Cruikshank to make sketches of a street performance by an Italian punchman named Piccini, who claimed to have introduced the show to England (see Figures 14 and 15). To accompany these illustrations, John Payne Collier provided a text that combined a transcription of Piccini's performance with his notes from a show he had seen as a boy in Brighton around 1805. The resulting text was very popular and went through numerous editions. Especially given that it was a conflation of two versions and that Collier was later to become a notorious literary forger, we cannot think of this (or any) script as "authentic" or "accurate." It can only gesture toward the vitality, diversity — and violence — of these street performances.

The Tragical Comedy, or Comical Tragedy, of Punch and Judy

Enter Punch

PUNCH: Judy! Judy, my dear! Judy! Can't you answer, my dear?
JUDY [*within*]:   Well! What do you want, Mr. Punch?
PUNCH: Come upstairs. I want you.
JUDY: Then want must be your master. I'm busy.
PUNCH [*singing, [to the] tune "Malbrough"*]:
Her answer genteel is, and civil!
No wonder, you think, if we live ill,
And I wish her sometimes at the Devil,
            Since that's all the answer I get.
            Yet, why must I grumble and fret,
            Because she's sometimes in a pet?
Though I really am sorry to say, sirs,
That that is too often her way, sirs.
For this, by and by, she shall pay, sirs.
        Oh, wives are an obstinate set!
Judy, my dear! [*Calling.*] Judy, my love! Pretty Judy! Come upstairs.

Enter Judy.

JUDY: Well, here I am! What do you want, now I'm come?
PUNCH [*aside*]:   What a pretty creature! Ain't she one beauty?
JUDY: What do you want, I say?
PUNCH: A kiss! A pretty kiss! [*Kisses her, while she hits him a slap on the face.*]
JUDY: Take that, then. How do you like my kisses? Will you have another?
PUNCH: No. One at a time, one at a time, my sweet pretty wife. [*Aside*] She always is so playful. Where's the child? Fetch me the child, Judy my dear.   [*Exit Judy.*]

PUNCH [*alone*]:   There's one wife for you! What a precious darling creature! She go to fetch our child.°

Reenter Judy with the child.

JUDY: Here's the child. Pretty dear! It knows its papa. Take the child.
PUNCH [*holding out his hands*]:   Give it me — pretty little thing! How like its sweet mamma!
JUDY: How awkward you are!
PUNCH: Give it me. I know how to nurse it so well as you do. [*She gives it to him.*] Get away!   [*Exit Judy.*]
PUNCH [*nursing the child in his arms*]: What a pretty baby it is! Was it sleepy then? Hush-a-by, by, by [*Sings to the tune of "Rest thee, Babe."*]

> Oh, rest thee, my baby,
> Thy daddy is here;
> Thy mammy's a gaby,°
> And that is quite clear.

> Oh, rest thee, my darling,
> Thy mother will come,
> With a voice like a starling —
> I wish she was dumb!

Poor dear little thing! It cannot get to sleep. By, by, by, by, hush-a-by. Well, then, it shan't. [*Dances the child, and then sets it on his lap, between his knees, and sings the common nursery ditty.*]

> Dancy baby diddy,
> What shall daddy do widdy?°
> Sit on his lap;
> Give it some pap.°
> Dancy baby diddy.

[*After nursing it upon his lap, Punch sticks the child against the side of the stage on the platform and, going himself to the opposite side, runs up to it, clapping his hands, and crying "Catchee, catchee, catchee!" He then takes it up again, and it begins to cry.*]

What is the matter with it? Poor thing! It has got the stomachache, I dare say. [*Child cries.*] Hush-a-by, hush-a-by! [*Sitting down and rolling*

She go . . . child: Since this script claims to reproduce Piccini's performance, it sometimes gestures toward his broken English. Following Piccini, some punchmen mimicked Italian accents and introduced some Italian words into their shows.   **gaby:** a simpleton, a stupid person.   **widdy:** with thee.   **pap:** soft food fed to infants, often a kind of porridge.

it on his knees.] Naughty child! Judy! [*Calling.*] The child has got the stomachache. Pheu! Nasty child! Judy, I say! [*Child continues to cry.*] Keep quiet, can't you? [*Hits it a box on the ear.*] Oh you filthy child! What have you done? I won't keep such a nasty child. Hold your tongue! [*Strikes the child's head several times against the side of the stage.*] There! — there! — there! How you like that? I thought I stop your squalling. Get along with you, nasty, naughty, crying child. [*Throws it over the front of the stage among the spectators.*] Hee! hee! hee! [*Laughing and singing to the same tune as before.*]

> Get away, nasty baby —
> There it goes over —
> Thy mammy's a gaby;
> Thy daddy's a rover.

Reenter Judy.

JUDY: Where is the child?

PUNCH: Gone — gone to sleep.

JUDY: What have you done with the child, I say?

PUNCH: Gone to sleep, I say.

JUDY: What have you done with it?

PUNCH: What have I done with it?

JUDY: Ay, done with it! I heard it crying just now. Where is it?

PUNCH: How should I know?

JUDY: I heard you make the pretty darling cry.

PUNCH: I threw it out at window.

JUDY: Oh, you cruel horrid wretch, to throw the pretty baby out at window. Oh! [*Cries, and wipes her eyes with the corner of her white apron.*] You barbarous man. Oh!

PUNCH: You shall have one other soon, Judy, my dear. More where that come from.

JUDY: I'll make you pay for this, depend upon it. [*Exit in haste.*]

PUNCH: There she goes. What a piece of work about nothing! [*Dances about and sings, beating time with his head as he turns round on the front of the stage.*]

[Reenter Judy with a stick. She comes in behind, and hits Punch a sounding blow on the back of the head, before he is aware.]

JUDY: I'll teach you to throw my child out at window.

PUNCH: So-o-oftly, Judy, so-o-oftly! [*Rubbing the back of his head with his hand.*] Don't be a fool now. What you at?

JUDY: What? You'll throw my poor baby out at window again, will you? [*Hitting him continually on the head.*]

PUNCH: No, I never will again. [*She still hits him.*] Softly, I say, softly. A joke's a joke!

JUDY: Oh, you nasty cruel brute! [*Hitting him again.*] I'll teach you.

PUNCH: But me no like such teaching. What! You're in earnest, are you?

JUDY: Yes [*hit*], I [*hit*] am [*hit*].

PUNCH: I'm glad of it. Me no like such jokes. [*She hits him again.*] Leave off, I say. What? You won't, won't you?

JUDY: No, I won't. [*Hits him.*]

PUNCH: Very well. Then now come my turn to teach you. [*He snatches at, and struggles with her for, the stick, which he wrenches from her, and strikes her with it on the head, while she runs about to different parts of the stage to get out of his way.*] How you like my teaching, Judy, my dear? [*Hitting her.*]

JUDY: Oh, pray, Mr. Punch — no more!

PUNCH: Yes, one little more lesson. [*Hits her again.*] There, there, there! [*She falls down, with her head over the platform of the stage; and, as he continues to hit at her, she puts up her hand to guard her head.*] Any more?

JUDY: No, no, no more! [*Lifting up her head.*]

PUNCH [*knocking down her head*]: I thought I should soon make you quiet.

JUDY [*again raising her head*]:   No.

PUNCH [*again knocking it down, and following up his blows until she is lifeless*]: Now, if you're satisfied, I am. [*Perceiving that she does not move.*] There, get up, Judy, my dear. I won't hit you anymore. None of your sham-abram.° This is only your fun. Have you got the headache? Why, you're only asleep. Get up, I say! Well then, get down. [*Tosses the body down with the end of his stick.*] Hee! hee! hee! [*Laughing.*] To lose a wife is to get a fortune. [*Sings*]:

> Who'd be plagued with a wife,
>   That could set himself free
> With a rope or a knife,
>   Or a good stick, like me?

[*This scene usually ends with Punch pushing Judy's body off the stage with his stick.*]

---

sham-abram: nonsense word meaning faking or counterfeiting. Punch accuses Judy of playing dead.

Analogues to Shrew Taming

Petruchio's taming methods are subtler than those used by the husband in *A Merry Jest* or by Punch. Petruchio transforms Katharine "from a wild Kate to a Kate / Conformable as other household Kates" (2.1.270–71) by "watching" her, or keeping her awake, and by starving her. Petruchio draws an explicit parallel between his method of domesticating his wife and the method used by falconers (4.1.159–65). He will "man his haggard" or tame his wild female hawk. Since Petruchio depicts himself as a falconer and Katharine as his hawk, who must learn to "come and know her keeper's call," it makes sense to compare his methods to those described in guidebooks on falconry.

There is another, more disturbing, analogue to Petruchio's methods. Roughly half a century after Shakespeare's play was first produced, authorities "watched" those accused of witchcraft, who were almost always women; in order to convince or coerce the accused, who were often old and frail, to confess, authorities kept them awake for several nights and denied them food. These two analogues differ in important ways. One comes from the realm of sport, the other from the realm of legal prosecution. One taming method focuses on birds, the other on humans. One is contemporary to Shakespeare's play; the other occurs almost half a century later. The consequences of success are also very different. If the falconer succeeds in manning his haggard, she will hunt for him yet not eat her prey; she will soar high but always return to his fist or her perch; she will be powerful and free but within limits that he determines. If those who watch witches succeed, the accused will confess; and on the grounds of that confession she will be hanged. Of these two images of the tethered haggard/hag, one tied to a perch, the other hanging from a gallows, the latter obviously depicts the most decisive defeat.

In both these analogues to Petruchio's politic reign, watching and/or starving is a strategy used by the powerful to break the spirit of — or at least to subordinate — one viewed as wild, strong, even supernaturally empowered. Yet the treatises on falconry also reveal the intimacy that can coexist with and enable domination.

FALCONRY

Because it was expensive and time-consuming, falconry was largely a sport of aristocrats. Like other forms of hunting, it became a mark of nobility. In the Induction to *The Taming of the Shrew*, for instance, the Lord enters with two "huntsmen" talking about their hunting dogs; the Lord's servants convince Christopher Sly that he, too, is a Lord by tempting him with the prospect of noble sports: "Dost thou love hawking? . . . Or wilt thou hunt?" (Ind. 2. 38–39). To engage in these sports, one must first own costly animals ("thou hast hawks"; "thy hounds"). By drawing on the language of falconry to describe how he will tame Katharine, Petruchio asserts himself to be a gentleman. Like taming a wife, taming a hawk is a way not only of dominating a wild and rebellious creature (who is invariably identified as feminine) but also of distinguishing one's self from other men. Petruchio's successful program to "man his haggard" is contrasted with Hortensio's failed attempt to woo Bianca, to whom he refers in defeat as "this proud disdainful haggard" (4.2.39). The final scene in which the three husbands wager on their wives makes this sporting competition especially clear.

Just as numerous texts were available to teach readers how to run their households and conduct their marriages, books were available to teach men the vocabulary and skills of falconry. Although George Turberville uses the subtitle of his book to claim that it is only "for the delight and pleasure of all noblemen and gentlemen," the very existence of guidebooks on the subject indicates that falconry was not a skill that aristocrats came by naturally or that was passed down from father to son; instead, it was a skill that men could learn, including those engaged in an individual or familial project of social aspiration.

The two works from which excerpts are presented below were both relatively popular, although they differ in tone and emphasis. George Turberville's *The Book of Falconry or Hawking; For the Only Delight and Pleasure of All Noblemen and Gentlemen* was published twice, first in 1575, and then, in a revised form, in 1611. Simon Latham's *Latham's Falconry, or The Falcon's Lure and Cure* went through four editions (1614, 1615, 1633, 1658); *Latham's New and Second Book of Falconry* was published in 1618, 1633, and 1658; a combined edition of the two works was published in 1662. Latham's greater success stemmed from the fact that he was a professional falconer who had learned from the grandson of Queen Elizabeth's "grand falconer" and who himself became an officer under the master of the hawks. In contrast, George Turberville was a younger son in an old and respected family who supported himself in various ways, publishing a great deal of work, mostly poetry, and even serving as Queen Elizabeth's ambassador to the emperor of Russia.

While Latham's text focuses on the details of caring for and training hawks, Turberville's book is more interested in the conduct of gentlemen and would-be gentlemen than of hawks. For instance, Turberville advises his reader to carry an extra supply of equipment into the field so that he can supply "his betters . . . if happily they want any such devices" (78). He also promises that his book will assure the reader "good pastime in the field, when other ignorant grooms shall both lack sport, and lose their hawks, the greatest corsie [grievance] that may happen to a gentleman that loves the game" (78). Turberville dwells here on the relationships among men "in the field" and the social advantages his readers can gain through masterful falconry; even the illustrations to his book depict hawks as accessories for stylish gentlemen and the hunt as an occasion for men to interact (see Figure 16). Latham also wishes to distinguish his readers from the man who "takes in hand to keep a hawk, [but] that having neither skill nor judgment, does not deserve the true title of a falconer" (C3).

But Latham is most interested in the relationship between keeper and hawk, who should be inseparable. He depicts this relationship as peculiarly intimate: "He that will be a falconer must be no sluggard. He must be up early, and down late, or else he shall never see how his hawk rejoiceth. Neither must he be tempted or drawn away with other mutabilities, or wandering affection, but remain and continue constant in the art he professeth" (8). For Latham this bond requires not only diligence but also, apparently, monogamy.

Because of passages like that, the most sustained inquiry to date into the falconry imagery in *The Taming of the Shrew* has read the relationship between keeper and falcon as a relatively positive model for marriage. Employing guides to falconry including those by Turberville and Latham, Ranald argues that "the compact between master and falcon is basically a voluntary commitment. When it soars, waiting for its prey, the bird is capable of flying away free, and only the kindness of the keeper and the consequent gratitude or indebtedness of the bird can keep it under control. So too with Kate and Petruchio" (Ranald 120). In Ranald's view, the relationship between keeper and falcon, like that between husband and wife, is reciprocal and equitable: "Each has duties and both have rights" (Ranald 132). Ranald finds this reciprocity even in the taming method of watching and starving the bird.

> This method of gaining obedience, though cruel, is one that lays equal demands on both bird and keeper. As long as the bird is "watched," an average of three nights, so long does the keeper have to go without sleep, suffering the same hardships as his falcon, until she stops her bating, or flying off the perch, and beating her wings in an endeavor to escape her leg restraints, or jesses. (Ranald 128).

Furthermore, both relationships require special attention at first, for the early days set the pattern that will be followed thereafter. This positive evaluation of falconry as a model for marriage downplays the significant disparities between the two parties: one is a human, endowed with reason

FIGURE 16 *A gentleman and his hawk, from George Turberville's* The Book of Falconry or Hawking (*London, 1611*). *The gentleman proudly displays his hawk, a prized possession and a badge of his high status, wealth, and accomplishment. The two also pose like a couple.*

and free will, the other an animal; one controls access to food, sleep, and flight, the other can choose only to resist or submit to circumstances she cannot control. The bond that results — reinforced as it is with leather restraints — is hardly between equals.

It is also worth remembering that although haggards are female hawks and *The Taming of the Shrew* and books on falconry depict "manning a haggard" as a taming by a male keeper/husband of his female bird/wife, the analogy to falconry also describes something women do to men. As we have seen, David Garrick's adaptation of *The Shrew* assigns language about manning a haggard to Catharine rather than to Petruchio. In *A Juniper Lecture* a mother advises her daughter to "torment and torture" her husband with her tongue, "as wild haggard hawks are tamed or manned, with being kept hungry, and continual waking" (*Juniper Lecture* Civ). When used by women, this method is usually depicted as ill-advised and inappropriately aggressive. But these examples suggest that a tamer is not inevitably masculine and that falconry provided a model for taming or dominating in a variety of situations.

Indeed, in John Fletcher's sequel to *The Taming of the Shrew*, *The Woman's Prize or The Tamer Tamed* (1611), Maria, Petruchio's second wife, celebrates her status as a "free haggard." After Livia announces "Let's all wear breeches" (1.2.146), Maria proclaims:

Now thou com'st near the nature of a woman.
Hang these tame-hearted eyasses,[3] that no sooner
See the lure[4] out, and hear their husbands' holla,
But cry like kites[5] upon 'em! The free haggard
(Which is that woman, that hath wing, and knows it,
Spirit, and plume) will make a hundred checks[6]
To show her freedom, sail in ev'ry air,
And look out ev'ry pleasure; not regarding
Lure, nor quarry,[7] till her pitch[8] command
What she desires; making her foundered[9] keeper
Be glad to fling out trains,[10] and golden ones,
To take her down again.   (1.2.147–58)

---

[3] **eyasses:** young hawks taken from the nest for training, or those whose training is incomplete.
[4] **lure:** a bunch of feathers attached to a long cord, in which food is placed during training. Falconers later use this to recall their hawks.
[5] **kites:** birds of prey.
[6] **checks:** false stoops, when the hawk forsakes the game she has been sent after to follow something else.
[7] **quarry:** the reward given to a hawk that has killed another bird.
[8] **pitch:** the height to which a falcon soars before swooping down on its prey.
[9] **foundered:** undermined, made to give way.
[10] **trains:** baits, enticements, but with the connotation of traps.

Although this speech ends with the free haggard being taken down by the bait or snare of her keeper, Maria's extended use of the language of falconry to describe a powerful and independent woman demonstrates the very different meanings that might be found in falconry as a model for gender relations (see also Latham's description of the haggard "while she is wild" below).

→ GEORGE TURBERVILLE

From *The Book of Falconry or Hawking* *1611*

First, let your hawk be taken on the fist and hooded. Then, let her be watched three days and nights before you unhood her; and feed her always hooded in an easy luster° hood. At the end of three days, you may unhood her, and feed her unhooded; and when she is fed, hood her again, so that she be not unhooded (but° when you feed her) until she know her meat. Then when she beginneth to be acquainted with you, hood her and unhood her oftentimes, to the end she may the better abide the hood. But use her gently, and be patient with her at the first. And to the end your hawk may be the better manned and the sooner reclaimed, you shall do well to bear her commonly in places where most people do frequent, and where most exercises are used. And when she is well-manned, make her come a little to the fist for her meat. And when you have showed her the perch or stock and tied her upon it, put with her upon the said perch or stock some pullet or other quick° fowl as often as you may, and let her feed thereon at pleasure until she be reasonably gorged. And do in like manner upon the lure until she know it perfectly. Afterwards, you may give her more liberty and lure her with a creance,° luring her twice a day, further and further off. And when she is thoroughly lured, you shall teach her to fly upon you, until she know both how to get to her gate,° and to fly round upon you. Then shall you cast her out some quick fowl, and when she hath stooped and seized upon it, you shall suffer her to plume° it, and to foot° it at her pleasure, giving her a reasonable

---

luster: a thin, light dress material with a highly lustrous or shiny surface.   but: except.   quick: living.   creance: a long fine cord attached to a hawk's leash, by which she is prevented from flying away while being trained.   get to her gate: get into flight.   plume: to pluck its feathers.   foot: to clutch it with the talons.

George Turberville, *The Book of Falconry or Hawking; For the Only Delight and Pleasure of All Noblemen and Gentlemen* (London, 1611), 79–80.

gorge thereon, as is before said, and continuing always to reward her upon the said lure, in such sort that she never find the lure without some reward tied upon it. And by that means she will always love the lure and her keeper well, and will not lightly rangle° or be lost.

rangle: rove, wander, stray.

→ SIMON LATHAM

From *Latham's Falconry* 1615

From Chapter 2, "A perfect description of the Haggard Falcon, with the manner and course of her life while she is wild and unreclaimed."

This Haggard falcon, slight or gentle, which[ever] you list to term her, hath for the most part all places both by sea and land left unto herself, where to rest and have her abiding. And where she best liketh, there she continueth certain, like a conqueror in the country, keeping in awe and subjection the most part of all the fowl that fly. Insomuch that the Tassell gentle,° her natural and chiefest companion, dares not come near that coast where she useth, nor sit by the place where she standeth. Such is the greatness of her spirit, she will not admit of any society, until such time as nature worketh in her an inclination to put that in practice which all hawks are subject unto at the spring-time.° And then she suffereth him to draw towards her, but still in subjection, which appeareth at his coming by [his] bowing down his body and head to his foot; by calling and cowering in his wings, as the young ones do unto their dam, whom they dare not displease. And thus they leave the country for the summertime, hasting to the place where they mean to breed.

From Chapter 3, "Here followeth the manner of reclaiming your Haggard, with the means how to enter her to the lure."

[Latham advises that a hawk who has just been taken from the nest should be left to rest quietly the first night.]

Tassell gentle: tercel-gentle, or male falcon.   that . . . spring-time: that is, mating.

Simon Latham, *Latham's Falconry, or The Falcon's Lure and Cure* (London, 1615), B3, C–C2.

The next day, easily take her upon your fist gently, and cease not to carry her the whole day continually, using a feather instead of your hand to touch and stroke her withall. And when you find her gentle and willing to be touched without starting, then may you alone by yourself pull off her hood, and quietly and gently put it on again, holding this course until she begin to feed. Then you must proffer her meat often, suffering her to take but a little at once, even to please her withall, never pulling off her hood, nor putting it on without a bit or two, both before and after, to quiet her. And draw her love unto the hood and yourself, not forgetting to use your voice unto her before you take it off and all the while she is feeding, and no longer; that as she reclaimeth and her stomach° groweth or increaseth, she may learn to know that when she heareth your voice, she shall be fed. Then, when through your diligent pains and this prescribed order in your practice you have brought her to feed boldly, then will it be fit time to teach her to jump to your fist, which you must do in this manner.

Set her down on a perch about your breast-high, or otherwise, if it be a low perch, then you must be on your knees, because your Haggard will be fearful and ready to start and bate° from you when she shall see you so high over her at the first, until she be better acquainted with you. Then unstrike° her hood, and lure her using your voice, with a bit or two of meat bestowed on her as she is hooded; for that will make her eager and to love your voice because she sees nothing to cross that humor in her. Whereas otherwise it may be as yet her coyness or her perceiving of one thing or other may provoke her to take dislike or to bate from you, and thereby catch some sudden fear, which at the first you ought to be careful to prevent. For it is hard to work that out again, which she is suffered to take at the first. And most commonly she will be subject to it ever after, whether it be good or evil. Therefore, it shall be your best course to hold this order until you shall find her familiar, and her stomach perfect. For it is that only that guides and rules her; it is the curb and bridle that holds and keeps her in subjection to the man; and it is the spur that pricketh her forward to perform the duty she oweth to her keeper; and that which he requireth from her to be effected. And without° that one only thing be preserved and carefully kept ripe, perfect, sharp, and truly edged, there is no subjection to be gained, nor no content to be received, but scornful disobedience and altogether offensiveness.°

---

stomach: appetite. More generally, Latham presents the stomach as the seat of the falcon's spirit and pride. bate: to beat the wings impatiently and flutter away from the fist or perch. unstrike: loosen the strings on the hood so that it can be readily taken off. without: unless. offensiveness: The margin here reads: "No subjection when the stomach is full."

Now by this time you may be bold to pull off her hood, and let her sit bare-faced, keeping yourself as yet close by her. And as you shall perceive her to have any untoward humor in her (as to stare about, or wry° herself to and fro), proffer her a bit of meat with your hand, and use your voice withall to draw her straight unto you, which when you have effected, and that you do find she will boldly attend, willingly receive bits at your hand, and jump readily to your fist, then will it be a fit time to set her to the lure, which order and practice (because I know the simplest falconer is not ignorant of) I will omit.

But to proceed, so soon as your hawk will come readily in the creance to the lure garnished with meat, nay not long in that kind, for she will soon begin to scorn it and look another way, then will it be convenient to let her see a live dove at the lure; and lure her unto the same, which when she hath killed and eaten the head, take her up very gently with a bit of meat and put on her hood. Then lure her again unto the dead pelt, and so use her two or three times and no more. For she will quickly begin to perceive your intent, and will grow loath to be taken off and her desire to keep it still in her possession will cause her to drag it from you, and thereby her love will rather abate than increase.

wry: to pull or twist, contort.

WATCHING A WITCH

Witchfinders or witchhunters were those who "specialized in accusing and finding witches" and who traveled from village to village searching for witches, collecting evidence and building cases against them, and earning money for each conviction they could secure (Macfarlane 135). Witchfinders contributed to the last gasp of witchcraft prosecution in England. To do so, they needed methods more extreme than those that had previously been used to pressure witches into confessing; they also gathered physical evidence more aggressively. In England witchfinders were most active in the middle of the seventeenth century (especially the 1640s) and helped to boost prosecutions. Matthew Hopkins and his assistant, John Stearne, remain the most notorious of the English witchfinders. Their efforts in Essex in 1645 resulted in the hanging of nineteen women, "the largest number ever executed at one time in England" (Laurence 218), despite the fact that, on the whole, executions were dwindling by this time; at least in Essex, they had reached their peak in the 1590s. Although Hopkins and Stearne profited from their efforts, it is also possible that they "really believed that they were performing a public service, dealing with a public menace" (Macfarlane 140). In their hunt for witches Hopkins and Stearne sometimes acted as detectives or prosecuting attorneys, sometimes as witnesses, sometimes as inquisitors (bordering on torturers). They did not use the kinds of torture that were illegal in England, and which the English contemptuously associated with the Inquisition in Catholic Europe; still, Hopkins and Stearne experimented with various new methods for convincing suspects to confess.

"Watching" was one of these. As the survival of texts in which Hopkins and Stearne defend the practice reveals, this innovation was controversial. It was also associated by those who opposed it with methods used to "tame a wild colt, or hawk." One sceptical critic, Thomas Ady, claims: "This trick will tame any wild beast and make it tractable, or any wild hawk and make it tame, and come to your fist." In the view of those who opposed the bounty-hunting witchfinders, methods used to tame animals were not appropriate for people.

Securing a confession, by whatever means, was crucial to the success of a witchcraft prosecution. Witchcraft was very difficult to prove in court; the rate of acquittal was always high, and even Hopkins had an acquittal rate of 42 percent (Shapiro 206). Seventeenth-century prosecutors (especially witchfinders) sought physical evidence to counter growing scepticism about both witchcraft and the prospect of proving it. For instance, juries of matrons searched suspects' bodies for "devil's marks." Any mark or irregularity on the body might be seen as a teat or pap from which the suspect was presumed to suckle "familiars" or imps (demonic domestic pets who served both as companions and as agents of mischief) or the devil himself. This suckling never occurred at the breast; the marks were most often identified near the genitals or anus. Hopkins and Stearne base their justifications of "watching" on their assumption that the relation between a witch and her familiars is somehow addictive. If she is kept awake, sometimes nude and cross-legged on a table in the middle of the room, her familiars will have to come out of hiding to suckle her. If, for whatever reason, they do not, she will be so dispirited that she will confess.

In the late 1640s, both Hopkins and Stearne wrote pamphlets answering objections to their work and justifying their methods; in the excerpts here, each of the veteran witchfinders defends the practice of watching witches. A decade later, Thomas Ady articulated the growing scepticism about witchcraft among learned people in a lengthy treatise challenging the beliefs and practices on which prosecutions relied. In the excerpts, he censures the watching of witches as particularly inhumane and corrupt.

Despite increasingly aggressive searches for physical evidence, the burden of proof rested on witnesses' testimony and, especially, on the accused's confession. This need for a confession spurred Hopkins and Stearne to employ methods that stirred controversy and condemnation. The disapproval of witchfinders in turn led to decreasing confidence in confessions extracted under such circumstances, scepticism about witchcraft, and, by 1736, the repeal of statutes against witchcraft altogether. After that, witchcraft ceased to be a crime. Although Hopkins and Stearne artifically inflated prosecutions by using extreme and objectionable methods, they may also have contributed to the decline and ultimate cessation of prosecutions and executions by the early eighteenth century.

→ MATTHEW HOPKINS

From *The Discovery of Witches*   *1647*

QUERY 8: *When these paps are fully discovered,° yet that will not serve sufficiently to convict them, but they must be tortured and kept from sleep two or three nights, to distract them, and make them say anything; which is a way to tame a wild colt, or hawk, &c.*

ANSWER: In the infancy of this discovery [of witches], it [i.e. watching] was not only thought fitting, but enjoined in *Essex* and *Suffolk* by the Magistrates, with this intention only — because they [witches] being kept awake would be the more active to call their imps in open view the sooner to their help, which oftentimes have so happened. And never or seldom did any witch ever complain in the time of their keeping for want of rest. . . . [And after it was prohibited by judges and other magistrates,] never were any kept from sleep by any order or direction since; but peradventure their own stubborn wills did not let them sleep, though [sleep was] tendered and offered to them.

When . . . discovered: That is, after the suspect has been searched and supernumerary teats found on her body. Hopkins here imagines or reproduces a frequently voiced query or objection, in order to answer it.

Matthew Hopkins, *The Discovery of Witches: In Answer to Several Queries Lately Delivered to the Judges of Assizes for the County of Norfolk* (London, 1647), B.

→ JOHN STEARNE

From *A Confirmation and Discovery of Witchcraft* *1648*

But I desire to answer one objection before I proceed further. That is, some say, and many will and do say: "But you watched them, and kept them from meat, drink, or rest, and so made them say what you would. A very unnatural part so to use Christians." I answer so it were. But I never knew any deprived of meat, drink or rest, but [they] had what was fitting till they were carried before some justice of peace to be examined, and had provision to rest upon, as bolsters, pillows, or cushions, and such like, if they were kept where no beds were. Yet I do not deny but at first some were kept two, three, or four days, perchance somewhat baser. But then it had been either when no justice of peace was near, or when the witnesses against them could not go sooner. But then they have had beds, and for other provision, I never knew any kept, of what rank or quality soever, but that they had better provision, either meat or drink, than at their own houses. For the watching, it is not to use violence or extremity to force them to confess, but only the keeping is, first, to see whether any of their spirits or familiars come to or near them; for I have found that if the time be come, the spirit or imp (so-called) should come. It will be either visible or invisible. If visible, then it may be discerned by those in the room. If invisible, then by the party. Secondly, it is for this end also: that if the parties which watch them, be so careful that none come visible nor invisible but may be discerned, if they follow their directions, then the party [being watched] presently after the time their familiars should have come, if they fail [to come], will presently confess. For then they think they have forsaken them. Thirdly, it is also to the end that godly divines and others might discourse with them, and idle persons be kept from them. For if any of their society come to them to discourse with them, they will never confess.

John Stearne, *A Confirmation and Discovery of Witchcraft, Containing These Several Particulars: That There Are Witches Called Bad Witches, and Witches Untruly Called Good or White Witches, and What Manner of People They Be, and How They May Be Known, with Many Particulars Thereunto Tending. . . . As Also Some Objections Answered* (London, 1648), C2–C2v.

→ THOMAS ADY

From *A Candle in the Dark*   *1656*

[Ady describes the tortures devised by the Roman church to get people to confess "impossibilities"; he includes among these one which is] one of the most devilish cruelties that hath been devised among men. And that is, to keep the poor accused party from sleep many nights and days, thereby to distemper their brains, and hurt their fancies,° at length to extort confession from them, and then to bring their own confession as an evidence against them. . . . This trick will tame any wild beast and make it tractable, or any wild hawk and make it tame, and come to your fist. How much more may it make men and women yield to confess lies and impossibilities?

.   .   .   .

[Ady also discusses trials that occurred in England in 1645,° including those at Chelmsford at which Hopkins and Stearne were the chief accusers. In these trials, according to Ady,] those poor accused people were watched day and night, and kept from sleep with much cruelty, till their fancies being hurt, they would confess what their inquisitors would have them, although it were a thing impossible, and flat contrary to sense and Christian understanding to believe. Where, for the removing of objections, it is to be noted that a fancy so hurt with watching cannot afterward of a long time recant, or deny that which they have confessed, no more than a hawk thoroughly tamed by watching can grow speedily wild again, although you give them their full sleep.

---

fancies: imaginations.   trials . . . in 1645: At these trials fifty were indicted, thirty-six were imprisoned or tried, nineteen were executed, nine died of jail fever, and six may have remained in jail (they were still there in 1648). See Macfarlane 135.

Thomas Ady, *A Candle in the Dark, or, A Treatise Concerning the Nature of Witches and Witchcraft* (London, 1656), O2, P.

Untamed Shrews

→ THOMAS HARMAN

From *A Caveat for Common Cursitors,*
Vulgarly Called Vagabonds   *1568*

In this story a woman describes how she, with a group of other women, helped
a wife teach her promiscuous husband a lesson. The story appears in a guide to
different types of vagrants, or homeless people unassociated with any household
or master. The storyteller, who is never given a name, is identified only as a
"walking mort,"[11] or, as one of the characters in her own story describes her, "a
poor woman that goeth about the country." The story was recorded by Thomas
Harman, a country gentleman of property, who, when confined to his estate in
Kent by illness, amused himself by questioning the vagrants who begged at his
door about how they lived. Insisting that the information he collected was accurate, Harman even made occasional visits to London to corroborate the vagrants' testimony. He published the results of his research in *A Caveat for
Common Cursitors,*[12] *Vulgarly Called Vagabonds.* Harman's title reveals that his
intention is not to expose the social problems of poverty and homelessness, nor
to elicit sympathy for those he interviews, but rather to warn readers about these
immoral criminals. In the service of education he also offers readers the pleasure
of vicarious bad behavior; page after page recounts the scandalous conduct of
various kinds of beggars. *A Caveat for Common Cursitors* was extremely popular,
with editions in 1566, 1568, 1573, and 1592. Two unauthorized editions further
attested to its popularity, as did other writers such as Thomas Dekker and Richard Head, who honored Harman by borrowing from him freely.

In this story Harman seems to offer two perspectives that the other materials included in this volume have not made available. First, he vividly describes
what it meant to be poor in sixteenth-century England, when poverty and
vagrancy were being defined as crimes through changing legislation (what are
now known as the Tudor Poor Laws) and changing social practices. Informal,
local systems of charitable relief were breaking down, and had not yet been
replaced by state-sponsored, institutionalized poor relief. Harman's "walking
mort," who tells this story, describes her pleasure in food she scrounges for
herself or receives from a friend, in a warm fire, in the gift of a petticoat; she
also conveys her gratitude and loyalty to the woman who often helps her.

[11] **mort:** a girl or woman, especially a "loose" woman, a "slut."
[12] *Cursitors:* tramps.

Thomas Harman, *A Caveat for Common Cursitors, Vulgarly Called Vagabonds* (London, 1568),
E4v-F3.

Second, this story dwells on women's attitudes and feelings more consistently than do any of the other texts included here. Apparently from the perspective of the kind of woman whose voice was rarely recorded, we learn not only about her own experiences but also about the threats and frustrations she shares with other women. The "walking mort" depicts a world in which even well-to-do married women are vulnerable to sexually transmitted disease from an unfaithful husband, or to rape. She describes marital betrayal in concrete, understated detail: the husband here occupies the time before his assignation with the vagrant woman by conversing with his wife and "feeding her with friendly fantasies." In this story marital conflict occurs not in isolation — as it does, for instance, in *A Merry Jest,* in which the husband and wife struggle violently in the solitude of their cellar — but within a larger community. The wife can appeal to her female friends for support. The women in this tale confide in and collaborate with one another, in contrast to the competing women in *The Taming of the Shrew,* and those in Snawsel's *A Looking Glass for Married Folks,* who are reformed by one of their number.

But this depiction of women's community is also acutely aware of the differences among women as well as of the conflicts between women and men. Harman lays the foundation for these differences by emphasizing that the "walking mort" is the mother of an illegitimate child whose father she cannot name; in his view she is the moral inferior of the other women with whom she collaborates. He seems baffled by the sense of ethics that leads her to resist her friend's husband's advances. How, he seems to wonder, could a promiscuous woman have any sexual ethics at all? But the story juxtaposes another morality to Harman's, a morality that unites women rather than making distinctions among them.

The women's revenge scheme also casts differently situated women (the wife, the female vagrant, the wife's friends) in very different roles. Each woman is cast according to her social and moral position as well as to her motives for participating. Further, this taming scheme is just as violent as that in *A Merry Jest.* Yet some readers may react differently to the violence here, in part because of the inversion of the gender relations we usually find in shrew-taming tales — female tamers and a male victim rather than vice versa.

Harman's text offers valuable access to the sort of voice that is usually missing from the historical record. But we cannot assume that this story is authentic or true. Harman himself describes how he secures the story by lying; after assuring the "walking mort" that he will not repeat what she tells him, he publishes it. Clearly, Harman does not feel that he has to honor his promise to such a person; furthermore, he piques the reader's interest by depicting the story as a guilty secret, revealed only through deceit. By interjecting himself into the story at various moments, Harman also reminds readers of his presence as examiner, recorder, and judge. Although the story at first seems to be told in the "walking mort's" voice, the voice soon begins to shift between the first person ("I") and the third ("she"), finally settling uneasily into the third.

Harman so allied his efforts with those of the constables and justices of the peace in controlling vagrants that he sometimes responded to vagrants' stories of their deceptions by confiscating their begging licenses and ill-gotten gains. By documenting the numbers of vagrants and their various illegal means of supporting themselves, he also fueled efforts to monitor the movements and activities of vagrants and to control poverty by making it a crime. His decision to tell the "walking mort's" fascinating story must be considered in the context of this larger project: to demonstrate the moral corruption of vagrants and to promote social order. But, although Harman certainly controls how this story is told and mediates between readers and the "walking mort," his informants and their stories sometimes evade his control. Perhaps vagrants told Harman the truth. Perhaps they did not. The complex underworld they described, a world turned upside down with its own language, customs, rules, and hierarchies, might have been a fiction they collaborated with him in forming. Through his questions Harman may have prompted them to depict their world as the inverted reflection of polite, mainstream society that he expected to see. It is unlikely that the life of transient people was so very structured. In the story below, despite Harman's interjections and judgments, we can still glimpse fragments of a story distinctly different from those that were endlessly repeated about shrewish women and the husbands who tame them; we can hear voices rarely audible in most texts from this period.

A Caveat for Common Cursitors, Vulgarly Called Vagabonds

The last summer, *anno dom[i]ni* 1566, being in familiar talk with a walking mort that came to my gate, I learned by her what I could, and I thought I had gathered as much for my purpose as I desired. I began to rebuke her for her lewd life and beastly behavior, declaring to her what punishment was prepared and heaped up for her in the world to come for her filthy living and wretched conversation.° "God help!" quoth she; "how should I live? None will take me into service, but I labor in harvesttime honestly." "I think but a while with honesty," quoth I. "Shall I tell you," quoth she, "the best of us all may be amended. But yet, I thank God, I did one good deed within this twelve months." "Wherein?" quoth I. Saith she, "I would not have it spoken of again." "If it be meet and necessary," quoth I, "it shall lie under my feet." "What mean you by that?" quoth she. "I mean," quoth I, "to hide the same and never to discover it to any." "Well," quoth she, and

---

conversation: way of life, behavior, especially sexual conduct.

began to laugh as much as she could, and swear by the mass that if I disclosed the same to any she would never more tell me anything.

"The last summer," quoth she, "I was great with child, and I travelled into east Kent by the seacoast, for I lusted marvellously after oysters and mussels, and gathered many. And in that place where I found them, I opened them and ate them still. At the last, in seeking more I reached after one and stepped into a hole and fell in into the waist, and there did stick. And I had been drowned if the tide had come. And espying a man a good way off, I cried as much as I could for help. I was alone. He heard me and repaired as fast to me as he might; and finding me there fast sticking, I required — for God's sake! — his help. And whether it was with striving and forcing myself out, or for joy I had of his coming to me, I had a great color in my face, and looked red and well-colored.° And to be plain with you, he liked me so well (as he said) that I should there lie still and° I would not grant him that he might lie with me. And by my troth, I wist° not what to answer, I was in such a perplexity. For I knew that man well; he had a very honest woman to his wife, and was of some wealth. And on the other side, if I were not helped out, I should there have perished. And° I granted him that I would obey to his will; then he plucked me out.

"And because there was no convenient place near hand, I required him that I might go wash myself and make me somewhat cleanly; and I would come to his house and lodge all night in his barn, whither he might repair to me and accomplish his desire. 'But let it not be,' quoth she, 'before nine of the clock at night, for then there will be small stirring. And I may repair to the town,' quoth she, 'to warm and dry myself, for this was about two of the clock in the afternoon.' 'Do so,' quoth he, 'for I must be busy to look out my cattle hereby before I can come home.' So I went away from him and glad was I." "And why so?" quoth I. "Because," quoth she, "his wife my good dame is my very friend, and I am much beholding to her. And she hath done me so much good ere this that I were loath now to harm her any way." "Why," quoth I, "what and it had been any other man and not your good dame's husband?" "The matter had been the less," quoth she. "Tell me, I pray thee," quoth I, "who was the father of thy child?" She studied awhile, and said that it had a father. "But what was he?" quoth I. "Now by my troth, I know not," quoth she. "You bring me out of my matter,° so you do." "Well, say on," quoth I then.

---

red and well-colored: Rosy cheeks were a mark of beauty among generally fair-skinned English people. In the case of a vagrant woman they might also make her look healthier than a poor diet usually allowed. **And:** if. **wist:** knew. **and:** so. **out of my matter:** beyond what I know.

"I departed straight to the town, and came to my dame's house, and showed her of my misfortune, also of her husband's usage in all points, and that I showed her the same for goodwill, and bade her take better heed to her husband and to herself. So she gave me great thanks and made me good cheer, and bade me in any case that I should be ready at the barn at that time and hour we had appointed. 'For I know well,' quoth this good wife, 'my husband will not break with thee. And one thing I warrant thee, that thou grant me a watchword aloud when he goeth about to have his pleasure of thee, and that should be "fie for shame, fie!" and I will be hard by you with help. But I charge thee, keep this secret until all be finished. And hold,' saith this good wife, 'here is one of my petticoats I give thee.' 'I thank you, good dame,' quoth I, 'and I warrant you I will be true and trusty unto you.' So my dame left me sitting by a good fire with meat and drink; and with the oysters I brought with me, I had great cheer.

"She went straight and repaired unto her gossips,° dwelling thereby; and, as I did after understand, made her moan to them what a naughty, lewd, lecherous husband she had, and how she could not have his company for harlots, and that she was in fear to take some filthy disease of him, he was so common a man, having little respect whom he had to do withall. 'And,' quoth she, 'now here is one at my house, a poor woman that goeth about the country, that he would have had to do withall! Wherefore, good neighbors and loving gossips, as you love me, and as you would have help at my hand another time, devise some remedy to make my husband a good man, that I may live in some surety, without disease, and that he may save his soul that God so dearly bought.'

"After she had told her tale, they cast their piercing eyes all upon her. But one stout dame amongst the rest had these words: 'As your patient bearing of troubles, your honest behavior among us your neighbors, your tender and pitiful heart to the poor of the parish, doth move us to lament your case, so the insatiable carnality° of your faithless husband doth insti- gate and stir us to devise and invent some speedy redress for your ease and the amendment of his life. Wherefore, this is my counsel, and you will be advertised° by me. For I say to you all, unless it be this goodwife who is chiefly touched in this matter, I have the next cause. For he was in hand with me not long ago, and company had not been present — which was by a marvelous chance — he had, I think, forced° me. For often he hath been tampering with me, and yet have I sharply said him nay. Therefore, let us assemble secretly into the place where he hath appointed to meet this

gossips: female friends.   carnality: sensuality, indulgence of his flesh and its appetites.   adver- tised: informed, directed.   forced: raped.

gillot° that is at your house, and lurk privily in some corner till he begin to go about his business. And then, methought I heard you say even now that you had a watchword, at which word we will all step forth, being five of us besides° you. For you shall be none because it is your husband, but get you to bed at your accustomed hour. And we will carry each of us a good birchen rod in our laps, and we will all be muffled for knowing.° And see that you go home and acquaint that walking mort with the matter, for we must have her help to hold, for always four must hold and two lay on.' 'Alas,' saith this goodwife, 'he is too strong for you all. I would be loath for my sake you should receive harm at his hand.' 'Fear you not,' quoth these stout women. 'Let her not give the watchword until his hosen be about his legs. And, I trow, we all will be with him to bring before he shall have leisure to pluck them up again.' "

They all with one voice agreed to the matter that the way she had devised was the best. So this goodwife repaired home. But before she departed from her gossips, she showed them at what hour they should privily come in on the backside and where to tarry their good hour. So by the time she came in, it was almost night. And [she] found the walking mort still sitting by the fire; and declared to her all this new devise above-said, which promised faithfully to fulfill to her small power as much as they had devised. Within a quarter of an hour after, in cometh the goodman, who said that he was about his cattle. "Why, what have we here, wife, sitting by the fire?" and "If she have eaten and drunk, send her into the barn to her lodging for this night, for she troubleth the house." "Even as you will, husband," saith his wife. "You know she cometh once in two years into these quarters. Away," saith this goodwife, "to your lodging." "Yes, good dame," saith she, "as fast as I can." Thus by looking one on the other, each knew other's mind, and so [she] departed to her comely couch.

The goodman of the house shrugged him for joy, thinking to himself: "I will make some pastime with you anon."° And calling to his wife for his supper, set him down and was very pleasant, and drank to his wife, and fell to his mammerings,° and munched apace, nothing understanding of the banquet that was a-preparing for him after supper. And according to the proverb ("sweet meat will have sour sauce") thus when he was well-refreshed, his spirits being revived, entered into familiar talk with his wife of many matters, how well he had spent that day to both their profits — saving some of his cattle that were like to have been drowned in the ditches,

---

gillot: a loose or wanton woman.   besides: in addition to, apart from, other than.   muffled for knowing: disguised, covered up so as to be unrecognizable.   anon: soon.   mammerings: mutterings, mumblings.

driving others of his neighbors' cattle out that were in his pastures, and mending his fences that were broken down — thus profitably he had consumed the day. Nothing talking of his helping out of the walking mort out of the mire, neither of his request nor yet of her promise. Thus, feeding her with friendly fantasies, [he] consumed two hours and more.

Then, feigning how he would see in what case his horse were in, and how they were dressed,° [he] repaired covertly into the barn, whereas his friendly foes lurked privily, unless it were this mannerly mort that comely couched on a bottle° of straw. "What? Are you come?" quoth she. "By the mass, I would not for a hundred pound that my dame should know that you were here, either any else of your house." "No, I warrant thee," saith this goodman, "they be all safe and fast enough at their work; and I will be at mine anon." And lay down by her, and straight would have had to do with her. "Nay, fie," saith she, "I like not this order. If you lie with me, you shall surely untruss you and put down your hosen for that way is most easiest and best." "Sayest thou so?" quoth he. "Now, by my troth, agreed." And when he had untrussed himself and put down, he began to assault the insatiable fort.° "Why," quoth she, that was without shame, saving for her promise, "And are you not ashamed?" "Never a whit," saith he. "Lie down quickly." "Now fie, for shame, fie," saith she aloud, which was the watchword. At the which word, these five, furious, sturdy, muffled gossips fling out, and take sure hold of this betrayed person, some plucking his hosen down lower, and binding the same fast about his feet, then binding his hands and knitting a handkerchief about his eyes, that he should not see. And when they had made him sure and fast, then they laid him on until they were windless. "Be good," saith this mort, "unto my master, for the passion of God!" and laid on as fast as the rest, and still ceased not to cry upon them to be merciful unto him, and yet laid on apace. And when they had well beaten him that the blood burst plentifully out in most places, they let him lie still-bound with this exhortation: that he should from that time forth know his wife from other men's and that this punishment was but a flea-biting in respect of that which should follow if he amended not his manners. Thus leaving him blustering, blowing, and foaming for pain and melancholy, that he neither might [n]or could be revenged of them, they vanished away, and had this mort with them, and safely conveyed her out of the town.

Soon after, cometh into the barn one of the goodman's boys to fetch some hay for his horse. And, finding his master lying fast-bound and grievously beaten with rods, was suddenly abashed and would have run out

---

dressed: groomed, cleaned and brushed.   bottle: bundle.   assault the insatiable fort: attempt to penetrate her sexually.

again to have called for help, but his master bade him come unto him and unbind him. "And make no words," quoth he, "of this. I will be revenged well enough." Yet, not withstanding, after better advise,° the matter being unhonest, he thought it meeter to let the same pass, and not, as the proverb saith, "to awake the sleeping dog." "And by my troth," quoth this walking mort, "I come now from that place and was never there since this part was played, which is somewhat more than a year. And I hear a very good report of him now, that he loveth his wife well and useth himself very honestly. And was not this a good act? Now how say you?" "It was prettily handled," quoth I. "And is here all?" "Yea," quoth she, "here is the end."

advise: consideration, reflection.

→ THOMAS HEYWOOD

From *A Curtain Lecture* 1637

In this story, a husband's attempts to tame his loquacious wife backfire. On his own initiative and in his own backyard, the husband resorts to what had become the standard punishment for scolds; he repeatedly dunks his wife in their well. But unlike the woman in "The Cucking of a Scold," whose resistance is, at last, overcome, this woman never gives up. Most stories about shrews and scolds depict their taming or silencing, even if they cast doubt on the permanence or sincerity of the woman's submission. But this story opens up another possibility — that women sometimes continued to resist, not only silently (which we can imagine but not prove) but openly.[13]

The context of this story must be kept in mind, however. Often attributed to Thomas Heywood, a prolific writer known best for his many plays, *A Curtain Lecture* is a collection of the speeches that scolds deliver to their husbands, published in 1637 and 1638. There were other works like this one published around this time, including Richard Brathwaite's *Ar't Asleep Husband? A Bolster Lecture* (1640) and John Taylor's *Diverse Crabtree Lectures* (1639) (see Figures 1, 2, and 3). All these texts have a curiously contradictory project. Providing scripts for the annoying lectures that women give their husbands, they invent or reproduce pages of female speech in order to make the

[13] A similar story is told in *The Anatomy of a Woman's Tongue* (1638); in it, a cucked scold continues to gesture when she is under water: "To signify, that then she could not talk, / But then she would be sure her hands should walk: / She had no power, but yet she had a will, / That, if she could, she would have scolded still" (278).

Thomas Heywood, *A Curtain Lecture* (London, 1637), H6–H7v.

case that women's speeches are extremely irritating. They also suggest that women's "lectures" are conventional; women never say anything new or interesting; women's voices are all the same. These books seem to be pitched at a male audience, to whom they offer evidence that women's speech disrupts domestic peace; female readers might also be shamed into reticence by these catalogues of all the aggravating things they might say, but should not. Yet, if women's speech is such a nuisance, why document it at such length? It is also possible to imagine a female reader who finds encouragement in all this female complaint or who picks up tips about things she might resent or insults she could level.

The anecdote below is as ambiguous as the project of the book in which it appears. Heywood goes out of his way to emphasize that the story is a fiction that does not depict recent events in England. Instead, Heywood borrows it from a joke book assembled by Poggius (Poggio), a fifteenth-century Italian humanist. If the story is a joke, it is not clear who the butt of the joke is or what purpose would be served by narrating this woman's resistance. This story could be seen as a cautionary tale about why husbands should employ policy, as Petruchio does, rather than force.

This story, then, offers a reminder that many different stories circulated in sixteenth- and seventeenth-century England, and that most of them could be read and interpreted in different, even contradictory ways. It also offers a closing reminder of the complexity of this culture's obsession with disorderly women. If the goal was simply to silence and subordinate these women, why talk about them so much, so often, in so many different ways? And why allow them, even if seldom, to talk back?

A Curtain Lecture

Poggius the Florentine, an excellent orator, in his *Facetiis*° reporteth this story. A woman amongst us (saith he) was so contrary unto her husband in all things, that whatsoever she had said, how absurd soever it were, she would maintain it even to death. Who, scolding and bitterly railing against her husband one day, amongst many other liveries° which she gave him to wear for her sake, she called him "lousy knave." At which words growing wondrous impatient, he beat her with his fists, and kicked her with his heels. Notwithstanding, she never ceased to iterate the same words over and over; and the more he struck her, the more she persisted in her

---

Facetiis: Gian Francesco Poggio Bracciolini (1380–1459) was an Italian humanist who translated Aesop's fables and wrote his own; "facetiis" are witty stories and jokes that Poggio collected from Latin sources.   **liveries:** suits of clothes or uniforms worn by all the servants in a household; livery served to identify an individual as a member of a group. Here the wife "dresses" her husband in insults that mark him as a member of a group to which he does not want to belong.

obstinacy. At length, having so tired himself with beating her that he was scarce able to lift his arms so high as his head, and yet vowing to himself that he would then get the mastery or never, he bethought himself of another course. And tying her fast to a cord, let her down into a well, there threatening to drown her unless she would cease that language.

But the more he menaced her, the louder she talked, not changing a syllable. At length, he sunk her body so far as to the chin, and yet nothing was in her mouth but "lousy knave!" which she often repeated. He then ducked her over head and ears, when, not being able to speak because the water choked her, what she could not do with her tongue she expressed with her fingers; and holding her arms above water, by joining the nails of her two thumbs together, she did that in action, which she was not able to deliver in words. In so much that her perverse obstinacy prevailing above his punishment, he was forced to draw her up again, being ever after a subject to her morosity and bitterness.

Bibliography

————————————— ✳ —————————————

Primary Sources

The Anatomy of a Woman's Tongue Divided into Five Parts (London, 1638). *Harleian Miscellany*. London: Robert Dutton, 1809. Vol. 4.

B., S. *Counsel to the Husband: To the Wife Instruction*. London, 1608.

Becon, Thomas. *A New Catechism Set Forth Dialogue-Wise in Familiar Talk Between the Father and the Son. The Works of Thomas Becon*. 3 vols. London, 1560.

Brathwaite, Richard. *A Bolster Lecture*. London, 1640.

Collier, J. P., ed. *The Tragical Comedy, or Comical Tragedy, of Punch and Judy*. London, 1828.

Dod, John, and Robert Cleaver. *A Godly Form of Household Government*. London, 1621.

T. E. *The Law's Resolutions of Women's Rights, or The Law's Provision for Women*. London, 1632.

Erasmus, Desiderius. *A Merry Dialogue, Declaring the Properties of Shrewd Shrews and Honest Wives*. 1557. *Tudor Translations of the Colloquies of Erasmus (1536–1584)*. Delmar, New York: Scholars' Facsimiles and Reprints, 1972.

Fletcher, John. *The Woman's Prize, or The Tamer Tamed*. Ed. George B. Ferguson. The Hague: Mouton, 1966.

Garrick, David. *Catharine and Petruchio. A Comedy, in Three Acts*. Edinburgh, 1756.

Gouge, William. *Of Domestical Duties: Eight Treatises*. London, 1634.

Griffith, Matthew. *Bethel, or A Form for Families*. London, 1634.

Harman, Thomas. *A Caveat For Common Cursitors, Vulgarly Called Vagabonds.* London, 1568.

Heale, William. *An Apology for Women, or An Opposition to Mr. Dr. G. His Assertion. Who Held in the Act at Oxford, Anno. 1608, That It Was Lawful for Husbands to Beat Their Wives.* Oxford, 1609.

Heywood, Thomas. *A Curtain Lecture.* London, 1637.

"A Homily of the State of Matrimony." *The Second Tome of Homilies.* London, 1623.

Hopkins, Matthew. *Discovery of Witches.* London, 1647.

A Juniper Lecture. With the description of all sorts of women, good and bad. From the modest to the maddest, from the most civil, to the Scold Rampant, their praise and dispraise compendiously related. The third Impression, with many new Additions. Also the Author's advice how to tame a Shrew, or vex her. London, 1652.

Latham, Simon. *Latham's Falconry, or the Falcon's Lure and Cure.* London, 1615.

Markham, Gervase. *The English Housewife.* Ed. Michael R. Best. Kingston and Montreal: McGill-Queen's UP, 1986.

A Merry Jest of a Shrewd and Curst Wife Lapped in Morel's Skin, for Her Good Behavior. London, c. 1550.

A Pleasant Conceited History, Called The Taming of a Shrew. London, 1594.

Rastall, William. *A Collection in English of the Statutes Now in Force.* London, 1603.

Rollins, Hyder E. *A Pepysian Garland: Black-Letter Broadside Ballads of the Years 1595–1639.* Cambridge, MA.: Harvard UP, 1971.

Snawsel, Robert. *A Looking Glass for Married Folks.* London, 1610.

Stearne, John. *A Confirmation and Discovery of Witchcraft.* London, 1648.

Tilney, Edmund. *The Flower of Friendship: A Renaissance Dialogue Contesting Marriage.* Ed. Valerie Wayne. Ithaca: Cornell UP, 1992.

Turberville, George. *The Book of Falconry or Hawking.* London, 1611.

Whately, William. *A Bride-Bush.* London, 1623.

Wing, John. *The Crown Conjugal.* London, 1632.

USEFUL COLLECTIONS OR EDITIONS OF PRIMARY TEXTS

Graham, Elspeth, Hilary Hinds, Elaine Hobby, and Helen Wilcox. *Her Own Life: Autobiographical Writings by Seventeenth-Century Englishwomen.* London: Routledge, 1989.

Henderson, Katherine Usher, and Barbara F. McManus. *Half Humankind: Contexts and Texts of the Controversy about Women in England, 1540–1640.* Urbana: U of Illinois P, 1985.

Kinney, Arthur F. *Rogues, Vagabonds, and Sturdy Beggars: A New Gallery of Tudor and Early Stuart Rogue Literature.* Amherst: U of Massachusetts P, 1990.

Klein, Joan Larsen, ed. *Daughters, Wives, and Widows: Writings by Men about Women and Marriage in England, 1500–1640.* Urbana: U of Illinois P, 1992.

Rosen, Barbara, ed. *Witchcraft in England, 1558–1618.* Amherst: U of Massachusetts P, 1969, 1991.

Roxburghe Ballads. Vols. 1–3 ed. William Chappell; vols. 4–9 ed. J. Woodfall Ebsworth. Hertford: Ballad Society, 1872–99. Rpt. New York: AMS, 1966. 7 vols.

Secondary Sources

Amussen, Susan Dwyer. " 'Being stirred to much unquietness': Violence and Domestic Violence in Early Modern England." *Journal of Women's History* 6.2 (1994): 70–89.

———. *An Ordered Society: Gender and Class in Early Modern England*. Oxford: Blackwell, 1988.

Andresen-Thom, Martha. "Shrew-Taming and Other Rituals of Aggression: Baiting and Bonding on the Stage and in the Wild." *Women's Studies* 9.2 (1982): 121–43.

Bamber, Linda. *Comic Women, Tragic Men: A Study of Gender and Genre in Shakespeare*. Stanford: Stanford UP, 1982.

Baumlin, Tita French. "Petruchio the Sophist and Language as Creation in *The Taming of the Shrew*." *Studies in English Literature (SEL)* 29.2 (1989): 237–57.

Bean, John C. "Comic Structure and the Humanizing of Kate in *The Taming of the Shrew*." *The Woman's Part: Feminist Criticism of Shakespeare*. Ed. Carolyn Ruth Swift Lenz, Gayle Greene, and Carol Thomas Neely. Urbana: U of Illinois P, 1980. 65–78.

Belsey, Catherine. *The Subject of Tragedy: Identity and Difference in Renaissance Drama*. London: Methuen, 1985.

Berek, Peter. "Text, Gender, and Genre in *The Taming of the Shrew*." *"Bad" Shakespeare: Revaluations of the Shakespeare Canon*. Ed. Maurice Charney. London and Toronto: Associated UP, 1988. 91–104.

Boose, Lynda E. "Scolding Brides and Bridling Scolds: Taming the Woman's Unruly Member." *Shakespeare Quarterly* 42.2. (1991): 179–213.

———. "*The Taming of the Shrew*, Good Husbandry, and Enclosure." *Shakespeare Reread: The Texts in New Contexts*. Ed. Russ McDonald. Ithaca: Cornell UP, 1994. 193–225.

Bradbrook, M. C. "Dramatic Rôle as Social Image: A Study of *The Taming of the Shrew*." *Shakespeare Jahrbuch* 94 (1958): 132–50.

Brunvand, Jan Harold. "The Folktale Origin of *The Taming of the Shrew*." *Shakespeare Quarterly* 17.4 (1966): 345–59.

Burnett, Mark Thornton. "Masters and Servants in Moral and Religious Treatises, c. 1580–c. 1642." *The Arts, Literature, and Society*. Ed. Arthur Marwick. London: Routledge, 1990. 48–75.

Burns, Margie. "The Ending of *The Shrew*." *Shakespeare Studies* 18 (1986): 41–64.

Burt, Richard A. "Charisma, Coercion, and Comic Form in *The Taming of the Shrew*." *Criticism* 26.4 (1984): 295–311.

Clark, Anna. "Humanity or Justice? Wifebeating and the Law in the Eighteenth and Nineteenth Centuries." *Regulating Womanhood: Historical Essays on Marriage, Motherhood, and Sexuality.* Ed. Carol Smart. London: Routledge, 1992. 187–206.

Cressy, David. *Literacy and the Social Order: Reading and Writing in Tudor and Stuart England.* Cambridge: Cambridge UP, 1980.

Daniell, David. "The Good Marriage of Katherine and Petruchio." *Shakespeare Survey* 37 (1984): 23–31.

Dash, Irene G. *Wooing, Wedding and Power: Women in Shakespeare's Plays.* New York: Columbia UP, 1981.

Davies, Kathleen M. "Continuity and Change in Literary Advice on Marriage." *Marriage and Society: Studies in the Social History of Marriage.* Ed. R. B. Outhwaite. New York: St. Martin's, 1981.

Davis, Natalie Zemon. *Society and Culture in Early Modern France.* Stanford: Stanford UP, 1975.

Dolan, Frances E. *Dangerous Familiars: Representations of Domestic Crime in England, 1550–1700.* Ithaca: Cornell UP, 1994.

———. "Gender, Moral Agency, and Dramatic Form in *A Warning for Fair Women.*" *SEL* 29 (1989): 201–18.

Dusinberre, Juliet. "*The Taming of the Shrew:* Women, Acting, and Power." *Studies in the Literary Imagination* 26 (1993): 67–84.

Ezell, Margaret J. M. *The Patriarch's Wife: Literary Evidence and the History of the Family.* Chapel Hill: U of North Carolina P, 1987.

Ferguson, Margaret W. "A Room Not Their Own: Renaissance Women as Readers and Writers." *The Comparative Perspective on Literature.* Ed. Clayton Koelb and Susan Noakes. Ithaca: Cornell UP, 1988. 93–116.

Fineman, Joel. "The Turn of the Shrew." *Shakespeare and the Question of Theory.* Ed. Patricia Parker and Geoffrey Hartman. New York: Methuen, 1985. 138–59.

Fleming, Juliet. "*The French Garden:* An Introduction to Women's French." *English Literary History (ELH)* 56 (1989): 19–51.

Garner, Shirley Nelson. "*The Taming of the Shrew:* Inside or Outside the Joke?" *"Bad" Shakespeare: Revaluations of the Shakespeare Canon.* Ed. Maurice Charney. London: Associated UP, 1988. 105–19.

Gowing, Laura. "Gender and the Language of Insult in Early Modern London." *History Workshop Journal* 35 (Spring 1993): 1–21.

Greenberg, Janelle. "The Legal Status of the English Woman in Early Eighteenth-Century Common Law and Equity." *Studies in Eighteenth-Century Culture* 4 (1975): 171–81.

Greenfield, Thelma. "The Transformation of Christopher Sly." *Philological Quarterly* 33 (1954): 34–42.

Haring-Smith, Tori. *From Farce to Metadrama: A Stage History of "The Taming of the Shrew," 1594–1983.* Westport, CT: Greenwood P, 1985.

Heilman, Robert B. "The *Taming* Untamed, or The Return of the Shrew." *Modern Language Quarterly* 27 (1966): 147–61.

Hibbard, George. "*The Taming of the Shrew:* A Social Comedy." *Shakespearean*

Essays. Ed. Alwin Thaler and Norman Sanders. *Tennessee Studies in Literature* Special Number 2. Knoxville: U of Tennessee P, 1964. 15–28.

Hodgdon, Barbara. "Katherina Bound; or, Play(K)ating the Strictures of Everyday Life." *Publications of the Modern Language Association (PMLA)* 107.3 (1992): 538–53.

Hogrefe, Pearl. "Legal Rights of Tudor Women and the Circumvention by Men and Women." *Sixteenth Century Journal* 3.1 (1972): 97–105.

Holderness, Graham. Introduction. *A Pleasant Conceited Historie, Called The Taming of a Shrew*. Ed. Holderness and Bryan Loughrey. Lanham, MD: Barnes and Noble, 1992.

Hosley, Richard. "Sources and Analogues of *The Taming of the Shrew*." *Huntington Library Quarterly* 27.3 (1964): 289–308.

Houlbrooke, Ralph. *The English Family, 1450–1700*. London: Longman, 1984.

Howard, Jean E. *The Stage and Social Struggle in Early Modern England*. London and New York: Routledge, 1994.

Hunt, Margaret. "Wife Beating, Domesticity and Women's Independence in Eighteenth-Century London." *Gender & History* 4.1 (1992): 10–33.

Hutson, Lorna. *The Usurer's Daughter: Male Friendship and Fictions of Women in Sixteenth-Century England*. London and New York: Routledge, 1994.

Ingram, Martin. "Ridings, Rough Music and the 'Reform of Popular Culture' in Early Modern England." *Past and Present* 105 (1984): 79–113.

———. " 'Scolding Women Cucked or Washed': A Crisis in Gender Relations in Early Modern England?" *Women, Crime, and the Courts in Early Modern England*. Ed. Jenny Kermode and Garthine Walker. London: UCLP, 1994. 48–80.

Jardine, Lisa. *Still Harping on Daughters: Women and Drama in the Age of Shakespeare*. Sussex: Harvester, 1983.

Jayne, Sears. "The Dreaming of *The Shrew*." *Shakespeare Quarterly* 17 (1966): 41–56.

Kahn, Coppelia. *Man's Estate: Masculine Identity in Shakespeare*. Berkeley: U of California P, 1981. 104–18.

Kermode, Jenny, and Garthine Walker, eds. *Women, Crime, and the Courts in Early Modern England*. London: UCLP, 1994.

Kussmaul, Ann. *Servants in Husbandry in Early Modern England*. Cambridge: Cambridge UP, 1981.

Laslett, Peter. *The World We Have Lost: Further Explored*. 3rd ed. New York: Scribner's, 1984.

Laurence, Anne. *Women in England, 1500–1760: A Social History*. London: Weidenfeld, 1994.

Leggatt, Alexander. *Shakespeare's Comedy of Love*. London: Methuen, 1974.

MacDonald, Michael. *Mystical Bedlam: Madness, Anxiety, and Healing in Seventeenth-Century England*. Cambridge: Cambridge UP, 1988.

Macfarlane, Alan. *Witchcraft in Tudor and Stuart England: A Regional and Comparative Study*. London: Routledge, 1970.

MacKinnon, Catharine A. "Feminism, Marxism, Method, and the State: Toward Feminist Jurisprudence." *Feminist Legal Theory: Readings in Law and Gender*.

Ed. Katharine T. Bartlett and Rosanne Kennedy. Boulder: Westview P, 1991. 181–200.

Maguire, Laurie E. " 'Household Kates': Chez Petruchio, Percy, and Plantagenet." *Gloriana's Face: Women, Public and Private, in the English Renaissance.* Ed. S. P. Cerasano and Marion Wynne-Davies. Detroit: Wayne State UP, 1992. 129–65.

Marcus, Leah. "The Shakespearean Editor as Shrew-Tamer." *English Literary Renaissance* 22.2 (1992): 177–200.

Martin, Randall. "Kates for the Table and Kates of the Mind: A Social Metaphor in *The Taming of the Shrew." English Studies in Canada* XVII.1 (1991): 1–20.

Mayhew, Henry. *London Labour and the London Poor: A Cyclopaedia of the Condition and Earnings of Those That Will Work, Those That Cannot Work, and Those That Will Not Work.* Vol. 3 (1851). New York: Reprints of Economic Classics, 1967.

McLuskie, Kate. "Feminist Deconstruction: The Example of Shakespeare's *Taming of the Shrew." Red Letters* 12 (1977): 33–40.

Mikesell, Margaret Lael. " 'Love Wrought These Miracles': Marriage and Genre in *The Taming of the Shrew." Renaissance Drama* n.s. 20 (1989): 141–67.

Morris, Brian. Introduction. *The Taming of the Shrew.* By William Shakespeare. London: Methuen, 1981.

Neely, Carol Thomas. *Broken Nuptials in Shakespeare's Plays.* New Haven: Yale UP, 1985.

Newman, Karen. *Fashioning Femininity and English Renaissance Drama.* Chicago: U of Chicago P, 1991.

Novy, Marianne L. *Love's Argument: Gender Relations in Shakespeare.* Chapel Hill: U of North Carolina P, 1984.

Okin, Susan Moller. *Justice, Gender, and the Family.* New York: Basic Books, 1989.

Orlin, Lena Cowen. "The Performance of Things in *The Taming of the Shrew." Yearbook of English Studies* 23 (1993): 167–88.

———. *Private Matters and Public Culture in Post-Reformation England.* Ithaca: Cornell UP, 1994.

Palmer, Daryl. *Hospitable Performances: Dramatic Genre and Cultural Practices in Early Modern England.* West Lafayette, IN: Purdue UP, 1992.

Perret, Marion D. "Petruchio: The Model Wife." *SEL* 23.2 (1983): 223–35.

Powell, Chilton Latham. *English Domestic Relations, 1487–1653.* New York: Columbia UP, 1917.

Quiller-Couch, Sir Arthur. Introduction. *The Taming of the Shrew.* By William Shakespeare. Ed. Quiller-Couch and John Dover Wilson. Cambridge: Cambridge UP, 1953.

Quilligan, Maureen. "Staging Gender: William Shakespeare and Elizabeth Cary." *Sexuality and Gender in Early Modern Europe: Institutions, Texts, Images.* Ed. James Grantham Turner. Cambridge: Cambridge UP, 1993. 208–32.

Radford, Jill. Introduction. *Femicide: The Politics of Woman Killing.* Ed. Radford and Diana E. H. Russell. New York: Twayne, 1992. 3–12.

Ranald, Margaret Loftus. *Shakespeare and His Social Context.* New York: AMS P, 1987.

The Revels History of Drama in English. Gen. Ed. T. W. Craik. Vol. 4 (1613–1660). Ed. Philip Edwards, Gerald Eades Bentley, Kathleen McLuskie, and Lois Potter. Vol. 5 (1660–1750). Ed. John Loftis, Richard Southern, Marion Jones, and A. H. Scouten. London: Methuen, 1976.

Roberts, Jeanne Addison. "Horses and Hermaphrodites: Metamorphoses in *The Taming of the Shrew.*" *Shakespeare Quarterly* 34.2 (1983): 159–71.

Rose, Mary Beth. *The Expense of Spirit: Love and Sexuality in English Renaissance Drama.* Ithaca: Cornell UP, 1988.

Rutter, Carol. *Clamorous Voices: Shakespeare's Women Today.* London: Women's P, 1988.

Saccio, Peter. "Shrewd and Kindly Farce." *Shakespeare Survey* 37 (1984): 33–40.

Seronsy, Cecil C. " 'Supposes' as the Unifying Theme in *The Taming of the Shrew.*" *Shakespeare Quarterly* 14 (1963): 15–30.

Shapiro, Barbara J. *Probability and Certainty in Seventeenth-Century England: A Study of the Relationships between Natural Science, Religion, History, Law, and Literature.* Princeton: Princeton UP, 1983.

Shapiro, Michael. "Framing the Taming: Metatheatrical Awareness of Female Impersonation in *The Taming of the Shrew.*" *Yearbook of English Studies* 23 (1993): 143–66.

Shaw, George Bernard. *Shaw on Shakespeare.* Ed. Edwin Wilson. New York: Dutton, 1961.

Shershow, Scott Cutler. *Puppets and Popular Culture.* Ithaca: Cornell UP, 1995.

Shurgot, Michael W. "From Fiction to Reality: Character and Stagecraft in *The Taming of the Shrew.*" *Theatre Journal* 33 (1981): 327–40.

Slater, Miriam. *Family Life in the Seventeenth Century: The Verneys of Claydon House.* London: Routledge, 1984.

Slights, Camille Wells. "The Raw and the Cooked in *The Taming of the Shrew.*" *Journal of English and Germanic Philology (JEGP)* 88.2 (1989): 168–89.

Smith, Steven R. "The London Apprentices as Seventeenth-Century Adolescents." *Past & Present* 61 (Nov. 1973): 149–61.

Speaight, George. *The History of the English Puppet Theatre.* 2nd ed. London: Robert Hale, 1990.

Stone, Lawrence. *The Family, Sex, and Marriage in England, 1500–1800.* New York: Harper, 1977.

Thomas, Keith. "The Meaning of Literacy in Early Modern England." *The Written Word: Literacy in Transition.* Ed. Gerd Baumann. New York: Oxford UP, 1986. 97–131.

Thompson, Ann. Introduction. *The Taming of the Shrew.* By William Shakespeare. Cambridge: Cambridge UP, 1984.

Todd, Margot. *Christian Humanism and the Puritan Social Order.* Cambridge: Cambridge UP, 1987.

Tomarken, Edward. *Samuel Johnson on Shakespeare: The Discipline of Criticism.* Athens, GA: U of Georgia P, 1991.

Underdown, David. "The Taming of the Scold: The Enforcement of Patriarchal

Authority in Early Modern England." *Order and Disorder in Early Modern England.* Ed. Anthony Fletcher and John Stevenson. Cambridge: Cambridge UP, 1985. 116–36.

Wayne, Valerie. Introduction. *The Flower of Friendship: A Renaissance Dialogue Contesting Marriage.* Ed. Wayne. Ithaca: Cornell UP, 1992. 1–93.

———. "Refashioning the Shrew." *Shakespeare Studies* 17 (1985): 159–87.

Wentersdorf, Karl P. "The Original Ending of *The Taming of the Shrew:* A Reconsideration." *SEL* 18.2 (1978): 201–15.

Wiltenburg, Joy. *Disorderly Women and Female Power in the Street Literature of Early Modern England and Germany.* Charlottesville: U of Virginia P, 1992.

Woodbridge, Linda. *Women and the English Renaissance: Literature and the Nature of Womankind, 1540–1620.* Urbana: U of Illinois P, 1984.

Wright, Louis B. *Middle-Class Culture in Elizabethan England.* Chapel Hill: U of North Carolina P, 1935.

Wrightson, Keith. *English Society, 1580–1680.* New Brunswick, NJ: Rutgers UP, 1982.

ACKNOWLEDGMENTS CONTINUED FROM PAGE IV

INTRODUCTION (continued)
Figure 2. Frontispiece from Richard Brathwaite, *Ar't Asleepe Husband? A Boulster Lecture* (London, 1640). STC 3555. Reprinted by permission of the Folger Shakespeare Library.
Figure 3. Frontispiece from Thomas Heywood, *A Curtaine Lecture* (London, 1637). STC 13312. Reprinted by permission of the Folger Shakespeare Library.

CHAPTER 1
Figure 4. Frontispiece from David Garrick/John Kemble, *Catharine and Petruchio* (1838 edition). Reprinted by permission of the Folger Shakespeare Library.

CHAPTER 2
Figure 5. John Dod/Robert Cleaver, *A Godly Forme of Household Government* (London, 1621). Signatures A7Y-A8. Reprinted by permission of the Folger Shakespeare Library.
Figure 6. Frontispiece from John Wing, *The Crowne Conjugall* (London, 1632). STC 25845. Reprinted by permission of the Folger Shakespeare Library.
Figure 7. "An Homilie of the State of Matrimonie" from *The Second Tome of Homilies* (London, 1563). STC 13663. Reprinted by permission of the Folger Shakespeare Library.

CHAPTER 3
Figure 8. "The Woman to the Plow, And the Man to the Hen-Roost" from *Roxburgh Ballad Collection* II. 534. © The British Library Board. All rights reserved 9/9/2013.
Figure 9. Woodcut of woman holding rods on page 54 of Nathaniel Crouch, *Delights for the Ingenious, In above Fifty Select and Choice Emblems* (London, 1684). Wing C7312. This item is reproduced by permission of the Huntington Library, San Marino, California.

CHAPTER 4
Figure 10. "The Cruell Shrow" from *Roxburgh Ballad Collection* I. 28, 29. © The British Library Board. All rights reserved 9/9/2013.
Figure 11. Frontispiece from *A Merry Jest of a Shrewd and Curst Wift Lapped in Morel's Skin* (London, c. 1550). This item is reproduced by permission of the Huntington Library, San Marino, California.
Figure 12. Illustration of a woman on a cucking stool by T. N. Brushfield, *Chester Archeological Society Journal* 2 (1855-62), p. 203. © The British Library Board. All rights reserved 9/9/2013.
Figure 13. Illustration of a woman wearing a scold's bridle on page 110 of Ralph Gardiner, *England's Grievance Discovered, in relation to the Coal-Trade* (London, 1655), Shelfmark 4° S.21.Jur. Reprinted by permission of the Bodleian Library.
Figures 14 and 15. J. P. Collier, *The Tragical Comedy, or Comical Tragedy, of Punch and Judy* (1828), George Cruikshank's illustrations of Punch and Judy beating each other. Reprinted by permission of Miami University, Oxford, Ohio.
Figure 16. Woodcut of gentleman and his falcon on page 75 of George Turberville, *The Book of Falconrie* (London, 1611). Courtesy of the University of Illinois at Urbana/Champaign.

Index

———————————————————— >‹‹—— ————————————————————